SCOTLAND
HISTORY OF A
NATION

SCOTLAND
HISTORY OF A
NATION

DAVID ROSS

LOMOND
BOOKS

For W. A. Ross

Picture Credits

Photograph of Donald Dewar on page 17 courtesy of the Scottish Executive.
Photographs on pages 19, 26, 32, 275, 280 and 288 courtesy of Hulton Getty Picture Library.
Illustrations on pages 47, 48, 66, 98 and 220 by Mike Lacey; on pages 83, 85 and 86 by Yanek
Matysiak; on page 91 by Susan Hutchison; on pages 148, 159, 160, 211, 228 235 and 236 by
Jane Taylor; on pages 206 and 223 by James Field; on page 252 by John Marshall
(all courtesy of Waverley Books Ltd)

Cover images: map based on map of the British Isles by John Speed *c*.1676;
portraits of Mary Queen of Scots by Jane Taylor (courtesy of Waverley Books Ltd);
portrait of William Wallace by Maurice Mechan; photographs of standing stones by
Dennis Hardley, Forth Bridge courtesy of the Illustrated London News, Oban Castle estate
courtesy of Corel

This edition published by Geddes & Grosset, David Dale House,
New Lanark, ML11 9DJ, Scotland, for Lomond Books Ltd

Text © David Ross 1998
First published 1998
Reprinted 1999, 2000
Updated & reprinted 2002

ISBN 0 947782 58 3

Printed and bound in Finland

Contents

CHAPTER NINE
From 1603 to the Union 175

Fact Windows

Foreword

'The Scottish versions of history seem to oscillate between extolling the virtues of passive suffering and glorifying moments of volcanic, almost involuntary violence. Where are the episodes in which the Scottish people, by holding together and labouring patiently and wisely, achieved something?' This question is asked by Neal Ascherson in his book *Games With Shadows*. These 'episodes', in as far as they existed, are noted in this book. Patience, even wisdom, may not be the chief characteristic of the Scottish people, but they often achieved things despite their rulers and the country's closest neighbours.

It is easy to sum up our history as a catalogue of internecine bloodshed, lost opportunities, tragic ironies, exploitation of the many by the few, with more battles lost than won, but such a picture is distorted. In seismic events, on the surface, there is always the sense of a people struggling to keep its being and its identity, to preserve something that every generation for a thousand years has thought worth preserving. That 'something' has grown more complex with the passage of time, and has acquired new facets through political and cultural change, but its essence has not changed. We still manage to do certain things in our own way.

The concepts of 'Scotland' and 'Scottish' are not only still meaningful, but strong enough to contain contrasting and mutually contradictory ideas – a good omen for a lively, if argumentative, future.

DAVID ROSS

Scotland through the Rear-View Mirror

THE OPENING OF PARLIAMENT

On 1 July 1999, the Queen opened the first session of the new Scottish Parliament. The First Minister, Donald Dewar, made a speech that recalled some of the past glories and achievements of the Scottish people, and a grand party was held in the old Parliament House.

Since the elections in May, there had already been intense political activity, as well as public scrutiny of the new parliamentarians. The system of proportional representation, cunningly devised, had resulted in Labour being the largest party but lacking an overall majority. A coalition with the Liberal Democrats was formed, despite ill-ease among many MSPs of the latter party. Scottish Nationalists and Conservatives formed an un-united Opposition, along with two kenspeckle Socialists and a solitary Green.

The attitude of Labour Party managers to the Parliament showed all the signs of parents who had given their child a new bicycle and suddenly realised that at the other end of the quiet cul de sac was the open road. Their very defensiveness on the subject – quite apart from the presence of 38 Nationalist members – ensured that the nature of the Union would continue to be an issue. But the focus of the legislative programme was necessarily on the bread-and-butter issues within the Parliament's remit: education, transport, health and welfare.

The parliamentary election managed to be hailed as some sort of victory by all four main parties. It signalled that Conservatism in Scotland, despite having no members in the Westminster Parliament, was by no means dead. It gave the Liberal Democrats their first opportunity in 78 years of sharing power at a national level. It returned enough Nationalists to show that many people did not believe that that party's historic role was now accomplished. Labour, in which a history of control over much local government might have encouraged a 'destined to rule' mentality, perhaps took least satisfaction from the result, despite being the dominant party.

THE REFERENDUM

The elections of May 1999 followed eighteen months of intensive work by civil servants after the referendum of September 1997. In this, the electorate voted by a substantial majority in favour of the reinstatement of a Scottish parliament. It was to have strictly limited powers and to operate under the aegis of the British Parliament. Electors also agreed to the possession of restricted powers to raise or lower income tax by this Parliament. The overall result was received with great public satisfaction. For some it represented as much independence as Scotland required. For others, whether supporters or opponents of the new proposals, the prospect of a new Scottish Parliament was seen as merely the first step towards the re-establishment of Scotland as a fully independent nation state.

Fifty years before, there had been little serious interest in setting up a Scottish Parliament. The reasons for this change in outlook are fascinating to examine: some of them are of recent origin and others can be traced back a long way into the experience of previous centuries. In the latter half of the twentieth century, the case for devolution of parliamentary powers from Westminster produced no compelling new arguments, and no outstanding figure gave it passion or command. A change in attitude came not so much from explicit political persuasion as from the private perceptions and thoughts of the electorate. Once upon a time, when the Scottish people wanted to make their wishes known, they had to express them, sometimes forcibly, in public, but secret ballots have made this unnecessary. In 1997 the country had made up its mind almost in silence. Even on the eve of the Scottish Referendum for a new Parliament the result was considered unpredictable. No one really knew if there would be a majority 'Yes' vote, especially as to whether that Parliament would be allowed taxation powers.

VOTING SYSTEMS

The new Parliament has little in common with its predecessors. The body that voted for its own dissolution in 1707 was a Parliament that had enjoyed full independence, but it was far from being the forum of the full nation. Only a tiny proportion of the male population had the right to vote. Its members were the nobility, the country gentry, and a selection of burgesses of the royal burghs, chosen by the town councils. Today everyone over the age of eighteen is eligible to vote for their new Members of Parliament – MSPs – using a system that includes a degree of proportional representation. This novel system provides both constituency members and members nominated by any party which wins a sufficient share of the total vote. Some welcomed it as a means of introducing able candidates to Parliament whose abilities might not include the robust business of local electioneering. It was also seen as a means for political parties to reward their faithful followers, whatever those people's personal talents might be.

PARLIAMENT BUILDINGS – AND THEIR OCCUPANTS

Since the 1970s a home for the new Parliament had been waiting in Edinburgh in the refurbished classical buildings of the Royal High School on the slopes of Calton Hill. The failure of the 1979 Referendum to achieve the necessary mandate for devolution left the building unused. Campaigners for a Scottish Parliament occupied the gateways of Calton Hill to publicise their continuing cause. It was a dominant site – perhaps too dominant for those who feared a Scottish parliament would soon try to extend its authority. In January 1998, it was announced that a new building for the Parliament was to be constructed for its inauguration in 1999. Shortly afterwards it became clear that a new building could not be completed in time and makeshift arrangements would be necessary. The news was received with derision and some dismay. Even before it had members to constitute it, there was the suggestion that the new body was more preoccupied with its accommodation than with its functions. The choice of a redundant brewery as the site, although close to Holyrood Palace, did little to improve matters. And the inevitable escalation of its cost created further argument.

No system of government will gain universal approval. In Scotland, a country that has never shirked argument over ideas, the prospect of a Parliament caused intense debate and conjecture against a background of fervent hope that the new Parliament would acquit itself well and become not just a regional council writ large but a true forum for deciding Scotland's future at the start of its second millennium as a nation. Donald Dewar, the Secretary of State, had worked hard to achieve the Referendum and the setting-up of the Parliament within a short timetable. Alex Salmond, the leader of the Scottish National Party, had vindicated the political risk he and the party took by accepting the limited-powers Parliament. But there was a hope abroad that a new political generation would emerge in the new Parliament and make it their own, unaffected by experience of, or aspirations towards, the Parliament in London.

Donald Dewar 1937–2000,
First Minister of Scotland 1999–2000,

ELECTION PATTERNS
PRIOR TO THE REFERENDUM

The 1997 Referendum came shortly after the election of the first Labour Government of Great Britain for eighteen years. Labour Party adherence to the idea of Scottish devolution, by no means whole-hearted, followed rather than led public opinion. But the tactical change in Labour policy suddenly made devolution seem practical politics to electors who did not want to vote for the full-independence agenda of the Scottish National Party. (The SNP itself had had to consider whether Labour's plan provided it with an opportunity or a potentially fatal trap; although some veterans resisted, it opted to take what was on offer, without prejudice to its ultimate ambition.) Through successive elections for the Westminster Parliament, the Scots had elected a Labour majority, only to see it engulfed by the Conservative majority elected by voters south of the Border. In 1997 Scotland elected no Conservative members at all. The regiment of Labour members elected in the urban seats was leavened by successes in the more rural areas for both the Scottish Nationalists and the Liberal-Democrats. But ever since the 1960s, the political debate north of the Border has been conducted well to the left of the political centre, as perceived in England. The Labour Party assumed itself to be the special beneficiary of this political outlook and received a rude shock in November 1967 when Mrs Winnie Ewing achieved the first significant parliamentary election result for the Scottish National Party by easily winning a by-election in the Labour stronghold of Hamilton. But in the 1970 General election, Labour swept back in Hamilton and forty-two Nationalist candidates lost their deposits. The volatility of the electors was shown four years later, in October 1974, when the SNP took eleven Scottish seats. Twenty-four years later, with Scottish Parliamentary elections in sight, Labour found it had fallen into the same old error of taking the support of the Scots for granted. Incompetence and malpractice in some areas of Labour local government were revealed, and the party saw the National Party overtaking it in public opinion polls.

POST-MODERN SCOTLAND

TRADE AND INDUSTRY 1970s–1990s

The large anti-Tory majority in Scotland was unable to prevent the vast impact on the Scottish economy of the radical policies introduced under Margaret Thatcher as Prime Minister, with her Britain-wide mandates. She had no truck with Home Rule and was reputed to care little for Scotland, which offered her little in return, except for some talented MPs, very much of her own persuasion, emerging from St Andrews University, which seemed to be a nursery of right-wing thought in a left-wing country. Tory Scottish Secretaries were somewhat beleaguered figures, open to the charge of being virtual colonial administrators, but nevertheless they were in power.

In the 1970s and 1980s most of the heavy industries that had created modern Scotland were swept away. The remaining coal mines were considered uneconomic and were closed. Steelworks in Motherwell were deemed an unnecessary duplication of facilities available elsewhere in the United Kingdom and were dismantled. Shipyards on the Clyde, despite a repeated and increasingly desperate pattern of rationalisation, mergers and increasing hostility between workers and management, found it impossible to compete with the low-waged Far East or with the highly paid Germans. Manufacture of cotton cloth and thread on an industrial scale fell victim to Far Eastern competition and to materials created by new technology. Huge factories, like the Singer Sewing Machine works, with its own railway station, were shut down. Nor was it only the older nineteenth-century industries that collapsed. Comparatively new motor works, aluminium works, wood-pulp mills, all built in the 1960s and 1970s with the aid of huge amounts of taxpayers' money, were closed. Staple industries that survived, like agriculture, tweed-milling and whisky distilling, found that technical advances enabled them to employ far fewer people. Distilleries once employed a dozen or more stokers simply to keep the furnaces burning beneath the stills. Now they just turned on the gas and ran the whole complex operation with only a dozen or so staff.

Miners' rally during the 1983–84 strike

The shock of such drastic changes, followed by the severe recession of the early 1990s, came after several decades in which the Scots had felt a growing attrition of their country's resources. Unemployment was high and always proportionally higher in Scotland than in England. The railway system had been much reduced in the 1960s. The fishing industry, which had once been a source of employment all around the coast, was much reduced and concentrated in only a handful of ports between Buckie and Aberdeen. Meanwhile the inhabitants of Coigach in the northwest could see the night sky illuminated by 'Klondikers' who had come from Eastern Europe, and beyond, to fill the holds of their factory ships. The teaching profession, always a significant element in Scottish society, was locked in a long and bitter struggle with the government over standards and its status.

Successive Conservative governments were sustained by faith in monetarism, belief in the effectiveness of competition and confidence in the ability of market forces to create a satisfactory basis for social life. This led to a widening gap between richer and poorer. Privatisation of national and municipal resources made it possible for a few determined and well-placed people to make fortunes on a Victorian scale. Many might have admired the energy with which some men and women took control of their companies and became wealthy, but they did not see better services on offer. Only public outrage at the selling of a national natural resource prevented the government from selling off the Scottish water authorities in the early 1990s. To use Scotland as the test-bed of the new poll tax, where local rates would be replaced by a tax on each person occupying a property, was an unwise decision that prefigured the shambles that would follow in England and Wales. Scotland saw the growth of 'quasi-autonomous non-government offices', or quangos – boards set up to run great swathes of the national life. Quango members were appointed, not elected, and often seemed able to maintain more than one highly paid position. The patronage dispensed by the Secretary of State rivalled that of his eighteenth-century predecessor, 'King Henry' Dundas. The sense of personal and public accountability diminished.

Scots were also keenly aware of the fact that much of their new or surviving industry and commerce was not rooted in Scotland, or even in Britain. America, Japan, Korea and Germany were the places where decisions were taken and often where basic research was done. International companies could change locations tactically and ruthlessly, depending on where the incentives were best. Scotland-in-Britain felt vulnerable on these counts. The frequency of government initiatives in job creation and investment policy from both major Parliamentary parties merely revealed, each time, the inadequacy of the previous scheme. Industrial relations, never easy in a country where master-servant roles had long been established, became stormier as industries declined and unemployment rose. Yet the clear threat of 'no investment without good behaviour' was a powerful one. New industries wanted assurances that they would have no strikes, and although their 'human resources' management often was good, they did not like unions. Trades unions had become a powerful force for industrial protectionism, but they lost both influence and membership with the abolition of the 'closed shop' policy. No longer had all new employees to join the union. No longer was the shop steward as powerful as the company director. In trades unions with vastly reduced bargaining power, or in no union at all, individual workers, within companies large and small, became isolated and felt a new insecurity both as employees and citizens.

British imperial pretensions were slower to end than the actual empire, but geopolitical changes culminating in the collapse of Communism had an impact on the Scottish economy as defence-related industries were weakened. Cuts in the army and navy not only struck at a sense of tradition but also increased unemployment. The inevitable protest movement arising from each regimental or depot closure reflected a real sense of national decline, in the perception that the old order was vanishing fast whilst the country was ill-placed to assess and take up new options.

COAL, IRON AND STONE

The great geologist Sir Archibald Geikie (1835–1924) published an essay in 1861 describing his boyhood discovery of fossils in a limestone quarry. The quarrymen, like kobolds in a fairy tale, still descended deep into the earth to extract limestone for burning in their kilns. Over the centuries many millions of tons of Scotland have been pick-axed, blasted and carried away by human agency. In the 1950s and 60s, more than two million tons of coal were still being mined each year. Now there is a Mining Museum but no working pit of any size.

Most Scottish roads in hill country still show traces of overgrown, small side-quarries where the stone to make the roadbed was dug out. But in a few places, on the mainland and in the islands, the hard rocks of Scotland are still being quarried for roadstone on a massive and landscape-transforming scale.

Ironically, the sites of the great ironworks, like Motherwell, Coatbridge, or Dixon's Blazes, have been bulldozed or rebuilt clear of all identity, while up and down the country, in remote locations, such as those by Loch Awe and Loch Maree, the ruined furnace houses of more primitive iron works can still be seen; and the slag heaps of prehistoric metalworkers can still be found on hillsides in the Southern Uplands.

GOVERNMENT ORGANISATION

Under the Conservative administrations of the 1970s to the 1990s, local government organisation in Scotland drastically changed. The burgh structures that had existed in one form or another since the thirteenth century were abolished. County councils of vastly varying sizes that had administered local life since 1889 were reduced to nine mainland regions: Highland, Grampian, Tayside, Fife, Central, Dumfries and Galloway, the Borders, Lothian and Strathclyde. Strathclyde stretched from Lanark to Argyll and contained about a third of the entire Scottish population. Lothian, too, was densely populated. Island councils were established for Shetland, Orkney and the Outer Hebrides and were considered an improvement in terms of local organisation. But the mainland arrangements, like all attempts to manage Scotland's mixture of dense urban areas and sparsely populated countryside, were not universally popular. Generally, local government was felt to have moved farther away from local people.

With the arrival of European Parliamentary elections there was, for a time, a four-tier system of elective government. In 1996 a further rearrangement took place which abolished district councils and restored unitary authority to the four cities of Glasgow, Edinburgh, Aberdeen and Dundee, which had previously been merged into their regions, along with twenty-four other 'single-tier' authorities.

SCOTLAND'S OIL?

North Sea oil and gas fields, discovered in the 1960s and 1970s, created a sense of new hope for economic growth and stimulated substantial investment in offshore industries. The Cromarty Firth, redundant as a naval base with the abolition of the Home Fleet, became a centre for servicing oil rigs. Other coastal locations also benefited from the oil industry. Aberdeen became one of the world's offshore oil capitals. But those who cried 'It's Scotland's oil', cried in vain. The huge profits and royalty revenues generated from North Sea oil did not remain in Scotland. The oil industry alone could not, in any case, provide an adequate counterbalance to the drastic slide into oblivion of the traditional heavy industries. Scots looked enviously at Norway, which was developing its oil-fields on a long-term basis and using its oil revenues for its own social development programmes. Only in Shetland, where the vast Sullom Voe terminal was established by agreements between the Shetland Council and the oil companies, sanctioned by the government, was a fund set up to use some oil revenues to improve the islands' amenities.

SCOTLAND IN EUROPE

The growing sense of marginalisation felt by Scots was perhaps the prime factor that led to the political annihilation of the Conservatives in 1997. Mrs Thatcher was not sympathetic to the view that Scotland was a separate country to be seen in its own terms. Her Scottish lieutenants – and her successor, John Major – were doggedly Unionist in outlook. Yet in many ways the country had never been so prosperous. Professional salaries were on a par with the rest of the United Kingdom. After joining the European Common Market in 1972 (from 1989 the European Community), farmers' incomes also benefited from the Common Agricultural Policy. But from 1994 onwards, the contamination of British cattle herds by the disease BSE severely damaged the important Scottish beef industry. Effective world-wide marketing of whisky and, to a lesser degree, of tourism brought in increasing amounts of foreign revenue. Meanwhile, many parts of Scotland became eligible for grants of 'euro-money', paid from the European Social Fund. These funds helped in the landscaping of many blighted industrial sites. Some of the most decrepit of Glasgow's tenement buildings were pulled down, and the city embarked on a slow and diffi-

THE STONE OF DESTINY

Ever since the 1850s, there had been feelings of annoyance in Scotland – not only among those who wanted self-government – at the extent of the anglicisation of Great Britain and the ways in which Scottish tradition and history seemed to be ignored, including a neglect of long-established Scots heraldry. When no provision was made in 1952 to proclaim Queen Elizabeth II of England as also Elizabeth I of Scotland, a few letter boxes bearing the new royal monogram were blown up. Prior to that, on Christmas Day 1950, in what was condemned by the government as a prank but which was a serious plan to arouse publicity, an independent group of young Nationalists removed the 'Stone of Destiny' from Westminster Abbey, where Edward I of England had installed it more than six hundred years before, and brought it back to Scotland. It was eventually deposited in Arbroath Abbey – source of the fourteenth-century Declaration that re-asserted Scotland's national independence – and recovered by the authorities on 11 April 1951. It was then returned to London. In 1996, the Stone was at last formally returned to Scotland, where it is now on display with the 'Honours of Scotland' in Edinburgh Castle.

cult transformation from smokestack industry to being a centre of high-technology factories, of light industry, of financial management and of cultural tourism.

The European connection was a source of confidence as well as funds. A majority of the population had voted for entry. London was no longer the sole place of last resort for Scottish questions: Brussels and Strasbourg also held power and purse strings. The slogan 'Scotland in Europe' offered the prospect of a national entity within the protective embrace of a multinational union. The Scots did not fail to notice the transformation of the Irish Republic's economy in the EC; and how that country's per capita income had overtaken that of Great Britain.

WELFARE

Although it was under extreme pressure, the edifice of the welfare state set up with such pride and hope in the 1940s still protected those who were registered as unemployed or who were disabled from the extremes of destitution. Definitions of poverty accepted in the 1980s, including the lack of a television set, would have brought a bitter smile from anyone who experienced hardship in the 1930s or earlier. Now television and, increasingly, the Internet were bringing Scotland into the ambit of a global culture.

The majority of Scots in the later decades of the twentieth century would be better housed, better clothed, better fed and better informed than they were in the 1950s. Central heating and deep freezers in the home would be taken equally for granted by the great majority. Twenty years before, such comforts would have been seen as transatlantic luxuries. Scottish consumers had a greatly extended choice of purchases, although charity shops and the 'everything-under-a-pound' shops also grew vastly in number. Scots took more foreign holidays, drank more alcohol, owned more cars and spent their money on a wider range of pastimes. Scottish children stayed longer at school, and by the end of the century they could face many educational choices at specialist colleges of higher education and at more than a dozen universities. Before or after higher education, many would travel or work abroad for a year, an opportunity almost impossible in the years before the jumbo jet.

SOCIAL CONDITIONS

Social legislation for the United Kingdom had abolished capital and corporal punishment. It was no longer thought tolerable for a husband to beat up his wife. European legislation would have a bearing on many aspects of

Scottish law: on the treatment of children, on equal opportunities for women, on racial equality and on work practices. The somewhat aimless gang warfare of Glasgow had given way to more organised and more discreet crime, often based on drug-dealing. This was not necessarily any change for the better, and a violent sub-stratum remained in society. By the end of the century Scotland had also become a far more secular community than it had ever been. The Church, whose doctrines and disciplines had once been central to national life, was now an external element in most people's lives. Fewer people went to church, and Sunday was now a day of many options on which shops, pubs and places of entertainment remained open. Football matches were played. Deplored by the traditionally minded and those still adhering to strict Presbyterianism, these changes were happily accepted by the majority and very quickly taken for granted.

But people were not satisfied by the state of the nation. In the complex pattern of progress and decline through the decades, one thing had become sufficiently clear: Scotland was at the mercy of social and economic forces that it had no instruments to control. Not only that – the same was essentially true of the greater political entity, the United Kingdom. At the time of the half-hearted devolution referendum of 1979 that dissatisfaction had still not taken a definite shape. The numbers for and against devolution were almost even, and the majority of voters did not vote at all. In 1997 the need to bring about a new order of things was far more clearly perceived.

MODERN SCOTLAND

THE 1950s TO 1960s

The Scotland of the 1950s had little of the stress or excitement experienced later in the century. Unemployment, although twice the British average, remained relatively low. Industrial and commercial structures created throughout the nineteenth and early twentieth centuries were still in place. There were over seventy working coal mines, and over two million tons of steel were being produced each year. The frailty and obsolescence of it all were apparent only to the prescient. There were six different banks with offices in the High Streets. Steam trains ran, increasingly emptily as the car and bus began to take over, to such places as Gatehouse of Fleet, Crieff and Ballater.

THE POST-WAR SOCIETY

In the first half of the decade before, war had raged across the world, with Scotland no backwater The war still echoed strongly in people's memories and attitudes. Six Highland and eight Lowland regiments were based in Scotland, and there were important naval bases at Rosyth, Invergordon and on the Gareloch. All males were liable for national service after their eighteenth birthday. Shops closed early in the evenings and all day on Sundays. Public houses opened only between eleven and three o'clock and between six and ten o'clock on most evenings – a little later on Saturdays. Any town with more than two thousand or so inhabitants had its pocket of industry at the gasworks where gas was made from coking coal. The same gas often lit the street lights. Tall tram cars ran with squealing wheels through the streets of Aberdeen, Dundee, Edinburgh and Glasgow.

Football League clubs recruited their players from their home towns. Bakers' boys delivered fresh morning rolls for breakfast, while horse-drawn milk carts trotted by. Men wore flat caps. Women scrubbed stairs or doorsteps wearing turban-like headscarves. People mainly lived in terraced houses or in tenements. Glasgow was just about to embark on the social disasters of its overspill estates and high-rise blocks. Girls and boys went to the high schools and academies in uniforms that had not changed in appearance since the 1920s. Their teachers all too often relied on a leather tawse to keep discipline. And only Catholic Ireland had a higher proportion of Sunday churchgoers than Presbyterian – mostly – Scotland. In the 1920s and 30s, apart from even fewer motor vehicles and many more horse-drawn ones, the scene would not have been greatly different.

Politically, the battle was between Tories and Labour. The divide was comparable to that in England, where industrial cities returned Labour Members of Parliament while middle-class suburbs and the farming shires returned Tories. The Union of Scotland and England was not in question for the great majority; the sense of British togetherness fostered during the Sec-

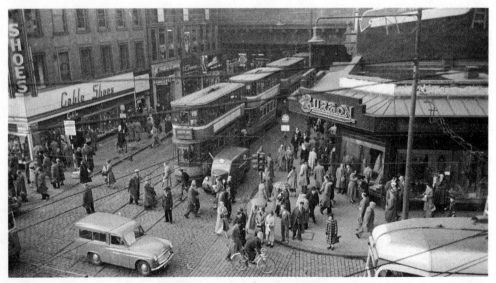

Tram cars in Glasgow, 1955

ond World War was still strong. The Nationalist cause seemed peripheral, and eccentric independent campaigners like the indefatigable Wendy Wood did not help to gain it serious attention. There was one freakish and brief immediate post-war result for the Scottish National Party, when Dr Robert McIntyre, its future leader, represented Motherwell at Westminster for six weeks in 1945, but they were not to repeat it until the Hamilton by-election of 1967. Labour had not achieved the massive majorities of later decades, and at times, as in 1955, the Tories secured both more Scottish votes and more seats in Parliament. No matter which party was in power, the United Kingdom Parliament allowed little time for Scottish matters. There was a revealing period from 1949 to 1951 during which time the maverick Nationalist John MacCormick organised the Scottish Covenant, a petition for a Scottish Parliament. Estimates of the number who signed it ran as high as two million, but it was completely ineffective and was regarded as a sentimental gesture with no weight of commitment behind it. At Westminster it was ignored, and no one took to the streets in Scotland as a result. Indeed, the country swung to the Conservative-Unionists in the 1951 General Election.

SCOTLAND AT WAR

SCOTTISH SOCIETY BETWEEN 1914 AND 1945

In the late 1940s, Scotland, with the rest of the United Kingdom, saw the introduction of the 'Welfare State', a system of social welfare that was achieved not without difficulty in the post-war years and which played a significant part in preserving an all-British ethos. It also saw the results of one significant act that had been passed under the wartime coalition government led by Winston Churchill, the setting-up of the North of Scotland Hydro-Electric Board. The war-time Secretary of State for Scotland, Tom Johnston, viewed the new Board as a powerful engine for the regeneration of the Highlands. Unlike the other regional power boards, it had a specific social remit. On a smaller and more hesitant scale it recalled Franklin D. Roosevelt's Tennessee Valley Authority Scheme of the 1930s in the United States. By the mid-1950s, virtually all the Highlands and Islands were supplied with electricity. The process was completed just in time for the installation of the national television broadcasting network. Many lochs, including Loch Awe and Loch Luichart, were heightened by damming, and completely new lochs, such as Loch Glascarnoch and Loch Faskally, were created in the most dramatic alterations to the Highland scene since the Ice Age. The Hydro-Electric Board is now Scottish Hydro plc, responsible not to the community but to its shareholders.

In the Second World War, 1939–1945, Scotland suffered far less loss of life through fighting than it had done in the trench carnage of the First World War of 1914 to 1918. The relative lengths of the lists of names on village war memorials is an accurate guide. As in the First World War, the country's strategic position between the Atlantic Ocean and the North Sea was of great importance. Naval bases at Rosyth, Invergordon, Scapa Flow and the Gareloch were enlarged. Loch Ewe became an assembly point for merchant convoys. But the most visible signs of war were the many military

THOMAS JOHNSTON (1881–1965)

Growing up in Kirkintilloch, close to the Antonine Wall, gave Tom Johnston an early interest in Scottish history. His father was a provision merchant, a trade not normally linked with socialist thinking, but Johnston was a radical socialist from an early age. When he left Lenzie Academy, a distant relative put him in charge of a printing works and two weekly papers. In 1906 he launched the socialist journal *Forward*, on a budget of £60, and edited it for 27 years. Conscious of his lack of higher education, he studied moral philosophy and political economy as an external student at Glasgow University in 1908. His outspoken book *A History of the Working Classes in Scotland* (1920) was a success and helped to sustain his political work. He held the parliamentary seat of West Stirling from 1922 to 1924, and after an interlude as an MP in Dundee, from 1929–31, and 1935–45. From 1929 to 1931 he was Under-Secretary of State for Scotland. His opposition to the National Government cost him his seat in 1931. As a backbencher from 1935, conscious of the threat of Hitlerism, he called the period up to 1939 "the years the locust ate". In 1939 he was made Regional Commissioner of Civil Defence for Scotland, with two peers, Lords Rosebery and Airlie, as his deputies; this post made him keenly aware of what the community of Scotland could do when held to a common purpose. In 1941, to his surprise, he was appointed Secretary of State. To help him, he asked for the setting up of a Council of State, composed of all living previous holders of the office. This body did not achieve a great deal, but was a useful public relations exercise. Tom Johnson's lasting achievement was the North of Scotland Hydro-Electric Board, but his term of office also included the formation of rent tribunals, the development of free hospital facilities in the Glasgow area, and the Scottish Tourist Board. In the context of a huge war effort, it was a remarkable achievement. In 1945 he resigned from parliament, refusing a peerage, and was chairman of the Hydro-Electric Board until 1959. He died in Milngavie.

airstrips laid out on both the eastern and western coasts. Scotland suffered relatively little by way of air raids compared to the cities of England, although in the Spring of 1941 there were air attacks on the Glasgow shipyards and on towns along the Firth of Clyde that caused serious damage and a number of deaths. Edinburgh, Leith and Aberdeen were also targeted. Children were evacuated from inner-city homes to country towns and villages. Ironically, the war, which devastated other countries and peoples, brought a degree of prosperity and increased social welfare to Scotland. More land was taken over for agricultural purposes and for forestry. Food rationing and price controls actually improved the diet of many people, and there was full employment. There was also a thriving black market in goods that were in short supply. To an even greater degree than their mothers had, twenty-five years before, women worked in industry, transport, on the fields and in the forests. The presence of large numbers of American troops helped the traffic in luxury items and also encouraged a change in attitudes in what was still a deferential society. The foreman, the factor, the bank manager, the 'big farmer' were all men who knew their power within small communities and liked to see it acknowledged.

The ironworks, brickworks, shipyards, textile factories and coal mines that laboured to help the war effort had stood quiet only a few years before. The Depression following the Wall Street crash of 1929 afflicted Scotland severely and unemployment ran as high as thirty per cent of the working population. In towns with only one main industry this could mean something closer to eighty per cent. The years between 1929 and 1939 marked the worst decade of the twentieth century for Scotland. Beginning in financial instability, they passed rapidly into industrial decline and ended in European war. There was no evidence of competent management from a National Government whose Prime Minister (to 1935), Ramsay Macdonald, was himself a Scot. Those who looked abroad to Europe saw only trouble. Even emigration, the answer so often before, had little to offer since the lands of opportunity were themselves in slump. The third novel in Lewis Grassic Gibbon's *Scots Quair* trilogy, *Grey Granite*, gives a graphic description of the period, set in a city with features of both Aberdeen and Dundee.

There were elements of progress. House-building programmes undertaken by local councils provided both work and an improved housing stock, with minimum standards of space and quality in building practice established by law. One of the distinctive aspects of Scottish life was the high proportion of tenanted homes – usually council tenants – in comparison to owner-occupiers.

Modern industries, the basis of the hi-tech and communications revolution to come later, were being set up. The technical inventiveness that had characterised the country for a hundred and fifty years did not disappear. But the Depression meant that much of Scotland's heavy industry, which had hardly been modernised since before the First World War, was both inefficient and obsolescent when the Second World War began.

The crisis in the capital markets did not result in a Marxian revolt of the workers. Scotland was essentially a country of the working class, although land-workers were less likely than industrial workers to see themselves in proletarian terms. Despite the apparent inability of government or the managerial class to improve matters, there were no great storms of protest. One or two Communist Members of Parliament were elected. The Labour Party had no cures to offer, drastic or otherwise. But even in 1932, when nearly thirty per cent of the working population were unemployed, the other seventy per cent who remained in work had something to hold on to. For the unemployed, apart from the state money, or dole – if they qualified for it – and charitable handouts, there was a strong national tradition of grim endurance, with a Scots word to express it. They had to thole it, and hope for better things to come.

The despondency of the 1930s was intensified by the memory of the Great War of 1914–1918 and by the growing anticipation of another war to come. Soldiers had returned home in 1918 to the promise of the Prime Minister, Lloyd George, of 'a land fit for heroes to live in'. Instead they encountered the inevitable post-war slump as the economy returned to peace-time conditions. Fifteen years later they were on the dole or forced to accept reduced pay in return for keeping their jobs.

In the early 1920s there was indeed a flurry of entrepreneurial activity, coinciding with high spirits, new music and new post-Edwardian fashions, that earned the sobriquet of the 'gay twenties'. Bicycles became a popular form of travel for individuals. Petrol engines, much improved in the course of warfare, came into their own. Army surplus trucks were converted into buses, linking villages to their market towns. Road haulage became a speedy affair. Competition made the distribution of goods, notably farm and dairy produce, less expensive, and pressures were put on local and national authorities to improve the roads. Main roads were much as they had been in the days of Telford and McAdam; side roads were variable in quality. Railways were still a vital means of bulk transport, but branch lines were already beginning to close. And across the land, the supremacy of the work-horse diminished rapidly. The cadger and his horse-drawn cart disappeared from the roads. On the big farms of the northeast, the hierarchy of the horse team, from 'orra loon' to first man, with all its prestige and lore, was reduced to the solitary tractor driver.

THE FOUNDING OF THE SCOTTISH NATIONAL PARTY

The first Labour government came to office in 1924, and individual Scottish Labour Members of Parliament presented drafts of Home Rule Bills to Parliament in 1926, 1927 and 1928, only to be 'talked out' by a combination of Unionist opposition and general indifference from their own party. Home rule had always been part of the Scottish Labour platform. It had also been Scottish Liberal policy. But by the late 1920s it was clear to those who wanted any degree of home rule that it would not come from a party that saw itself in a United Kingdom context. The Scottish Home Rule Association had been refounded in 1918, with its roots in the left-wing Independent Labour Party and Roland Muirhead as its Secretary. By 1929 it had collapsed, although Muirhead remained prominent in Nationalist politics for many years. The Scots National League, which had been founded in 1921 by Ruaraidh Stuart Erskine of Mar, also had a radical standpoint in politics, sufficient for the aristocratic and Catholic Erskine to work with the atheist and communist John Maclean. In 1927, Erskine's party was renamed the National Party of Scotland. In 1932, the Scottish Party was founded, from the other side of politics, following a revolt among Scottish Unionists. This party merged with the National Party of Scotland – after some acrimonious debate – to form the Scottish National Party on 20 April 1934. These small parties or pressure groups had varying aims, from full independence to management of home affairs, or home rule within a sort of federal version of the British Empire. They had little organisation in the country and aimed to persuade Members of Parliament rather than to galvanise the population. It would be 1948 before the Scottish National Party forbade its members to join any other political party. In 1934 the country was in the economic and social depths of the Depression. Nationalism in Italy and Germany was not an encouraging spectacle. Semi-independent Ireland was locked in a bitter and violent power struggle.

In a party with one overriding motive there were inevitably many different points of view about the political nature of an independent Scotland, and many prickly, combative personalities. Although the ethos of the Scottish National Party emerged largely from the Independent Labour Party, there were right-wing, even fascist, sentiments expressed by some members. Three decades of argument, internal disputes, breakaways, failed initiatives and public indifference were to follow, but the Scottish National Party nevertheless held together, produced a comprehensive 'Statement of Aim and Policy' in 1946, and under the unglamorous but careful leadership of Dr Robert McIntyre and William Wolfe, it gradually built itself up from local bases, with concentration on local issues, into an effective national political force.

HOME RULERS AND NATIONALISTS

In the nineteenth century, the promoters of Scottish devolution were almost all talking in terms of Home Rule, that is to say, Scottish management of its own domestic affairs through a Parliament. Foreign and Imperial affairs were to remain the concern of a London Parliament with Scottish members. There were natural reasons for this. The British Empire was still a reality, and Scotland had made vast investments of people and capital in it. Scottish politicians did not not want to lose that stake. The Scottish Home Rule Association, founded in 1886, and supported both by Liberal and Labour figures, made this clear. Despite Liberal and Labour support for Home Rule, a Scottish National Party had been mooted at least since 1903. But it was not until the second decade of the twentieth century that complete separation from the United Kingdom became a clear strand of Scottish political thought. The First World War, the Russian Revolution, the growing signs of British weakness, disillusion with the British political parties, all sharpened the ideas of Ruaraidh Erskine of Mar, John Maclean, and Hugh MacDiarmid, who began to articulate the notion of an independent Scottish nation. This took shape with the formation of Erskine's Scots National League in 1921, the first organised party with full independence as its aim. Those who still felt home rule was sufficient joined the

Hugh MacDiarmid (Christopher Murray Grieve) (1892–1978), poet and passionate nationalist

Scottish Home Rule Association, which had withered away before 1914 but was refounded in 1918. The two strands were uneasy allies in the young SNP, leading to dissidence and the breakaway of John MacCormick's Scottish Union, later Scottish Convention, which organised the grand but futile gesture of the 1949 Scottish Covenant.

HOUSING

Despite the Housing Act of 1924, which had been passed by the first Labour Government and sponsored by the Clydeside MP John Wheatley, the standard of most Scottish housing was poor and often deplorable. New houses of only two rooms, or even one room, the notorious 'single-ends', were still being built to house whole families. The typical Scottish town had always

SCOTTISH INTROSPECTION IN THE 1930s

Some Scottish writers, like Hugh MacDiarmid and Lewis Spence, were actively associated with the Nationalist movement in the 1930s (and after, although the SNP found MacDiarmid too hot to hold and expelled him). Eric Linklater and Compton Mackenzie, highly successful novelists, lent their support (Linklater's novel *Magnus Merriman* gives a rumbustious account of the times). Others, like Lewis Grassic Gibbon (Leslie Mitchell) and Edwin Muir, either ignored it or were tepid in support. But in the 1930s there was intense interest and concern about the condition and soul of the nation, explored by writers and journalists in a series of notable books. These include William Power's *Scotland and the Scots*, Edwin Muir's *Scottish Journey*, George Malcolm Thomson's *Caledonia*, Lewis Grassic Gibbon's and Hugh MacDiarmid's *Scottish Scene*, George Scott-Moncrieff's *Scottish Country* and Colin Walkinshaw's *Scots Tragedy*. Some of these probed delicate tissues more fiercely than others. Power shows sentimental attachment to Kailyard themes. *Scottish Scene* set out to shock the unco guid. Edwin Muir exudes a mournful horror at what he saw. Walkinshaw goes right back to the Union of 1707 as the source of disaster. What they all do is to see Scotland as separate from the rest of the United Kingdom, and to identify its problems and their solutions as specifically Scottish. In this way they provide a parallel to the political argument. These books, widely read by people who saw the National Party as eccentric or irrelevant, played a significant part in shaping the thought that Scotland had to face its own past and tackle its own problems. Harold J. Hanham, in his excellent study, *Scottish Nationalism*, suggests the intellectuals damaged the Nationalist cause by attacking such Scottish icons as Presbyterianism: it is much more likely that they broke up the concrete of national mythology and played a vital part in establishing a more open and analytical attitude to the past and the future.

been close-packed, with relatively tall tenement-style dwellings at the centre and rows of cottages at the outskirts. There was a preference for, or habituation to, such proximity. And there was a definite desire to keep rents to the lowest possible, to which landlords, whether municipal or private, responded by providing minimal accommodation.

Social and economic factors combined to make Scottish housing among the most squalid, and consequently disease-ridden, of Europe. James Maxton, a schoolteacher before he became an MP in 1922, noted that in one class of sixty children thirty-six could not stand up straight because of rick-

THE LALLANS CONTROVERSY

The question of language has never been far away from the argument for Scottish independence. It is no coincidence that Hugh MacDiarmid, poet, communist, nationalist, also became an ardent advocate of using Scots (the term 'Lallans', from Lowlands, has never caught on) as a literary language. Despite their use of words that had to be extracted from Jamieson's *Dictionary of the Scottish Language* of 1823, his poems in *Sangschaw* (1925) and his *A Drunk Man looks at the Thistle* (1926) have the vibrant vitality he sought. Other poets like William Soutar and Sydney Goodsir Smith also wrote convincingly in Scots, and the notion of a 'Scottish Renaissance' was canvassed. Cold water was poured on this by Edwin Muir in 1936, when he wrote that the writer who roots himself deliberately in Scotland 'will find there, no matter how long he may search, neither an organic community to round off his conceptions, nor a major literary tradition to support him'. The debate was heightened by the fact that the country's two leading poets had taken opposing stands. Scottish writing since the Second World War shows neither point of view to be wholly right, or relevant. In recent years an assured use of current vernacular Scots, mixed with English, by novelists such as James Kelman and Irvine Welsh, and the work of many poets in Scots and in English, suggests that the vitality and self-assurance of the nation is the crucial factor in establishing an authentic literature. These aspects were at a low ebb in the 1930s: sixty years later, though again in an economic recession, the spirit was different.

ets. Tuberculosis, then incurable, was a scourge in these tightly packed and insanitary dwellings, made worse by the damp and cold that prevailed for much of the year. Coal fires from domestic stoves and from industry polluted the air and coated every building in soot. (It would be a satisfying visual shock later in the century when the many colours of Glasgow and Edinburgh stonework were again revealed by restoration and cleaning.)

THE EFFECTS OF WAR

The mild euphoria of the 1920s expressed the relief of communities after the heavy losses in the recent war. A stoic, melancholy pride accepted the torrent of deaths in Flanders. An innovation in every high street after the First World War was the town or village war memorial. The British commander-in-chief had been a Scotsman, Earl Haig, who was presented with the stately home of Bemersyde, which had long been associated with his family name. The number of Scots in the armed forces had never been so great. Regiments increased the number and size of their battalions and maintained much of their Victorian panoply in the face of ferocious mechanised warfare. Highland regiments fought in the kilt for the last time.

At this time, organised labour showed itself as more tigerish than it would do in the Depression. The war economy, which by 1916 was as tightly managed by the government as any Soviet commissar might have desired, placed heavy demands on industry, simultaneously stripping it of manpower. The huge munitions industry that grew up in the Glasgow area would have collapsed without thousands of women workers. The jute industry of Dundee, which boomed exceptionally, had always relied chiefly on low-paid female labour. Women's contribution to the war effort was one of the reasons given for women over the age of thirty being given parliamentary votes in 1918. But without the previous agitations of the Suffragettes, it might not have been considered necessary by a male-dominated society. The long struggle of the trades unions to achieve mass membership and negotiating power now put them in a strong position when maximum output was demanded. Their keenness to avoid exploitation by employers and landlords, who were doing well out of the war, led to strikes at the work-place and to a rent strike in 1915 against opportunistic rent rises by the landlords. But there were also the kinds of demarcation dispute that would be a contributory feature of the later decline of the shipbuilding industry. These were not sudden or petty matters. The tradition, practice of, and pride in craftsmanship had grown up through the centuries with such divisions of labour. They could not suddenly be blown away.

Fuelled by a great demonstration in George Square, Glasgow, in January 1919, which caused a nervous Government to call out tanks and troops, a myth of 'Red Clydeside' grew out of all proportion to the activity, aims or achievements of the intensely vocal syndicalists, socialists, communists and pacifists who made up the political community of Glasgow and its environs.

PRE-WAR SCOTLAND 1900–1914

The Great War, with its grisly mortality rates and its social and economic consequences, really marked the start of the twentieth century for Scotland. The decade and a half between 1900 and 1914 was in most respects far more the continuation of the Victorian period than the advent of a new order. 'Before the War' became, retrospectively, a golden age. Viewed in a forward perspective by the generation growing up in the 1890s, it looked rather different (*see* Chapter 12).

Scotland came into the twentieth century as a prosperous province of Great Britain. For the first time, the general level of people's income in Scot-

JOHN MACLEAN

John Maclean was born in Glasgow in 1879 and spent his life in that city. He became a teacher, like his contemporary James Maxton, and was a founder member of the Glasgow Teachers' Socialist Society. Strongly involved with Labour-related causes, he was a staunch internationalist, in correspondence with the International Workers of the World in America and the revolutionary movement in Russia as well as with the trade union and Co-operative movements closer to home. In 1914 he affirmed his pacifism, and in 1915 he supported the Rent Strike. He was jailed for a year for agitation. After the Bolshevik Revolution he was appointed the first Soviet Consul in Great Britain, a post the government did not acknowledge. In April 1918 he was arrested again and jailed for five years, but after protests against the severity of the sentence, it was reduced to six months. He died in 1923.

land matched that of the English. It was the world's greatest shipbuilding centre, the South Korea of the time. The demand for intercontinental transport, resulting in ever bigger and better-equipped passenger ships, was combined with a need for more and bigger cargo vessels. These serviced a strong export programme of manufactured goods, from sewing machines to steam locomotives, and returned with imports of food and raw materials on a steadily increasing scale. Just as once the Scottish pedlar had walked the roads of northern Europe, now the Scottish tramp-steamer wandered the sea routes of the world, collecting and landing cargoes everywhere between Valparaiso and Rangoon. Public funds and private money – the hugest example being the donations of the Scots-American steel tycoon Andrew Carnegie – maintained the late Victorian practice of erecting florid public buildings containing such social amenities as public libraries and baths. New railways were still being built, with the extension of the western Highland lines to Mallaig and Kyle of Lochalsh. Glasgow, wreathed in smoke and garlanded with soot, with its million-plus population, was proud to call itself 'the second city of the Empire'.

In 1905 Norway, an ancient ally and trading partner, for centuries under the rule first of Denmark and then of Sweden, re-established itself as a wholly independent kingdom. This was noted in Scotland. Nationalism was by no means dead, and was much discussed on the left of politics, but Scotland was doing well out of the British Empire and could not muster the passion that had never gone away in Ireland. The Labour movement led by Keir Hardie looked favourably on limited self-government for Scotland and for Ireland but was more concerned about developing its own organisation and structure. As these became stronger, the ambitions of the Labour leaders moved on to a broader British scale with the prospect of a Labour Party majority at Westminster.

The Liberal Party, ostensibly in favour of home rule for Scotland, was actually divided. Back in power from 1905, its previous leader, Lord Rosebery, was at odds with the Prime Minister, Sir Henry Campbell-Bannerman. Both were Scots, one from the aristocracy and the other from the Glasgow mercantile bourgeoisie. In 1911, Winston Churchill, in his Liberal incarnation and sitting for Dundee, had got as far as drafting a plan that allowed for regional parliaments throughout the United Kingdom before he was transferred from the Home Office to the Admiralty. Political debate in the first decade of the century raged furiously around other issues of equal concern both to Scotland and to England. One was the imperial theme of free trade against protectionism. Another was the growing power and assertiveness of Germany. A third was the British domestic theme of where political power should lie. The constitutional struggle between the House of Commons and the House of Lords ended with the Parliament Act of 1911, which established the supremacy of the Commons and salaries for Members of Parliament. For at least half the adult population there was another commanding issue. Women had no parliamentary vote and would not vote on equal terms with men until 1928.

Well within a centenarian's lifetime, that confident placing of a United Kingdom at the industrial hub of a world-wide British Empire would vanish with the Empire itself. Britain would no longer be in charge of its own destiny. The world around Scotland would change radically too. In the later decades of the twentieth century there would be a new interest in the realities, as distinct from the popular myths, of Scottish history. This in itself was expressive of a revived sense of national identity and responsibility. The British doctrine, impressed into successive generations of schoolchildren, was that Scotland had failed as an independent nation. The Union with England, they were told, had been both inevitable and necessary. Now, after almost three hundred years, the Scottish people had seen the rise and fall of a British Empire in which they had enthusiastically collaborated. This perspective of a shrunken, uncertain, post-imperial Great Britain helped the Scots to see their own past in a different way. It was no longer a shackle, with the label of national incompetence attached to it: simply a set of experiences that they could, at last, confront and learn from. From 1948 onwards, they had seen the rise of a new European political framework that accorded full participation to small nations. The possibility of – and the need for – a new beginning were clear.

CHAPTER TWO

Back to the Beginning

AFTER THE ICE AGE

It used to be said that the history of Scotland began with the arrival of the Romans in AD 79. Agricola, a Roman general, was accompanied by the historian Tacitus, who provided the first written description of the people and of the region called Caledonia at that time. But the suggestion of a sudden beginning to Scottish history is of course false.

The country we now call Scotland had been continuously, if sparsely, inhabited for some four thousand years, stretching almost halfway back to the time of the last Ice Age when the newly scraped-out landscape re-emerged from its thick mantle of ice. The North Sea had not fully formed. Hardy communities of hunter-gatherers and semi-nomadic pastoral groups made settlements around the coasts. Inland there were dense and thickly matted forests, marshes and peat bogs, grass and heather plateaux above which rose bare peaks of rock. Wild oxen, roe deer, wild pigs, beavers, bears, wolves and wolverines lived in these forests. Reindeer cropped the mosses of Caithness. Grouse, blackcock and capercaillie lived on upland moors. Cranes were common at the water's edge and the great auk joined with the other sea birds in competing for both shellfish and dorsal-spined fish which were the rich haul of the sea.

Slow, spasmodic waves of immigration came up the shallow coasts of the North Sea and overland through what was not yet England. These new settlers with their already tamed cattle, sheep and goats came from Europe, where *Homo sapiens* had been established for twenty thousand years. Pigs and dogs may have been domesticated from local wild stock. But making a home in a forest clearing was the hardest task for people equipped only with stone blades.

Even from the earliest times, the inhabitants of Scotland were part of a wider economic structure. As immigrants, they knew where they had come from. Stone Age Europe, with thousands of years of inherited and hard-gained knowledge, knew where essential resources lay. They would travel long distances in the best-made vessels of the time, dug-out canoes, or coracles, to secure them. Flint, for example, has always been rare in Scotland and so quality flints were imported goods. Eagles' feathers or whale oil could be taken back to Europe as a primitive form of export in an economy of barter and exchange. In the wider northern world, Scotland, with its central isthmus and its Great Glen was also an important portage route which avoided the Pentland Firth and stormy northern seas.

Early inhabitants of Scotland may have had as many languages as those of New Guinea still do. The people who lived in stone-built and stone-furnished houses at Skara Brae in Orkney may have had no kinship with those who lived in wooden lodges in the eastern glens. Progress was likely to have been uneven as groups arrived from different starting points at different times. Some of the settlers appear to have practised new farming techniques developed in Europe and brought into Britain around 2200 BC which involved saving seed corn to grow wheat and barley annually. New forms of farming needed agricultural tools, digging sticks and primitive hoes. These farmers also made clay pots and vessels whose style and structure can be dated. At the same time there were other more traditional hunting-gathering communities whose livelihood might remain perfectly viable. What is clear is that by around 1500 BC some of these groups had a well-developed culture both in terms of ideas and of technology. The people who built Maes Howe, the great chambered tomb on Orkney, commanded both highly skilled craft workers who could cut stone and substantial labour resources to bring building materials to assemble the covering mound. This and similar if smaller tombs suggest a socially stratified society or a dominant warrior caste able to direct and command many people at a time. This society had also evolved a theory of its place in the universe.

Artist's impression of a Roman altar found at Birrens in Dumfriesshire

METAL USERS

Even as the inhabitants of Scotland reached the high point of stone tool technology, knowledge of metal-craft was working its way westward towards them. Its harbingers were the prospectors. In the far southwest of the island of Britain, these prospectors found tin, which was rare, and vital in the making of bronze. Looking elsewhere, they found copper and gold. From now on, incoming settlers were often metal-users, at first on a very limited scale, perhaps only for ceremonial occasions. They were a more homogeneous group, coming from the northern part of what is now Germany, with a distinctive form of pottery. They favoured a separate rite and burial place for each individual rather than use a collective chambered tomb. These people used the bow and arrow and perhaps established themselves by force, like later settlers in America. They wore woollen clothing fastened with buttons in addition to the furs that were still plentiful. They were probably the builders of stone circles, the sites of many of which can still be traced and some of which still enigmatically stand. By the middle of the second millennium, settlement, in the more favoured areas at least, must have been either by invitation or invasion. But perhaps the natural outwards drift, from already settled and expanding communities, was opening up new areas of habitation, like the islands, with few or no 'waves' of immigration.

Easily workable copper deposits helped with the development of metal-working, although trade links with those who controlled the tin mines of Cornwall were essential to make bronze. For a period of perhaps a thousand years, coming close to the start of the Christian era, a bronze-using culture developed and existed, about which little is known. By this time the population had grown considerably from minimal beginnings but was still largely based around coastal areas and the islands, for practical reasons – including the availability of seal and whale oil and blubber – and where people could maintain easier communication with one another. The interior landscapes of Scotland remained a virgin jungle of oak, elm and ash trees, with rowan, birch and pine forests in the more exposed areas. These areas were rich hunting grounds to which tribal communities were probably already staking their claims. A tribal social structure with its hierarchy, functions and degrees seems the likeliest form of social association. Cultural changes included a gradual change in the pattern of burial to cremation from inhumation of the dead. Peoples' lives may have been relatively stable and peaceful, and certainly the evidence of extensive walls and fortifications comes from a later period.

THE COMING OF THE CELTS

Centres of world civilisation and technical progress lay far away to the east. But with a huge growth in human numbers, central and eastern areas of Europe and the plains of Asia were swarming with an unprecedented mass of human beings seeking to expand south and west into areas where there was a dispersed and conquerable population. The first waves of the great folk movements in Europe were under way. By around 600 BC the people speaking Celtic languages had spread themselves in ever thinner but ever overlapping layers across Europe from Bohemia to France. During this process of migration, they acquired the use of iron tools and weapons and were thus in a superior technological and military league to the peoples whom they overran. They were expert horsemen and used the war chariot. By the middle of the fifth century BC they were establishing settlements in England. Although they were never organised as a central power, these groups organised themselves in temporary and shifting alliances between tribes and they were formidable opponents. In 386 BC they sacked Rome.

Celtic tribes appear to have been relatively slow to move into Scotland in significant numbers. Their relationship, conducted from their southern strongholds, may have involved a mixture of activities from violent raiding to peaceful trading. When settlement began in earnest around 100 BC, the newcomers built themselves hill-forts from which they could control small tracts of countryside. Many of their forts, as far north as Easter Ross, were constructed with walls of wood and stone which are now preserved and remain in vitrified form because, by accident or design, the wood of their construction was burned and the walls fused into a single craggy mass.

The language they spoke was of that branch of the Celtic languages which includes Welsh. Their houses were round, with timber frames and walls of sticks and mud, known as wattle-and-daub. Some were isolated dwellings, but settlements of fifteen or so within a palisade were common. Single dwellings were often crannogs, built on an artificial island in a loch or marsh with a wooden causeway that could be easily moved. Crannogs remained popular for centuries afterwards, and by no means all examples are truly ancient ones.

There may already have been a Celtic element in the population of Scotland, at least in terms of language. However, the fort-builders established themselves as an aristocracy who bore iron weapons but who were also highly mobile. They did not wipe out the previous inhabitants, some of whom probably spoke a language that was neither Celtic nor even Indo-European. The invading Celts were in touch with a wider world both on the Continent and in Ireland, where the already established Celts spoke a different language which was an ancestral form of Gaelic.

'THEY MAKE A DESERT AND CALL IT PEACE'

The Romans were no strangers to the Celts. The Roman invasion of AD 79, although it led to what must have been by far the biggest battle yet to take place on the territory of Scotland, was neither an ending nor a beginning, despite its interest for historians. The continuity of population was not affected by the Roman incursion. The nameless dwellers of prehistoric Scotland were awarded tribal identities and a generic name by the taxonomically minded Romans. It is possible that all Scotland was already under the control of Celtic tribes at the time the Romans arrived – but if not, the power of the Celts was certainly supreme by around AD 100.

Numbers can only be guessed at, but clearly the tribes were substantial enough to offer significant resistance to the Romans. Thirty thousand warriors – probably an exaggeration – were said to have fought at Mons Graupius. By inference, a population of approximately three hundred thousand actually lived in the country.

With customary speed the Romans set up roads from their English province of Britannia and began to build forts in southern areas. Excavations which revealed the statue of a carved lion have shown how Cramond, near Edinburgh, may have been a significant port for the Romans. Spies gathered information and traders reported back to Roman garrisons from the hinterland. The boundary of Roman occupation was set as a line from the River Forth to the River Clyde, and the invading force began to build a chain of forts. But the native population did not remain behind the turf walls and ditch, and they made constant incursions from the north. In 83 BC the Roman General Agricola set out to destroy the Caledonians. He spent a winter camped at Inchtuthil, where the River Earn joins the River Tay, then marched north while simultaneously a fleet of ships advanced along the east coast and burned settlements as they went. The historian Tacitus, who accompanied him, ascribes a famous, bitter quotation to Calgacus, the Caledonian leader: 'They make a desert, and call it peace.' (In later years, other leaders in Scotland were to learn how to turn scorched earth to their own advantage.)

At Mons Graupius – which has been traced to several different places but may well have been Bennachie in Aberdeenshire – there was a pitched battle. Despite the fact that the Romans were surprised at being confronted by war chariots, which were long in disuse elsewhere in the world, the invaders won a hard-fought victory. The survivors of the Caledonian army were chased into the woods and disappeared. But the Romans did not follow up Agricola's victory. In the following year the general was recalled to Rome and the tribes resumed their control over the centre and the Southern Up-

HADRIAN'S WALL – WHY WAS IT BUILT?

It seems odd that the Romans, who had conquered so much of the known world, should have failed to conquer the tribes who inhabited Scotland. The Hadrianic and Antonine Walls were expensive to build and maintain. Why mark the limits of such a vast empire less than three hundred miles from the Pentland Firth? The landscape, wet, boggy, forested, was not too difficult to penetrate through its major glens and passes, but impossible to police in depth without an army that would have been unsustainably large. The Romans, since their shattering defeat in the forests of Germany, were chary of forest warfare. All in all, a war of extermination against the Caledonians would have been too great, risky and expensive, whilst the costs of the Wall and the garrison, year by year, were manageable.

lands of Caledonia. Somewhat later, in the early second century, the Ninth Legion was sent north from York on an expedition to reassert Roman authority, but it was never heard of again.

THE ROMAN BOUNDARIES OF CALEDONIA

In AD 122 the Emperor Hadrian fixed the boundary of the Roman province and ordered a frontier wall, now known as Hadrian's Wall, to be built. Twenty-four years later the Roman governor, Lollius Urbicus, passed beyond the limits set by Hadrian with three legions and reclaimed an area to the north, marking another boundary, known as the Antonine Wall, which was completed about AD 143, on the earlier boundary line. The zone between the two walls was not a colony or a province but a military area. A garrison of ten thousand Roman soldiers lived in fortified camps sur-

Boundary slab from the Antonine Wall

rounded by a largely hostile population. There were uprisings in AD 155, forcing a temporary Roman retreat to Hadrian's Wall. About the year AD 158, the Romans returned and re-garrisoned the Antonine Wall, but by AD 180 they had finally withdrawn to Hadrian's Wall again.

By the beginning of the second century the northern tribes had banded together in a military alliance of two main groups. South of the Forth-Clyde line were the Maeatae and to the north were the Caledonii. In AD 208, Emperor Septimius Severus took his army into Caledonia with the intention of destroying the tribes' ability to invade. No pitched battle was fought this time. The native peoples adopted a form of guerrilla tactic, and despite marching up through Strathmore and the Mearns, Severus was unable to engage them in battle. A treaty was made, however, and the Romans enjoyed fifty years of comparative peace.

Hadrian's Wall remained the Roman frontier. South of it was Britannia, a province of the Empire, with governors, paved roads, villas, hot baths, and a system of administration that reached back to Rome and even Constantinople.

North of Hadrian's Wall was Caledonia with its shifting alliances of Celtic tribes. There they maintained a warrior culture with bards to recite their history, genealogies and exploits; with druids to preserve their religion, a version of nature worship; and there they preserved an inter-related network of chiefs and petty kings. To the Romans, they were simply barbarians who tattooed or painted their bodies and grew their hair long. These barbarians sometimes went into battle stark naked, but when clothed they might wear colourfully outlandish garments, including trousers.

PICTISH SOCIETY

The Romans classified some fifteen tribes in the north and loosely identified the territories they occupied. They also observed that tribal chiefs had a religious as well as a royal function. Women could have such a role, as was the case with Boudicca of the Iceni. The succession of leaders was matrilineal: it mattered more who their mother was than who their father was. Since it is possible that women may indeed have had more than one husband, the matter of succession could be complex. Later Romantics sometimes regarded this Pictish society as democratic, but it was in fact full of social differentiations.

Under the tribal leader there was a class who maintained chariots and fought from them. These charioteers had the status of barons, owned cattle and land in their own right, and usually they owned slaves who worked their land and served in their homes. These slaves were normally war prisoners although their status was often hereditary. There may also have been raids to obtain slaves from other tribes and vulnerable coastal communities south of the frontier. Between the ranks of barons and slaves were the freeholders who owned shares in the common land of each group of households. With their families, they tilled the land and shared the other tasks. Cattle were probably common property among them. In any battle they would fight on foot. Among the freeholders were numbered specialist crafts-workers like blacksmiths, weapon makers and bards. Some bards may have enjoyed a more exalted status and the leader's or king's bard had special privileges. Druids formed a class apart, although in the role of the leader or king their functions were joined with the concerns of the rest of the community. Our knowledge of this society comes largely from similar groups in ancient Ireland. It may well be that among the Pictish tribes, who were themselves far from a homogeneous group, there were important but unknown differences. When the Scots later established themselves, they found significantly different customs among the Picts.

The Romans coined the generic name *Picti* for these northern barbarians. This ambiguous word may mean 'painted people' or may be a Latinised version of their own name for themselves. Alternatively, it may have been the name of one tribe alone. In the period of four hundred years between the invasion of the Romans and the immigration of the Scots many changes must have occurred. In the early years of the Roman invasion the threat of attack and perhaps conflict among the tribes themselves had prompted a movement of population into the hitherto unpopulated northwest as well as to the islands. The islands, well populated at a much earlier date, appear to have been largely abandoned by the first century.

The new settlers evolved a new and distinctive dwelling based on the model of the old round houses. It was built of stone and rose high above the ground, with an entrance door at an upper level. This was the broch, of which well-preserved examples remain in Glenelg and Orkney. Often placed close by the sea, the brochs' structure indicates the need for defence against attack from both sea and land. The Pictish homes thus show the degree to which people adapted to changing conditions. In the evolution of Pictish society other changes may have been in the organisation rather than the basic structure of society, with the inevitable tendency of tribal units to improve their own security by absorbing their neighbours. In doing so there was a gradual process of change in the language they developed. By the fourth century it seems likely that Celtic speech was the main language of the whole northern region. Traces have been detected of pre-Celtic language but they are insufficient to give it much identity or to establish its degree of use. It bears no apparent relationship to any Indo-European language (some scholars dispute this) and must be presumed to have been, like modern Basque, a continuing memento of some of the earliest people to occupy the terrain.

In the late third century the Maeatae once again stormed Hadrian's Wall. The Romans were distracted by trouble on other, longer eastern frontiers. In AD 360 the Picts and their Irish allies were freely overrunning the province of Britannia and reached as far as Londinium in the south. In 369 AD the Empire sent the able general Theodosius to maintain the Roman presence in the area and to restore the damage to Hadrian's Wall, but after his departure it was breached again in AD 383, and not repaired. In AD 407, as the Western Empire of Rome was crumbling in the face of onslaughts from Goths and Huns, the last legionaries were recalled from Britannia. The Picts responded by streaming back across the abandoned Wall. The so-called Dark Ages had well and truly begun. In a sense, though, for Scotland, which had never really experienced the *Pax Romana*, the dark ages were just coming to an end.

Several hundred years of proximity to civilisation, however hostile the attitude, could not fail to have some impact on the inhabitants of Caledonia. Tribal kings were impressed, if not overawed, by the wealth and sophistication of the Empire on whose outermost fringes they dwelt. The kings began to describe themselves using the Latin word *rex*, or 'ruler', by which the Romans designated them (hence Gaelic *righ*), and set out their own styles and titles in somewhat crude Latin. There is evidence that even remote tribes traded with the Romans and that the Hebridean wool trade began as a result of Roman demand. The tribes of the south of Caledonia, *Votadini* and *Damnonii*, made and broke a series of pacts with the invaders from Rome without becoming Romanised. But these tribes were the most open to ideas coming from the greater world, whether about Christianity or good agricultural practice.

CHRISTIANITY IN PICTLAND

During the fourth century Christianity gained acceptance among some Latinised Britons. Missionary zeal took some enterprising messengers of the Gospel into the land of the savage and pagan tribes. Cumbrians south of the Roman walls were the same people as those in North Cumbria, although living under very different circumstances. It was from South Cumbria that two evangelising saints emerged. St Ninian was to establish the first Christian Church in Scotland at Whithorn in AD 397; and St Patrick, whose first acquaintance with Ireland was as a kidnapped slave, returned in AD 432 to complete the conversion of the islanders to Christianity.

Ninian's success is more difficult to assess than that of Patrick. He is reputed to have travelled widely through the country, although some scholars believe his name was given to other mission houses by disciples and that his reputation spread in the manner of a cult. Like the later Columba, he was reputed to be of noble birth, which helped his cause among the aristocratically minded Picts. But, apart from his church of Candida Casa and the monastic school at Whithorn, seat of his bishopric, there is little evidence of his enduring success. Pictland remained pagan, with only a few isolated pockets of committed Christians. The ambitions of the Pictish kings were focused on booty to be found in the old Roman province of Britannia, where the Celtic population was fighting for survival against successive invasions of pagan races from Northern Europe. The Gospel of Peace found little attention.

CALEDONIA AD 400–800

During the fifth and sixth centuries the colonisation of Argyll by the Scots of Dalriada took place. Latin writers had referred to both *Hibernii* and *Scotti* as tribal groups from Ireland. Undoubtedly there was a significant amount of contact across the North Channel, which stemmed from shared political and commercial interests. But in or around AD 498 a definitive event occurred when a group of 'Scotti', led by a prince named Fergus Mor MacErc, left the Glens of Antrim to settle just across the water in Argyll. The Scotii, or Scots, named their kingdom Dalriada, using the name of their original home, and they appear to have been tolerated by the resident Picts. Two generations later they became more predatory under Aidan MacGabrain and began to take part in widespread fighting. By the end of the seventh century – within the time span of one hundred years – the Scots spread from the west across the centre of Caledonia. Place-

Artist's impression of the restored Iona Abbey

THE BOOK OF KELLS

This celebrated hand-drawn text, now the pride of Trinity College, Dublin, is named after Kells in Ireland, at whose abbey it was preserved, but there is little doubt that it was begun and perhaps completed in the scriptorium of the abbey of Iona, during the late eighth and early ninth centuries. It represents the high point of an art that had developed over the previous hundred years in widely spread Irish-founded monasteries. Lavish care and art were devoted to these illustrated transcriptions of the Gospel texts; and the artists drew on their own traditions which predated the arrival of Christianity, just as the Celtic Brid assumed the lineaments of Christian St Bridget. The intricacy of pattern and ornament is imbued with a mystical significance we have lost but which would have been strong in the mind of the illustrator. We still can appreciate the plastic subtlety of the line, and the remarkable way in which real shapes are always indicated yet never exactly delineated. Particularly since the 'Celtic Revival' of the later nineteenth century, the motifs of Celtic art have exercised a strong influence on the graphic arts far beyond the Celtic lands.

Artist's impression of a monk writing an illuminated manuscript

names such as Earn (Erin) mark their progress. 'Pictland' was not a single kingdom and the Picts were not politically united until AD 685 under Brude MacBile. This political division is likely to have assisted the establishment of the Scots.

The arrival of Columba on Iona around the year AD 563 and his energetic transformation of St Oran's church into a monastic school and Christian mission was of profound political and linguistic as well as religious significance. When King Conall of the Scots died, Columba was sufficiently influential to establish his own candidate to succeed to the throne. He chose

Aidan as a new king for the Scottish Dalriada, and in AD 575 accompanied Aidan to the Synod of Drumceatt in Ireland. At this summit meeting, Columba – who had been born in Donegal and educated in Derry – helped to negotiate an agreement that no more tribute would be paid to the king of Irish Dalriada, although some other services were still to be retained. He also made a celebrated visit to King Brude of the Picts at Inverness, encountering an early form of the Loch Ness monster.

It is almost impossible to trace the languages or dialects of the Picts and to assess their degree of resemblance to the Gaelic of the Scots, but it is plain that the use of Gaelic spread steadily. The prestige of Columba in the region may have played a part, as did the fact that Gaelic was the language of the new Christian religion. Gaelic may also have been a useful common speech within a set of various languages belonging to a variety of small communities.

Thus while the united Pictish kingdom dominated politically as far afield as the Western Isles and Orkney, the influence of the Scots on language and culture was overwhelming. The spread of Christianity as a religion was slow and uneven. It was unaccompanied by the miracles related by Columba's hagiographer, St Adamnan, but owed much to the patient and unspectacular work of missionaries like Moluag and Kentigern. Iona was the religious centre and would remain so until the raids of the Vikings.

South of the Roman walls, which by this time were crumbling, the Pictish peoples had observed immense changes. The new composition of settlers in South Britain caught up with them by the middle of the sixth century. To the southeast the Picts faced an aggressive new kingdom of people known as the Angles. This kingdom, Bernicia, was centred on Bamburgh and extended from the River Tees to the River Forth. Other new kingdoms had also been established farther south. The British tribes had been pushed westwards. From the southwest of Scotland the Welsh-speaking tribes now formed part of a larger British, Celtic-speaking area that stretched continuously down the west coast of Britain to Cornwall.

Throughout the sixth, seventh and eighth centuries these groups of tribes pursued a tortuous series of wars and alliances. In AD 603 the Scots under King Aidan of Dalriada were overwhelmed by the forces of Aethelfrith, whose kingdom of Bernicia was now making inroads into Cumbria. By AD 613 the Welsh-speaking tribes in Strathclyde were cut off from their natural allies to the south. Under Aethelfrith's successors, Bernicia became the kingdom of Northumbria, which was converted to Christianity by monks sent from Iona. By AD 657 Oswy of Northumbria was overlord of the Scots and perhaps also of a southern Pictish kingdom. In 671, when the Picts invaded southwards, they were defeated by Ecgfrith, king of the Angles. But in a crucial battle in AD 684 at Nechtansmere – probably Dunnichen in Angus – Ecgfrith in turn was defeated and killed by the Picts, and the imperial venture of Northumbria came to an end.

Picts, Scots and Britons lived and fought on among themselves. The next significant Pictish king to succeed to the throne after Brude MacBile was Aengus, who fought his way to power in AD 731. Five years later he captured Dunadd, the royal centre of Dalriada, and in 756, in league with the Northumbrians, he overcame the North Britons in their stronghold of Dumbarton. From then on, the political and cultural identity of the North Britons declined steadily. But in less than a hundred years from the battle of Nechtansmere all the Northern tribes had to face a new enemy.

NORDIC INVADERS

From the great Scandinavian land-mass to the northeast came the Norsemen, spurred on by the dynamics of land-hunger and political rivalry. They were fuelled by a culture of warfare and hero-worship. They were also equipped with superbly designed sea boats. Within Pictland there had been relative peace. Churches, monasteries and settlements lay open to attacks from the sea. The pagan raiders spared nothing and no one. In AD 795 they systematically plundered areas from Skye to Iona. By AD 807 the island of Iona could not be defended from the Norsemen any longer and the abbey was transferred to Kells in Ireland. A brief, brave, suicidal attempt was made to revive a community on Iona by St Blathmac in 825.

THE KINGDOM OF THE PICTS AND SCOTS – THE ORIGINS OF SCOTLAND

In 839 Eoganan, king of the Picts, was killed fighting the Norsemen. In the same year Kenneth, son of Alpin, became king of the Scots, and by AD 844, traditionally by means of an organised massacre of Pictish chiefs, he also became king of the Picts. In the past, through dynastic marriages and matrilineal succession, Picts had ruled the Scots and vice versa. It is highly possible that Kenneth's mother was a Pict, and therefore he had a claim to rule her people as well as the Scots. But a fundamental change had taken place. From now on the descendants of Kenneth continued to rule the combined peoples. Although the Pictish kingdom was far larger than that of the Scots, Kenneth and his successors did not forget that they were by origin kings of Scots too, and when Donald II took the title of 'King of the Scots' in AD c.889, he accepted it as his senior title. Pictland as a political concept was obsolescent. By the end of the first millennium Scotland was the coming reality.

CHAPTER THREE

The Celtic Kings

THE TURMOIL OF THE NINTH CENTURY

Alba, the unified Pictish and Scottish Kingdom ruled by Kenneth MacAlpin, may have offered better defence against the raids of the Norsemen than before but, for more than a century after AD 843, the country endured a series of fearsome batterings. By now the Norsemen were more than pirates and seasonal raiders. They had established bases on Orkney and in the Western Isles and probably in Caithness. They were settlers and took their land without the permission of or duty to the Alban kings. Ironically, in turn their own settlements were to become subject to raiding by later generations from Scandinavia.

Much of their war effort was directed to subjugating the peoples of Strathclyde, and in AD 839 they had already sacked the stronghold of Dumbarton. But coming to the assistance of the beset kingdom, more Picts were moving in. The Picts did not act out of generosity. They were taking advantage of the weakness of Strathclyde to establish themselves. Already most of the area of the Lennox had been ceded to them. Still the Norse aggression continued and was not confined to coastal areas. Through glens and over passes, they could move quickly overland. The army of the Picts and Scots was defeated by Norsemen in AD 874 and again in AD 876. The country must have been in danger of succumbing entirely to Norse rule had it not been for the fact that the Norsemen themselves at this time were not united. The line of Alban kings was preserved and some kind of rule was maintained during this stormy and chaotic time. Despite ample evidence of aggression from outside, there was also civil war, or at least struggles for the kingship ending in assassination. The sword and not the sceptre was the essential item a king required.

KING KENNETH MACALPIN
AND THE ALBAN KINGS

The centre of administration of the Pictish kingdom in the ninth century was Forteviot on the River Earn. Close by at Dunkeld, King Kenneth

MacAlpin set up a new religious centre about AD 850. This was an acknowledgement of the fact that Iona was now no longer tenable as a religious capital, although the monastery was eventually re-established and it remained the burial place of Pictish kings until the time of Donald Ban. While the record is one of almost constant strife at this time there must have been periods and localities where normal life continued without interruption, and the Picts practised the arts that still survive in fine sculpture and perhaps others that have perished.

Artist's impression of the round tower, Brechin

The Pictish kings, who were warriors first and foremost, must have summoned fighting men from all their chiefs and headmen, although the numbers involved in these battles may not have been very great. Exposed communities took the brunt of the fighting. It is likely that at this time many ancient brochs were rebuilt and occupied while new ones were also constructed. A new defensive building development, perhaps copied from Ireland, was the tall round tower, of which examples remain at Abernethy and Brechin.

The sea was still a vital food source and communications route, and although coastal communities must have lived in suspense and fear for much of the time, even the limited trading of the times was essential and had to be maintained. Warfare demanded weapons, and many daily items required metal. Chiefs' households wanted foreign luxuries: hides, wool, amber and copper were all being shipped out in return.

Kenneth MacAlpin died in AD 858 and was succeeded by his brother, Donald I. In his reign there was a change from the previous law of succession to the Scots form of tanistry.

Conflict with the Norse invaders continued. Forteviot was burned and Dunkeld was raided. The civil government was moved to Scone, to which Kenneth MacAlpin had already carried the coronation stone of the Scots in AD 850 after it had been rescued from Iona. Around this time, perhaps because of the burning of Dunkeld, Abernethy became a religious centre. But St Andrews, with a legacy of Celtic Culdee – from the Gaelic *Cele Dei*, friends of God – monasticism, as well as the growing

TANISTRY

Inheritance in Celtic Scotland was not a matter of the eldest son assuming the rights and titles of his father. Primogeniture was established gradually in the twelfth century, in an imitation of Norman practice. Even then, it was at first only used in the royal succession, and other lordships continued to be inherited by the former system. This method has acquired the name of Tanistry. The tanist was the heir presumptive, and his right to the throne was conferred not by his father but by his mother. Matrilinear succession, in one form or another, was typical of the Celtic kingdoms. The tanist was very often the son of the reigning king's sister. Whatever the roots of the custom, its effect was to ensure that a capable adult was available to take over – a vital consideration when the king was the war-leader. The defect of the system was the often murderous rivalry it promoted when there were a number of possible successors.

cult of St Andrew, based on the legend that the apostle's bones had been brought there, eclipsed other places as a place of pilgrimage and an ecclesiastical centre.

In the reign of Donald II, the first monarch to be called 'King of Scotland' or *Ri Alba*, from AD *c*.889, Harold Fairhair established the Norwegian kingdom. Shetland, Orkney, Caithness and the Hebrides were *de facto* his possessions and became Norwegian earldoms. The ruler of Alba could do nothing about this, or to stop the activities of predatory Norwegian earls. Nevertheless, the grim, dour persistence of the MacAlpin kings and their people preserved the greater part of their realm while other kingdoms vanished. At least three kings of Alba died fighting the Vikings; one was killed fighting the Britons and others fell to internal strife.

In AD 911 the formation of the duchy of Normandy caused attention to turn to France. Calls for alliances came from Mercia and Northumbria, who were now facing menaces from all sides. A battle at Corbridge in AD 918 held the Norsemen south of the Tyne. Before long the Norse forces became firmly established as a power in Northumbria, and Constantine I, king of Scots, was making treaties with them.

In AD 926, Athelstan, king of Wessex and Mercia, took over Northumbria, and in 934 he invaded the Scots both overland and from the sea. By 937 the Scots, Britons and Norsemen retaliated with a landing on the Solway coast. Athelstan, supported by other factions of the Norsemen, won the resulting battle of Brunanburh. Constantine I, like a number of his predecessors, retired to a monastery in St Andrews and was succeeded by his nephew, Malcolm I.

In AD 945 Malcolm negotiated the possession of Cumberland from Eadmund of England in return for his collaboration. This means that this part of the kingdom of Strathclyde had become detached from the 'Scottish' end and had passed to English control at an earlier and unknown date.

Malcolm's successor was his cousin Indulf. During the reign of Indulf, attempts were made to regain Northumbrian – once Bernician – territory, and Lothian may have been annexed at this time. Some time later, around 971, Eadgar of England formally ceded Lothian to Kenneth II. Southern gains were balanced by northern losses. By AD 987 the Norwegian Earl Sigurd the Mighty of Orkney was also master of northern Scotland as far down as Moray.

THE ACQUISITION OF LOTHIAN

When Kenneth II died in AD 995, the negative aspects of tanistry were plainly visible, not for the first time. Competition for the title of king was fierce and the prized position was frequently contested. The family trees of this time are extremely complex, as was the pattern of murders and battles for the inheritance of lands. Malcolm, son of Kenneth II, had given way to the succession of Constantine III, of Kenneth III and of Grig before he became King Malcolm II in AD 1005. Malcolm's reign lasted nearly thirty years, during which time, despite continuing warfare, he appears to have brought a degree of internal stability and strong rule to his kingdom. During his reign Scots fought both for and against the Irish under Brian Boru in the great Battle of Clontarf, which ended the Norse overlordship of Ireland. That was in 1014. Four years later, in a battle of more local significance at Carham, Malcolm II routed the Northumbrians and shortly afterwards became the master of Lothian which he had lost to Northumbria early in his reign. From now on Scotland's southeast frontier was the River Tweed. The region had a population that was largely of Anglian descent and predominantly Anglian-speaking. This was to have important cultural consequences. Perhaps significantly, it was around this time that the Gaelic name Alba – still the Gaelic name today – was supplanted by the hybrid word Scotland.

Cnut, king of England and Denmark, is recorded as having advanced into Scotland to accept the homage and submission of Malcolm II in AD 1033. In 1034 Duncan I succeeded his grandfather, Malcolm II. Duncan appears to have already held the kingship of Strathclyde, and some records indicate that because Malcolm granted captured lands there to Duncan, the old king was murdered. Whatever the case, Strathclyde was by this time a shadow of its former self and was changing rapidly because of pressures from northern, eastern and western groups. From the west, the Gall-Gaels, who were a piratical mixture of Viking and Irish forces, had fought their way into the area and bequeathed their name to Galloway; from the north and the east, Gaelic-speaking Picts overran some of the area.

As king of Strathclyde, Duncan had more prestige but probably little more power than the provincial rulers of the old territories of Pictland – such as had not, like Caithness, gone into Norwegian possession. These provinces – Atholl and Gowrie, Fife and Fothrif, Angus and Mearns, Mar and Buchan, and Moray and Ross – were governed by mormaers, literally, great stewards. The mormaers had great authority; they had quasi-royal status and, indeed, they were often members of the royal family from which kings were chosen. The power of the mormaers underlined the substantive nature of the kingship. Despite – perhaps because of – the pressures from all sides, the kingdom of Scotland did not disintegrate but slowly and painfully grew both in size and in internal unity.

DUNCAN AND MACBETH

When Duncan became king, his elevation was resented by Macbeth, mormaer of Moray. Macbeth was also a grandson of Malcolm II, but in addition descended through his father from Kenneth III and considered himself to be next in line to Malcolm by the rules of tanistry. The royal descent of his wife, Gruoch, further reinforced his claim to the throne. A northern league against Duncan was formed by Macbeth with their first cousin Thorfinn, earl of Orkney, Caithness and Sutherland under the king of Norway. The league confronted Duncan in AD 1040, resulting in the defeat and death of the king. Macbeth assumed the kingship, and his reign remained sufficiently stable although his northern power base drew hostility from forces south of the Tay, and there was a battle at Dunkeld in 1045 in which Crinan, titular Abbot of Dunkeld and father of Duncan I, was killed. But in spite of such opposition, Macbeth was able to travel abroad and leave his kingdom unattended, and that would have been impossible if there had been any serious threat to his power at the time. He is known to have travelled to Rome on a journey that would have combined aspects of a diplomatic mission – to foreign potentates and the Pope – and of a religious pilgrimage.

Government in the west was at a relatively primitive stage at this time. The king and his immediate council would decide policy. It was more than an assembly of war-lords, as it included at least some representatives of the

Church, who had already been diplomatic mediators in the past. Because of their education, their knowledge of legal matters, their international networks and the privilege and sanctity which their priestly status gave them, the clergy had an important role in running the country. It was important to know of developments in neighbouring kingdoms for trading as well as security purposes. When a powerful court, like that of Charlemagne or Athelstan or Cnut, gained extensive influence, the Scottish king would seek to establish a friendly relationship with it. His own personal prestige would be enhanced by the acknowledgement of other kings. And, as with dynasts and would-be dynasts through the ages, he did not hesitate to make accommodations or give vague understandings of homage if these were necessary to maintain or improve his own position.

MALCOLM CANMORE AND MARGARET

By contrast, this diplomacy could be counterproductive. It could encourage interference from other power bases. The sons of Duncan I had fled to Northumbria, and it was with the help of their mother's cousin, Siward, earl of Northumbria, that Malcolm Canmore gained first Lothian and Strathclyde in 1054 and went on to defeat and kill Macbeth in battle at Lumphanan in Aberdeenshire in 1057. Even then the northern chiefs put Gruoch's son, Lulach, up as king, and he was installed at Scone. A further battle, at Eassie in Angus in 1058, was necessary before Lulach was killed and Malcolm III or Canmore (from the Gaelic *ceann* 'head' and *mor* 'great') became King of Scots.

Malcolm III married Ingibiorg, the widow of Thorfinn, in what may have been an effort to improve his position by gaining the territories of Moray and Ross. Such dynastic marriages indicate the close linkages there were between the Scots and the Norse.

From historical records largely based on battles, it can be inferred that there were prolonged periods of peace in which there was easy trading, diplomatic and legal negotiation and a degree of linguistic interaction. Ingibiorg bore Malcolm a son called Duncan and perhaps two other children before she died. Around 1069 Malcolm married Margaret, the great-granddaughter of Aethelred Unraed, king of England. By now England had been conquered by William of Normandy, and Margaret and her brother Edgar Atheling, claimant to the throne of England, were exiles, in a situation comparable to that of the Jacobite 'Pretenders' of later history. To give them a foothold in Scotland would not necessarily have pleased William I of England.

Even now, Scotland and England were not wholly clear entities. Current knowledge of Scottish history before 1000 is a matter of interpreting extremely scanty evidence. Written records are scarce and were often the product of tendentious chroniclers anxious to extol the supremacy of Anglo-Saxon kings. In the eleventh century, however, the Scots knew their own history. Not only did they have the records kept by Church scribes, they had above all the orally transmitted knowledge passed on in the schools of bards and seannachies. The kings were in no doubt about their historic rights.

The king of Scots traditionally had a strong claim to Cumbria as part of the kingdom of Strathclyde, which stretched at least as far as Westmorland. The feudal overlord of Northumbria had reason to regard Lothian as part of his historic domain; the Scots king, however, saw Northumbria as an unattached sub-kingdom to which his own claim as over-king was as good as anyone else's. And whatever treaties had been made with the Norsemen, the kings of Scots would not be allowed to forget that the Pictish kingdom had once embraced all those parts of the mainland, the Orkneys and the Hebrides which now gave allegiance to the king of Norway. Confirmation of the royal boundaries would be a prime concern throughout the eleventh and twelfth centuries.

Malcolm III made raids into Northumberland, and in 1070 William I of England responded by invading Scotland. At Abernethy he met Malcolm, and together they came to some form of agreement. Malcolm sent his eldest son, Duncan, south as a hostage and guarantee of his good faith. In 1079 Malcolm again invaded Northumbria but was repulsed by William's son, Robert, who in 1080 ordered the construction of the castle at Newcastle. Malcolm invaded once again in 1091. While Malcolm failed to gain control of Northumberland, William Rufus of England marched up on the west and took control of Cumbria in 1092, establishing a stronghold at Carlisle. After this Malcolm III travelled to Gloucester on a diplomatic mission to have his lost province restored but William Rufus refused to see him. Warfare resumed, and in 1093 Malcolm III was killed while besieging Alnwick in Northumberland, and his queen, Margaret, died only a few days after him.

The lengthy reign of Malcolm III was mainly focused on the south. Although he was finally unsuccessful in his strategic territorial aims, in many other ways he achieved much of what he and his strong-minded wife desired. Malcolm and Margaret had not been intrinsically anti-Norman but they had been fiercely committed to maintaining their interests. The southward focus and the international connections of the Athelings had a strong effect on Scottish trade, language, religion and culture.

THE COURT AT DUNFERMLINE

The Scottish court had now been established at Dunfermline and was fully informed of the extraordinary changes in the Anglo-Saxon kingdom. The Athelings, as long as they kept their ambitions in check, were well treated by the Conqueror, and despite the occasional outbreaks of war, brief spells in Malcolm's thirty-five year reign, personal contacts between Scotland and England were regular and frequent. Malcolm's eldest daughter married the new Norman Lord of Richmond in Yorkshire. Margaret's sister Christina became Abbess of Romsey, and it was from there that her Scottish niece Matilda was released from her vows to become queen to Henry I of England (the only Scots princess ever to marry an English king, though many English brides went to Scotland).

Queen Margaret was a strong figure in her own right. She was pious and was responsible for the installation of Benedictine monks at the abbey of Dunfermline, replacing the Culdee community. But Margaret was also wise to the world, a cosmopolitan figure brought up as a royal refugee in Hungary. She knew the courts of Europe and had met some of its leading churchmen. Her reputation survives as an exemplary figure in every way. She bore numerous children, most of whom survived into adulthood and all of whom she trained with a firm hand for royal careers.

REFORM OF THE CHURCH

The Church in Scotland in the eleventh century was ripe for reform well before the queen-saint applied her broom to it. Its organisation was still along the lines of the tribal society from which it had emerged. As was to be the case four hundred years later, local magnates were often lay abbots who collected Church revenue and delegated the religious function to anointed priests. Clerics themselves were free to marry, and religious observation in general appears to have been casual. The Culdee communities, who were semi-monastic, had originally gathered together in an austere protest against the lax morals of the time, but had themselves become property owners and passed their time increasingly in secular lives. Some members kept wives, though not within the Culdee settlement itself. Many of the clerics had no knowledge of Latin and used Gaelic for their services. Since the religious reforms of Whitby in 664, priests had observed Easter with the rest of the Christian world but did not celebrate Mass on Easter Day, and they kept a shorter Lenten season. The role of King Malcolm within the Church is unclear, but he convened a conference and introduced a number of reforms, chiefly of a formal nature. These appear to have included the banning of Gaelic from the Church service. The queen was present at this assembly and embarrassed clerics by knowing proper procedure better than they did and having Papal manuals to quote from.

Gaelic continued to be the national language. The upper class spoke Gaelic although they must also have used Anglo-Saxon and, increasingly, Norman-French in dealing with the south. People in Lothian spoke mostly Anglian. Pockets of Welsh-speaking people probably still existed in remoter areas to the west and in Strathclyde. In the areas still dominated by the Norsemen, Gaelic and Old Norse were spoken, except in Orkney which almost certainly was populated entirely by people of Nordic stock who spoke a form of Norwegian. Latin was the language of the church, of learning and of diplomacy. Writing was predominantly in Latin, especially for legal and religious matters. It was a multilingual community.

Queen Margaret however did not speak Gaelic. It was known that she identified the language with the irregular state of the Church, the roughness of manner of the people and the rough-and-ready approach to ceremony adopted at court. Bards, harpers and druidic old men who knew and recited the ancestry of Malcolm III back to Adam were not to her liking. She disapproved of the married abbots and grizzled warriors who expected King Malcolm to carouse with them. To the queen all these courtiers appeared to treat the king with a familiarity she had never seen elsewhere and it did not please her. While Gaelic could not cease to be the language of the court of the king, it was definitely not the language for the queen.

Even before the arrival of Malcolm Canmore in the Gaelic area of Fife, Dunfermline had become a royal capital. But already, earlier kings had established a hunting lodge on a steep rock, Dun-eideann, in the Anglian-speaking area just across the Firth in Lothian. It had probably been a fortified site at least from the first century BC. Lothian was fertile, populous, peaceful and not at all Celtic. The queen liked Edinburgh, and a chapel dedicated to her name was built there on the orders of her son, King David I. It appears to be the first Romanesque building in Scotland and still stands preserved after long use as a gunpowder store. Margaret is also remembered from the 'Queen's Ferry' (hence the name of modern Queensferry) which was established to carry pilgrims to St Andrews without charge at a crossing point by boat to Fife. The ferries ran for eight hundred years until the building of the Forth Road Bridge. And it was in Edinburgh Castle that Margaret died shortly after the death of her husband.

The queen's confessor, Turgot, recorded how Margaret introduced luxury and ceremony not only into the court but into the lives of the magnates of the realm. More people could afford luxuries because Scotland experienced a degree of political stability that stimulated commerce both at home and abroad. The gold and silver that began to adorn royal tables and church altars had their source in the activity of workers in the fields, of the fur trappers, the fisher people and the people who dug for minerals. There would have been economic and social progress under Malcolm III even without his modernising queen, but its form would have been very different.

DONALD III

The backlash of Celtic conservatism was felt immediately after the death of Malcolm. His brother, Donald III, known as Donald Ban or Bane, 'the fair', who had been living in relative obscurity in the Hebrides, raised an army and sped to Edinburgh. Four turbulent years were to follow, during which time Donald Ban tried to reverse many previous reforms. Meanwhile the sons of Malcolm III struggled to oust him. By the rules of tanistry Donald was fully entitled to be king, but tanistry was acquiring an old-world air, along with many other of the country's traditional practices.

The English relatives of Queen Margaret fled. Donald Ban's reactionary approach may have gratified many people, especially in the north and west, but he had little opportunity to make a strong mark. William Rufus still held Duncan II, the eldest son of Malcolm, at his court in England. Supported by a Norman army, Duncan came north and drove Donald Ban back into the Celtic hinterland in the summer of 1094, and Duncan II was established king. Six months later he was assassinated and Donald Ban was back in power. William Rufus then gave Edgar, fourth son of Margaret and Malcolm, a large army. Instead of a full-scale fight the issue appears to have been determined by a battle between appointed champions from each side, in which the Scots lost. Donald was deposed and blinded, and there were rumours that he ended his days scrubbing clothes. Such scurrilous remarks are normal when a faction triumphs. In fact, he died a prisoner in 1099, was given a royal funeral and was the last king of Scotland to be buried on Iona. Edgar was now confirmed as king. Neither he nor the brothers who succeeded him had any time for the Celtic party. They had other ideas for exercising their kingship, which owed much to their mother and nothing to their uncle.

CHAPTER FOUR

The Scoto-Norman Kingdom

THE VIEW FROM NORTHERN ENGLAND

The installation of Edgar as king in 1097 was a new political departure, although it was not taken account of as such at the time. He was not the first or the last king to be helped to the throne of the Scots with the assistance of forces to the south. Now, however, the powers of the south were no longer divided. Predecessors like Malcolm III could have looked to Northumbria for tactical alliances, kinship and support when aid was needed. Similarly, for Northumbrian earls, a Scottish alliance would strengthen their position against the powers to the south. Scotland and the Anglo-Saxon kingdoms had mutual interests and dealt with each other on something like equal terms.

Now England was a unified Norman state, and its power and resources far exceeded those of Scotland. Norman kings administered a feudal system, which was firmly based on the tenure of land. Those who held a piece of land, however small, did so on a basis of service to the next man in rank above them. Their service might be given in payment as rent, in the supply of labour under certain conditions and in military duties, again under set terms, in war. A large estate, whether an abbey or a lordship, would supply provisions, weaponry, men at arms and a specified number of fully armed knights to the service of its superior, who might be an earl. In turn an earl owed service to the king and was required to muster his resources at the king's request. In return, layer by layer, each successive superior gave security and protection to the people in his service. Failure to do so entitled a 'man' to withdraw his obligations formally. The system was hereditary, based on the succession of the eldest son or nearest male heir.

Scottish kings relied on service through the mormaers and the chiefs and headmen below them. Military service was known as 'Scottish service', and it was summoned by a message, signal or symbol from the king. The king was also due 'rights of cain and conveth', that is, food and hospitality, from his subjects and, in return, had to dispense both of these in generous measure.

The Norman kings of England knew Scotland well enough and certainly travelled its southern borders. Their records told of the expedition of William I to Abernethy and the submission of Malcolm Canmore. The Normans, assiduous land-grabbers, were anxious to assert legal control to lands wherever they had settled and liked to have charters, establishing rights, duties and, above all, confirmation of ownership. They rapidly became part of a pan-European system that provided legitimacy through recognition by both Pope and Emperor. But where was the Scottish king's charter? To the Conqueror and his sons, accustomed to the notion of feudal supremacy over semi-independent duchies or principalities, Scotland appeared just another such, ready to be incorporated into their ever expandable structure.

From the Scottish point of view, English kings and English government have often been portrayed as predatory and imperialistic, seeking to impose an alien rule. From the twelfth-century Norman point of view, the Scottish kingdom seemed an anachronism and an anomaly.

SCOTTISH CLAIMS TO THE THRONE

It was as the 'man' of William Rufus, or William II, of England, that Edgar was crowned. Others, especially William, the son of Duncan II, had a better claim to the throne. Primogeniture – the succession of a first-born son – was not yet the established method of succession. But the sons of Malcolm Canmore had made a powerful bond with England: their sister Matilda was its queen. When Edgar died at Dundee in January 1107, he left a will in Norman fashion as if his kingdom were his to dispose of. Unmarried, he declared his brothers Alexander and David to be his heirs. Alexander was to be king, but David was to have Cumbria and Lothian. This settlement, made with the approval of, and even perhaps at the behest of, Henry I of England, was briefly contested by Alexander before the two brothers settled into a form of joint rule in which Alexander was titular head but David exercised power in the south. In 1114 David also became Earl of Huntingdon and Northampton in England.

The fact, as well as the method, of these arrangements created resentment in some circles in Scotland. William, son of Duncan II, who was established at the Norman court in England, appears never to have pressed his own claim. But his son Donald reverted to Celtic tradition and established a line of MacWilliams in the north who maintained and periodically tried to enforce, their claims to the Scottish succession. The descendants of Lulach, who were still mormaers of Moray, were also to cause trouble for some time to come, using their claim to the throne as a means to gain influence even if they did not expect to become kings. In the north of Scotland Alexander faced double trouble. King Magnus III of Norway, known as Magnus Barelegs, violently resumed control of the Western Isles after laying waste to them. Edgar, who wanted peace in the north, had formally acknowledged Magnus as ruler of the Hebrides in 1098. There was a rebellion in Moray and the Mearns to which the warlike Alexander took a small but swift and well-armoured force who fought all the way as far as Ross. The campaign put an end to the rebellion, and Alexander founded the Augustinian Abbey at the already sacred site of Scone as a gesture of gratitude for his success.

THE CANMORE LEGACY

When Edgar died he was buried in Dunfermline Abbey. Seventeen years of the reign of his brother Alexander I followed. In turn Alexander was succeeded by his brother David I as sole monarch and he had a reign of twenty-nine years. During those decades the MacMalcolm kings introduced revolutionary changes. Although they themselves had no Norman ancestry, they identified fully with the 'commonwealth' of Norman enterprise that had established kingdoms from England to Sicily, and were enthusiasts for the system of government that sustained the Norman states. They had been educated at a Norman court, and David in particular was considered by the Norman grandees as one of themselves.

Scotland itself was regarded from outside as a barbarous country by those who were able to set their opinions down in writing, like the English chronicler-monk Ailred. This may only have meant that Scotland was not Norman and, as such, not civilised. Despite the reforms of Malcolm III and Queen Margaret, the country still retained many of the simple institutions and traditions of the Picts and Scots, including the rites of succession among chiefs and mormaers through the laws of tanistry. The Church in Scotland still remained idiosyncratic in many ways. So far, the commercial life of Scotland had not reached a level where a currency was required, and no Scottish coins had been minted. Coinage did circulate: Anglo-Saxon coins from the eighth century have been discovered as far north as Moray.

The three main foundations of the rapid change in Scottish life were the castle, the sheriff and the burgh. The Norman incomer had by now fully developed the business of establishing himself on his newly awarded land. A castle would be speedily built on a strong point or artificial mound. At first it would be only of wood; a stone keep would come later. The land would be marked out and awarded to the baron's leading men and subdivided again and again until it reached the area that only one or two men could effectively till. Hunting grounds would be identified and kept strictly for their owner; poachers would be summarily hanged. Charters would define every level of ownership. The king took for granted his right to dispose of the land. Some of the land holdings given by David I were quite small and provided only enough to sustain an individual knight and his small band of retainers. These knights were significant as they owed their loyalty directly to the king. Other holdings were vast, like the two hundred thousand-acre Lordship of Annandale given to de Brus (or Bruce). Knights installed on these lands would owe loyalty first to their lord. At certain strategic points the king built royal castles, occupied by sheriffs, who were royal officials. However well ordered in theory, it was a military society, and an element of crown control was vital. The sheriff, like the Celtic thane, perhaps often the old thane with a new designation, was there to secure the king's rights and administer the king's justice.

Alexander I had already employed a chancellor, a chamberlain and a constable, who had not been drawn from the ranks of the mormaers. These positions rapidly became hereditary. Subsequently, in the reign of David I, the presence of Norman lords and the feudalisation of Celtic lordships hardly went beyond the shores of the River Forth, but it set a model that was to be followed in later reigns. Already there were enough Normans in the country for the king to make proclamations to his 'Scots, French and English' people. These were references to language. Scots was Gaelic; English was the Anglian speech of the people of Lothian, now evolving into Scots; and French was the Norman-French of the new nobility and the reformed court.

TRADE AND COMMERCE IN BURGHS AND TOWNS

Perhaps the most dramatic change in the time of the MacMalcolms was the growth of town life. On the one hand, Queen Margaret and her cultivated manners encouraged the use of new consumer goods at court. On the other hand, the Normans brought trade and the market-place with them. A more developed form of local government, a more cosmopolitan outlook on the part of the lords and a more intensive approach to agriculture – partly to cope with the increasing domestic demands – all promoted the existence of towns, however small. Merchants and craftsmen found more opportunities for trade and became increasingly interdependent. Imports and exports grew.

The times were such that the security of a fortified wall was still necessary to protect the towns. The first towns in Scotland were also on strategic landward or coastal sites and existed as protected enclaves against invaders: Dunfermline, Berwick, Roxburgh, Perth, Stirling, Aberdeen and Edinburgh.

Burghs were tied firmly into the royal management of the country. In return for the privilege of holding a market, engaging in export trade or having a monopoly on certain imports, they paid rents and customs duties. They dealt in currency as well as in barter, and David I established mints at Roxburgh and Berwick, introducing silver pennies as the first Scottish coins in direct imitation of the English model.

Because of their small size and their need to grow or purchase their own food, the towns could never be truly detached from the land around them. But in their early days towns were separate little enclaves full of foreigners. This was especially the case in the seaports, of which Perth was one, with a part-settled, part-transient population of English, Flemings, Burgundians and other North Sea peoples.

Towns were places of interest and often envy to the country-dwellers, who were rigorously excluded from living in them. By the end of the twelfth century, they were an important source of royal revenue not least because they paid in cash, in silver or gold, rather than in goods. A common interest was soon identified among the burghs, and the quartet of Berwick, Roxburgh, Edinburgh and Stirling formed the Court of the Four Burghs, which met to settle disputes and discuss matters of mutual interest, chiefly concerned with the maintaining and extension of burgh rights.

RELIGION AND POLITICS

Alexander I and David I both had strong links with the Church. They may well have been genuinely and naturally pious, but the distinction between spiritual and political conduct in the role of kings was not necessarily clear. The sons of Margaret were keen to foster the idea that their mother should be advanced to the immense honour of sainthood and, in doing so, enhance the political and religious status of their own family. Later monarchs would see the Church as a sort of natural resource that was there for them to exploit. These kings set the Church on its path to wealth and power. In the wars of independence, their successors would have reason to be grateful.

The Celtic Church had enjoyed great prestige during and after the time of Columba. Established while the Papacy was in a weak situation, the early church had developed in its own way but by the eleventh century it was an exhausted institution. Bishops had never held territories on their own behalf; their functions were spiritual and they were subject in other things to the abbots. But the abbots now were often laymen and their ecclesiastical functions were neglected or ignored. The Celtic Church was not alone in its need for reform. Alexander I, aware of the various reforms being undertaken in Europe, began to import them. With Papal sanction, he founded the bishoprics

*Artist's impression of the Church of
St Rule (Regulus) in St Andrews,
built around 1130*

of Dunkeld and Moray, and at this time there was a vacancy for the bishopric of St Andrews.

Now that the church of Alexander had been brought back within the sway of Rome, a dispute arose involving the Archbishop of York, the Archbishop of Canterbury and the Bishop of Durham as to who should consecrate the new Bishop of St Andrews. The see of York claimed primacy over the bishoprics of Scotland. This was a claim that Alexander and the Scottish bishops refused to accept. They knew they had inherited a church with an unbroken tradition going back to before St Ninian. It had been sending out missionaries when Canterbury was still a pagan capital and York a Roman ruin inhabited by ravens and rabbits.

In the end, Turgot, a Saxon who had been confessor to Queen Margaret, was consecrated Bishop of St Andrews by the Archbishop of York. The Archbishop reserved his rights, and the Church in Scotland did likewise. Eadmer, another Saxon, was to succeed Turgot, but when he claimed that the English see of Canterbury had primacy over the whole island of Britain, Alexander stoutly resisted the idea and as a result Eadmer was never able to take up his position. This controversy between the Scottish and English Churches would continue, with appeal and counter-appeal to Rome, until 1192 when the Scottish Church was finally made the 'special daughter' of the Pope.

The dispute, which has an apparently nationalistic tinge, was in fact more likely to have been the product of Alexander's desire to protect his own authority and prestige as king rather than any religious quarrel. Also, he had only to look as far as Durham to see what worldly power a bishop could wield. A wealthy bishop, owing his authority to the English king, would be dangerous and difficult to control. At this time England was in a state of virtual anarchy. The Church was beyond the simple political claims of national loyalties but its provinces tended to correspond with kingdoms. Thus the Church in the Northern and Western Isles at this time formed part of the widespread Norwegian diocese of Nidaros (Trondheim).

In the reign of David I, a full episcopal structure of nine bishoprics was established. St Andrews was the leading see, although it did not have metropolitan status. The others were Glasgow, Aberdeen, Dunkeld, Dunblane, Brechin, Ross, Whithorn and Caithness. David established numerous abbeys under different forms of the monastic rule. The great Border abbeys of Melrose, Kelso, Jedburgh and Dryburgh began to rise. David also founded Holyrood Abbey in Edinburgh to house a venerated relic brought to Scotland by his mother – the Black Rood – believed to contain a fragment of the cross on which Christ was crucified.

The last Culdee communities were turned into Augustinian canonries. The new abbeys and cathedral churches were given large tracts of land. At this time, too, an embryonic system of parishes began to form. Not yet on Scottish territory, in the same year that Jedburgh Abbey was founded, the great cathedral of St Magnus was founded at Kirkwall in Orkney. It was instituted by Earl Rognvald, who then sailed off with a flotilla of longships to visit Constantinople.

NORMAN INFLUENCES

Lands given to Norman barons and Norman abbeys were not simply empty spaces waiting for new owners. Some passed into Norman hands through the legacies of marriage or death but some were also transferred by force. Many local *toiseachs*, or chiefs, became sub-tenants of new tenants-in-chief. At the bottom of the social heap there were serfs, other people's property whose role did not change when the estate changed hands. Some of the husbandmen who tilled the soil can have experienced little change. Others acquired new masters with new ways of life: no longer the tribal chief, with his long, hospitable hall, but a Norman stranger, with charters and prejudices about barbarians as well as a hostility to the old patriarchal traditions. The native people of Scotland were required to work and fight, not for the tribal lands and the tribal heritage but in the name of something abstract: the law. The tribal lands had gone, the heritage was withering.

In AD 1130 there was conflict once again in Moray, led by Angus, the grandson of Lulach, with the help of Malcolm MacHeth. But by 1134 David I had established control there, and Angus was killed, while Malcolm MacHeth was captured and confined to Roxburgh Castle for many years. David seized the opportunity to Normanise the province. With peace in Moray the Scottish king could now direct his attention to the confused events to the south of his kingdom. England was in a state of civil war. Since David I was also the Earl of Huntingdon, he was an important landowner in England. He had other family interests at stake.

THE STRUGGLE FOR NORTHUMBERLAND

Stephen of Blois – married to one of David's nieces – was challenging Edith (Maud or Matilda in English) in Northumberland. David campaigned for Matilda but in his own interest, hoping to maintain and secure the region of Northumberland. For three years David terrorised the north of England. The brutalities of the time helped to define and clarify who the Scots were and who the English were. Nationality along the Border became clearer as the Scots were identified as hated raiders. There was a full-scale battle on 22 August 1138, in which the Scots were routed by an English army, inspired by the speeches of Thurstan, Archbishop of York, and by the standard, or emblem, that he had sent out to rally the soldiers. The event became known as the Battle of the Standard.

Two of Scotland's magnates, Robert de Bruis, or Bruce, and John Balliol, had Scottish lands but also great English land holdings: they refused to support the Scottish king and fought against him. David continued his raids, and in 1139 his only son, Prince Henry, was awarded the earldom of Northumberland. For a time Scotland's southeastern frontier stretched to the River Humber. When Earl Henry, David's only child, died in 1152, his eldest son, Malcolm, was a boy of ten. David I, determined to maintain his own line of succession, named his grandson Malcolm as heir to Scotland; Malcolm's brother William became heir to the earldom of Northumberland. David I died in 1153 and was buried in Dunfermline Abbey.

Northumbria remained in contention. Henry II of England, despite an earlier assurance to David I, regained control there in 1157, having persuaded Malcolm IV to 'resign' it. Malcolm's behaviour suggests vassalship to the English king. He went with the English army to Toulouse in 1159, and Henry assisted him against a rebellion of six earls in 1160 and in the subjugation of Galloway in the same year.

Well beyond the control of Malcolm IV, there was warfare in the Western Isles, which was ultimately resolved by a partition in 1156. In the split, the Outer Hebrides remained with the Norwegian King of the Isles, but the Inner Hebrides were ruled by Somerled, Lord of the Isles, a Norse-Celtic kinsman of the descendants of Lulach, who was later killed trying to raid Glasgow in 1164. The balance of power in the west had changed.

Malcolm IV, whose religious devotion and unmarried state earned him a posthumous by-name, 'the Maiden', died aged twenty-four in 1165. His robust younger brother William I was to reign for forty-nine years. William's policy was aimed at the recovery of Northumberland, in which he had the title of earl, with the single-mindedness of the jouster. Taking advantage of the warfare between Henry II and his son, he instigated Border wars.

SUBJECTION TO HENRY II

In 1174 William was caught in a surprise attack at Alnwick in North-umberland and was sent as a prisoner to Falaise in Normandy. To obtain his release he had to submit himself, the whole of the kingdom of Scotland and his castles at Berwick, Roxburgh and Edinburgh to the power of Henry. Having thus bought his freedom, William returned to face a rebellion in Galloway which he managed to quell. But then in 1179 he was forced to lead a campaign to the north, where Donald Ban MacWilliam, grandson of Duncan II, with wide support was challenging his authority. Two years later Donald was master of Ross and Moray. Bringing a warlord from one end of the country to help deal with a warlord at the other seems a risky venture. Nevertheless, in 1181, Roland of Galloway, sent by William, came upon Donald at the back of Ben Wyvis and in the ensuing battle Donald was killed.

The homage of William to Henry threw the status of the Church into doubt again. There was a lengthy wrangle between William I and no fewer than five successive Popes over the appointment of a bishop to the see of St Andrews, each vetoing the other's candidate. The English intervened on the side of the Pope, and in 1181 William was excommunicated by the Arch-bishop of Canterbury and subsequently the entire Scottish people were ex-communicated by the Bishop of Durham. Only two years later, matters had changed so radically that the Pope sent William I the Golden Rose as a spe-cial tribute to a king of exceptional religious zeal. With the special relation-ship to Rome instituted in 1192, the integrity of the Scottish Church was assured — as was the royal say in the appointment of prelates.

Three years before these events, and perhaps as a necessary preliminary, the humiliation of Falaise had been bought away. Richard I of England, seeking cash for the Third Crusade, released William from his previous bond of allegiance to the English Crown for the sum of ten thousand marks. A special council was convened at Musselburgh to arrange taxes to pay for this consideration. The contract was concluded by the Quitclaim of Canter-bury in 1189.

William I never fulfilled his ambitions to regain Northumberland. Even Richard would not sell it, and John of England, far from giving ground, built a castle at Tweedmouth and in 1209 obtained hostages and a payment of fifteen thousand marks to avert a battle there. William was more success-ful in the north, where he regained Moray and all the Norwegian territories on the mainland from Earl Harold of Orkney in 1196. Nevertheless, royal control of the far north remained slight. The MacWilliams were still active, in the person of Guthred, son of Donald Ban MacWilliam, who in 1211 came from Ireland and made himself master of Ross. With the help of cavalry borrowed from England, Guthred was defeated, delivered up in the end by his own men and his head sent to the king. William I died in the winter of 1214, a king of venerable years who was thereafter called 'the Lion'.

THE ENERGETIC REIGN OF ALEXANDER II

The last of the descendants of Duncan II, Donald MacWilliam, invaded Moray almost as soon as the sixteen-year-old Alexander II was proclaimed king on the Stone of Destiny. Donald MacWilliam was joined by Kenneth MacHeth in this uprising, but King Alexander had a new champion in Fearchar MacTaggart, lay Abbot of Applecross, who defeated the forces of MacWilliam and MacHeth in 1215 and was himself made Earl of Ross.

The troubles of King John of England with his barons were a natural opportunity for the Scots. The young Alexander II hoped to win back the northern English earldoms and, in anticipation, laid them waste. John, distracted by other matters, could not prevent it, and in 1217 Alexander led his army through England all the way to Dover, where he made contact with Louis, Dauphin of France, and paid homage. Then he made his way back to Scotland, unchallenged because of the death of John, but without new territories or titles. In 1221 he married Joanna, sister of Henry III of England, and ceased to interfere in matters south of the Cheviot Hills.

In his reign further efforts were made to pacify the restive north of Scotland and to regain the Western Isles. In one incident, the Bishop of Caithness had been stripped, stoned and finally burned to death in September 1222. The Earl of Caithness had done nothing to stop it or to arrest the killers. Alexander II made the long march north from Jedburgh to Wick and confronted the earl. The culprits were produced and tortured to death; the earl made his peace with the king. Nine years later, however, the Earl of Caithness was burned to death in his own castle.

The Normanising policy did not cease. By now the process had reached even the remoter parts of the land. When the Lord of Galloway died in 1234 leaving three daughters, the king procured three eligible Normans to marry them and divided the province into three parts. The Galwegians, conscious that they had enjoyed an adventurously separate past and would suffer an all too predictable feudal future, rebelled in favour of Thomas, the illegitimate son of their old lord. A fierce battle was fought and the forces of the king seemed trapped in marshlands. But in a dramatic counterpoint to Roland of Galloway's exploit in Ross, the able MacTaggart, now Earl of Ross, led his Highlanders around the morass and attacked the Galwegians in the rear. Thomas was defeated, but Alexander showed him and the people of Galloway mercy. Although Galloway retained some of its own archaic laws and customs for many years, it was no longer a Celtic power base.

When his first wife, Joanna, died in 1238, Alexander's second marriage to Marie, daughter of the French Count de Couci, opened a period of worsening relations with England. Henry III, seeing a French-oriented foreign policy develop, demanded homage from Alexander, which was refused. By 1244, as a new war seemed imminent, with armies mustered on both sides, Alexander offered terms for peace which Henry, with troubles threatening on his Welsh border, was pleased to accept.

In 1242 Alexander II had offered to buy the Western Isles from Haakon, and his emissaries had been treated with laughter and derision. Ewan, Lord of Argyll in the Scottish kingdom, had refused to give up doing homage to Norway for the possession of the Inner Hebrides. It was clear that remaining Norwegian territories would be regained only by force. In the summer of 1249, Alexander II was in full campaign with his fleet to achieve this when he died suddenly on the Isle of Kerrera.

In all these campaigns, Alexander II himself led his troops. For the king to lead his army was typical of this and much later times. But even to bring an errant, though not rebellious, earl to heel, the king of Scots had to challenge his wayward subject in person. There was an hereditary constable, but clearly there was no practical possibility of delegating the authority of the king. The mormaers of the past had by now become earls. Some were Norman, some were Celtic, most were a mixture of both. There were lordships as great as the earldoms. Although Alexander II had shown that none of these nobles was beyond his reach, their power still had wide limits and their capacity for intrigue was endless.

WALTER COMYN AND ALAN DURWARD

The eight-year-old Alexander III had been king for only a few days when two factions began to struggle for control of his small person. One was led by Alan Durward, the Justiciar of Scotland, supported by the Bruces and the Earl of Dunbar; the other was led by Walter de Comyn, Earl of Menteith and head of an ambitious and much ramified baronial family.

There would not be another coronation at Scone until 1292, and that would be a somewhat half-hearted event. Here, in 1249, the full, ancient, semi-pagan ceremonial was observed in the abbey churchyard. The Stone of Destiny, placed beneath a tall Celtic cross, was spread with silk embroidered in gold. The procession approached it from the abbey. The young prince sat, as the Earl of Fife placed the crown on his head and the Bishop of St Andrews performed the Act of Consecration. The moment the boy became king was when he was presented with a wand by the chief bard, or ollave. The earls of Scotland cast their mantles down before him. Then an aged sennachie approached, fell to his knees, and recited the pedigree of the young king in Gaelic: 'Alasdair macAlasdair macUilleam macEanruig . . .' and all the way back, not merely to Fergus mac Erc but far beyond him, to 'Iber the first Scot, son of Gaithel Glas, son of Neoilus, King of Athens, begotten of Scota, daughter of the Pharaoh Chenthres, King of Egypt.'

Two years after his coronation there was a splendid marriage at York. Alexander III and the eight-year-old Princess Margaret of England were made husband and wife. After the wedding, Alexander was to do homage to Henry III for his English possessions and titles. When asked to perform homage for his whole country, the boy, who had been well coached, refused diplomatically. He made it clear that this was a difficult matter on which he had not yet consulted with his chief men. The issue was not pressed. But Henry III's subsequent interventions in Scottish affairs went beyond the paternal concerns of a benevolent father-in-law.

The king returned home with his juvenile queen to be kept in Edinburgh Castle while Walter Comyn ruled the land in their name; Alan Durward went to Henry III to complain. The dispute between Comyn and Durward has been seen by some historians as the first appearance of distinct parties in Scotland, one set on maintaining independence, the other set on a closer and subservient relationship with England. It is more likely that the dispute marks the beginning of a long series of attempts by ambitious nobles to use the power of England to lever themselves into control in Scotland. Whilst one side courted Henry, the other perforce had to play the patriotic card.

In the summer of 1255 a plot was put into effect: the Earl of Dunbar seized Edinburgh Castle, and Alexander and his queen were transferred to Roxburgh and thence to Wark where Henry III was waiting. Then they returned to Edinburgh with Durward. The Comyns were out, Durward was in. The king's principal councillor was his good friend Henry III. Two years later the Dowager Queen Marie took the Comyn side, who once again seized the king, and the Durward faction fled to England. Henry III began to mobilise an army and the Comyns did likewise. At a late stage, concessions were made by both sides during a long conference in Jedburgh in September 1258, and war was averted. The death of Walter Comyn came very shortly after the conference, assisting Alexander, now seventeen, to rule in his own right.

DUNS SCOTUS

The by-name of 'the Subtle Doctor' is far more fitting to this highly intelligent man than the word 'dunce'. According to tradition, he was born in Duns, around 1265, and died in 1308. Educated at Oxford and Paris, he taught in Cologne and was a philosophical opponent of St Thomas Aquinas. Duns Scotus believed that our reason deals only with the natural world, and that free will and faith are quite distinct from it. He had many followers, and even when the dispute was settled in favour of Aquinas, the followers of Duns maintained his ideas. They were called 'dunses', and the contempt of their opponents for their hair-splitting reasonings eventually led to the word being equated with stupidity.

THE WESTERN ISLES

Throughout the first half of the thirteenth century relations with Norway had been poor. Scots settled and traded with the Inner Hebrides, and the feeling grew that these islands, so close to and visible from the mainland of the Scots, should not belong to Norway on the other side of the North Sea. Pressure was put on the Lords of Argyll to give up their vassalship to the Norwegians.

In AD 1263, King Haakon IV, who had ruled Norway and its island empire for over forty years, set out to reaffirm his control of his lands. With one hundred and twenty ships packed with fighting men, he appeared off the island of Arran in the month of August. Negotiations with the Scottish king began to take place. While they prepared to resist the onslaught of the Norwegians, the Scots also managed to extend the diplomatic parleys into September. Their hope was that lack of food or incidence of bad weather would send the Norsemen away.

Haakon became tired of these long debates and sent half his force, dragging their ships over the two miles of land from Loch Long to Loch Lomond, to invade the Lennox. The Norwegians met little resistance to their invasion but a storm destroyed ten of their ships. The same storm drove some ships ashore near Largs, and on 3 October 1263 Haakon landed with about nine hundred men to retrieve what they could. During the operations, the Scottish army appeared, led by Alexander. Haakon's men forced their king to return to his ship while they stayed and fought a rearguard action on the shore. The stormy weather prevented Norsemen on the ships from joining the battle, but the nine hundred forced the Scots back and then escaped to the ships. It was no victory for Alexander III, but his general strategy was justified. Haakon, with his fleet largely intact, withdrew. Three months later he died in Kirkwall.

Magnus succeeded Haakon as the king of Norway and was more amenable to reaching a settlement with the Scots. In the summer of 1266, an agreement was concluded. The king of Scots would hold dominion over the Western Isles and the Isle of Man on payment of four thousand merks and a further hundred pounds a year in the future. The new friendship was sealed by the marriage of the daughter of Alexander III, Margaret of Scotland, to Eric II of Norway in 1281.

THE ENDING OF THE 'GOLDEN AGE'

The reign of Alexander III was largely peaceful, as his father's had been. His barons indulged their taste for fighting by joining Henry III in English wars and by going on Crusade. Farming, hunting, forestry and trading could be carried on without military interruption. In the last year of the reign of William I, lords had been ordered to give their richer peasants (owners of four cows) more land to take into cultivation. This sign of a need for greater food production indicates an increase in population in the twelfth century. Bad weather might still mean poor harvests and shortages: the milder climate that had ushered in the second millennium was now coming to an end. But the wealth of the country increased. Extra inflictions like the 'ransom' for William I as well as the Norwegian payment could be absorbed.

The number of burghs expanded dramatically. By 1283 most of the towns of Scotland, with the exception of a few in the West Highlands and Hebrides, had come into existence and were given charters either from the king, as royal burghs, or from the local magnate, as baronial burghs. Lords and

---

'BAGIMOND'S ROLL'

In 1275 the Pope sent Benemund de Vicci to Scotland to re-assess the funds of the Church. The Italian's arrival, with his clerks and counters, must have caused apprehension among the higher clergy. The Church had been paying about three per cent of its revenues to Rome. But the assessment in use was an ancient one, and the wealth of the abbeys and cathedrals had grown greatly through the thirteenth century. 'Bagimond's Roll' took account of all this, and Benemund duly reported back to the papal chancery. Keen to raise crusading funds, the Pope raised the levy to ten per cent. There were anguished protests from Scotland, but the Pope did not relent.

---

abbots readily saw the financial and social advantages in having a market and manufacturing centre in their own domain. The location of industries such as coal mining and salt panning was governed by geography, but any town could make cloth if the enterprise and the will were there.

THE 'MAID OF NORWAY' AND THE CRISIS OF 1290

Alexander III and Queen Margaret had three children at the time she died in 1275. By January 1283 all three were dead and his only direct heir was a baby granddaughter in Norway. Known as the 'Maid of Norway', she was the daughter of Eric II of Norway and Alexander's daughter Margaret. She was proclaimed heir, but Alexander remarried in October 1285. His new bride was French, Yolande of Dreux. It was to be with her at Kinghorn, in Fife, that he rode from Edinburgh after a meeting with his council on 19 March 1286. It had been a stormy day and it was a stormy night. He crossed the Firth of Forth safely on Queen Margaret's ferry, but lost his escort on the shores of Fife and fell from his horse in the dark. His body was found below the cliffs the following morning.

Alexander III had done all he could in ensuring the Scottish succession. There may even have been an uxorious anxiety in his haste to return to the queen through the storm. It is possible too that the storm has been exagger-

---

THE CULTURE OF THE ALEXANDRIAN ERA

Normally, a period of relative peace and increasing wealth, such as Scotland knew at this time, is also a time of flowering of cultural life. Of the arts in Scotland, as of most other parts of Europe, sadly little is preserved from this time. On the mainland of Europe it was the time of the Minnesingers in Germany, elaborating the formalities of courtly love. The French already had their grand epic in the *Song of Roland*. In Italy, Dante was already established as a poet before Alexander III's death. Middle English had not yet emerged in Chaucerian vigour, but the Norsemen had the Sagas. From Scotland, there is nothing. Yet the Scots had epic centuries of struggle to look back on, and it is hard to believe there was no account of it. But it would have been in Gaelic, a language already outlandish to the court and preserved only in the oral tradition. Yet the great ancient legends of Cuchulain and of the Fianna survived: perhaps their cult absorbed later hero tales. In any case, Scotland had to wait for further heroes and poets to establish a national epic in literature.

ated and that the king was drunk. The collapse of the state, which followed not on his death but on that of the Maid of Norway in 1290, showed how much the fabric of the realm owed to the king: not only the person of the king but the very fact of the continuing kingship.

The Scoto-Norman kings were the best that Scotland was to have. They maintained the integrity of the nation and developed its prestige and resources in a way that was exemplary for the time. They preferred negotiation to war, but negotiated from strength. Their inability to create institutions that could survive the crisis of 1290 was shared with their officials and councillors, and exacerbated by their feudal tenants-in-chief. The message was clear – Scotland would not survive without a strong and resourceful leader.

The Struggle for Survival

THE COMPETITORS

Following the death of Alexander III, six Guardians, lords and bishops, were appointed to rule on behalf of his nominated successor, Margaret, the 'Maid of Norway'. In the Treaty of Birgham, of March 1290, these royal representatives accepted a proposal from Edward I of England that the Maid should marry his own son, Edward of Caernarvon, so long as the independence of Scotland was assured. Eric II of Norway duly sent his daughter to her kingdom, but she died in Orkney without ever seeing Scotland. There was no obvious heir to the throne. Robert Bruce, Lord of Annandale, claimed that Alexander II had long ago named him as heir in such an eventuality. He raised an army and marched on Perth with the intention of being crowned at Scone, nearby. The Bishop of St Andrews, a Guardian, feared there might be an outbreak of civil war and wrote to Edward I asking him to help preserve the peace. The adherents of Bruce also wrote to Edward I to ask for his support. The geese had invited the fox to dinner. Meanwhile other claimants came forward as the news of the vacant throne spread, and in the end there were thirteen claims in all.

Edward I had been, as far as is known, the personal friend of Alexander III. They had exchanged affectionate letters. Alexander and his predecessors had in their maturity acted as undoubtedly independent kings. This independence may be deduced not only from the freedom of their actions but also from the assertions made by Scottish ambassadors to the Pope, which constantly contradicted English claims that the Scottish kingship was, or ought to be, subject to the crown of England.

Edward I had every possible archive in England searched in order to find substance to his claim of feudal superiority over the northern kingdom. His aim was to put an end to the dispute once and for all, taking advantage of the Scottish succession crisis to establish a full, active and permanent suzerainty. At a stroke he would have extended his empire, enhanced the Plantagenet prestige, neutralised any threat from the north and increased his income. Searches of many documents established numerous instances of homage paid by Scottish kings to England over hundreds of years. There had been no doubt that William I gave total submission to England, but there was the Quitclaim. What had the Scots bought back with their ten thousand merks in 1189? The Alexanders, landholders in England, had performed homage for those lands, and perhaps for Lothian, which an English king had ceded, but specifically saving their kingdoms. Alexander III is recorded by a Scottish annalist as stating it categorically on his visit to Edward I in Westminster in 1278: 'I become your man for the lands which I hold of you in the realm of England, for which I owe you homage, saving my realm.' This was challenged by the Bishop of Norwich, and Alexander replied, 'No one has a right to homage for my kingdom save God alone, and I hold it only of God.'

This was precisely the position defended by Scottish envoys to the Papacy in Rome. It may be noted that the English record of the same event said nothing of either the exception or the intervention. But it made no mention of the kingdom of Scotland at all. Edward felt that his researches had sufficiently established his historic right. He challenged the 'high men' of Scotland to disprove his claim. The Guardians dodged the issue, pleading that it was a matter for a king when one was appointed. Far more to the immediate point, every one of the competitors agreed with him, and faithfully promised to hold Scotland under the sovereignty of the Lord King Edward of England.

All the competitors for the Scottish crown could prove some distant kinship with the line of Malcolm Canmore, but Robert Bruce and John Balliol patently had the strongest claims. Some had come not for the throne itself but to claim that the kingdom should be broken up in order that they could take their rightful share. Balliol and Bruce both traced their ancestry to David, Earl of Huntingdon, the younger brother of William I. Balliol was the grandson of the earl's eldest daughter. Bruce, now elderly, was the son of the earl's second daughter, Isabella. He was one degree nearer, but his rival stemmed from the elder daughter, Margaret. The commissioners acted without haste, allowing time for Count Florent of Holland to find documents to back his claim, which unfortunately were never found. In the end Balliol was selected on grounds of primogeniture, and he was crowned King of Scots in November 1292.

THE LUCKLESS KING JOHN

As King John, Balliol set about his task as the leader of the Scots. In the ten kingless years, the north and west had slipped easily into old habits of private war and banditry. The new king set up sheriffdoms in Skye, Lorne and Kintyre. Four parliaments were held, and arrears of justice and payments were tackled.

The seal of King John Balliol

But before long Edward made the terms of his role as English overlord very clear. He allowed Scottish legal cases to be heard by his courts, and the English courts were able to summon King John to answer for Scottish issues to them. In 1294 a Bordeaux wine merchant took his lawsuit to London for the unpaid wine bills of Alexander III, and King John was ordered to appear to answer in person.

In the same year, military service to Edward's Gascon war was demanded of the Scots. Balliol's council, which included representatives from six burghs of Scotland, not only refused to send men but, with the approval of their king, made an alliance with Edward's French enemies. In 1296 Edward responded by capturing and burning Berwick, Scotland's chief trading town. The Scots army met him at Dunbar, but the cavalry ran away without fight-

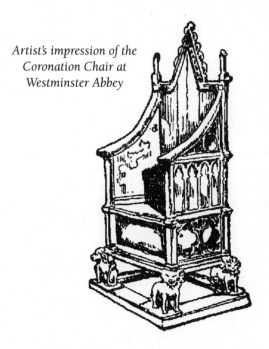

Artist's impression of the Coronation Chair at Westminster Abbey

In 1292, John Balliol became the last king to be enthroned on the Stone of Scone, or the 'Stone of Destiny', in Scotland. The stone had been used as part of the enthronement ceremony of the Scottish Kings since the 9th century. In 1296 it was removed by Edward I of England and installed in the Coronation Chair at Westminster Abbey.

ing and the foot-soldiers followed them. Only one Scots knight, Sir Patrick Graham, stayed. He died with his honour intact. Great castles surrendered to Edward with undignified haste. In the hall of Brechin Castle, Balliol was ceremoniously stripped of his royal vestments and forced to abdicate. He went to London as a prisoner. Also removed were the Stone of Destiny, the Black Rood of St Margaret, the kings' regalia and the Scottish official records. Military and civil governors were appointed to rule the land for the English king.

RAGMAN ROLL

Not all the Scots magnates had agreed with the anti-English policy. One competitor, Bruce, had died, but his son and grandson fought for Edward against the Scots. With lands in both Scotland and England, they and many others were accustomed to thinking in terms of personal loyalty rather than nationality and felt no loyalty to Balliol or to Scotland. The twenty-two-year-old grandson of Bruce, Robert, would go through a painful process of education in this matter. But their attitude in 1296 was entirely conventional and was shared by many people who did not have great vested interests to preserve. When Edward demanded sealed vows of loyalty, even those who in the past had been notable in their anti-English stance, like the Comyns, hastened to oblige. The thirty-five parchment sheets subscribed at Berwick that year, known as the Ragman Roll, contain the names of nearly all the men of substance in Scotland.

The Scots now knew their fate. As Edward I described it to them, theirs was the land of Scotland, not the kingdom. The son of the Competitor Bruce asked Edward for the kingship on the terms that Balliol could not swallow and was sent off with a flea in his ear. Edward had no plans for future kings of Scotland. Suddenly it had become an occupied province. Until March 1286, everything had seemed strong and stable. Now, all that was missing from the same structure was the king, and yet everything had sprung apart. Scotland had fallen into the hands of Edward Plantagenet like a harvested apple, with little effective resistance. Where were the proud earls of long lineage? Where were the great officers of state, the Marischal and the Steward? Some, like Comyn of Badenoch, had been sent to England. Three earls, Atholl, Menteith and Ross, had made a swift raid into Cumberland in response to the siege of Berwick. They had occupied Dunbar Castle, where they were captured and were sent to the Tower of London. But they were soon under King Edward's peace. Others did nothing and said nothing. No attempt was made by the magnates of Scotland to resist the English king.

BALDRED BISSET

Baldred Bisset, Master of Arts of the University of Bologna, never attained to high preferment in the Church. His assiduous attendance at the Vatican, as an advocate for Scotland, shows the calibre of the lower ranks of the clergy in the early fourteenth century. Sent with two colleagues by Sir John Soulis, the Guardian, as a diplomatic mission to represent Scotland, Master Baldred put forward a forcefully argued *Processus* against the claims of sovereignty being made by England. He drew on the familiar national legend of eastern origins, saying that the Egyptians might claim more rights in Scotland than the English. Clerics like Bisset, learned men and passionate patriots, were powerful propagandists both inside and outside Scotland.

THE COMMUNITY OF THE REALM

What then happened established beyond all possible doubt that there was something called Scotland and that it was more than a geographical expression or a name on an official charter. An enigmatic but resonant phrase, 'the community of the realm', emerged and found its way into documents of no official standing. What its authors meant is not entirely clear, but this phrase clearly did not refer to the king's council, or any single sector of the community. It may have been a line of propaganda designed to make those who read or heard it feel commitment to the message that went with it. There were able propagandists among the opposition to Edward. But it undoubtedly struck home to the people of Scotland and brought a new dimension into their political thinking that afterwards never quite disappeared.

Those who did not swear loyalty to Edward were by definition outlawed, and in this way William Wallace was an outlaw even before he killed Sheriff Hazelrigg of Lanark and set the town ablaze. He may have had personal reasons to take up the fight. The rule of Justiciar Ormsby and Lord Treasurer Cressingham was marked by arrogance, callousness and greed, and many people suffered from it. As the younger son of a country squire, Wallace owed his prime loyalty to his feudal superior, James the Steward. His family home was at Elderslie, and he may already have known Robert Wishart, Bishop of Glasgow. With cheerful cynicism this prelate had sworn allegiance to Edward, one of only three of the twelve Scottish bishops to do so. He was to repeat his oath whilst continuing to conspire against English rule.

The role of the churchmen is one of the most striking features in the re-sistance to England. They provided money, supplies, encouragement and spiritual support even under the threat of Papal interdict. Above all they provided the brains to support and guide a long and often apparently hope-less campaign. Self-interest has been suggested as their motivation since, in 1297, Edward gave orders that only English priests should be appointed to Scottish benefices. But it is much more probable that this order was the re-sult, and not the cause, of resistance from the Scottish bishops. Wishart was already in league with James the Steward who, although unwilling to lead, was ready to play a more discreet part in organising resistance.

The first important stroke was in May 1297, when an attack led by Wallace and Sir William Douglas was made against Ormsby the Justiciar, who was based at Scone. Ormsby narrowly escaped his opponents, but they were able to seize much valuable booty. At the same time, Andrew Murray (or de Moray), son of a prominent landholder who had been Justiciar of the North under the Guardians, raised a force in the north and in a short cam-paign established control of all Scotland north of the River Tay. Murray and Wallace were named Guardians in a new context. Their deeds roused many others to come out and fight, one of whom was the young Robert Bruce, Earl of Carrick, whose father had offered to be a puppet-king under Edward. In June 1297, Bruce, the Steward and the Bishop of Glasgow made a half-hearted bid to fight a battle at Irvine against an English force, but sur-rendered in a manner similar to the disgrace at Dunbar. Bruce's learning process was beginning. At this time, he still thought in terms of classical warfare and formal battles.

THE BATTLE OF STIRLING BRIDGE
AND THE ROLE OF WILLIAM WALLACE

Undaunted by the inglorious side-show at Irvine, Murray brought his force south to link up with that of Wallace. On 11 September 1297, their com-bined armies met the forces of John de Warenne, the Earl of Surrey, and the Lord Treasurer, Hugh de Cressingham, just outside Stirling. Gathered on the Abbey Craig to the north of the River Forth, the Scots army formed into schiltroms, or shield rings, which were circular formations of men armed with spears or pikes, protected by shields. The schiltrom was a novel forma-tion and perhaps Wallace's own invention. The English army, which in-cluded many Scots knights and their followers who were loyal to Edward, stood on the south side of the River. For battle to begin, a narrow wooden bridge across the river had to be crossed. Received wisdom at the time was that armed knights on horseback could not be beaten by soldiers on foot.

As Wallace and Murray had no cavalry force, Surrey may have felt perfectly confident that his army would triumph when, after two false starts, it began to cross the bridge. Wallace waited until a sufficient force had crossed, then charged with his men. The schiltrom was suddenly revealed as a formidable offensive weapon. The English army was cut in two and totally defeated at what was called the Battle of Stirling Bridge. Surrey fled to Berwick, while Cressingham was killed, strips of his skin becoming Scottish souvenirs. Andrew Murray was badly wounded and died shortly after the battle. Wallace went on to capture Berwick and to make raids on Northumberland. He claimed to correspondents in Hamburg that he had achieved 'the liberation of Scotland'. He became Sir William Wallace – probably knighted by James the Steward – and was now sole Guardian in the interest of John Balliol.

The forming and training of an army continued, with enforced conscription. There was a winter campaign of raids in northern England. The Battle of Stirling Bridge had not won a war, and it was inevitable that the English would return. Wallace, however, intended to fight the kind of campaign in which he had a chance of winning. When Edward I appeared with a large army at the end of June 1298, Wallace hung back, hoping that supply problems and lack of food in the countryside would demoralise and weaken the other side. But too soon for him, Edward's loyal Scottish followers, the Earl of Angus and the Earl of March, revealed his position and Edward led his men in a rapid march to force a battle. On 22 July, near Falkirk, the Scots were defeated in a hard-fought struggle. As at Dunbar, their small cavalry force had mostly run away, but the foot-soldiers stayed grimly on. English archers and repeated cavalry charges destroyed them. Wallace took refuge in the forest, and his Guardianship, although not his part in the resistance, was at an end.

Artist's impression of the Battle of Falkirk, 22 July 1298

The Battle of Falkirk did not mean that Scottish forces had entirely lost the war. Only the southeast could be said to be under English rule; elsewhere, with the Earl of Carrick (Robert I) and John Comyn of Badenoch as Guardians, Edward could not enforce his rule completely. From Scotland itself, and with the help of the Scottish delegation at the French court, there was a sustained effort to win the active support of the Pope in having John Balliol returned to his throne. Whilst the Pope gave favourable replies and addressed stately remonstrances to Edward I, Balliol remained a prisoner, although now under Papal custody. Edward was angered when two new Scottish bishops, Lamberton and Murray, were appointed.

William Lamberton was appointed to St Andrews and David Murray to Moray, and both men were firmly committed to the national cause. Lamberton became chief Guardian to Bruce and Comyn. He was a man of determination and strong character, whose qualities were severely tested by the mutual jealousy and conflicting interests of his fellow Guardians. By May 1300 Bruce was no longer a Guardian. Although the reason for this is not clear, even at the time of the battle at Irvine it was rumoured that Bruce's aim was to establish himself as King Robert and not to reinstate King John. In February 1302 Bruce renewed his allegiance to King Edward. At this time the return of Balliol seemed likely – there was intense diplomatic activity and the appointment of Sir John Soulis as Guardian in May 1301 may have been in anticipation of it. But in the context of relations between England and France, the Scottish question was a minor one. With France and England at war, Scotland had purchase on France and French diplomacy.

When France and England made peace on 20 May 1303, however, Scotland was left out in the cold. Balliol would not be sent back with French aid. The Pope had lost interest in the Scottish cause, and Edward I was free to concentrate on his recalcitrant province. His lieutenant, Sir John Segrave, had suffered a sharp defeat at Roslin on 24 February 1303, at the hands of Comyn and Simon Fraser. In response Edward I gathered a large army and remained in Scotland through the winter of 1303–1304, based at Dunfermline. One by one the castles were restored to English control; and one by one the great men of Scotland once again renewed their pledges of allegiance to Edward. The last castle to fall was Stirling, on 20 July 1304. Sir John Soulis did not submit to the English but left for France. Sir William Wallace did not submit, and he did not leave the country. He continued his guerrilla campaigns, but on 3 August 1305 he was captured and turned over to the English by Sir John Menteith. Twenty days later he was subjected to a show trial, condemned to death and hanged, drawn and quartered as a traitor to the king of England.

Artist's impression of William Wallace being dragged to his execution in London

EDWARD I'S NEW DISPENSATION

The brutality of Wallace's execution, compared to the relatively mild way in which Edward I dealt with the other leaders of Scotland, ensured that the memory of the indomitable Guardian was seared into the Scots spirit. The vindictiveness of the English king earned him contempt in Scotland. Nevertheless, the regulations imposed by Edward in 1296 had actually been more oppressive than the new declarations he made in the Ordinance of September 1305. His new constitution for Scotland included a council of earls, barons and bishops. All executive power rested with the appointed lieutenant, chancellor and chamberlain. It remained a set of provisions for a conquered territory, and the resistance continued.

Even as they both formed part of the royal retinue who watched the bombardment of Stirling Castle in 1304 in the presence of King Edward, William Lamberton and Robert Bruce had made a secret pact, or 'band', of support for each other. In March of that same year Bruce's father had died and Robert was now the bearer of the Bruce claim to the throne (and still a great landowner in England). Seven months after the death of Wallace, with Balliol still alive, Bruce made a move of extraordinary boldness, in extraordinary circumstances – he arranged his own coronation as king of Scotland.

THE COMING OF ROBERT I, 'THE BRUCE'

A short time before, a crime that horrified a God-fearing nation was committed on 10 February 1306. Having arranged a meeting with John Comyn

Artist's impression of Stirling Castle at the time of Robert Bruce

in the Greyfriars' Church in Dumfries, Robert Bruce and his supporters had killed Comyn in front of the altar. Murder and assassination were not unusual happenings – but to break safe-conduct to commit such a crime defied all codes of knightly conduct; to add sacrilege made it an atrocity.

John Comyn was a magnate of power and authority. In the eyes of the nation, his record in the war of independence and at the victory of Roslin would have seemed considerably more distinguished than Bruce's switches of loyalty. He had friends and relations throughout the nobility of Scotland – his great-uncle had been Walter Comyn. Bruce had summed up his situation in desperate terms: his bid for the throne needed Comyn to give him firm support – or he would have to get rid of him. He offered Comyn the Bruce lands to add to his own great domains in return for that support. Comyn refused. The two men had always been rivals and Bruce struck with personal as well as political motives. Was the killing premeditated? It seems likely that this may have been the case, although the matter is beyond proof.

The effect was to force Bruce onwards to his goal. There was no going back. In the following weeks the Bruce party secured as much as they could of the southwest. In this matter more than any other, the role of the clergy is remarkable. Bishop Wishart of Glasgow gave the red-handed Bruce every possible help and even supplied the robes in which he would be crowned. He gave Bruce absolution for his mortal sin. It is impossible to avoid concluding that the bishops were privy to Bruce's plans, although not the

Comyn murder, and had already committed their support. For them, too, there was no going back.

Bishop Lamberton, president of Edward I's council, had hurried from Berwick to Scone to officiate at the coronation. Efforts were made to replicate the ancient rituals, in the absence of the Stone of Scone and the royal regalia. The coronation was also held without the approval or presence of many nobles who were supporters of the Comyn family, who were still loyal to King John or who simply believed Bruce was vainglorious and was doomed to failure. He was crowned twice, once on March 25th, and again on March 27th, by which time the Countess of Buchan, sister of Macduff, Earl of Fife, had arrived to perform that family's traditional role of placing the crown on the king's head.

The ceremonies at Scone punctuated a time of intense activity. King Robert I ranged the country from Galloway to Strathmore, confirming loyalties, seizing castles from those who refused allegiance, setting in motion the process of raising an army. The supporters of the new king had recruiting methods that were not gentle – gallows were set up for those who refused the call to join the forces. The English king reacted by sending one of his distant relatives, an experienced soldier, Aymer de Valence, who was also brother-in-law to the murdered Comyn, to Scotland with orders to 'burn and slay and raise dragon'. The emblem of the dragon was a battle standard which meant that no quarter would be given. By June, the forces of de Valence had captured Perth. Robert and his army approached from the

---

BANDS

B and is Scots for bond, and the word refers to a practice, common among the nobles and prelates of Scotland for centuries, of swearing a secret agreement for mutual support. This might not mean immediate action. The band between Bishop Lamberton and Robert Bruce in 1304, when both were sworn supporters of Edward I, did not take effect for two years. The band made by Moray and his fellow nobles when Mary, Queen of Scots married Darnley had an immediate effect. Sometimes the band was dependent on a potential happening, like the Earl of Montrose's Cumbernauld Band of 1640, which was aimed against Argyll becoming supreme. The effect of the band was to increase the uncertainty of politics and the likelihood of treachery. Its last manifestation was in the Stair-Breadalbane conspiracy of 1689 which led to the Massacre of Glencoe.

west but de Valence led his men out in a surprise attack at dawn on the morning of 19 June 1306 and routed the Scots army at Methven.

King Robert became a fugitive. With his forces reduced to a few hundred, he was confronted and defeated near Tyndrum by MacDougall of Argyll, an adherent of the Comyn family. Robert sent his queen, his brother Neil (or Nigel), his sister Marjorie, and Isabella of Buchan north for refuge in his castle of Kildrummy while he took to the hills. The women had to leave Kildrummy on the approach of de Valence and were arrested in Tain by the Earl of Ross. Edward may have felt betrayed by Robert; he certainly had been fooled, and displayed the normal reaction of the totalitarian mind by malevolent vengeance, which included the imprisonment and display of the Countess of Buchan and of Mary Bruce in wooden cages.

Bishop Lamberton and Bishop Wishart were sent to England in chains. Those who had fought for Bruce were executed as traitors. The case of King Robert seemed desperate. Whatever chance his cause had, depended on his survival. To stay in Scotland would have been suicidal. He left his kingdom narrowly ahead of the pursuit, and sailed to Rathlin Island off the Antrim coast. For four months he vanished into the Hebridean mists.

THE EDUCATION OF A KING OF SCOTS

Robert I's education as King of Scots was now fully under way, and proved painfully expensive to himself, his family and his country. None of his successors had the opportunity of repeating it, or of learning the same lessons. The chivalric young Earl of Carrick, with a feudal army at his disposal and a family tradition of self-serving ambition, gradually turned into a patriotic leader and respected king of his people. Robert I still kept the support of the

The seal and counter-seal of Robert the Bruce

bishops, the Steward and numerous barons. In effect, the organising power of the resistance was only temporarily in abeyance. It was now that the people began to put their faith in Bruce. Nearly ten years of struggle had shown that the Scots would not give up their concept of a kingdom. Now, in dozens of small military actions, in secret meetings, in speeches made in forest glades, in stories of daring that spread through the land, they found they had a king worthy of that concept.

Bruce's maturity was both military and political. He realised that Scottish war must be guerrilla war, a bitter affair of attrition and burnings, of sudden appearances and swift disappearances, and he made himself a master of it. He fought alongside his men and not on an armoured charger. When Perth was retaken in 1313, a French knight observed with some amazement that King Robert was wading across the moat up to his neck in water with the advance party that stormed the walls. To be successful, such war required the consent of the people. For them, Robert had developed a message that went beyond the patriotic cause. It concerned freedom. At the lowest ebb of his career, he found that people were supporting him not through duty but of their free and independent choice; the same choice by which they renounced any oaths extracted from them on behalf of Edward I.

BRUCE EXTENDS CONTROL

Robert I had made himself king by ambition and boldness. The Scots confirmed him as monarch because they yearned for a king who would guarantee the integrity of the kingdom. In return, as his quoted words before Bannockburn show, he spoke to them as, 'My lords, my people accustomed to enjoy that full freedom for which in times gone by the kings of Scotland fought many a battle.' Scotland under Robert I was not a free society in a way that people of the twenty-first century would understand. It still possessed serfs, and the feudal structure remained in place; but there was a bond between king and nation that was to find its clearest expression in the Declaration of Arbroath.

Between 1305 and 1313, Bruce's campaigns went steadily on. In Scotland he still met the opposition of the Comyns and Balliol's party. John Balliol had not been formally deposed by the Scottish parliament or nation, and no Scottish patriot could regard Edward I's deposition of him as legal. To Bruce and his supporters the answer to this was to treat the entire Balliol episode as an aberration, and they insisted on making the immediate predecessor of Bruce Alexander III.

For the government of England, just as much after Edward I's death in

1307 as before it, Scotland represented unfinished business. Edward II, however, was more sluggish in pursuing it. Robert I, on the other hand, did not waste time. He invaded the Comyn province of Buchan, laid waste to it, and brought in many new inhabitants from the south. In this way Buchan rapidly changed from a Gaelic-speaking to a Scots-speaking area. In 1308, he challenged the Earl of Ross, outfaced him, pardoned him and turned him into a faithful supporter. Around the same time, Robert took revenge for the losses at Tyndrum by defeating John Lorne MacDougall in the Pass of Brander, which brought most of Argyll under his control. Robert's brother Edward overran Galloway and forced out the anti-Bruce chieftain Dungal MacDowell, although he failed to take such crucial castles as Lochmaben, Dumfries and Ayr.

From 1308 Bruce was able to govern much of Scotland, and on March 1309 he held a parliament at St Andrews. He was already in correspondence, as acknowledged king, with Philip IV of France. This parliament officially established the Bruce doctrine that Balliol had been put on the throne by a foreign power despite the better claim of the Bruces.

CONFLICT WITH ENGLAND
AND THE BATTLE OF BANNOCKBURN

In 1310–11 Edward II mounted an invasion of Scotland, but Robert prudently avoided a battle and the English withdrew. Robert then went on to raid systematically into Cumberland and Northumberland and as far as Durham, making rich hauls of cattle, spoils and cash payments in return for truces.

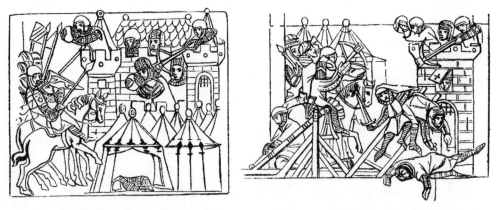

Summoning a castle to surrender   *The assault*

Scenes from a fourteenth-century manuscript depicting a siege

England still held many of Scotland's strong points. Banff and Dundee were not recaptured until 1310; Perth and the castles of the southwest not until 1313. When, on 24 June 1313, Edward Bruce made his rash agreement with Moubray, the (Scottish) commander who held Stirling Castle for Edward II, the English were still also holding Edinburgh Castle and the fortresses of Linlithgow, Berwick, Roxburgh and Jedburgh. The agreement was that Stirling would be surrendered if an English army did not come within three miles of the city before twelve months had passed.

This was a typically chivalric compact of the kind that Robert I deplored. If Edward II had been sluggish before,

Artist's impression of an archer at the time of Robert Bruce

he was now presented with a challenge to which all knightly Europe was witness. Scotland had a year to prepare for the inevitable response. During this time the castles of Linlithgow, Roxburgh and Edinburgh were retaken by the Scots, using the now perfected means of surprise night attacks, light scaling ladders and diversionary attacks. On 23 June 1314, Edward II came within three miles of Stirling, with a cavalry division of around three thousand and fifteen thousand foot-soldiers.

Robert I faced him with a Scottish army of perhaps ten thousand infantry with some five hundred light cavalry. Bruce had by no means decided to give battle. His experience and instinct must have been against it and his disposition was made as much for withdrawal as for attack. Nevertheless, important preparations had been made, which included the digging of pits armed with three-pronged spikes, known as calthrops, on the ground where the English horse would advance. The Scots army also carried with it the nation's most venerated remaining relic, the eighth-century Brecbennoch of St Columba, now known as the Monymusk Reliquary, believed to contain fragments of the bones of the saint.

On that same day an adventuring English advance party came upon an equally incautious Robert I, alone, reviewing the line of his troops. Recognising the king, Sir Henry de Bohun levelled his lance and charged. Bruce, on a small horse, avoided the lance of his attacker, rose in his stirrups and felled the knight with his battle-axe. The rest of the English party were put to flight. This minor incident created a dangerous moment followed by a sense of good omen for the Scots. More significant was a belated but successful effort by Moray to stop an English cavalry detachment from outflanking the Scottish army and reaching Stirling on the higher ground. The schiltrom formation advanced and in a hard action defeated the mounted knights. During the night, a Lothian landowner, Sir Andrew Seton, deserted from the English side to Robert. He told the doubtful Bruce that the English were in poor heart and could be beaten. After discussion with his captains, Robert agreed to attack in the morning.

Edward Bruce led the attack, with the Earl of Moray's schiltrom almost abreast on the left and the Steward to the left and slightly to the rear of Moray. As the English watched, Edward Bruce's men knelt to pray. Edward Plantagenet, observing this, is recorded as saying, 'These men kneel to ask for mercy.' Sir Ingram de Umfraville, a Scots knight and formerly a Guardian, replied, 'You are right, they ask for mercy. But not from you. They ask it from God, for their sins.'

Led by the Earl of Gloucester, the English heavy cavalry charged, but the schiltrom threw them back. Both armies heaved and pressed together. The English bowmen were poorly marshalled and the Scots cavalry, useful for once, scattered them. Robert then sent his Highlanders and Islesmen forward in a screaming charge. The English force, pushed back and separated by the schiltroms, now began to disintegrate. King Edward II left the field with five hundred knights, and his departure brought English resistance to an end.

THE ISLE OF MAN

Man, strategically placed between Great Britain and Ireland, was part of the Norwegian possessions and was the base of a Norse princedom of the Sudreys, as they called the Western Islands. Its language was not Norse, however, but Manx, a close relative of Gaelic. In 1266 Man passed to Scotland under the treaty of Perth, and was covered by the Scottish payment. In 1290, during the Interregnum, it was overrun by the English. Under Robert I it was regained but was subsequently lost again to the English. Strategically it was more important to England and its loss was not significant to Scotland. Bizarrely, after a long history of rule by the Stanley family, it passed to the dukes of Atholl, who sold their sovereignty to the British Parliament in 1764.

Edward made first for Stirling Castle, then changed plan and rode for Dunbar, vainly pursued by Sir James Douglas with a small cavalry force.

Bannockburn was a decisive battle which confirmed the position of Robert as the king and leader of his people in Scotland. It was a necessary preparation for the eventual English acknowledgement of that position, although that was still fourteen years away. English captives brought opportunities for ransom. They also offered the chance for an exchange of prisoners which would free the queen, sister and daughter of the Scottish king, as well as the aged Bishop Wishart of Glasgow, from English captivity. But the war continued with regular and intensive Scottish raids far into northern England. Only the strongest castles were safe against the forces of Bruce. These highly profitable raids might have achieved even more if it had not been for the ambitions of the Bruce family.

EDWARD BRUCE AND IRELAND

Despite their Norman origins and English titles, the members of the family of Robert I, by virtue of their Scottish connections, were also by this time drawn by kinship and the location of their Scottish domains into the Gaelic-speaking Celtic world, which had its own agendas. Ireland, where they already held land, was a complex structure of Celtic earldoms and Anglo-Norman feudal baronies.

Edward Bruce, while he had a reputation for flamboyance and recklessness was also considered to be a strong soldier. The king of Tyrone asked for his assistance to oppose English troops in Ireland in 1315. With support from the Irish, Edward Bruce defeated the English in a series of small battles, and was crowned king of Ireland at Dundalk in May 1316. He was not master of the country, however, and Robert I brought an army to support him in the autumn of 1317 which failed to consolidate Edward's position. By the end of 1318, Edward Bruce was killed in battle at Dundalk and the adventure was at an end.

A Bruce kingship of Ireland would have been strategically extremely valuable for Robert in maintaining pressure on England. But the campaign was essentially an opportunistic piece of family imperialism.

THE STRUGGLE FOR RECOGNITION

England north of York and Lancaster became a reluctant but hapless supply source to the Scots. The English King Edward II was barely in control there and had other difficulties in his own kingdom. In 1320 the English secured

a two-year truce in these northern provinces. In 1322 a large force commanded personally by Robert I came south and burned Lancaster. Edward
II rallied enough of his barons to lead another army into Scotland and
reached Edinburgh, which he burned, but was forced by the Scottish
scorched-earth policy to retreat. Robert pursued Edward south with a large
force and almost captured him near York, seizing instead his baggage train.
The Scots had won the struggle for survival. Now the emphasis of their
policy moved to the struggle for recognition.

CHAPTER SIX

Confirmation of the Kingdom – and a New War of Independence

SCOTTISH FINANCE

The wars of independence would have been more damaging to the Scottish economy if the Scottish economy had been less rudimentary than it was. The country was self-sufficient in food production. There were craft-workers capable of making the arms and armour that the Scots army required. The loss of Berwick and its international trading community was a blow, and although trade moved to other ports under Scottish control, imports and exports must have been seriously disrupted.

The conflicts with England had not caused a blockade, though occasional Scotland-bound ships were captured off the English coast. Scottish sea lanes were of great importance however. After the Battle of Stirling Bridge, Wallace had quickly sent a 'business as usual' message to Lübeck and other northern European ports. North Sea trading links were an important concern for the parliaments of Robert I. But the richest part of Scotland, Lothian and the Borders, was largely held by barons opposed to Bruce. It was extensively fought over. In 1322 fighting in the area was so fierce that it was said that the invading English found only one cow alive between Berwick and Edinburgh. Despite this report, it may have been the case that the profits of raiding the farms and blackmailing the northern counties of England, and the booty of Bannockburn, were so great that the wealth of Scotland actually increased – despite the costs of fighting a war.

A NEW SYSTEM OF TAXES

The extent of the spoils of war, however, did not correspond to the regular trickle of royal funds through the sheriffs, customs officers, or custumars, and tax gatherers in the counties. The income of the king had become much reduced. Customs duties on exported goods, market taxes, fines imposed at law, feudal contributions could be collected, but the war meant that such sources of royal finance were smaller in yield and more sporadic in payment than usual.

It was proposed that one tenth of the annual value of freeholds be granted to the king. To help achieve this, delegates of the burghs were summoned to a parliament which met at Cambuskenneth in 1326. This was a significant change, although it was made not to exemplify the 'community of the realm' but merely to ask for their money. The burgesses were well aware of this and did not attend the summons with any enthusiasm. Robert I called frequent parliaments. He showed himself to be an effective king in civilian as well as military terms. He dealt with large and small economic matters, and his enactments included provisions for a variety of activities such as the close season for salmon fishing. Nevertheless, the defender of the people's liberties also spelled out their duties. Every man worth more than ten pounds was to equip himself with a hat and coat of iron, a spear and a sword. Anyone who owned at least one cow was ordered to have a good spear or a bow and two dozen arrows. In small ways he was dealing with bigger issues: the proverb, 'If you wish for peace, prepare for war' was taken literally.

PAPAL INFLUENCE IN DIPLOMATIC ISSUES

Raids into northern England were the bloodthirsty and noisy forefront of intense diplomatic activity. The focus of diplomacy was to gain the support of the Papacy in Rome. Papal recognition of Robert as king would cancel out the English claims that first of all Scotland was not a kingdom and that in any case Bruce was a usurper. As ever, the Scots' efforts were vigorously countered by envoys from England. Pope Clement V was a firm supporter of England, and his successor in 1316, Pope John XXII, although no partisan of the English, was no friend to the Scots either. Anxious to mount an anti-Turkish Crusade, Pope John wanted the king of England's collaboration and saw the dispute between the Scots and English as an annoying distraction from the main issue.

THE DECLARATION OF ARBROATH

In particular, the status of Balliol and the murder of Comyn remained unresolved. King John Balliol had died in 1313, but his son Edward maintained his right to inherit the kingdom. Pope John XXII tried to impose a two-year truce in 1317. The Scots ignored the truce, as they also ignored his subsequent excommunication order on four of their bishops as well as his interdict of the entire nation. The Pope received a response, written at Arbroath

Abbey and dated 3 April, 1320. The Abbot, Bernard of Linton, was also the Chancellor of Scotland. Known now as the Declaration of Arbroath, this celebrated document spelled out with great clarity the views of the community of the realm.

> 'At length it pleased God, who alone can heal after wounds, to restore us to liberty from these innumerable calamities, by our most serene prince, king and lord Robert, who for the delivering of his people and his own rightful inheritance from the enemies' hand, did, like another Joshua or Maccabeus, most cheerfully undergo all manner of toil, fatigue, hardship and hazard. The divine providence, the right of succession by the laws and customs of the kingdom (which we will defend till death), and the due and lawful consent and assent of all the people, made him our king and prince. To him we are obliged and resolved to adhere in all things, both upon account of his own right and his own merit, as being the person who hath restored the people's safety in defence of their liberties. But after all, if this prince shall leave these principles he hath so nobly pursued, and consent that we or our kingdom be subjected to the king or people of England, we will immediately endeavour to expel him as our enemy, and as the subverter of both his own and our rights, and will make another king who will defend our liberties. For so long as there shall be but one hundred of us remain alive, we will never consent to subject ourselves to the domination of the English. For it is not glory, neither is it honour, but it is liberty alone that we fight and contend for, which no honest man will lose but with his life.'

The document was sent to the Pope in the names of eight earls and thirty-one high officers of state, of members of the nobility, of freeholders and of the community of the realm. Perhaps because of the Papal interdict, the bishops and abbots did not sign the letter. The Declaration's tribute to Robert, its emphatic defence of the kingdom and its utilitarian view of the role of the king are notable. Pope John ultimately returned a somewhat evasive reply but cannot fail to have noticed that Scotland saw and did certain things differently to the other kingdoms of Christendom.

Despite the ringing endorsement of the Arbroath letter, King Robert had a troubled year in 1320. An alliance of Balliol and Comyn nobles plotted to take his life, but their plans were exposed. They were impeached before a parliament at Scone in August, called by some the 'Black Parliament'. There were six executions, and the Countess of Strathearn and William de Soulis were imprisoned for life.

In January 1323, perhaps despairing of his own monarch, Andrew Harcla, Earl of Carlisle, entered into direct peace negotiations with Scotland. For this he was executed by the English in March of the same year. In May, a thirteen-year truce was negotiated between the two countries. One of its conditions was the ending of England's diplomatic war at the papal curia. Instead, this campaign intensified. Nevertheless, Pope John acknowledged Robert as king of Scotland in January 1324, although his excommunication was not yet lifted.

The coronation of Edward III of England in February 1327 brought the truce to a premature end. In June a large Scottish army went to England and took part in some inconclusive chasing about, which nevertheless discomfited the English government. Heavier fighting took place in Northumberland which continued into 1328. Yet in October 1327 negotiations for peace began again and by March 1328 they were concluded. A treaty was signed in Edinburgh on 17 March and ratified by the English parliament at Northampton on 4 May. In October of the same year, the Pope lifted the bans he had placed on Robert the Bruce and his kingdom.

DAVID II SUCCEEDS TO THE
THRONE OF ROBERT THE BRUCE

The man the English propagandists had mocked as 'King Hob' was now 'the lord Robert, by God's grace illustrious king of Scots, our ally and very dear friend.' The treaty guaranteed that 'the kingdom of Scotland shall remain for ever separate in all respects from the kingdom of England, in its entirety, free and in peace.' The new relationship was to be sealed by the marriage of seven-year-old Joan, the sister of Edward III, to the four-year-old David, son of the Scottish king, and they were married at Berwick on 16 July 1328.

A year later, on 7 June 1329, Robert I died at the country house he had built at Cardross on the banks of the Firth of Clyde. He had accomplished everything he had set out to do in Scotland, but he had never realised his ambition to join in the Holy Wars against the Turks and Saracens. In his will, he asked for his heart to be taken on Crusade by Scotsmen. Sir James Douglas, who had long been a friend and fellow-warrior, carried

Artist's impression of the seal of David II

out the wishes of his king and died fighting in Spain. The heart of Bruce was brought back to Scotland and buried in Melrose Abbey. Another faithful captain of Robert Bruce, Thomas Randolph, Earl of Moray, assumed the regency and kept up, or possibly enforced more firmly, the rule of law. The young David II was crowned at Scone on 24 November 1331 and was the first Scottish king to be anointed with the papal unction.

THE GUARDIANS AND BALLIOL

Under the terms of the peace treaty, Scotland had undertaken to pay the sum of twenty thousand pounds to England, perhaps as compensation for the raids they had made on the north. Once payment was complete, the English government began to dispute the treaty. Edward III claimed his signature was invalid as he had been a minor at the time. The situation was made worse by the claims of the 'disinherited' nobility in England, who had forfeited their estates in Scotland, and by the complaints of the Scots who had fled to England. Edward III interceded on their behalf without success and then turned a blind eye to their invasion of Scotland by sea in August 1332 under the nominal leadership of Edward Balliol. The Earl of Moray had died in February; the Bruce generation was gone. Under the new Guardian, Donald of Mar, an over-confident Scots army set out to repel the invaders. On 11 August, the Scots were routed at Dupplin Moor and Mar was among those killed. Edward Balliol was set on the throne by the Earl of Fife and proclaimed King of Scots. He had already pledged his allegiance to his patron, Edward III.

Although Edward Balliol had supporters, the government of Scotland was not yet in his possession. A new Guardian was appointed: Sir Andrew Murray, son of the Guardian who had died after the Battle of Stirling Bridge. Inauspiciously, Murray was soon taken prisoner and replaced by Sir Archibald Douglas. With the young Robert the Steward and John of Moray, Douglas made a surprise attack on Balliol at Annan, and the vassal-king fled half-naked to Carlisle. Edward III prepared for war and laid siege to Berwick. On 19 July 1333, Scots and English met in battle at Halidon Hill, not far from the town. The Scots, forced to attack uphill against a rain of arrows, were heavily defeated. Guardian Douglas was among the dead. Edward Balliol re-established himself as King of Scots and began the process of rewarding and reinstating the disinherited magnates.

David II and his young English queen were in the safety of Dumbarton Castle, where Robert the Steward joined them. In May 1334 they were transferred to France by invitation of King Philip VI. Young Randolph, whose earldom of Moray had been taken away by Balliol and given to the English Sir Henry Beaumont, was now named Guardian with Robert the Steward, and they proceeded to re-establish control over the southwest. Edward Balliol had ceded great tracts of the Borders to Edward III, and these were brought back into the Guardianship.

Sir Andrew Murray was released from captivity on the payment of a ransom and returned to oppose Balliol once again. Edward III, like Edward I before him, found that his dispensations did not last long. In the summer of 1335 he marched as far as Perth with an army some fifteen thousand strong and attempted to re-establish the basis for Balliol's rule. When his own lands were threatened, Robert the Steward made his peace. Sir Andrew Murray remained aloof. When the lieutenant in the north who had been appointed by Balliol, David of Strathbogie, laid siege to Murray's castle of Kildrummy, Sir Andrew hurried back there to defend his property and defeated Strathbogie in a small but fierce battle. In spring 1336 Murray was named Guardian of Scotland once again.

Edward III returned once more to Scotland, could not coax Murray – well versed in the style of Scots warfare – to fight him, and burned Aberdeen. Most of the castles in Scotland had been destroyed by Robert I, but now Edward III and Edward Balliol set about rebuilding them. As soon as the walls went up, Murray and his men went up over them and then pulled them down. As well as using the techniques of destroying castles perfected by Bruce, the Scots were sufficiently strong and resourceful to employ siege engines, including the formidable 'Bustour', or buster, that broke the walls at St Andrews and of Bothwell. Edward III tired of a campaign that offered little chance of glory or plunder, and delegated command in Scotland to the Earl of Warwick while he planned for war in France.

Murray's guerrilla campaign went on remorselessly, extending raids into Cumberland. Once again Lothian was devastated as armed bands ranged up and down the countryside. The lands around Perth were so bare that people may have practised cannibalism. A substantial English force under the Earl of Salisbury and the Earl of Arundel was sent to oppose Murray and the Scottish forces. They besieged Dunbar Castle but it was defended by the Countess of March, known as 'Black Agnes', who held them off with military zeal and spirited mockery in the absence of her husband, and the matter ended in a negotiated truce.

In 1338 Murray died, and Robert the Steward, now twenty-two and heir presumptive to David II, his fourteen-year-old uncle, became Guardian. He did not emulate Murray's vigour, but the return of John Randolph from imprisonment in England led to more attacks, and in April 1341 Edinburgh Castle was taken back into the hands of the Scots.

BLACK AGNES

Two generations of heroic Scotswomen supported and suffered in the Bruce cause, nearly all of them as nameless as their sons and husbands who did likewise. They could all take heart from the example of Black Agnes Randolph, Countess of Dunbar and sister to Thomas Randolph, Earl of Moray. Mistress of the strategic Dunbar Castle, controlling the coastal route to Edinburgh, she took charge in 1337 when the Earl of Salisbury besieged it. Asked to surrender, she is said to have replied:

'Of Scotland's king I haud my house,
He pays me meat and fee;
And I will keep my gude auld house,
While my house will keep me.'

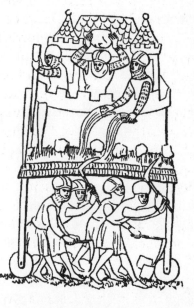

The English had a battering ram, 'the Sow', covered by a wooden roof. Agnes had a large stone dropped through the roof, scattering the men beneath. She and her attendants ostentatiously flicked the parapets with their handkerchiefs where English shot had cracked or scraped them. When her brother, in English custody, was brought in front of the castle and threatened with death, she scorned them, saying that if he died, she would be the earl of Moray.

On 10 June 1338, the English gave up and raised the siege.

Artist's impression of 'the Sow', from a fourteenth-century manuscript

THE RETURN OF DAVID II

On 2 June 1341 David II returned to Scotland aged seventeen, old enough to commence his personal rule. In his time as a guest of the French at Chateau Gaillard he had learned how to be a French prince but not how to be a King of Scots. He had learned a lot about the kind of chivalrous and courtly behaviour that his father had set aside, and he wanted to have fun and cut a dash in the world. Relations with Edward III became a curious mixture of formal jousting encounters and bloody raids on English farms and villages.

The gallant young king was not the man to rein in the excesses of his knights. When Sir William Douglas was made the Lord of Liddesdale, he had Sir Alexander Ramsay, Sheriff of Teviotdale, killed. David was not able to resist a request from Robert the Steward that his friend William Douglas be pardoned for his act.

Prompted by treaty obligations to France and the opportunity of making progress in the continuing English war, David II entered England at the head of an army in 1346. The people of northern England assembled an army under the Archbishop of York, and on 17 October 1346 at Neville's Cross they defeated the Scots and took their king prisoner. One third of the Scots army, under Robert the Steward and the Earl of March, ran away without fighting.

Once again Edward Balliol asserted his claim to the throne and once again the bulk of the nation ignored it. He remained in Galloway where ancestral loyalties to him prevailed. Meanwhile the Steward resumed his office as Guardian. But the territories which had been ceded by Balliol, the sheriffdoms of Berwick, Roxburgh, Selkirk, Peebles and Dumfries, were taken back into the possession of England in 1347 by Edward III.

BUBONIC PLAGUE

Those who had grown up in the reign of Robert I must have wondered what had happened to the rulers of the country. But they were also congratulating themselves that their land had been spared the Black Death, which raged in England in 1347. It spared the Scots until the winter of 1349, when plague spread throughout the country. This new, silent, insidious horror caused terror and panic. It was a virulent pneumonic form which brought death within two days. In any place where people lived in close contiguity, which was everywhere in Scotland except for a handful of castles, it claimed about a third of the lives. No war had been so devastating to human life. With very little medical knowledge of any value and unable to move from their close-packed and insanitary dwellings, the Scots did what they already had long practice of: they tholed it.

DOMESTIC POLICY IN THE REIGN OF DAVID II

David returned to Scotland in 1357 after eleven years' absence and an agreement to pay a ransom of 100,000 merks. He had made a brief visit to Scotland on parole during 1352 in the course of abortive negotiations for his release. Robert the Steward's concept of rule was to delegate internal powers to his fellow territorial magnates in their own domains. He had left the

Bishop of St Andrews to manage the protracted negotiations for the release of the king. When David returned to Scotland he had forcibly to re-assert his authority since law and order had become local matters. The western and northern Highlands seemed to have practically no links with the national government at all.

The finances of the Scottish court were in considerable disorder and arrears had been left unpaid. Not only had the ransom to be raised, but the household of King David had to be reformed and its costs met. The burgesses were once again summoned to attend councils and parliaments. In November 1357 their role was recognised in the use of the phrase 'the three communities' of the nobility, the clergy and the burgesses, which became known as the Three Estates. With peace established again, trade expanded rapidly and the towns, which had suffered both war and plague, began to prosper. Epidemics of plague were to return both during and after 1362 but their devastating effects were less. David initiated some reforms: he extended the privileges of the burgh merchants; holdings and property were reassessed; taxes were collected; money from the 'great customs' were put aside to pay for his ransom; and exchequer audits were held regularly. Yet the ransom itself was soon being paid irregularly and was subject to two further rounds of renegotiation while David was able to divert some of the funds into his own coffers. David II also began the practice of devaluing the currency. The silver penny introduced under David I had been of equal value to the English one, but now he increased the number of pennies to be had from a pound of silver from two hundred and fifty-two to three hundred and fifty-two.

Haphazard administration of justice was at least partially replaced by new central controls. Royal attention was given to the work of the sheriffs, who provided part of the king's income as well as dispensing his justice. Parliamentary councils were formed to speed up the reviewing of legal disputes and financial claims.

Gradually the king imposed himself on the earls and barons. The murder of his mistress, Katherine Mortimer, in 1360 helped him to realise that if he did not rule them, they would rule him. He appointed men of lower rank as household officers and to hold his strategic castles. As his Stewart successors would do later, he developed skill in picking off barons one at a time isolating them, and putting them at his mercy. When the childless Queen Joan died in 1362 and he proposed to marry Dame Margaret Logie, the Steward made a band with other nobles, with the aim of getting rid of David's upstart councillors and of Dame Margaret too. David dipped into his hoarded funds to muster an army which he led to confront James, second Earl of Douglas, at Lanark. Douglas fled and the other conspirators surrendered. The king duly married Margaret. The Steward submitted but tasted prison again in 1368.

There were other occasions when the king had to assert his authority. In 1369 a royal expedition to Inverness was required to bring John of the Isles, who had been living virtually as an independent power and who had been dealing with Edward III in his own interests, to accept that he had committed 'certain negligences' in his duties to his king and the country. John was made to offer up hostages and to accept taxation from David.

David II's foreign policy was inevitably linked to the need to raise money for the English ransom. Until his death he was engaged in complex negotiations on the subject, progressively managing to bring it down as his own wealth increased. He relished his pleasure trips to London, and he wanted also to achieve a final peace settlement with England, but here he was less successful. By threatening to reactivate the French Alliance, he was able to delay ransom payments and negotiate them down. But Edward III had a goal in mind: a new way of satisfying the ancient urge to nullify the Scottish power. He wanted to succeed David II in Scotland. If that was not acceptable, he wanted one of his younger sons to be the heir to the Scottish throne. In return he offered to make various restorations of selected hostages and the return of some territory. The separate existence of Scotland would be guaranteed. David II put the proposals to his parliament which summarily rejected it, leaving the king 'richt wae and angry'. The Stewart interests were mustered against it, but then nothing suggests David II was an admirer of the qualities of Robert the Steward. His own remarriage failed to produce an heir to the Bruce line. He divorced the protesting Margaret Logie and appeared to be preparing to marry the daughter of Black Agnes of Dunbar when he died suddenly on 22 February 1371.

CHAPTER SEVEN

The Stewart Kings: From Robert II to James III

'TURBULENT, RAPACIOUS AND IGNORANT'

When King David II died without a direct heir in 1371, peace with England was still unresolved though neither country was actively at war with the other. The Scottish realm was intact, prosperous (at least in Scottish terms) and better organised than before. A dynamic and efficient new king would have had a promising basis on which to build. But such a king was not to be.

'The Scottish nobles from the fourteenth to the sixteenth century were probably the most turbulent, rapacious, and ignorant in Europe'. The words are John Buchan's. It was from the ranks of these nobles that Robert the Steward, great-nephew of Robert I, was drawn to become king. Even before the coronation, a rival in the form of James, second Earl of Douglas, made a bid for the throne, but Robert II was duly anointed and crowned at Scone on 26 March 1371, establishing the Stewarts as a royal house. Robert was fifty-five. He was a man who looked every inch a king, and every inch deceived. He had taken part in previous battles at Halidon Hill and Neville's Cross but had no reputation either for fighting or for government. There was a dispute about the legitimacy of the children of Elizabeth Mure of Rowallan, his first wife, partly because some of them were born before their marriage but also because Robert and Elizabeth themselves were said to be too closely related. Only the legitimacy of the four children born of his second wife, Euphemia Ross, was not in dispute.

THE STEWARDSHIP OF THE STEWARTS

As a great landowner himself, Robert II maintained the self-interest of a territorial baron, and had neither the will nor the personal qualities to win the obedience and respect of his fellow-barons. Despite his sheriffs and the royal castles, the king's hand lay lightly over the provinces of Scotland. Short of rebellion or extreme contumacity, barons were secure and supreme on their own ground. Many estates were designated regalities, which meant that within his territory all royal rights, apart from ultimate feudal loyalty to the king, were vested in the landholder. In these conditions, a noble family could flourish. Robert I had given land and power to magnates whom David II had already found dangerously overbearing. Among them the Douglas family were pre-eminent and still gaining power in the Borders. They had the prestige of being heirs to the great 'Black Douglas', the ferocious warrior and Crusader who was also known as 'The good Sir James' because of his long association with Robert the Bruce.

Whether Robert II had any theory about the role of the king beyond that of a figurehead is doubtful. His internal policy was to 'stewartise' the ranks of the nobility as much as possible by marrying his daughters to them and by granting any available estates to his sons. As he had fathered more than twenty children from his two marriages and many liaisons, his opportunities to do so were plentiful. If the proverb 'A' Stewarts are no sib to the King' was quoted – that is, all Stewarts are not the king's relatives – it had a tinge of sour ambiguity about it. A great many of them were. However, it was also normal practice at the time for dependants and tenants to take the surname of their overlord if a surname was required. The result of saturating Scottish baronies with Stewarts was to raise the aspirations of the nobles and simultaneously reduce the distinctive status of the king.

What the Scottish nobles did, they did for themselves. Beyond Stewart territories, the Lord of the Isles, tamed by David II, now resumed a form of independence. The Douglas family kept the Border but their wars with the Percy family in Northumberland were almost private affairs. For the nobles, their sheriffdoms were regarded as opportunities to make money, and Alexander, one of the sons of Robert II, Justiciar of the North, used his appointment as a form of licensed banditry. Dismissed from his post in 1388 for 'negligence', Alexander descended on Elgin with his brigands and burned both town and cathedral. Known as 'The Wolf of Badenoch', Alexander occupies a stately tomb in Dunkeld Cathedral.

Rivalries among the nobles resulted in murders, which resulted in blood feuds. The king, placidly patriarchal amidst hot-blooded ruffians, was always ready to issue pardons in the hope that he would avoid confrontation. The trend towards anarchy was partly stemmed by the Scottish parliaments, whose tone of injury and complaint increased as the reign wore on. Finally, in 1384, Robert II assigned the task of keeping the common law everywhere throughout the kingdom to his son and heir John, Earl of Carrick, who later became Robert III. Parliament passed some acts to speed up the course of justice but there is no record to show that the earl did any more to stop lawless behaviour among the nobility than did his father.

THE CHRONICLERS OF SCOTLAND

From the fourteenth century, there is a series of writings which set out the history of Scotland, as seen at the time. Andrew of Wyntoun (*c*.1350–*c*.1424) composed an *Orygenale Cronykil of Scotland*, which takes the Creation as its starting point. Though written in rhyming Scots couplets, it has no literary merits. John of Fordun, who lived in the mid-fourteenth century, wrote his *Scotichronicon* in Latin; it was continued by Walter Bower, who died in 1449. These early chroniclers made use of annals and records that have since perished. Their successors often took them as fact, but much of the material relating to the remoter ages is dubious or fantastic. Within their accounts of the Scots' wanderings from Scythia or Egypt may be preserved at least the ghost-record of the Celtic transmigration to the West. The Scottish academic John Major (1467–1550), apostle of British union, wrote a more analytical account in his *Historia Majoris Britanniae* of 1521. Hector Boece, though principal of the university in Aberdeen, wrote, again in Latin, a more credulous account in his *Historia Gentis Scotorum* of 1527, soon translated into Scots by John Bellenden. Robert Lindsay of Pitscottie's *Historie and Cronicles of Scotland* is certainly the most readable of older histories of the country. A Fife farmer or small laird, who lived from around 1520 to around 1565, probably a graduate of St Andrews, he set out to continue Boece's account into his own times. This work was not published until 1778. A Latin work by the great humanist George Buchanan, *Rerum Scoticarum Historia*, was published in 1582, the year of his death. This, despite many inaccuracies and distortions, remained the standard account for some two hundred years.

NEW WAR WITH ENGLAND

In England, the death of Edward III in 1377 removed a long-standing threat to Scotland's integrity and independence. David II had left a continuing legacy of ransom payments, made to perpetuate the truce between Scotland and England, and these were promptly ceased. A new French alliance, the Treaty of Vincennes, had been made in 1372, and it was inevitable that when the Catholic Church entered the great Schism of 1378 Scots should favour the French-backed Clement VII of Avignon while England would support Urban VI of Rome. The Papal dispute brought Scotland its first cardinal, Walter Wardlaw, formerly Bishop of Glasgow, who was promoted to maintain the interests and cause of Clement.

The status of the truce waxed and waned as Dunbars and Douglases felt

THE BRUS

This is the first extant poetic work in Scots, written around 1375 by John Barbour, a cleric who was first precentor of Dunkeld Cathedral, then archdeacon of Aberdeen. From 1378 he received a royal pension. Barbour is believed to have compiled a genealogy of the Stewarts for king Robert II, in addition to his great work, and may also have produced other works, now lost. *The Brus* is a lengthy poem in octosyllabic verse recounting the deeds of Robert I and of Sir James Douglas in the War of Independence. It includes the celebrated Address to Freedom. With Barbour the tradition of a Scots-writing court poet was established.

inclined. Border territories ceded to Edward III were gradually taken back into Scottish control, despite the protests and threats of John of Gaunt, Duke of Lancaster. John of Gaunt himself was forced to take refuge in Edinburgh from the English 'Peasants' Revolt' in 1381. In 1384 he returned to Edinburgh, this time with an army, but he was bought off by a ransom. It was a demonstration of what England could do. Undaunted, the Scots arranged for a French contingent to land in May 1385.

*Artist's impression of a fourteenth-century
ship with a galley in front*

HENRY SINCLAIR'S VOYAGE

Henry Sinclair (*c*.1345–*c*.1400), of a Lothian-based family, became the first Scottish earl of Orkney, although he paid homage for it to the Norwegian king. With a sailor of Venetian descent, Antonio Zeno, he made a voyage in 1391 from Orkney to Greenland, and is credited with the 'rediscovery' of that territory. More speculative accounts suggest that he reached North America, on the coast of what is now, by coincidence, Nova Scotia.

John of Gaunt returned again to Scotland with his young king, Richard II, and this time Edinburgh was attacked and burned, but the allied Scots-French army was not drawn into battle; it instead left scorched earth in Lothian and went off to plunder Cumberland. The French detachment went home without a chivalric battle and with sour stories of the beggarly and primitive Scots. Raids into England, however, did continue. At Otterburn on 5 August 1388, the Earl of Douglas engaged the Earl of Northumberland in a battle that became famous as the very model of a chivalric encounter. It ended with Northumberland giving his surrender to Scottish forces at the very time when the Earl of Douglas died on the battlefield.

JOHN, EARL OF CARRICK, AS ROBERT III

Robert II virtually abdicated in what seems to have been a confrontation with his general council on 1 December 1388. The king submitted himself and his eldest son, John, Earl of Carrick, fully to the will of council. Carrick was physically disabled – some said by a kick from a horse – and his younger brother, Robert Stewart, Earl of Fife, was appointed Guardian. The Earl of Fife would hold power for thirty-two years. Robert II died on 19 April 1390; John, Earl of Carrick, then took his father's name to become Robert III when he acceded at the age of fifty-three and carried on his administration in much the same style as his father.

During his sixteen-year period on the throne, the administration of the country continued to decline. Earl Robert, the new king's brother, maintained his role as Guardian, a position that was renewed, perhaps with little choice by successive parliaments. It was a role which was not exercised for the nation but for his own enrichment. Meanwhile the north slipped completely out of royal control. Clan warfare there was endemic, and raids out of the Highlands into Strathmore were assuming the nature of a small-scale war. In September 1396, sixty champion warriors of two feuding clan

The seals of Robert II and Robert III

groups, Kay and Chattan, met on the North Inch of Perth to fight to the death. Like a latter-day Roman emperor, Robert III with a retinue of invited guests supervised the slaughter.

Far beyond the control of King Robert or the Guardian, their uncle, Donald MacDonald, Lord of the Isles, was able to receive missions from England. Donald's brother, Alastair Carrach, was blackmailing landowners in the east of Scotland to keep the peace. Farther north, Orkney was undergoing the same process of assimilation to Scotland which had happened earlier in the Hebrides. The Earl was a Scot of Norman ancestry – the de St Clair, or Sinclair, family – doing homage to the king of Norway for Orkney and to the King of Scots for his Scottish holdings.

In 1398, in a fine ceremony at Scone that aped procedures adopted in England, the Earl of Fife was named Duke of Albany. His nephew, Prince David, the heir apparent, was named Duke of Rothesay. Not long afterwards, in 1399, the Duke of Rothesay became lieutenant of the kingdom and a power struggle began between him and his uncle, the Duke of Albany. This rivalry ended in 1401 when the headstrong and foolish Rothesay was locked up by Albany in Falkland Palace, where he died – either of dysentery or starvation. Albany could be ruthlessly decisive when his own interests

NAMES AND SURNAMES

An enduring stability in Scotland's land-based society is seen in the preservation of distinctive names in all parts of the country. Scott is still a very common name in the Borders. Macdonalds have gone across the world, but they still make up an impressive proportion of the Western Isles telephone directory. Traills and Baikies are still found in Orkney, Gunns in Caithness, Cheynes in the northeast, Macdowells in the southwest.

Surnames began to be used in Scotland from the twelfth century, and became common in the fourteenth. At first they were the preserve of the nobility and clergy, and showed a man's estate, like Bruce of Annandale, or his function, like MacTaggart, son of the (hereditary) priest. When lists began to be kept in writing, it became necessary to identify a far greater number of tenants and sub-tenants, suppliers and debtors. As a great many men were called John, a further name was all the more necessary. Some of these came from personal features – a brown complexion produced Brown, or Donn in Gaelic. Trades gave rise to names like Smith, or Gow from the Gaelic. Father's names were extremely common in Scots and Gaelic, like Johnson/ MacIain, and Thomas/Tawse. Sometimes a man was named from his birthplace, like Wemyss or Abernethy. It was common practice to take a lord's name: when Sinclair became earl of Caithness, many people became Sinclairs, and it remains a local name. Surnames at first were shifting things, and it took several generations for a name to become established within a family. Even then, under external pressures, it could change. When the surname of the MacGregors was forbidden by law for most of the seventeenth century, they became Campbells, or Comries, or Whites. Some eventually changed back; some did not.

were touched. In the same year as the death of the Duke of Rothesay, the fourth Earl of Douglas invaded England with a Scots army and was heavily defeated at Homildon Hill near Newcastle. Albany's eldest son, Murdoch, was taken prisoner.

Robert III had another legitimate son, James, who was still a young boy. Mindful both of the way Albany had dealt with his elder son and of the new vulnerability to England, the king arranged to send the eleven-year-old James to France 'for his education' in 1406. On the way to France, James was captured at sea by the English and sent to London. In that same year King Robert III died on 4 April, having requested to be buried on a dung heap. His death meant no more to the state than his life had.

WAR IN THE HIGHLANDS

Nothing was to change. The Duke of Albany was appointed Governor of the Realm on his nephew's behalf. Conflict in the kingdom continued. Open war broke out in the Highlands in 1411. Despite his Stewart connection, Donald of the Isles resented the wholesale Stewart annexation of earldoms around him. A dispute had been simmering since the earldom of Ross became vacant in 1402. Donald had a claim to it through his wife, but the Duke of Albany intended it for his own son, John, who was already Earl of Buchan. Donald took a chance, seized the earldom of Ross, and in 1411 advanced eastwards towards Aberdeen to claim other lands and properties belonging to the earldom. On 24 July, he was met at Harlaw by Alexander Stewart, Earl of Mar – son of the Wolf of Badenoch – with a locally recruited army. After the resulting battle, both sides claimed to have won. Donald retreated to the west but continued to act as an independent power, and Albany recovered at least part of the earldom on behalf of his son.

Among the forces of the Earl of Mar had been a detachment of burgesses from Aberdeen, fearing that the Islesmen were out to burn their city. They had businesses as well as families to protect. Aberdeen had not been attacked since the days of Edward III. Following the 'herschip', or harrowing, of Buchan by Robert I, the lands around Aberdeen had become largely Scots-speaking. An invasion of Gaelic-speaking Highlanders may have been seen as a terrifying attack by alien savages. Other significant towns like Perth, Stirling, Glasgow and Dumfries still adjoined Gaelic-speaking areas and may have seen the clansmen as uncouth but nevertheless accepted them as fellow-Scots. Whether the clansmen saw themselves as Scots at all is doubtful, particularly at this time when they led lives largely independent of the government and when the kings were passive figures, not national war-leaders.

GROWTH OF THE BURGHS
IN THE FOURTEENTH CENTURY

In the political swamp of the guardianship of the Duke of Albany, the burghs did not fare too badly. Their rights and freedoms were often guaranteed by the local magnate, and if their taxes were siphoned off before reaching the royal exchequer, that was not their problem. The burghs kept trading, and money in circulation was a good thing. The demand for luxury goods was rising. The Scots nobility wished to maintain the kind of style they saw in France and England: as long as the merchant was there to supply the goods as well as to lend the money to pay for them, the nobility would buy them. The burgh councils of Edinburgh, Dundee, Perth and Aberdeen underwrote the 'ransom' of James I.

Although many fortifications and castles had been wrecked in the wars of independence, Scots burghs maintained stout walls and some had castles with royal garrisons to protect them. While national government grew less, the burghs increasingly developed their own local government. The whole life of the burgh was rigidly organised within a social structure that was intended to perpetuate a miniature oligarchy of merchant burgesses. The burghs were still very modest townships, whose importance was relative to the poverty and backwardness of the country. Even the merchants of Edinburgh, by now the principal town, would have felt that they were poor relations in cities like Ghent or Dijon. But perhaps, in Bergen or Riga they could feel like great men. The burgesses at this time did not hesitate to ask for concessions. In April 1394, Perth was allowed to form its own sheriffdom. The four prime burghs still held their own 'parliament' once a year to discuss appropriate matters, and from 1405 delegates from the royal burghs south of the River Spey were required to attend this body.

THE FIRST UNIVERSITY
FOR THE SCOTS

The Church was less involved in the affairs of the nation than it had been in the early part of the century; its battle for independence had been largely won and the travails of the wider Church claimed its attention. Despite the barbarities of their reigns, the Stewarts were devout, and the Church was one of the elements that held their unsteady kingdom together. The Church was wealthy and its leaders were great landholders on behalf of their institutions and still included men of calibre and integrity. Bishop Wardlaw of St Andrews, who had graduated like any other educated Scotsman on the Continent (although some attended Oxford or Cambridge when circumstances allowed), founded the first university in Scotland at St Andrews in 1410.

There was a delay in approving the new university, and the papal bull recognising its institution was not issued until 1413. The Schism may have prompted the need for an acknowledged university in Scotland. An independent Scottish university could provide a defence of orthodoxy for the country's own Church against the growth of pre-Protestant heresy – an English Lollard had already been burned at Perth in 1406. Clearly a general need was also perceived for providing higher education to the future clerics and young nobility of Scotland without them facing the risks and the costs of foreign travel.

THE REIGN OF JAMES I

By the time King James I reached the age of seventeen, he was not content with his comfortable confinement in London. In 1413 his release seemed close, but the death of Henry IV changed the situation. Henry V found it convenient to have the king of Scots in his custody while he himself sought the crown of France. The release of James' cousin, Murdoch Stewart, in 1416, however, would have done nothing to soothe his impatience. Nevertheless, eight years were still to pass before his return. War between England and France produced a confused situation. Many Scots were in the service of two different French factions, the forces of the Duke of Orleans and of the Duke of Burgundy, who were at war with each other. At the same time, the Scots carried out minor raids over the English border, but eventually, in 1418, the Dauphin sent an appeal for serious aid and a force was assembled, commanded by the Earl of Buchan. Meanwhile King James went to France in the retinue of Henry V and found himself confronting his own countrymen. Scotsmen sent to France under the orders of the Scottish government were being hanged as traitors to the Scottish king. A modest victory of the Scots and French on 22 March 1421 at Baugé, in a battle against the English in which the Duke of Clarence was killed, compounded the embarrassment.

Robert, Duke of Albany, died early in September 1420. His son Murdoch succeeded him as duke and Guardian and saw no reason to change the style of government. When King Henry V died in August 1421, the Protector, the Duke of Gloucester, instigated negotiations for the release of the King of Scots, encouraged by the powerful Beaufort family. Joan Beaufort had won the heart of the poetically gifted young king. A ransom of sixty thousand merks, ostensibly to pay for the cost of keeping James in England and for the cost of his 'education', was called for. Twenty-one members of the Scots nobility were required as hostages in England until the full sum was paid. At last, on 5 April 1424, James came back to Scotland with his English queen.

THE 'REVOLUTION' OF 1424

A revolution was imminent. But left to itself, what sort of kingdom might have evolved from those first Stewarts? Their behaviour had been almost reactionary, tinged with aspects of old Celtic traditions, in their sense of the family, their tolerance of violence and their acquiescence in such things as trial by combat. But they were *rois fainéants*, or phantom rulers, not warrior kings, even if they relished the panoply of chivalric life. Its basis of a military society draped in fake mythology suited them well. Presiding over a state that was, more than most, half medieval and half straining towards the Renaissance, the Stewarts did not try to influence developments. The two strands of medieval and Renaissance thinking could not survive long together. The agents of progress were dynamic; the maintainers of archaic ways were inert or defensive. Bishop Wardlaw and his new university, the merchants who traded with the Hanseatic League, the mercenaries of all ranks who went abroad, and sometimes returned — every link with the outside world tugged at the ancient roots to which the Stewarts, in the novitiate years of their kingship, seemed to be clinging. (They did achieve one thing, and that was to die in their beds, after long life. Even Albany did, escaping the storm to come; but it would be a long time before another king of Scots lived out a natural term.)

There was no doubt about the modernising zeal of James I. Already he knew much about the state of Scotland and about its leading citizens. The country had involuntarily bought him a very expensive education, and he did not arrive in Scotland without a plan. The plan had several aspects, but James' first intention was to destroy the house of Albany. Within the year, Murdoch, two of his sons and his father-in-law were arrested, then tried and executed. Murdoch was the heir presumptive to the crown and a sense of shock went through the whole country. The motives of James I may have been partly rooted in personal vengeance but it was also plain that the Albany Stewarts were obstacles to, and not allies in, what he wanted to accomplish.

JAMES I AND SOCIAL REFORM

James wanted to restore law and order and to re-establish the finances of government on a regular basis. In a memorable phrase, he wanted 'the key to keep the castle, and the bracken bush the cow'. Parliament became his main instrument for reform, and a torrent of legislation affecting every aspect of Scottish life was to ensue. Apart from the magnates, those who were summoned to attend parliament were clerics, representatives of the smaller landowners and of the royal burghs who were likely to support the reforms. James was further aided by the way in which parliament operated. Since 1370 a smaller governing group with members from all the Three Estates and known as the Committee of the Articles, had been responsible for framing acts of legislation, and the full parliament met only to approve or reject these laws. James I and his successors were to find the Lords of the Articles a convenient body to pack with trusty men.

In 1426 parliament abolished all laws other than the king's; it annulled the 'laws of the Macduffs', 'laws of the Galwegians' and other legal preserves maintained by certain earls and lords. Law reforms included the provision of free advocacy for those who were unable to speak for themselves or who could not afford to engage someone to do so. Justice was to be administered equally to poor and rich: a clear sign that this was not currently the case. Men of importance when summoned to appear before a judge usually brought along a substantial body of armed men: this intimidation was now forbidden. Again in 1426, a committee of parliament was selected to hold sessions, or meetings, three times a year, chaired by the chancellor, to review difficult cases. This was the beginning of the later Court of Session. As the king still relied on the holders of heritable jurisdictions, namely the great landowners, to dispense his justice, legal reforms were applied unevenly. There were no salaried judges. In a parliament of 1434, the hot-tempered king angrily denounced the laxness of his sheriffs and of the Lords of Regality in carrying out their legal functions.

In August 1428 James I carried out a purge of the semi-independent nobility. He summoned some fifty of the leading men of the north to a gathering in Inverness and imprisoned them all. Executions and banishments followed. Alexander, Lord of the Isles and Earl of Ross, submitted but then escaped and in 1429 set Inverness on fire. James pursued him. Faced with the royal standard, the allies of Alexander abandoned him and once again the Lord of the Isles was forced to submit to the king. But nothing changed. Two years later Alexander's cousin, Donald Balloch, defeated an army sent to pacify the West Highlands, at Inverlochy.

James's strategy for the Highlands was attempting too much, too quickly. On the fringes and south of the Highlands, the policy of the king seemed more successful. By pressure on nobles to forfeit their lands and by confiscation on quasi-legal pretexts, the crown obtained control of the earldoms of Buchan, Fife, Menteith, Lennox, Strathearn, Dunbar and Mar. But enormous resentment and anxiety built up against the king among the dispossessed landowners and those who waited for his next move. Sir Robert Graham is said to have attempted to arrest the king in parliament, in the name of the Three Estates. Lack of support from the military leaders who would normally have supported the king may explain the humiliating abandonment of the siege of the English-held Roxburgh Castle in August 1436 after only two weeks.

MONEY AND THE CHURCH

James' concern for the economic life of the nation went far beyond raising finance to pay his ransom. In fact, the ransom fell rapidly into arrears along with such payments as the Hebridean rental. Work was done to develop trade and restore a balance that had gone far in the direction of imports, with consequent losses to the country's stock of gold. Efforts were always being made to find gold, and alchemists in every country pursued the dream of creating it from base metal. Gold was being mined in Scotland, if only to a limited extent, and James claimed all gold and silver mining rights for the crown, taxed the export of bullion and imposed several other taxes, not particularly successfully. Much of the country's internal trade and most of its rents were based on payment in kind, not cash. More realistically, Scottish envoys had been trying for some time to establish a 'staple' port on the Continent giving them privileges, rights and security abroad, and in 1407 Bruges agreed to provide Scottish traders with a gateway to the Continent.

One source of financial outflow was the Church, since the Scots Church, like all others, had to pay dues to Rome. The Great Schism had ended in 1418, with Scotland as the last kingdom to come into line and give allegiance to Pope Martin V, the masters of St Andrews arguing forcefully against a reluctant Albany. The Papacy had, in its need for money, devised the system of 'provisions', a method of nominating a successor to a high office before a vacancy occurred, in return for a fee. Further fees were payable to Rome on the installation of the nominated cleric. Ambitious churchmen would go to Rome to make such arrangements. Clerics were now forbidden to leave the country without permission from their bishop or the king and the practice of trafficking in Church appointments, or barratry, was banned. From this ban arose a long dispute between the king and two successive popes which brought Aeneas Silvius Piccolomini, the future Pope Pius II, on a diplomatic visit to Scotland. He was not impressed by what he saw of the country, caught rheumatics, and the mission was a failure. However, James was not an irreligious king. He founded a Carthusian monastery at Perth, the last in Scotland. He also saw the need in 1425 to warn the abbots and priors in his kingdom of 'the downhill condition and threatening ruin of most holy religion' and asked for higher standards of Church life. The heretic burnings intended to deter and prevent the spread of Hussite and Lollard views were strongly supported by the king.

No detail of social life was too small for James to turn his attention to. His belief in the powers of legislation ran well ahead of their real effectiveness. People found playing football were to be fined. Only the senior members of the merchant class might wear furs. Taverns – the establishment of which he had encouraged – must not serve ale after nine at night. None of this was arbitrary: he wanted men to practise archery; he wanted to discourage expensive imports; and he wanted quiet, law-abiding streets at night.

A FAMILY REVENGE

James I was assiduous in his pursuit of the 'commoun wele', or general welfare. He was a king for the nation, determined to make it function, to advance it and to regulate it. To do this he did not hesitate to draw on English models and experience. The entire process was anathema to the Scots nobility whose traditional powers and privileges were under attack. But to the Stewart nobles, it was even worse — it was treachery. James' concept of the role of the king was quite alien to them; it was beyond their imagination to view the kingship as anything other than a family benefit. The fact that a stronger and richer kingdom also made a stronger and richer king stuck in the gullets of his uncles, aunts and cousins, who could only see James taking for himself what was theirs and not merely neglecting but judicially murdering his relations. Traditionalists that they were, they prepared for a traditional solution. The king, who appeared to prefer Perth to Edinburgh, was lodged with his family in the Blackfriars' monastery there. His half-uncle, the Earl of Atholl, was in charge of the arrangements for his comfort. But on the night of 21 February 1437, Atholl, Sir Robert Stewart and Sir Robert Graham burst into the royal apartments. James hid in the outfall below the privy, and there, in a slimy, stinking pit, was stabbed to death.

JAMES II, WILLIAM CRICHTON AND ALEXANDER LIVINGSTON

James I had brought about a revolution that was his alone. None of the great men of the realm gave their commitment to it; there was no friendly conspiracy of bishops to maintain it. His helpers had been men of modest rank, officials who owed their allegiance and their fortunes directly to him. Among them were Sir William Crichton, Sheriff of Edinburgh and Warden of its castle, and Sir Alexander Livingston, Governor of Stirling Castle. Parliament moved smoothly to avert further crisis. The Earl of Douglas was appointed Lieutenant-General of Scotland and the six-year-old James II was crowned, not at Scone, close to Atholl's lands, but in the Abbey of Holyrood.

   The men who murdered James I were in turn brutally put to death themselves in the Grassmarket of Edinburgh, and Atholl, who may have sought the crown for himself, received instead a crown of red-hot iron. It was a period of bad weather, poor harvests, famines and recurrent plague. Beggary, looting, piracy at sea and ambushes on the roads would have been problematic enough, but the barons now felt free to act as they liked, and there was an outbreak of raids and feuds which the Lieutenant and the Justiciar of the

North, Alexander of the Isles, did nothing to check. Meanwhile the person of the young king was being passed to and fro like a parcel, indeed once actually in a clothes-basket, between Crichton in Edinburgh and Livingston in Stirling. In 1439 William Crichton was appointed Chancellor, just before the Earl of Douglas's sudden death.

In 1440 Livingston still had custody of the king, but in September of that year Crichton lifted him during a hunting trip, probably in a plan hatched with the queen mother. Faced with the swagger of the new Earl of Douglas, the two functionaries, Livingston and Crichton, appear to have buried their differences and united against the Douglas family. William, the sixth Earl of Douglas was aged about seventeen, but his behaviour was a precocious indication of trouble to come and his potential military strength was vastly superior to theirs. On 29 November 1440, the earl, his brother David and his adviser Sir Malcolm Fleming came to dine in Edinburgh Castle with the boy king, his chancellor and the governor of the castle. In a grisly ritual, the chancellor placed a black bull's head on the table and the Douglas brothers were seized, dragged out and beheaded. The ten-year-old James's introduction to Scottish politics was a harsh and violent one.

The house of Douglas remained formidable although it was now less of a threat to the king. James 'the Gross' Douglas was Earl of Avondale and

THE CURSE OF KENNEDY

Bishop James Kennedy of St Andrews (*c*.1408–65), founder of St Salvator's College, was the outstanding churchman-patriot of his generation. On the deposition of Crichton in 1443, he became Chancellor and was immediately plunged into the toils of Douglas-Livingston-Crichton rivalry. Siding with Crichton, he was opposed by the formidable trio of Douglas, Livingston and the Earl of Crawford. Crawford swept the bishop's lands in Fife with destruction and death, but Kennedy had a resource that none of the others had. 'He cursit solempnitlie with myter, and staf, and buke, and candil, contynually a year.' Crawford, who was a Lindsay, became involved in a war with the Ogilvies. Crawford's equally ruffianly son, later known as the Tiger Earl, or Earl Beardie, had been ousted by an Ogilvie from the Justiciarship of Arbroath Abbey. Lindsays and Ogilvies came to battle over this profitable post, and a year to the day after Bishop Kennedy had raised his staff, the earl was killed. His body lay unburied for four days, no one daring to touch it until the bishop gave his sanction.

grand-uncle of the murdered William and David. Some believed he too was implicated in their murder. He now became seventh Earl of Douglas and retained the bulk of the Douglas lands. Meanwhile, for several years there were spasmodic disputes and reconciliations between Livingstons and Crichtons, until the Livingstons allied themselves to the Douglases and other southern families, including the Kennedys. The Crichtons were cornered but fought back, gaining powerful allies in Bishop Kennedy of St Andrews and the 'Red' Douglas, Earl of Angus; it took more than a year to prise them, with a surprising lack of bloodshed, out of their posts and castles.

AN EXPENSIVE WIFE

Despite this continuing power struggle, there was also busy diplomacy based on a wider range than the eternal triangle of Scotland, England and France. The independent duchy of Burgundy was Scotland's main trading gateway into Europe. Scottish troops were still active in France and entered Orleans with the victorious Joan of Arc. Five of the six sisters of James II married royal or ducal husbands in Europe. James himself was betrothed to Mary of Gueldres, niece of the Duke of Burgundy, at that time perhaps the richest potentate in Europe, and their marriage took place in suitably grand style in Holyrood Abbey in July 1449. To maintain his queen in the style to which she was accustomed proved a severe financial problem: her income had been guaranteed at five thousand pounds a year, which was more than of the king.

THE FALL OF THE BLACK DOUGLASES

Now aged nineteen, James II began to assert himself and moved against his erstwhile Guardian, Alexander Livingston, and his family. In January 1450, two members of the Livingston family were beheaded for treason and the family estates were forfeited to the crown. Gradually, however, the Crichtons now glided back into the king's favour and William Crichton regained the role of Chancellor. James now summoned parliaments and seemed to be pursuing the same general aims as his father. Indeed, this was the only course to follow other than submit to being the puppet-king of one or other faction. And, a faction in itself, there stood the entrenched power of the Douglas family. The son of James the Gross, William, had by 1443 become the eighth Earl of Douglas and had formed a bond, or 'band', with the Earl of Crawford and Alexander of the Isles, Earl of Ross, making a triumvirate whose power far eclipsed that of the king. William Douglas went in state to Rome for the jubilee year of 1450, and in his absence the king seized some of his castles.

James announced himself to be Lord of Galloway, a title Douglas believed to be his own. In 1451 the earl returned in some haste to Scotland. James and William staged a public reconciliation in which the king yielded William all his lands except Wigtown – which the King gave back to him, under pressure, later in the year. Douglas had outfaced the king, and in January 1452 tried but failed to capture the Chancellor Crichton. Against the background of these events, the earl accepted a promise of safe-conduct from the king to attend a meeting in Stirling Castle at which James asked him to break his band with Crawford and Ross. When Douglas refused to break away from his colleagues, he was stabbed in the neck by the king. The attendants of James II completed the job. It was a pointless act of treacherous violence, and although a well-packed parliament subsequently absolved the king of murder, the Douglases who dragged the dead earl's safe-conduct through Stirling on a board knew that they had right on their side in this at least.

Three years of hostilities with intervals of phoney truce followed. Fighting at first was on three fronts against Crawford, Ross and the new Earl of Douglas, James. Few of his nobles supported James II, who created numerous new earldoms and lordships for his loyal friends: the hereditary Marshal, Keith, became Earl Marischal; the Constable, Hay, became Earl of Errol; Colin Campbell became Earl of Argyll; George Leslie became Earl of Rothes; and Stewart of Darnley became Lord Darnley.

An enthusiast for mechanised warfare, King James purchased massive cannons, including 'Mons Meg' which can still be seen in Edinburgh Castle. This artillery was used against the castles of his enemies. In May 1455, with the Douglas lands devastated and their castles destroyed, the Earl of Douglas decided to escape. His three brothers fought a final battle at Arkinholm near Langholm in early June and were defeated; one fled to join the earl; one was killed in the battle; and one was tried and executed. The problem of the Black Douglases had been solved for the time being.

The way he dealt with the Douglas family demonstrated the combination of ruthless and dogged qualities which were part of the character of James II. In 1455 he was still only twenty-five. He was an able and resourceful leader of men and capable of getting out of a tight corner. He was persistent and, despite the temperament that had led him to stab the eighth Earl of Douglas, he was usually able to exercise a strategic patience. He took a scientific view of warfare but was also popular with the pikemen of his infantry and took pains to cultivate their support.

With no serious rival and with the support of the earls and lords he had created, and a confused political situation in England, James II might have achieved a great deal.

FIRST MONARCH KILLED BY A GUN

The political skill of the Scots council was tested by the rivalry of York and Lancaster in England. The Lancastrians generally wooed the King of Scots, promising the return of Berwick. The Yorkists mostly wooed his enemies. James II played a double game himself with both York and Lancaster; on all sides there were mixed motives often cloaked by fair words or insult. In 1455 James II genuinely feared an English invasion and set up beacons on the Border summits. An insulting message in 1456 from Henry VI to 'James, calling himself King of Scotland' impelled James to lead a demonstrative foray into Northumberland. Roxburgh remained a substantial English fortress controlling Scottish soil. James I had failed to capture it and his son made the attempt in 1460, far better supplied and with more united support. On Sunday 3 August, his queen came to give him encouragement. Standing close to a cannon whose barrel burst, he was struck in the thigh and died from loss of blood.

QUEEN AND BISHOP

There was no collapse of government, and the siege of Roxburgh went on until the redoubtable castle fell. The eldest of the five surviving children of James II, a boy of nine, was crowned James III in Kelso Abbey, close to the army. The Queen Mother, Mary of Gueldres, and Bishop Kennedy of St Andrews were now the leaders of the Scots council, with very different ideas, and they rapidly formed two parties. Bishop Kennedy was pro-Lancastrian and Mary veered from one English side to another. In April 1461 the deposed English King Henry VI and his court were refugees in Scotland. They surrendered Berwick back to the Scots. After a century of English possession, Berwick's commercial importance was vastly reduced but it remained a strategic and psychologically important site.

In the following year, Edward IV of England made a confidential pact with John Macdonald, Lord of the Isles and Earl of Ross, who invaded and took over the crown lands around Inverness in support of the 'Treaty' of Westminster and Ardtornish. This treaty was made without the knowledge of the Scots government. It was an outline plan, made in the interests of York and the English king against the Scots, which would have later repercussions. It proposed to break up the realm of Scotland. The Lord of the Isles and the exiled Earl of Douglas would share the territory of ancient Scotia north of the Forth as vassals of Edward IV of England, who would have the rest.

The convolutions and variations of policy at this time reveal the divisions within Scotland and also the degree to which Scotland, independent nation as it was, was affected by events in England. Without strong control, the greed and jealousy of the grander Scots nobles invariably led them to try to get the power of England to support them. They had no sense of nationhood. Macdonald and Douglas were not out to save the nation but to dismember it for their own benefit. Apologists for Macdonald refer to the tradition of semi-independent conduct of the Lordship of the Isles; apologists for Douglas suggest that because he had been disinherited he had a right to re-establish his interests. The fact remains that both men were unprincipled opportunists. As such they were typical, but most of their smaller fellow-magnates were content to keep their ambitions within the realm of Scotland. Thus on the deaths of Bishop Kennedy and Queen Mary, there was intensive haggling and 'banding' among the newer, minor nobility who had held administrative powers under James II and James I before him. As a result of this, the Boyd and Kennedy families took possession of the young king in 1466 and Lord Boyd became chamberlain while his son, Thomas, became Earl of Arran and married the King's elder sister, Mary.

THE PLEDGING OF ORKNEY AND SHETLAND

The Boyd 'government' can take the credit for the diplomacy that brought Orkney and Shetland under the Scottish crown. Already in 1460 there had been negotiations with the kingdom of Denmark and Norway over the arrears of payment of the Hebridean rental. In the process of negotiations, the marriage of Prince James to the daughter of the Danish King Christian I became part of a settlement. But these talks had collapsed. In 1468 a grand embassy was sent from Scotland to Copenhagen and the marriage was arranged once again. The settlement now included the abolition of the 'Norway annual' and of the arrears. In addition, sixty thousand Rhenish florins were to form the dowry of the princess. Since King Christian could find only the cash for a down payment of ten thousand florins, he agreed to pledge Orkney for the rest. In the end he could actually not produce more than two thousand florins and added Shetland to the pledge. Such pawning was not unusual, especially for Christian, who had a sprawling and restive Scandinavian empire; and it is almost certain that he anticipated redeeming the pledge when he could. James III and the twelve-year-old Margaret were married in Holyrood Abbey on 10 July 1469.

On 17 September 1470, Earl William Sinclair was bought out of his claim to the lands of Orkney and the still-unredeemed islands were to be held by the crown. The Scots did not delay in colonising the islands. On 20 February 1472 they were officially annexed to the crown of Scotland. The boundaries of Scotland, save for a few adjustments in the 'bateable lands' of the Borders and the twentieth-century annexation of Rockall, were now established.

In a repetition of previous history, James III, who was now eighteen, took action against the men who had controlled his childhood and his minority. Lord Boyd and the Earl of Arran fled the country, and their kinsman, Sir Alexander Boyd, was caught and beheaded. The Boyd lands of Arran and part of Ayrshire were forfeited to the crown, which made them, together with Bute, Renfrew and Cowal, the inalienable territory of the crown prince. At this time there was no prince, but the future James IV was born on 17 March 1473.

THE STATE OF THE NATION
UNDER JAMES III

The twenty-eight-year reign of James III from 1460 to 1488 was a period of relative international peace, at least as far as Scotland was concerned. For much of the time there was a depression in international trade, which had an impact on the Scottish economy. By the time that James was twenty, the Stewart kings had ruled Scotland for a century. Their dynasty was firmly established and the role of the king was respected. The hundred years of Stewart rule had brought many changes but little progress. If Robert II had returned from the dead, he would have recognised most of the features of the realm of Scotland. King James III, however, was richer in lands than previous kings had been, and his new palaces testified to this increasing difference in status. Towns in Scotland had become larger, especially Edinburgh, which was now a conurbation of the Old Town, the Canongate and Leith. Here there was already increasing pressure on living space, causing tall tenements to be built. There was a small galaxy of new earldoms and lordships but the old familiar earldoms still remained, essentially unchanged in style and attitude. The greater churches and abbeys still remained and still functioned as before, receiving their teinds, or tithes, and tenancy payments, and the clergy kept running the Church estates. Farmers scratched at the earth with implements that their forefathers had used.

Despite the many edicts of James I and the energetic campaigns of James II, Scotland was still a backward country. The hand of government was light and the size of the administration very small. The seat of government depended on where the king was to be found. Laws were archaic, often unclear and liable to the manipulation of any local baron. By old custom there was toleration of a high level of violence in every walk of life from the blood feud to the penalties of the courts and down to the domestic level of schoolroom and household. There were a few rich men, mostly among the nobility, though their wealth did not match their pretensions.

The vast majority of the population, perhaps about three quarters of a million but growing steadily, were poor. They had little or no money and lived on subsistence agriculture, on barter and on charity. Every visitor to Scotland commented on the poverty of the country and the swarms of beggars, often disabled, maimed or leprous. This poverty was partly the result of appearances. The country manufactured only coarse, drab, grey cloth, and this was what most people necessarily wore. Houses were still simple in construction, especially in the countryside where they were usually turf huts built around a wooden framework with no windows, and a door made of animal hide. In the Highlands families often still lived in crannogs and migrated seasonally with their livestock to summer hill camps which were even more rudimentary than their winter homes.

The towns were dangerous fire traps of close-packed wooden houses with thatched roofs. Churches were generally simple buildings of wood or stone thatched with heather. The greater stone buildings, the castles and abbeys, rose up out of groups of humbler dwellings in daunting force or splendour. Most castles remained, however, simple tower houses which were like a single tooth of masonry with a door on the first floor, limited inner space and few comforts. The owner might be a laird eligible to attend the parliament but he would resist the summons because of his lack of means. He was expected to pay his own expenses there, and would not be keen to display his poverty. Most of his income would be in corn, cows, and eggs.

As a society, fifteenth-century Scotland was distinctive. The population at this time was small, smaller than the present population of Glasgow. The nation was far from being a free society. Although the feudal structure was becoming less marked in its strict application, it still prevailed. Barons handed out the law of the king and had wide powers while the lords of regality had even greater influence. In one respect, however, Scotland was more advanced than many richer countries. The condition of serfdom, perhaps never widespread, had disappeared. Not since 1364 had a lawsuit for the recovery of a runaway serf been pursued, and transactions involving the gift or sale of people had ceased.

The difference in power and status between the lord in his castle and the peasant in the field was immense, but there was a tie of ancient custom between them that predated feudalism and had imprinted itself into the attitudes of the nobles of Norman descent. The tribal groups which once formed the Pictish kingdom had evolved and been reshaped and regenerated into a different world, leaving a legacy that was apparent in loyalty to land and leader. In its idealised form, this loyalty was not subservient but was given with good will and accepted in the same spirit by a lord who had obligations to maintain his followers and keep them secure. This was particularly so in the Highlands and the Uplands of the south. When times were hard, all suffered together, even if the peasant suffered most. A rental paid in kind could not be the same in a year of bad harvest as in a year of good yield.

The struggle of people to make a living in a system that required co-existence and co-operation promoted social cohesion. Traditional forms of cultivation were standard throughout the country, and influenced social life. The primitive farm implements of the time, the undrained soil and the relative weakness of the small horses and oxen meant that farming was labour-intensive. Eight or more labourers and as many animals might be needed to get the ploughing done.

Houses were set in random clusters with lands which spread away from them. The 'in-field', or the best ground, was near the houses. It was parcelled into strips known as 'runrigs'. Overall, the runrigs were held and worked in common by all the tenants. Individual strips of land were probably allocated by picking lots and then farmed in turn, giving everyone a chance to have a particularly good strip at some point. The runrigs would be constantly manured, and cultivated with barley, oats and sometimes also peas or beans. Beyond them, usually extending up a hillside was the 'out-field,' treated mostly as pasture land. Parts of the out-field would be sectioned off and more intensively grazed, and thus manured, then ploughed and cropped, and left to go fallow again. This pattern of land use, especially in the more fertile parts of the Lowlands, was not inflexible. The gradual introduction of feuing, or leasing, land was already taking place during the reign of James III, and the tendency of lairds to increase the size of their herds and encroach into the land of smaller tenants was strong enough for laws to be passed against it even in the time of William I.

THE HIGHLAND-LOWLAND GAP WIDENS

The cultural gap between Highlands and Lowlands was steadily widening. Scots was now almost the universal tongue of the towns, the Lowland countryside and the east coast. Gaelic speech survived only in pockets. Eastern and southern Scotland, in spite of all the remnants of a Celtic way of life, were also consciously part of the consciously modernising Western Europe.

In the Highlands and Islands, where Gaelic was their only language, people were aware that they were not part of a wider and expanding culture. With Galloway and Ireland, they were redoubts of an older civilisation. They were numerous enough for this to be a matter of pride rather than anxiety, and in some ways their lives were influenced by new ideas imported from the Continent and the world beyond. But despite the continuing high levels of achievement in the oral arts, no one beyond the Celtic world took an interest in their culture. The Celtic world had nothing to contribute to the climate of inquiry and experiment that was arising in Renaissance Europe.

Other countries, like France and Burgundy, struggled to impose national unity as political control was extended over different racial and cultural groups. Scotland was most unusual in that its society had evolved from a largely Gaelic-speaking people into a divided one separated not by race but by a steadily increasing divergence of language and custom.

THE ISOLATION OF JAMES III

James III was the king and chief of chiefs of this strange land. Gaelic bards still chanted his genealogy back to Iber. Such things were of no account to him, and it is unlikely that any king between the reigns of Robert III and James IV knew any but the most formal Gaelic. The interests of James III were not traditional but modern and intellectual: he had a remote temperament; his mental processes tended to the abstract and speculative and his interests to the new sciences. Things that were capable of mechanical explanation appealed to him; he was a discriminating patron of architects and a keen student of astrology and alchemy.

Nothing in his own history or that of his family made him feel well disposed towards the old nobility, and his distrust of them increased his isolation. His closest associates were Robert Cochrane, the architect who is believed to have designed the Great Hall of Stirling Castle, and the musician William Rogers. The king was also said to have given undue favour to his tailor, Hommil.

James III could be stirred to take decisive action. When, in 1475, the Treaty of Westminster and Ardtornish between King Edward IV and John, Lord of the Isles, came to light, he sent an expedition after the Lord of the Isles. John of the Isles was brought to Edinburgh where he duly begged for forgiveness from James but the earldom of Ross was taken from him.

In contrast to the king, his younger brothers, Alexander, Duke of Albany, and John, Earl of Mar, were men of the old school, knightly, grand-mannered public figures, interested in the finer points of chivalry and courtly behaviour. However, they were also capable of rallying support against the king. Pre-empting any potential threats from his brothers, the king imprisoned them on separate charges of using witchcraft against him, in 1479. Albany escaped from gaol in dashing style, killing the governor of Edinburgh Castle and sliding down the rock on tied bedsheets. Mar died in unexplained circumstances – possibly murdered or clumsily bled in a bath by an inept doctor.

ANGLO-SCOTS RELATIONS

James III made a startling change to the country's foreign policy by cultivating friendship with England. No positive benefits came to either side. There was a diplomatic setback in Anglo-Scots affairs when Margaret, the sister of the king, was betrothed to Earl Rivers, brother-in-law of Edward IV, but was found to be pregnant by Lord Crichton. Relations between England and Scotland rapidly deteriorated and were exacerbated by the French-Burgundian conflict. In 1481 there were hostile appearances of English vessels in the Firth of Forth. From April 1482, Edward IV had the Duke of Albany in his pay, as well as the exiled Lord Boyd and the Earl of Douglas.

THE CAPTURE OF THE KING

None of the policies of James III was calculated to appeal to his nobles, who were in touch with the opposing forces of Edward and the exiles. In 1481 the king mustered his army and set out for the Border, only to disband it on receiving an earnest plea from the Pope. But once again provoked in 1482, James set out again to meet the invading English. On the way, at Lauder, there was a confrontation. According to some records, James had made Cochrane Earl of Mar, which had been the title of his dead brother John. The barons summarily hanged Cochrane and some other friends, or 'familiars', of King James from Lauder Bridge and took the king himself into custody. The Scots army was sent home and the leaders of the coup prepared to negotiate a rapid truce with the English. The Duke of Albany returned to Scotland supported by the Duke of Gloucester's English lances.

CHANGING FORTUNES

Returning south, the English army once again reclaimed Berwick, which remained an English possession thereafter. Alexander, Duke of Albany, supported by his and the king's uncles, the Earl of Buchan and the Earl of Atholl, attempted to take control of government by being appointed Lieutenant-General. King James was released though apparently powerless. However, by March 1483 James III had regained control of affairs and Albany was compelled to resign. In May Albany was formally accused of treason and, foreseeing the outcome, fled to England. Just how James accomplished the change in his fortunes is not clear. He may have done little except float back on a tide of hostile reaction among the middling nobility, the lairds and the burgesses, against the notion that the kingship of Scotland was at the bestowal of the king of England.

Albany's vassalship to Edward IV must have been all too apparent, even if it was not formally acknowledged. In July 1484 he and the forfeited Earl of Douglas raided Lochmaben; Douglas was captured and imprisoned, while Albany fled to France where he died of a tournament wound in 1485.

The victory of Henry Tudor in 1485 signalled a period of relaxed relations with England. James, perhaps over-confident now, proceeded to make enemies among the Border families. He had already been urged by parliament in 1484 to bring the great lords into friendship and concord, but he seems to have done the opposite. By proposing to turn the Collegiate Church of Coldingham, the revenues of which were gathered by the Home family, into a Chapel Royal, he set the Homes – a house of considerable power since the fall of the Douglases – and their allies against him. Peace with England was not to their profit or liking either. On 2 February 1488, the governor of Stirling Castle allowed the Homes to seize the heir to the throne, then aged sixteen. The young duke was not unwilling to be kidnapped and accepted the title of Governor-elect.

A MYSTERIOUS END

Provoked by this act of defiance, James III was taken across the Forth by his loyal admiral, Sir Andrew Wood, to raise support in the north. At Blackness, on the southern shore of the Firth of Forth, there was sporadic fighting while talks went on. A patched-up peace agreement did not last long and there was no submission of the son to the father. Once again each side mustered its army and met at the Sauchie Burn, not far from Bannockburn, on 11 June 1488. Both sides displayed the royal standard of Scotland. This time there was hard fighting, and the unwarlike James III, equipped with the sword of Robert I, but seemingly in a state of extreme nervous agitation, was advised to leave the battlefield. His army fought on all through the day but was eventually forced back and put to flight. On the same day, close to the battlefield, James III was murdered in circumstances that remain highly mysterious. The chronicler Lindsay of Pitscottie relates that the king fell from his horse and was taken into a miller's house by the Bannock Burn, where he lay in a swoon. Eventually he called for a priest; the miller's wife ran out and found a stranger who said, 'Here am I, ane priest' entered the house, and stabbed the king to death.

CHAPTER EIGHT

Scotland Reformed: James IV to James VI

SCOTLAND, EUROPE AND ENGLAND

The death of James III had been unintended by his opponents. They had hoped to force a legal abdication and were ill-prepared for the shock caused by the death of the king and the way it had happened. Now, people interested in the laws of the land asked who should be brought to justice for the death of the king. Unfortunately, the answer could not exclude the new king, who had flaunted the royal standard so brazenly at Sauchieburn. The coronation of James IV must have been an unusually diffident occasion, although it marked the beginning of a flamboyant reign.

The Stewart monarchs were the product of their mothers as well as their fathers, a banal truth which the dynastic name often overshadows. James IV, King of Scots, was part-Danish and part-Flemish. His mother had been born in Norway and was half-Danish. His grandmother had been the part-Flemish Mary of Gueldres. Aunts and cousins were spread among the kingdoms and principalities of northern Europe. The new king had good reason to be European in his outlook. It was an outlook shared by his subjects, most of whom had a much less exotic ancestry. No thinking person would have felt Scotland could or should stand alone, simply sharing its island with its larger neighbour. Scots looked to Orleans and Bologna for their legal instruction, to Rome for their religion, to Paris for their education, to the Low Countries for their knowledge of trading and commerce and also increasingly for ideas on domestic building. France and the Low Countries had been and remained sources of inspiration for some of the most notable architecture in Scotland. The complex double-apsed design of Kelso Abbey came from the Ottonian minsters of Low Germany; the great castles of Doune and Tantallon, which combined the functions of fortresses with the amenities of palaces, were French in style; the new turreted palaces of Holyrood and Falkland were also drawn from the architectural designs of France.

And yet the greatest influence, the constantly felt presence, the true measure of Scotland's success and failure, was always England. A little continent in itself, larger, more populous, richer, patronising in friendship, jealously defensive in trade, unrelenting in hostility, England was inescapable. However fractured and crazed its own internal affairs from the days of William I to those of Henry VIII, England had not ceased in its efforts to make the Scots feel they lived on sufferance at best. Even the treaty of 1328 had been framed in such a way as to suggest that its terms were dictated by a generous England. Robert I and his advisers had had the good sense to be generous in that respect. The first five Stewart kings had generally been wary of direct confrontation with England. James IV, abounding in confidence and endowed with a powerful will, believed that it was time for Scotland to play a positive part in the affairs of Christendom. Not only for that reason, he was one of the most disastrous kings that Scotland has had.

NEW MEN, OLD METHODS

In the first parliament of the new reign, held after a judicious interval in October 1488, it was agreed that the death of the late king was due to the defeated party and their bad advice. The Homes and Hepburns, who had taken up arms against James III, were appointed to positions of power, but their allies, Lord Lyle and Sir John Stewart of Darnley, who was now Earl of Lennox, felt they had been passed over, and took up arms in rebellion. In September 1489, Lord Forbes and the Earl Marischal, claiming as their symbol the 'bloody shirt' of James III, made an improbable alliance with the Earl of Lennox. But the affair petered out, and the revanchists and the premature king made peace with each other.

NEW FOREIGN POLICIES

It was 1492 before parliament offered a reward for the detection of those who had killed James III. No one claimed it. In June 1493, James anticipated his twenty-first birthday with an Act of Revocation. This was the traditional sweeping away of pledges and agreements made by the monarch in his youth – a situation that the country at large was by now extremely familiar with. He began to establish his authority and his actions reveal a number of policies. Within the kingdom of Scotland he wanted to extend his rule to the Highlands and Islands. Beyond the existing borders of Scotland he wanted to be a force in European affairs. One way to do this was to have a navy, which he proceeded to build. There were other valid reasons for building up a fleet. Piracy was a regular activity for Scots, English and Continental adventurers. They were a serious menace to merchant shipping; and the only way to police the West and the Isles was by sea.

James did not seek to pursue his father's policy of peaceful co-operation with England. When the impostor Perkin Warbeck claimed to be the Duke of York whom Richard III had murdered in the Tower of London, he was welcomed to Scotland and married to the daughter of the Earl of Huntly. James proposed to invade England on his behalf, and despite Spanish dissuasion – the Spaniards wanted English support in Europe without the complication of Scotland attacking in the rear – summoned the Scottish army and invaded England in September 1496. The English did not rally to the banner of Perkin Warbeck and the invasion soon turned back, but in August 1497 James returned once again. He tried to capture Berwick and when he failed, vainly besieged Norham Castle instead. The Earl of Surrey advanced with his army but James declined a battle, offering single combat instead, which Surrey declined as too great an honour for a mere earl. The Spanish Ambassador, Pedro de Ayala, arranged a seven-year truce. James then changed his policy towards England. He asked Henry VII to allow him to marry his daughter Margaret Tudor. He was twenty-five and she was nine years old. Henry VII took his time to agree, but on 24 January 1502 the marriage treaty was concluded and was accompanied by the second Treaty of Perpetual Peace between the two countries. On 8 August 1503 James married the now thirteen-year-old Margaret in a splendid ceremony in Holyrood Abbey.

LOVE AND LIFE IN THE COURT
OF KING JAMES IV

James IV's love life was no secret to his people. Marion Boyd had borne him a son in 1493. Margaret Drummond had been his mistress from 1496, but she died suddenly and rather suspiciously with her two sisters, after a breakfast in 1502, conveniently one year before the king was to celebrate his grand dynastic marriage to Margaret Tudor. In 1501 James had granted the castle and lands of Darnaway, near Forres, to 'Flaming Janet' Kennedy at around the time she bore him a son, James Stewart, who was later to become the Earl of Moray. In 1512 Queen Margaret also produced a son, James Stewart, as the heir to the throne.

James IV wished to be seen and admired in kingly practices. His tournaments, hunts, concerts and feasts made his court colourful and alluring and at a more political level helped to keep the nobility out of mischief. Unlike his father and grandfather, he enjoyed entertaining his nobles. He shared his father's interest in architecture, the arts and the curiosities of science. He was responsible for endorsing a rather odd experiment in which two infant children were sent in the care of a dumb woman to the isle of Inchkeith to

A dance in the gallery

A tournament

Preparing for the joust

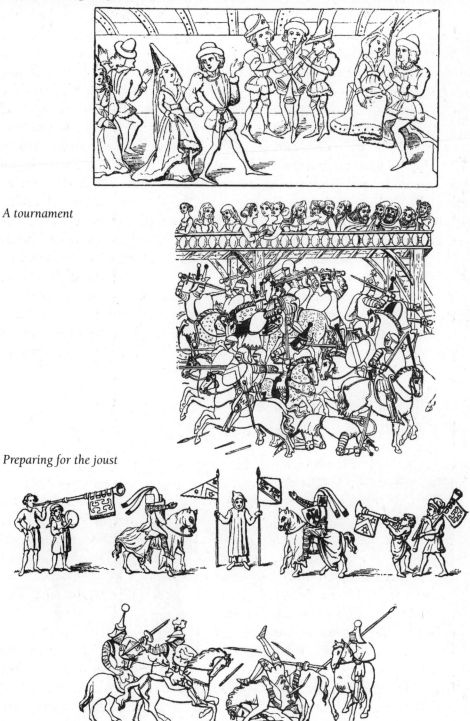

Artist's impression of scenes from court life in the fourteenth century

find out what language they would ultimately speak. His protégé, the alchemist Father Damian, made an early attempt at man-powered flight from the heights of Stirling Castle.

On a higher note, literature had a place at the court of King James. The king himself was known to have written love poems to Margaret Drummond, and he appointed a court poet in 1500. This was William Dunbar, whose range of work exemplifies the demands put upon him. He was equally capable of splendid religious poetry, like *Ane Ballat to Our Ladye*, as of the scurrilous badinage of *The Treatis of the Twa Maryit Wemen and the Wedo* whose recital no doubt caused great mirth among the more boisterous element at court. Social satire was a major element of the poetry of Dunbar. His mockery of such groups as the urban craftsmen helps to show the virtual absence of any element in society between the court and the ordinary people at the time. The courtiers laughed because the objects of Dunbar's rude humour were so familiar to them. Something of the character of the Scots of those days and the racy expressiveness of their language comes across in the verse form of 'flyting', a poetic exchange of views often at the level of a slanging match between two contrasting figures. The dialogue form was extremely popular in the sixteenth century and was still visible in works over two hundred years later, like *The Twa Dogs* by Robert Burns. The poems of William Dunbar were among the first books printed in Scotland.

The court of James IV also cultivated music. The king's new Chapel Royal in Stirling Castle was a centre of church music distinguished by the presence of Robert Carver whose masses and motets for church ceremonies are

Colophon and title page from Chepman and Myllar's edition of Dunbar's poems

still performed. English ballads, French dances and Flemish music were performed at court, along with Scots songs, reels and recitals of Highland music for both bagpipe and harp.

JAMES IV'S FOREIGN POLICY AND DEALINGS WITH THE CHURCH

There was peace and even friendship with England until Henry VII died in 1509. James IV looked farther afield in diplomatic matters. The treaty with Denmark was renewed in 1492, and in 1502 Scottish ships and men were sent to help King Hans in his fruitless attempt to stem a Swedish revolt. For several years after that, Andrew Barton, the chief naval captain of King James, kept ships on active patrol in the Baltic Sea.

James also corresponded with the Pope about the prospects of a new Crusade, and Julius II sent him the Golden Rose of papal approval and a ceremonial sword that is still part of the regalia of Scotland. At the same time, and with a degree of financial cynicism on both sides, there was a current of friction between Scotland and the papacy on the subject of benefices. Barratry, or the buying and selling of church privileges, was once again a problem. James made strenuous efforts through parliament to prevent Scottish ecclesiastics going to Rome to buy, pawn or traffic in positions of wealth and power in the Church. He wanted to be the sole channel of this traffic. Whilst a proper regard for clerical probity, and for the Scottish bullion supply, may have played a part, it is also the case that James first pro-

---

DON PEDRO DE AYALA

In the fifteenth and sixteenth centuries, the institutions of international diplomacy were already in place. For a country of lesser importance, like Scotland, ambassadors or legates would be sent or exchanged only if the international situation required it. In 1498, Spanish anxiety to keep Scotland and England at peace was responsible for the sojourn in Scotland of Don Pedro de Ayala, an affable aristocrat whose detailed messages and commentaries provide much information and inspired guess-work on Scotland at the time. Don Pedro enjoyed life at James IV's court, but had a shrewd eye for the king's character. 'He esteems himself as much as though he were Lord of the World,' he wrote, and, forebodingly, 'He is not a good captain, because he begins to fight before he has given his orders.'

SCOTLAND IN EUROPE

A useful corrective to excessive Scottish pride is to examine some general histories of Europe, whether originating in England, France or Germany. Almost without exception, their authors find it entirely possible to write the political and social history of Europe without reference to Scotland at all, save for the occasional mention of the Reformation, which in Scotland 'went further' than in any other country, and of the Union of 1707, seen in a context of development of the English state. *Europe: A History* by Norman Davies is a notable exception.

---

cured the appointment of his brother, Duke of Ross, to the rich archbishopric of St Andrews while he himself took over the Duke's territories, and then, on the duke-archbishop's death, he installed his own eleven-year-old illegitimate son on the throne once occupied by William Lamberton. It was financial raiding and spiritual debauchery all in one.

There were other instances where secular bishops were installed to Church positions. Andrew Forman, who had collected customs taxes north of the Spey as a custumar to the king, became Bishop of Moray. Many other abbots and bishops were in one way or another in crown service. But the Church remained by far the biggest and wealthiest institution in the country. Church revenue was ten times greater than the revenue of the state, and the Church as an institution still retained a creative power. In 1490 a new Scottish liturgy in the form of the Aberdeen Breviary, compiled by Bishop Elphinstone, was put out, accompanied by a carefully researched list of seventy Scottish saints. It was still an age of public piety and of demonstrative religion, led by the king, who made frequent pilgrimages to St Duthac at Tain, by way of Darnaway Castle, and also to Whithorn; and he established and endowed the Chapel Royal at Stirling Castle.

MERCHANTS AND CRAFTSMEN

James IV managed the picturesque and demonstrative aspects of kingship with aplomb. He cannot be held responsible for the trade slump that appears to have taken place by the end of the fifteenth century but his government did little or nothing to remedy the situation. A general recession in European trade hit the Scottish burghs quite badly. The debasement of Scottish coinage had gone far below the levels experienced in the time of King David II. Merchants in Scotland normally used a considerable amount of foreign silver coins. As business diminished, so did the supply of foreign money. With fewer foreign coins, the merchants increasingly experienced difficulties in meeting their commitments and these difficulties in turn put pressure on the Scots currency.

The king took no action over the money crisis and he appears to have called no parliament after 1509, governing through a council that consisted of selected members of the nobility and clergy. Even before that, Parliament had become steadily less representative of the lairds and burgesses. The burghs themselves had become the possessions of little self-perpetuating groups of merchants. Both parliament and king had backed the constant efforts of the merchants, who as burgesses ran burgh affairs, to keep down the craftsmen, who were often the actual and potential generators of wealth. Jealous of their status and privilege, the merchants fought every attempt by the craftsmen to import raw materials directly, to form guilds ('gilds' in Scots) or to exert any control on prices. The parliament under James III had encouraged craftsmen to elect deacons in order to maintain quality standards and to keep discipline: under his successor these acts were repealed.

Nevertheless, perhaps because the burghs were in a poor economic state, the craftsmen's position gradually improved as a result of their own agitations. Edinburgh led the way in this with a number of craft guilds being allowed to establish themselves under the Burgh Seal of Common Cause. Hatters and skinners took the first initiatives in 1473 and 1474; in 1500 the waulkers (cloth-makers) and tailors were incorporated and the barber-surgeons followed them in 1505. A new trade began in 1507 when Walter Chepman and Andrew Myllar set up the first printing press in Scotland. The printers had gained the approval of the king to start their business and they were to print the Aberdeen Breviary under the patronage of Bishop Elphinstone in 1510. Authors were now forbidden to send their manuscripts for publication beyond the borders of Scotland.

THE LEGAL SYSTEM

James IV took no action to improve the long-standing problems of Scots law. The laws had still not been codified and formed a chaotic collection of rules and judgements, some of them going back before the reign of Malcolm III. Enforcement and prosecution were the tasks of hereditary justiciars and sheriffs whose training and ability to discharge their office were variable. Many wrongdoers were able to bribe their way out of trouble; even if they were convicted of a crime they could appeal to the king to grant a remission or pardon. As the fount of justice, the king could and frequently did grant remissions as his predecessors had done, and for similar financial consid-

PIRACY

The North Sea, crossed by shipping lanes between all the ports in Great Britain and Northern Europe, was a rich field for those who preferred the risks of piracy to those of trade. The Frisians and the Scots appear to have been the worst offenders. In 1412 the Hanseatic League wanted to suspend all trading with Scotland, as a form of economic pressure to stop the piracy; its two main trading partners, Danzig and Stralsund, resisted, but between 1416 and 1436, there was an embargo. Later in the century, the English complained of James IV's ships intercepting their vessels, and there had long been a string of complaints from Scotland about English semi-official pirates. Long wrangles often ensued. A century later the position was no better. The town council of Edinburgh sent an emissary to Elizabeth I to protest about English privateers. Burghs tried to prevent the sale of pirated goods, with little effect, and raised funds to recompense those who lost goods through piracy. The practice of piracy went on until the early nineteenth century, by which time it was intimately involved with smuggling.

erations. No previous king had succeeded in reforming the legal system. James IV in the years of peace under his reign had the best opportunity to do so. The country now possessed three universities: following St Andrews, Glasgow was founded in 1451, and Aberdeen received the Papal Bull to authorise its foundation in February 1495. It is hard to believe that there were no scholars who could have undertaken the task, even though the universities themselves had no law faculty (although Bishop Elphinstone of Aberdeen hoped to establish one). Graduates who sought training in law still had to travel to the mainland of Europe, usually to Orleans. But there was no shortage of lawyers in Scotland.

THE HIGHLANDS AND ISLANDS
IN THE TIME OF JAMES IV

An undoubted achievement of the reign of James IV was to bring about the subjection of the Lord of the Isles. It was an attractive feature of the king that he encouraged the music and poetry of his Gaelic-speaking subjects. He had some command of the Gaelic language, the first king since the time of Robert III to do so, and the last also. In 1493 the titles and the lands of the Lord of the Isles were annexed to the crown. John of the Isles submitted, but it remained for the king to establish the authority that had been granted

by parliament. James IV made visits to the west in 1493 and 1494 and renovated the old castle of Robert I at Tarbert in Kintyre, but he did not find a
submissive population. When the royal forces established a garrison at
Dunaverty in south Kintyre they were attacked and forced out again; the
attackers hanged the leader of the garrison on the battlements while the
royal squadron was still in sight. In 1495 the king made a major sea-borne
expedition to the Isles. Again, in 1498, no fewer than three expeditions
were undertaken, after which James lost interest in making his presence felt
there. It was easier to get a island chieftain to promise submission than to
get him to keep it.

James gave the governorship of Tarbert Castle to the second Earl of Argyll
and in 1500 made the earl his Lieutenant-General in Argyll and the Isles. A
similar commission was given to the Gordon Earl of Huntly in 1501. Fundamental to the activities of these overlords was the power to grant tracts
(or 'tacks') of land in areas where no one could show a pre-existing charter
to prove ownership. In the Highlands and Islands, local communities had
in some cases held their land since the days of King Magnus Barelegs or
King Constantine and had nothing to show to prove their title to the land.
Generations of settlement were treated as irrelevant. Others had charters
from the Lord of the Isles, but these were now declared null and void. From
then on, the rise in power and spread in numbers of the Campbells and
Gordons was swift.

James may have temporarily thought he had solved the problem of the
Highlands and Islands, but between 1504 and 1507 a small war had to be
waged against the supporters of Donald Dubh, an illegitimate descendant of
the deposed and now dead John of the Isles, who now arose to claim the
Lordship of the Isles. Resentment among the numerous, many branched
and dispossessed clan of MacDonald was strong. Lesser clans had to accept
Campbell or Gordon supremacy and intrusion or move away. The numbers
of dispossessed families and broken men without land or chief increased,
and beggary and lawlessness were more rife than they had been when the
Lord of the Isles held sway. The privileged Campbells and Gordons consoli-
dated their power bases. James IV had exchanged one over-mighty subject
for two, and the Highlands and Islands remained with their population of
'wild Scottis', only partly integrated into the kingdom of Scotland.

THE FLEET OF KING JAMES IV

From 1492 the New World of the Americas – which may already have been
visited by Irish monks and even, in 1391, by the Earl of Orkney – was a
known fact and an incalculable new factor in international politics. James

IV took a commendably keen interest in technical innovation, which included the new developments in shipbuilding. Ships were now being designed to carry guns, and a fleet was becoming an important element in a coastal country's arsenal. James had already found naval power useful in the Western Isles. He commissioned the creation of a harbour at Newhaven, by Edinburgh, and initiated the purchase and building of a fleet. Centuries of timber exploitation without replanting and replacing trees had left Lowland Scotland with little of the dense forest that had once covered much of the terrain. Visitors to Scotland now remarked on the bareness of the landscape. When the biggest vessel in the fleet of King James, known as *Great Michael*, was said to have used up 'all the woods of Fife', it may have been that there were few woods left in Fife to be used. Timber was in short supply and already being imported from Scandinavia.

Despite the new enlargement of the world, the king had few mercantile, and fewer exploratory, ambitions for his ships: Scotland was to stake its claims to a wider empire much later. James sensibly wanted to eradicate piracy in the North Sea and establish Scotland's power there. Less sensibly, he wanted to help equip and lead in person an international expedition to fight the infidel Turks, who in 1453 had captured Constantinople and were spreading westwards. Such an initiative from Scotland, however noble, was never likely to be put into action seriously and it was not taken up by the larger powers.

A NEW KING IN ENGLAND

From 1509 there was a new king of England to contend with, James's brother-in-law – the youthful Henry VIII. The new English king confirmed his father's Treaty of Perpetual Peace with Scotland, but it soon became clear that he would not follow a peaceful policy. The marriage of 'the Thrissil and the Rose' already began to bedevil the English-Scots relationship. Until Henry VIII produced an heir, Queen Margaret of Scotland was his heir presumptive, and in 1509 she produced a son. Disputes between the two countries became more intense. The English regarded the fleets from Scotland, with some reason, as no better than pirates themselves, and the Scots commander, Andrew Barton, was defeated and killed in a small sea battle off the coast of southeast England, where he was allegedly trying to capture Portuguese vessels.

In 1511 Henry VIII entered the Holy League of Pope Julius II and prepared to make war on France. King Louis XII asked Scotland to renew the ancient Treaty of Alliance and promised James an army for his Crusade once peace was secured. He went further and promised support for any justifiable claim to the English crown. Despite the peace treaty with England, a new treaty with France was signed that committed Scotland to make war on England if the French did so. Scotland was caught in the periphery of a power struggle between larger European states. James IV made efforts to reconcile France and the militant and military Pope as well as to secure the support of Denmark if Scotland were drawn into war. The English tried to secure Scottish neutrality on these matters without offering any concessions in return. The tide of events led remorselessly in the direction of war. James increasingly turned his diplomatic strategy to concentrate on securing the best reward he could get from France if he broke the treaty with England. He asked Louis for an army to back up his own invasion; Louis in turn offered to re-equip the Scottish fleet. James decided that his best hopes for dynastic and crusading glory lay with France and he mobilised his fleet in July 1513, just as Henry VIII set off on his invasion of France. But in a delaying move, James sent his ships north around Cape Wrath to help his Irish allies, commanded by O'Donnel, to attack the English fortress of Carrickfergus.

THE BATTLE OF FLODDEN

In August 1513 James summoned the Scottish forces and on the 17th, sent seventeen pieces of heavy artillery southwards. It was the largest and best-armed force that had ever invaded England and it was not the least confident. By the end of the month, the Scots had captured the castle of Norham and had besieged two others.

Meanwhile the Earl of Surrey was marching northwards and gathering more troops as he advanced. He was supported by men and guns landed from a fleet commanded by his son, Thomas Howard, admiral of England. Heraldic exchanges took place between the two armies. Having been eluded once before by James, the Earl of Surrey may have been keen to force a confrontation and both sides agreed to fight at mid-day on 9 September. The Scots army took up a strong position, with artillery carefully placed to cover the anticipated line of attack, but Surrey, in a bold manoeuvre, divided his army, marched it around the Scots and took up a new position between them and Scotland. The Scots discovered the English move too late and had to make a rapid and complete change of position. Before they could accomplish this, the English attacked. Wind and rain made archery difficult and the English cannon were more effective than the hastily repositioned Scottish artillery. Seeing his ranks shaken and depleted by the gunfire, James ordered the army to advance. The battle developed with terrible rapidity. The Borderers on his left pushed their way through the English right and then dispersed. The Highlanders on his right charged but were thrown back without breaking the English line. The centre developed into a grisly tussle. It was an infantry battle between two large armies, around twenty thousand men on each side, wielding pikes, lances and swords. James disregarded the advice of his captains to stay in the rear, swept with the central division of his army far into the English centre and was killed in the fighting. Many in his army fought grimly on, long past the time when it was clear that the day was utterly lost. The numbers of dead and hopelessly wounded were reckoned at ten thousand; on the English side the losses too were great and Surrey's army was too weary to let him follow up his victory.

At Flodden, James IV was engulfed by the crowning disaster of his career. His death was needless. Perhaps the memory of his father at Sauchieburn played a part in his desire to rush to the attack. His military judgement had not matched the tactics of Surrey. But even as he died his myth took life. In so many ways he was the king the Scottish people wanted – grand and yet human, active, generous, gallant, susceptible and devout. For much of his reign he had presided over comparative peace at home and abroad. He had put colour into the lives of the grey-clad peasants and humdrum townsfolk. For a time, the nation in which they had a sometimes forlorn pride had seemed substantial at the councils of Europe. James IV was a 'larger than life' figure who seemed even larger in the years to follow. Above all, he died fighting the old enemy. The Scots could not but forgive a bonny fighter.

A FRENCH REGENCY

As had happened before, the small apparatus of government came together and maintained the realm. The citizens of Edinburgh hastily built the still-visible Flodden Wall, against the expected arrival of Surrey and his army. A regency was established under Queen Margaret. Also as before, the surviving lords of Scotland (some twenty of them were among the ten thousand who fell at Flodden) set about turning the weakness of government to their own advantage.

When in 1514 the queen remarried within a year of James IV's death, she disqualified herself from remaining as regent. Her husband was the ambitious Archibald the 'Red' Douglas, Earl of Angus, whose sympathies were very much pro-English. The role of regent was then assumed by John Stewart, fourth Duke of Albany, who was firmly pro-French. As son of the exiled Duke of Albany, John 'Stuart' had been brought up as a French aristocrat and spent time in France even during his regency. His appointment was bound to cause tension between his pro-French and the queen's pro-English loyalties.

Dissension with Lord Home, who was chamberlain, the Earl of Angus and the first Earl of Arran involved the Regent Albany in a pattern of reconciliations, betrayals, sieges and submissions in which the only certain thing was that he had the baby King James V in his safe keeping. In June 1517 Albany returned to France, leaving a Council of Regency in charge which rapidly polarised between the Earl of Arran, head of the house of Hamilton, and the Earl of Angus, head of the house of Douglas and husband of the queen. Angus held Edinburgh and the king.

Late in April 1520, the Earl of Arran failed to displace his rival, Angus, in a battle that was fought in the very centre of Edinburgh, and that Gavin Douglas, Bishop of Dunkeld – scholar and translator of the *Aeneid* into Scots but also the brother of the Earl of Angus – had tried in vain to prevent. The fight passed into popular lore as Angus's effort to 'cleanse the causey'. The Earl of Angus held power until Albany returned from France in November 1521, but then Henry VIII demanded the regent's removal. The Scots parliament refused and in 1522, Henry sent a fleet to the Firth of Forth. The Regent Albany summoned the Scots army, but the shadow of 1513 was still a long one and his captains would not follow him into England. It was clear to them that he was fighting for his true master, Francis I of France, who was at war with Henry VIII. Having secured a few French troops, Albany besieged the castle of Wark but could not capture it and the failure was blamed on the Scots Border troops. Albany finally departed for France and let his regency lapse in the spring of 1524.

THE REIGN OF JAMES V

By this time, James V had reached the age of twelve. Scotland rapidly became a Douglas kingdom in all but name, with his step-father, the Earl of Angus, filling virtually all posts of authority with his relatives. By 1526 the young king was already trying to rid himself of the oppressive tutelage of his step-father. The chronicler Pitscottie describes how the Earl of Angus 'rullit the king as he pleissit and caussit him to ryde throw all the pairtis of Scotland under the pretence and collour of justice to punisch thief and traitour; bot nane was greattar nor was in thair awin companie' [ruled the king as he pleased; he made the king go all over Scotland on the pretence and appearance of handing out justice, to punish thieves and traitors; but there were no greater thieves or traitors than those in their own entourage].

In the summer of 1528, James V escaped Angus's custody and rode through the night from Falkland Palace to Stirling. Within a few days he was advancing on Edinburgh at the head of two thousand men. The Earl of Angus fled to a hospitable welcome in England while the royal *putsch* rap-

Artist's impression of Falkland Palace at the time of James V

idly resulted in dismissals, forfeitings and executions among his kinsmen.

So began the personal rule of James V. Once again royal authority had to be restored to the parts of the country where it had become purely nominal. James was not in a hurry to make his presence felt, because, first of all, it was essential to establish some sort of administration, to review the royal finances and to learn what was what in his kingdom. In due course he made an expedition to the Borders, in 1530, and combined hunting deer with hanging Liddesdale reivers, one of whom was Johnnie Armstrong who became the subject of a famous ballad. The raid left the Borders severely disaffected.

Under the lieutenancies of the Campbells and Gordons, the Highlands remained largely quiet; though local affrays were frequent and bloody, they did not threaten the state. In one of the worst of these local fights, in 1527, Hector MacIntosh burned down a castle with twenty-four members of the Ogilvie family inside it. James sailed around the North and West of Scotland in the summer of 1540. His trip included a visit to Orkney and was more of a royal tour of inspection than a punitive expedition.

James's self-assertion was as vigorous as that of any of his predecessors. He went further in some respects. The limited powers of the old Court of Session were changed and recast when a new College of Justice was founded on the orders of the king. Finance was provided to pay the judges through a tax agreed with the bishops. The Session Court thus launched proceeded to evolve, becoming a two-tier structure in the 1550s, which enabled it to function both as a High Court and a Court of Appeal. The laws of Scotland, however, still had no formal structure and remained a jumble.

THE DECAY OF THE CHURCH

It was remarkable that James should earmark any large sum for any purpose other than enlarging the royal funds since, as his reign progressed, it became clear that he was obsessed with the accumulation of money. Even in his youth, court poets like Sir David Lyndsay had spotted this avarice and warned him against it. Naturally he turned his attention to the Church. Like his father, he combined the public display of demonstrative piety with a keen eye to the opportunities of diverting the ecclesiastical revenues for his own purposes. Moreover, he had a large family to support. He appears to have fathered at least nine illegitimate children. With a cynicism on which no later propagandist could improve, he informed the Pope that, by his bestowing the priory of St Andrews on a six-year-old son, 'the royall dignitie of the boy will put a restraint upon the impious.'

Neither James nor his nobles seems to have appreciated the harm being

Woodcut engraving of John Knox (c.1513–1572), Scottish Protestant reformer, from Theodore Beza's Icones *(1580)*

done to the Church. Its great offices gradually filled with younger sons, bastard sons, indigent uncles, nearly all of whom were secular figures with no religious vocation, who took the very large revenues of the bishoprics, abbeys and priories and paid back very modest amounts to the professional clerics who were expected to do the work. This trend developed rapidly, as the growth of Protestantism forced the Papacy on to the defensive. In 1520 Martin Luther had been declared a heretic but Lutheranism had spread throughout Germany and beyond. In 1532 Jean Calvin had begun to preach in Paris. As a sound and reliable Catholic king, James found he could obtain favours from a grateful Pope. The authorities in Rome feared he would go the way of Henry VIII, who in 1534 had made himself supreme head of the Church of England. By 1539 there was hardly a monastic house left in England. The condition of the Church in Scotland was made worse by the fact that very many of the parishes were administered by abbeys, often remote. At the very lowest level of Church organisation, parish priests lived on a pittance while the abbey's officer made sure that the parish sent its due contribution to its patron. The priesthood ceased to be a ladder of opportunity for the clever boy of low or modest social origin. The priests themselves, exploited and ill-paid, often became negligent or restive. John Knox, born around 1513, was already among their number during the reign of James V.

LAND RIGHTS IN SIXTEENTH-CENTURY SCOTLAND

At this time the custom of feuing land, whose tentative beginnings went back to the fourteenth century, became commonplace. Lands had normally been rented to groups of tenants on a term lease, for two to five years. Subsequently the landholder and tenants would renegotiate terms to extend or end the lease. Such leases often included duties and services ranging from the full feudal obligation to military service down to giving labour or regular payments in kind. To sell the feu for a cash sum and to obtain a low fixed rent provided instant capital for the landholder and security for the tenant, who could pass on the land to his inheritors so long as the annual rent was paid. James IV had been a determined collector of crown lands and turned them speedily into cash by feuing them, and the royal practice was adopted by the Church even before its higher positions were filled by the cash-hungry nobility. The initiative was often taken by the superior of an abbey or monastery, and the occupier of the land would have to buy the feu or move. Purchasers of feus could only be those already rich enough to have cash in hand. They included landowners keen to establish cadet branches of their families, bishops and abbots providing for their illegitimate children, court officials whose positions enabled them to take bribes or engage in peculation and embezzlement, and the more prosperous burgesses.

The amount raised by a feu depended on the size of the property, which ranged from a cottage and its field to the entire lands of the earldom of Strathearn. Feuars, tenants of feus, could then sublet in the old manner. The rush to sell feus put a lot of cash into circulation but it did nothing to stimulate economic growth. And even the most devious superior found it difficult to sell a feu twice. These transactions among the well-to-do left the bulk of the population in a situation in which they continued to work and pay their rents, as before, or worse off, under a new and more aggressive tenant seeking a good return on his investment. Some tenants found the money to pay the new rents, but others joined the growing numbers of wandering beggars. The gap between rich and poor in Scotland grew wider.

The new official insistence on documentary proof of ownership in the form of charters for lands themselves, for the sale of feus and for the resultant effective transfers of ownership, was an unwelcome revolution to the Scots peasantry in both Highlands and Lowlands. The commercialism of the feu system caused outrage and distress among those who were displaced by it. At this time the expression 'kindly tenants' came to the fore. In one petition to parliament in 1578, the tenants of the Bishop of Dunblane, who were about to become tenants of the Earl of Montrose, saw their fate all too clearly and referred to themselves as 'native tenants and kindly possessors' of their land who, if removed, would be reduced to beggary. These were tenants who held their smallholdings as part of the landowner's wider family, or kin (hence kindly). Often the rental was small and partly exchanged by service. The protests of these kindly tenants was evidence of the survival of arrangements that ran back to a more ancient Scotland. Fostered by the patriarchal tradition, the general illiteracy, and the long-standing feeling that the land was the tribal group's to inhabit by right of ancient possession, not the chief's to arrogate to himself, the sense of identity with their land was strong among the people. Despite 'Normanisation' and all that had come after it, even a landowner with a charter himself might be influenced by these feelings. The new legal requirements for documents could not accommodate such old-world sentiments and attitudes. At least since the accession of James IV, there had been a sense of changing times in the air. Lord Lindsay was one of those who had denounced the first parliament of James IV as 'false lurdans and traitours' [two-faced dullards and traitors] and he was dismissed as 'ane man of the auld world'. The new-world Scots were not alone in perceiving the past as something to shake off; the same attitude was even more widespread elsewhere in Europe.

THE ETERNAL TRIANGLE

Scotland's foreign policy was once more reduced to the eternal triangle of Scotland, England and France. James V and his Council were inclined to favour France, but the persistent urgings of his English uncle, Henry VIII, could not simply be ignored. In 1534 another Treaty of Perpetual Peace between Scotland and England was signed. Henry had been excommunicated by the Pope in 1533 and had made himself head of the Church of England in 1534. Here was a further reason for him to put pressure on Scotland, a Catholic state from which a counter-Reform campaign could easily be launched against England. The English king did not want any challenge to his authority.

Henry VIII was anxious to meet James V personally, and meanwhile in 1535 sent him a long anti-Papal treatise that he had composed himself. James evaded Henry's invitations, sailed to France and married the daughter of Francis I in Paris on 1 January 1536, returning in May; eight weeks later she died.

Against the advice of Henry VIII, James found another French bride. She was the widow of the wealthy first Duke of Lorraine, Claude Guise, and as Mary of Guise she brought James another substantial dowry within a short space of time. They were married in St Andrews in 1538.

Artist's impression of Mary of Guise

In religious matters the Scots government became more severe in its views of heresy, and the trial and burning to death of heretics became familiar. Although parliament acknowledged the declined state of the Church, it also made it a capital crime to dispute the Pope's authority. Scotland once again could boast a cardinal, in the person of David Beaton, Archbishop of St Andrews. Henry repeated his invitations to James to come and meet him and his requests turned into provocations. When James protested against these, he was invited to come to England to discuss the matter of redress. James did at last agree to a meeting at York in 1541 which Henry attended, but James decided not to go after all. By now the disease, nervous or physical, that killed James V at the age of thirty had taken hold.

Henry became more menacing, and in 1542 an English fleet harried shipping bound to and from Scotland. His army briefly crossed the Border and returned hastily, leaving prisoners behind. There were further manoeuvres and counter-manoeuvres on the Borders, with the Scottish leaders resolute only in their refusal to cross into England, and the king clearly not playing a leading role. Finally, in November 1542, a large Scottish army was thoroughly routed by a smaller English force close to the Border at the Battle of Solway Moss. James had been at Lochmaben, not far from the battlefield, and now retreated first to Edinburgh, then to his queen at Linlithgow, then to Falkland. He was no longer capable of managing affairs. In the last days of his life, Mary of Guise, having already borne him two sons who had died, delivered a third child, a daughter. As recounted by Pitscottie, the king 'turnit his bak into his lordis and his face into the wall'. By the time the baby girl was a week old she was Queen of Scotland.

COLLAPSE OF A KING

The sudden and total decline of James V has been puzzled over without any clear conclusion as to how it should have happened. In the first years of his reign he had showed resolution as well as a strong will, and in his relations with Henry VIII he had showed, if not very skilfully, that he was a man of independent judgement. Among the nobles he was unpopular, but there was never any suggestion that they would revolt against him. He had powerful friends in France. The defeat of Solway Moss, although it was a source of shame and distress, was not a catastrophe and the country was not in immediate danger. The situation was far from irretrievable. But by a savage irony, the first of the Jameses to die in his bed provoked by doing so a crisis more threatening than any the country had seen since the boyhood of David II.

The consistent, almost rhythmic but wholly accidental pattern of premature death and child succession which marked the Scottish monarchy from 1406 to 1567, with its well-known side-effects of disturbance and power struggles among the noble families, tends to obscure the more consistent and purposeful trends of national administration. Each successive king found a machinery of government that had never quite disappeared, and individuals who expected to play a part in the system. In the later reigns, each king found his administration to be a little more substantial and each reign reinforced the tradition and practice of royal government. James III's new nobility, consciously created to counterbalance the old, may soon have developed the habits of the long-established lords but they did not have the primeval power bases. Their estates were smaller and they were more dependent on royal favour and patronage. Their prestige came from their functions around the king as chamberlain or chancellor, justiciar or sheriff.

At a lower social level there were landowners or tenants not grand enough to be lords of parliament but important enough to be lairds, ranging from almost peasants to almost lords. Their sons went to school and university. The burghs governed themselves closely and had slowly developed as a network of mutual self-interest from the old 'Four Burghs' to the Convention of Royal Burghs. All these groups took a keen interest in what had happened to the English religious houses between 1534 and 1538. The Church in Scotland was far from being an entirely separate institution; it was integrated with the state in many ways as a landowner, as a source of revenue and as the provider of charity and education. There were men like Bishop Forman of Moray, who was also Justiciar of the North, who combined secular and Church roles. Cardinal Beaton was to become Chancellor. Leading Churchmen had a vested interest in peace and good order, as well as religious and moral

Artist's impression of Cardinal Beaton's house in Edinburgh

responsibility to help maintain these. Their presence in government was taken for granted.

Even during the worst disorders, although they might have been unable to exert enough influence to prevent conflicts, parliament and council did not disappear. At the height of his power, the Earl of Angus had found it necessary to insist that he governed in the name of James V and with the consent of the king. The country never collapsed into anarchy and was never in any real danger of doing so. The task of maintaining government in a royal minority still continued to be difficult and daunting. In 1542 the Council entrusted the regency to the Earl of Arran, head of the house of Hamilton, as a tribute to his closeness to the throne rather than to his abilities as a national leader.

It soon emerged that there were two parties in Scotland, the aims of which gradually became clearer. This was a new development in Scottish affairs and marks a new political consciousness that is modern rather than medieval.

Scotland had previously had factions motivated by such simple considerations as greed, loyalty and the blood feud. Ideas and principles played a scanty part in their actions. Now the parties opened up two ways of viewing the future. One was the pro-French and Catholic group which naturally gathered around the strong-minded Mary of Guise, the Queen Mother, and her ally, Cardinal Beaton. The other was the pro-English and ultimately Protestant group, the form and leadership of which were much more fluid. Initially the Earl of Lennox, a rival to the second Earl of Arran for the role of king if the infant queen were to die as her brothers had done, was its leading figure. Captured at Solway Moss, Lennox returned to Scotland in the pay of Henry VIII of England, as did numerous others. Between these groups many people vacillated in a torment of indecision between the Catholic and Protestant, French or English sympathies. Whilst the political momentum still made a French alliance the expected option, people increasingly began to ask what advantage the Scots had enjoyed from their links with France since Flodden.

A NEW SET OF CHOICES

These questions were open to the whole nation. It was a pregnant period. Fiery-eyed renegade priests, armed with the truths established in Paris and Geneva, were offering their countrymen something they had never had before — a real choice. With the choice of religion went the future of the country, with advantages and disadvantages attaching to either option. Whilst the canny man might study the way the laird was thinking, he need not, and often did not accept the laird's opinion. In those early years of the Reformation, the voiceless people of Scotland had a new freedom. All the energy of government and all the inertia of tradition could not prevent its slow and inexorable articulation.

THE ROUGH WOOING

For a brief time supporters of the English party prevailed. Cardinal Beaton was imprisoned. Henry VIII's intentions were plain. Equally hostile to Catholics and Lutherans, he wanted a reformed church in Scotland on the model he had created in England. Now that he had a male heir, his interest in dynastic union revived, and the Treaty of Greenwich of July 1543 included arrangements for the betrothal of his son, Prince Edward of England, to the child Queen Mary. Henry had a benevolent regard for his great-niece which was all too possessive and awoke fears that the English Tudors would achieve what the Plantagenets and Angevins had failed to do. The Earl of Arran and his council changed from their pro-English stance and

Artist's impression of Mary of Guise's Oratory in Edinburgh. The Guise Palace was erected after the English invasion of 1544. Its position on Castle Hill meant it was under the protection of the Castle's guns.

returned to the pro-French line that was being strongly urged by Cardinal Beaton, who had been released from prison. Arran had hopes that his own son, James, would marry the little Queen Mary. Scottish forces were beginning to reassemble against Henry, whose response was to begin his 'rough wooing'. In 1544 Edinburgh was assailed by sea and land, and the town burned for four days. Sporadic warfare continued along the Border and in February 1545 the Scots, led by the Earl of Arran, won a battle at Ancrum Moor which nevertheless did not alter the basic state of affairs.

THE ORIGINS OF THE REFORMATION IN SCOTLAND

With the pro-French policy went the anti-Protestant one. The doctrines of Reform were being brought into Scotland from France and Switzerland, often by priests who had been part of the established Catholic religion but who had become disaffected – such as John Knox. Despite efforts to prevent it, books and pamphlets were imported. The new ideas were unstoppable. They had a particular appeal to a small but influential class: the relatively important lairds who often had official responsibilities, like Sir William Kirkcaldy of Grange, who had been Treasurer to James V.

The Council took violent action against the new ideas, and George Wishart, the leading agitator, was burned to death at St Andrews in March

1546. Three months later, Kirkcaldy of Grange led an armed band into St Andrews Castle, assassinated Cardinal Beaton and hung his naked corpse out on the battlements. The Reformers had declared war.

THE QUEEN SENT TO FRANCE

Although their aim was to obtain an English alliance, neither the religious Reformers nor the pro-English party were a coherent or cohesive group. The death of Henry VIII and the rule of the Protector Somerset did not alter English policy, especially as it was now clear that the Scots government had no intention of letting the marriage of the young King Edward to Queen Mary take place. Somerset, who as Earl of Hertford had harried Edinburgh in 1544, returned to Scotland with a large army in September 1547 and trounced the Scots, led by the Earl of Arran, at Pinkie, near Musselburgh. The battle was fought close to the shore and caught the Scots between cannon fire from the English fleet and the English land artillery. The number of dead was little less than at Flodden. It did not have the desired results, however. Events in France had produced for the young Queen Mary a potential husband of impeccable eligibility, the Dauphin Francis, who was heir to Henry II of France. The interest of Scotland, as perceived by the queen mother, Mary of Guise, the interest of the Guise family themselves and the safety of the queen, all coalesced in one decision: the young Mary would be sent to France. On 7 August 1548, a French vessel left from Dumbarton with the queen, her retinue of 'four Maries' (Mary Fleming, Mary Beaton, Mary Livingston and Mary Seton) and an escort of Scots lords and ladies.

Artist's impression of a sixteenth-century man-of-war

THE BALLADS

The Scots ballads are in their origin folksongs, though we now treat them as poetry. They are songs that tell a story, often with a tragic theme, using narrative and direct speech, and with little elaboration or comment. They have a distinctive rhythm, and the typical, though not the only, form is a four-line stanza of which the second and fourth lines rhyme.

They begin to appear from the sixteenth century, though many of their themes have a much more archaic feel. The two great centres of the ballad tradition are the Northeast and the Borders, though the collector and classifier Francis Child believed 'That the best Scottish ballads come from the North, there can be no doubt.'

The original singers of the ballads are unknown, and they were passed on by word of mouth before finding their way into print. The first great collector of the ballads was Anna Gordon (1747–1810). Some were 'improved' in the process of collection, and the poet William Motherwell referred witheringly to 'the Alembic established at Abbotsford for the purification of Ancient Song' – a dig at Sir Walter Scott and his *Minstrelsy of the Scottish Border*.

In the spare, vivid Scots of the oldest known versions, the ballads bring this world together with unseen worlds, express the tragedy of human destiny, the fickleness of fate, the power of love, and view with a hardy realism the frailty of life. One of the most interesting aspects of the ballads is the fact that many of them are paralleled in other literatures; just like the folk-tale, they appear to emerge from an early European consciousness. But it was from Scotland that the ballads were re-exported to Europe, particularly to Germany, in the Romantic enthusiasm of the late eighteenth century and, taken up by Bürger and Goethe, reinvigorated poetry there. Ballad-making has never died in Scotland, but it has never excelled the songs that first created the tradition, like *Tam Lin*, *The Wife of Usher's Well*, *May Colvin*, *Sir Patrick Spens*, and many others.

> And see ye not yon bonny road
> That winds about the fernie brae?
> That is the road to fair Elf-land,
> Where thou and I this night maun gae.
> (From *Thomas the Rhymer*)

A SECOND FRENCH REGENCY

After some uneasy years of co-existence between Mary of Guise and the Earl of Arran, the queen mother finally obtained the regency in 1554 and Arran was paid off with the French duchy of Châtelherault. Mary of Guise's two brothers, one a duke and the other a cardinal, were the most influential men in France. With the help of French money – not as much as she requested – she was able to hire mercenary troops from France and Italy. The Protestant party had been somewhat embarrassed by the accession in 1553 of the Catholic Mary I to the throne of England; Mary of Guise was embarrassed by the French-Spanish War and the refusal of her nobles to invade England on behalf of the French. On 25 April 1558, Mary of Scotland was married to the fourteen-year-old Dauphin Francis, and in November of the same year, with the sanction of the Scottish parliament, he became king of Scotland. In theory at least, Scotland was, or was steadily becoming, a subject-state of France. Its queen had become a significant piece in the European power game.

When Mary I of England died at the end of 1558, the king of France lost no time in proclaiming Mary I of Scotland as rightful queen of England. The actual queen of England at that time was Elizabeth I, stigmatised by the Catholic world as illegitimate because of her father's chequered marital history, who saw in Mary Queen of Scots not merely her heir presumptive but an active and dangerous rival. And the Scottish Protestants again had an ally, if a wary and prickly one, in Whitehall.

Mary of Guise did her best to maintain an island of French and European culture at her Scottish court. There was much French music for both dancing and singing. The recently evolved style of the *chanson* was adapted to Scottish texts, and Scottish tunes were given to French words. Contemporary French poets like Ronsard were read and admired. There was also literary talent to be found closer to home. Alexander Scott gave the fashionable theme of unrequited love a Scottish flavour:

> 'Luve is ane fervent fire,
> Kendillit without desire;
> Short pleisure, lang displeisure,
> Repentence is the hire;
> Ane puir treisure without meisure:
> Luve is ane fervent fire.'
>
> [Love is a burning fire,
> Kindled without desire;

> Short pleasure, long regret
> Repentance is the price;
> A pure treasure without measure;
> Love is a fervent fire.]

In 1540 Sir David Lyndsay completed *Ane Pleasant Satyre of the Thrie Estatis*, the first genuine drama in Scots. It was based on the form of the medieval morality play but with a far greater and wittier relevance to the contemporary scene. The regent's bilingual courtiers might already have read the French version of Castiglione's *Il Cortegiano*, which was also available in English by 1561. The very fact that the court was such a trigger- or dagger-happy group made it vital to have some kind of social code, even if it was often ignored. The courtiers combined a veneer of polished official deportment with a tendency to revert to savagery. As with so many aspects of Scottish behaviour, this was by no means restricted to Scotland but often seemed to be carried there to a greater degree. Lord Darnley, who could turn out a ballade as readily as he could kick a citizen out of the way or pull his knife on a Riccio, was typical. Those who disapproved of the regime and its religion did not distinguish between the separate aspects of gaiety, artistic talent, frivolity and viciousness; they saw it as all of a piece and, as such, to be struck down.

CHURCH AND STATE

The Church in Scotland took action in parliament to defend itself and its creed, and at the same time, set up successive councils to study its own reform. In 1552 it produced a catechism, but the crucial questions were left to one side. On the mainland of Europe, the Council of Trent was already addressing itself to the disciplines required by an effective Counter-reformation.

In Scotland, older ways still prevailed. The new Archbishop of St Andrews held his office because he was a member of the Hamilton family, and he was in any case far from being the man to conduct a rigorous moral crusade.

THE LORDS OF
THE CONGREGATION

Against the fervent preachings of the Reformers, who made trenchant, public and all-too-valid criticism of the manners, morals and spirituality of the established clergy, the Church scarcely replied. John Knox, who had assumed the religious leadership of the Protestants after Wishart had been burned, organised the Protestant nobles, including the fourth Earl of Argyll and the illegitimate son of James V, Lord James Stewart, into the 'Lords of the Congregation' in 1555. When Mary of Guise tried to take action against militant Reformist preachers in 1559 and outlawed Knox and his followers, there was an immediate reaction. Knox preached a sermon in Perth, the effect of which was to rouse his listeners to a riot in which they despoiled the parish church and stormed into the two monasteries nearby, smashing images and vessels, stealing vestments, breaking furniture, and eradicating every trace of 'idolatrie'.

Artist's impression of the Mercat or Market Cross, Edinburgh

This finally prompted Mary of Guise to call out her French and Italian troops, but the Protestant party had also prepared an army of its own, which was ready and willing to fight under the command of the Earl of Glencairn. Calvinist zealots stripped St Andrews Cathedral and burned Scone Abbey, then advanced to Edinburgh, stripping bare the churches as they came to them. In the words of a contemporary, 'they were alluret with hope of prey, of Libertie, and a nue kind of Lyf' [they were burning with the prospect of loot, of Liberty and a new kind of life]. Mary of Guise took refuge in Dunbar, and the insurgents, as they had now become, proclaimed their government from the Market Cross of Edinburgh. Mary began to negotiate with the Reformers and agreed to suspend the laws against heresy if the Lords of the Congregation withdrew their forces from Edinburgh. She established herself in Leith and arranged for its walls to be strengthened while French supplies of men and munitions were shipped into the harbour.

The Lords of the Congregation took the old remedy of the Scots rebel and asked for help from England. Queen Elizabeth I supplied them with a fleet of sixteen vessels and an army of eight thousand soldiers, complete with siege artillery, which arrived before the walls of Leith in March 1560. Mary of Guise was by now fatally ill and had removed to Edinburgh Castle, where she died in June of that year. King Francis accepted the inevitable defeat of the Scottish and French forces in Edinburgh. He sent ambassadors to England who proceeded to Scotland, where, on 6 June 1560, the Treaty of Leith was signed by the three nations of Scotland, France and England. It arranged for all French troops to leave Scotland within twenty days and stated that no Frenchman could hold any public office in Scotland. A council would govern the country on behalf of Francis and Mary I and the Protestant party would have a majority. A parliament was called in the name of Queen Mary on 1 August, and decreed that the jurisdiction and authority of the Pope in Scotland should be abolished and that anyone who acknowledged the Pope's supremacy or issued decrees in his name should be banished and lose his goods. The celebration of the Mass was forbidden and the Protestant Confession of Faith accepted as 'hailsome and sound doctrine groundit upon the infallibill trewth of godis word' [wholesome and sound doctrine grounded on the infallible truth of God's word]. More than a hundred of the country lairds attended this parliament. They were men who, like their fathers before them, had never seen much point in coming. Now they had come to savour their victory, and in many cases to be in on the rich pickings from the carcass of prelacy.

The naive expectation of the religious Reformers was that the revenues of the old Church would simply be diverted to the new. They were quickly disappointed, and to some degree their own doctrines were to blame. The descendants of families who had endowed collegiate churches and abbeys with large amounts of money in order that perpetual prayers could be made for their souls were now informed that the prayers had been of no avail and would certainly not be permitted to continue. Like any victim of fraud, but with more than usual hope of success, they wanted their money back. Many wished to retain the benefices that they already possessed, some wanted newly looted church property back and others wanted to be rewarded for changing their allegiance. The result was that changes to Church organisation and structure were slower than the political changes. An accommodation was reached allowing for around a third of Church revenue to go to the crown and from this revenue the new Kirk would be funded.

MARY RETURNS

The Protestant party was well established in power when Mary I became a widow at the age of nineteen and returned to Scotland in August 1561. She had been brought up as a princess of France, in the kind of security and luxury far removed from the normal Stewart childhood. Nobody had expected her to exercise any real power and her education had extended only to the things an intelligent and modern queen consort was expected to know. Her kingdom was both familiar and foreign to her, and it was still in the throes of a massive religious and political upheaval. The physical impotence and early death of her husband had prevented her from providing

France with a dauphin, and her political importance to the Guise family was no longer significant. But she was still the Catholic claimant to the English throne, occupied or usurped by another queen regnant. The Treaty of Leith had provided that Mary would formally renounce her claim to the English throne, which was something that she certainly did not want to do without some compensatory gesture from England, such as her confirmation as Elizabeth's heir. This was not acceptable to Elizabeth herself. Diplomatic exchanges were conducted by Mary's Secretary of State, William Maitland, a master of analysis equal to Sir William Cecil, the Secretary of Elizabeth I.

THE COLLAPSE OF MARY'S RULE

Maitland and the most prominent of the Scottish nobles, Mary's half-brother, Lord James Stewart, made Earl of Moray by his sister, were both moderate Protestants, and on their advice the government did not try to overturn the religious revolution. Indeed, domestic politics of the old-fashioned military sort forced her to take action against one of the greatest

Artist's impression of Mary Queen of Scots, based on the portrait by an unknown artist in the Scottish National Portrait Galllery, Edinburgh

Catholic lords, the Earl of Huntly, in a nervously exhilarating campaign that took her into the Highlands as far north as Inverness.

Queen Mary was diplomatic about the issue of religion. She maintained her own Catholic practice and observance on a private basis. The ruin of her reign began in July 1565 when the much debated question of her second marriage was ended by her decision to marry her first cousin Henry

Artist's impression of Lord Darnley, Mary's second husband

Stewart, Lord Darnley, son of the Earl of Lennox who had changed to the side of the English after Solway Moss. He too had Tudor blood in his veins, and the marriage was seen as a confirmation that Mary still sought to claim the English crown. Her decision to marry Darnley brought her no support from Catholic Europe and raised screeches of protest from London. The Scottish Protestant nobles, instructed to treat this arrogant English-born playboy as King Henry, reacted with an armed revolt that was led by the queen's half-brother and erstwhile adviser, the Earl of Moray. The skirmishes that followed were called the 'Chaseabout Raid'.

Mary's interest in, and respect for, her husband diminished rapidly. 'King Henry' Darnley performed only one positive service to the Scottish nation. This was to engender a son who was to be the future James VI, born in June 1566. Three months before his birth, his mother had witnessed the murder of her private secretary, David Riccio. He had been dragged screaming from her room by her husband, Darnley, and his friend Lord Ruthven to be stabbed to death on the staircase in Holyrood Palace. Lord Darnley may have been trying to organise a *coup d'état* rather than simply make a jealous strike at a resented favourite who was in the queen's confidence. But if it was an attempt to make his nominal kingship a reality, it was certainly a failure, and Mary made a public reconciliation with him to separate him from his associates. Darnley became ill and faded from public attention until the dramatic events of the night of 9 February 1567, when the house in which he was recuperating in Edinburgh, known as Kirk o' Field, was blown up by gunpowder. Darnley was already lying dead in the garden, strangled. The crime was blamed on the Earl of Bothwell, who had become the new recipient of Mary's favours, and few people believed the queen was wholly innocent. Bothwell was acquitted of murder, in a trial courtroom that was packed inside and out with his armed supporters. Shortly afterwards, on 24 April, he took possession of the queen, ostensibly for her protection and almost certainly with her consent. Bothwell obtained a divorce from his wife on 7 May, and on 15 May, only three months after Darnley's death, they were married in a Protestant ceremony.

Scotland, which had tolerated murders by its kings and had winked at their often notorious extramarital adventures, was profoundly shocked. For those who liked the grand concept of kingship, the marriage of Queen Mary to Darnley was a deep disappointment, but her marriage to Bothwell was infinitely worse. For Calvinists, who viewed the role of the monarch in terms of a Protestant chief magistracy, the morality and the conduct of the queen made her an agent of hell.

The uprising of the nobles this time, urged on by the preachers, was no chaseabout. At Carberry Hill on 15 June 1567 the queen was present with her men, but her army was so much smaller than that of her opponents that no fight took place. Bothwell discreetly left the scene, and Mary was taken as a

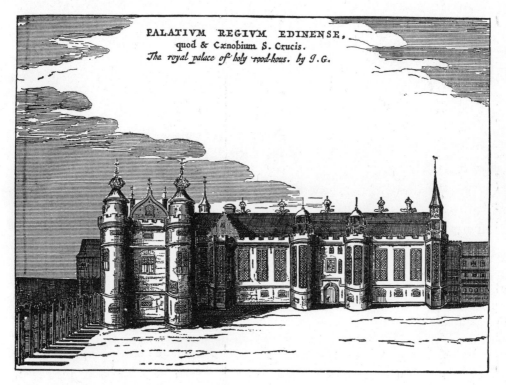

Engraving of the Palace of Holyroodhouse in the sixteenth century

prisoner to the island castle of Loch Leven. In prison she was threatened and bullied into an act of abdication in favour of her infant son. Her escape from Loch Leven took place in circumstances that would seem like a historical romance if they were not established fact. It encouraged a brief resumption of hostilities between her mainly Catholic supporters, led by the Hamilton and Seton families with the equivocal assistance of the fifth Earl of Argyll, against mainly Protestant barons led by the Earl of Moray, who had been named as regent in her imprisonment. At the Battle of Langside on 14 May 1568, Mary and her army were decisively beaten and she fled south into Dumfriesshire. By May 19 she had crossed the Solway Firth by boat to England, where captivity, execution and legend awaited her.

Despite the sea of ink that has been spilt about her life, Mary I's real contribution to the history of Scotland is minimal. Apart from giving birth to a successor, she did nothing to make a lasting impact on the country. The crises of her reign were self-created and irrelevant to the underlying tide of events.

The revolution-reformation went on, neither helped nor hindered. Commercial life pursued its established trends. Most people were preoccupied by frequent foul weather, famine resulting from bad harvests and outbreaks of plague across the country. It is the force of Mary's personality alone, her adventures, the lurid incidents and her fate, all immensely interesting in their own right, that have made her Scotland's best-known monarch. But as far as the history of Scotland is concerned, they are a side-show, part *fête champêtre*, part *grand guignol*.

QUEEN'S MEN
AND KING'S MEN

When Mary left Scotland there were nevertheless serious political repercussions. There remained two parties in the land, but the issues that divided them were now different. The developing hostility between Protestants and Catholics kept the pro-French party in being, while the Protestants still saw England as their ally. But the imprisonment in England of a crowned queen of Scotland, whose abdication had been under duress, disturbed many people and cut across the religious divide in Scotland. Protestant fighters like Kirkcaldy of Grange became Queen's Men allied to the Catholic power bases of the Hamiltons and Gordons. The ineptitude and lack of skill of Queen Mary seemed less important to them than the need to preserve the long-established principle of kingship.

On the other hand, the governing party had a perfectly legitimate, if very young, Stewart king who was currently undergoing what was considered an appropriate education for a Calvinist monarch. These tensions, added to the normal rivalries that arose in a royal minority, resulted in civil war. A further new element was the intensely vocal and politicised Protestant clergy. They had no power other than their influence over the people, but that was very strong. With their eyes still fixed firmly on the revenues of the old Church, they were forced to stay in alliance with the Protestant lords.

The Protestant lords, nevertheless, had already shown hostility to the more far-reaching plans of the Reformers. They too had intentions for the Church lands and funds that had nothing to do with the ministers' plans for salaried clergy and the establishment of schools in every parish. Some of the nobles were implicated in the death of Darnley, who had, after all, been the young king's father. At some time in the future James VI might seek revenge for the murder of his father. Such conflicts of interest and loyalty made matters even more unstable. In 1570 the Earl of Moray, who was still regent, was shot dead in the street in Linlithgow by a member of the Hamilton family; in 1571 Archbishop Hamilton was hanged in Stirling as an accessory to this murder.

In September 1571 the Earl of Huntly failed in an effort to snatch the young king from Stirling Castle, but the new regent, the Earl of Lennox, was killed in the affray. The Earl of Mar now took over the regency. In small, bloody battles and burnings of houses, no quarter was given and prisoners were hanged. Even Lindsay of Pitscottie, a supporter of the King's Lords, wrote: 'the kingis lordis tuik nane regaird to the common weill of the cuntrie nor to the kingis honour nor proffeit nor yit to the maintinance of the glorie of god nor the trew kirk therof bot to thair awin particular proffeit' [the king's lords paid no regard to the common good of the country, nor to the honour of the king or gave proper respect to the glory of God or the true Church but simply considered their own financial interests].

Artist's impression of Edinburgh Castle before 1573

Woodcut depicting the appearance of the streets of Edinburgh in 1573, from a sixteenth-century manuscript

THE ADMIRABLE CRICHTON

James Crichton of Eliock, born around 1562, was son of the Lord Advocate. In 1575 he graduated from St Andrews University and went on to polish his studies and knowledge of the world in Europe. As a teenager he spent two years in the French army. His intelligence and accomplishment made a great impact on those who met him, so that he became known as 'the Admirable Crichton', admirable then meaning marvellous rather than simply worthy of praise. A contemporary document from Mantua records that: 'The Scotsman, James Crichton . . . is master of ten languages, Latin and Italian in perfection, and Greek so as to compose epigrams in that tongue, Hebrew, Chaldaic, Spanish, French, Flemish, English and Scots, and he also understands the German. He is most skilled in philosophy, theology, mathematics and astrology . . . . His memory is so astonishing that he knows not what it is to forget. In his person he is extremely beautiful: his address is that of a finished gentleman. A soldier at all points, he has attained to great excellence in leaping and dancing and to a remarkable skill in the use of every sort of arms. He is a remarkable horseman and an admirable jouster.'

This paragon died in a street brawl in Mantua in 1582, putting a premature end to what might have been a great career. Sir Thomas Urquhart established his fame in *The Discoveryie of a Most Exquisite Jewel* (1652), and Sir J. M. Barrie borrowed the name for his perfect butler in the play of the same name in 1902.

A truce was organised at the end of July 1572 but it did not last. Mar died, and the Earl of Morton replaced him as regent, with the distinction of being almost as much detested by his own side as by the Queen's Men. Determined to break out of the long stalemate of conflicting interests in Scotland, he appealed to Elizabeth I of England, who gave money and promises of more support, and most of the opposing lords submitted. Kirkcaldy of Grange, along with Maitland of Lethington, remained defiant in Edinburgh Castle, but Morton brought in English guns and gunners who virtually destroyed the castle, and it was surrendered on 29 May 1573. Maitland died, possibly by suicide; Kirkcaldy was hanged as a traitor to King James. With English support, Morton continued as regent until 1581, but even if his strong-arm tactics had brought an end to fighting, they created only a surly peace during which he ruthlessly amassed a fortune for himself by expropriations, fines and taxes.

CHURCH AND KIRK

Protestant ministers were still relatively few in number, but they were steadily at work in the towns and villages. Great swathes of the country, especially where the earl was a Catholic, remained hostile or apathetic to Reform and to Protestant theology. The act forbidding the Mass was given as much obedience as was normal for Scottish acts of parliament, especially in places to which Edinburgh was just a name. The celebration of Catholic rites went on, while Catholic clergy as well as some of their congregation escaped to Europe by sea or plotted for the restitution of both queen and Church. The Kirk's dream, which had been spelled out in the Book of Discipline of 1560, of inheriting the wealth of the old Church, had long since faded. Under Morton, a new set of bishops and an archbishop were appointed. Rapidly named 'tulchan bishops' by the people, their prime function was to ensure that the teinds, or tithes, were still paid and to pass them on to the laymen who were now the owners of the Church estates. A tulchan calf was a straw dummy in the skin of a dead calf, placed by the mother cow so that she would continue to yield milk. The ministers did not like this development, despite the fact that the new bishops had no supervisory powers, and the Protestant clergy were free to continue to establish the Presbyterian structure of superintendents, ministers, readers, elders and deacons.

Nor did the ministers like the way Morton collected – allegedly on their behalf and in the interests of efficiency – the third of Church income due to be passed to the new Kirk. Their missionary and teaching work often had to be financed by the charity of the new congregations. John Knox, spokes-

THE EARL OF MORTON
AND CAPTAIN CULLEN

The story of Captain Cullen helps to explain the resentment felt against Morton. Cullen had served both Mary of Guise and Mary, Queen of Scots. He was implicated in the murder of Darnley, and was said to be the one who advised strangling the victim, explosions being capricious things. He was arrested but allowed to escape. Later he took service with the Queen's Men under Kirkcaldy of Grange. Caught in a skirmish, he was found hiding in a meat-safe. He had a pretty wife, so Morton had him hanged and lived with the wife. The Reverend Douglas of Dunglas protested to Morton about this, whereupon the Regent had him first tortured, then hanged.

man and historian if not architect of Reform, had died exhausted in 1572. Under the leadership of Andrew Melville, the growing Kirk reorganised itself and produced a Second Book of Discipline in 1578. This abolished the bishop-like superintendents and the readers. It provided for the establishment of the kirk session as the governing body for each church. It also set out the overall organisation of the Kirk, from the level of local churches as presbyteries, of presbyteries into provinces regulated by provincial synods, to the whole structure regulated by the General Assembly as supreme ecclesiastical court. The Second Book of Discipline also demanded the entire revenues of the old Church for the new, and sought to extend Kirk control over the government of the state to ensure that the state in its dealings did not transgress the principles of the new religion. Scotland was to be a model to the world: a state wholly obedient to the word of God as expounded by the Calvinist church.

KING JAMES VI GROWS UP . . .

Someone was growing up in Stirling Castle who would have strong views on the relations between Church and state, in complete opposition to those of Melville. James VI was only twelve years old when the Second Book of Discipline was published, but a court was forming around the precocious young king that had no loyalty to the Regent Morton and from which he was effectively excluded. Its leader was Esmé Stewart, another Franco-Scottish figure who had turned up in Edinburgh from France in 1579 and was generally assumed to be an agent of the French king. By September 1580, he was Earl of Lennox and Lord High Chamberlain. At the end of the year, James Stewart, captain of the royal bodyguard, accused Morton of the murder of Darnley. The regent was arrested and, despite the protestations of Elizabeth I, was beheaded on 2 June 1581. His accuser was made Earl of Arran.

  Suddenly Scottish policy veered towards warm relations with France. In a manner reminiscent of old times, Arran and Lennox made ostentatious use of their influence over the boy king, provoking the jealous fear of their fellow-nobles who in due course formed a band. In August 1582, on a hunting expedition, James VI was snatched away by a party led by the Earl of Gowrie. Lennox was sent back to Paris and Arran was imprisoned. Gowrie, Glencairn and the other members of the band were Protestants, and the Kirk now found more official backing. But James VI was now sixteen years of age and could not be held down, and the Earl of Arran was restored. A further effort by the Protestant lords, to seize Stirling Castle, was botched and Gowrie was executed, his colleagues taking refuge in England. Policy towards the Kirk was summarily reversed. In May 1584, it was announced through parliament that the authority of the king was supreme over all three estates and that the king was the supreme judge in all ecclesiastical matters. His power would be exercised through a hierarchy of bishops. Public criticism of the king was banned. Ministers and teachers must sign a declaration of obedience or lose their offices for ever. These were the 'Black Acts'. Andrew Melville had already fled to England and many ministers followed him.

English diplomacy now held a number of strong Scottish cards, from the Catholic ex-queen to the apostles of Calvinism. It also had

An artist's impression of 'the Maiden', an early form of the guillotine, said to have been invented by the Regent Morton, who perished by it in 1581

an ace up its sleeve. By this time it was clear that the fifty-one-year-old queen of England, even if she should yet marry, was most unlikely to be mother of an heir. All the pleasures that Paris could offer him were nothing compared to James VI's awareness that London could be his. Realism and self-interest pointed in the same direction, and on 31 July 1585 a Treaty of Alliance was signed between England and Scotland. James was promised a pension of five thousand pounds a year. Shortly afterwards Elizabeth I sent back the exiled lords, and Arran, having failed to raise a force against them, fled. The treaty and the pension survived the shock of the execution of Mary Queen of Scots at Elizabeth's orders on 8 February 1587, and the war between England and Spain.

Of his mother, James VI had said not long before her death, 'Let her drink the ale she brewed'. There was official mourning, an official protest, then official oblivion. As to Spain, the General Assembly of the Kirk prevailed over the resistance of the Convention of Royal Burghs to make parliament ban trade with the Spanish nation on grounds of religion. The king supported the ban on purely diplomatic grounds: his foreign policy had a single aim, which was not to antagonise England. The shipowners and merchants, picking up a lot of the Spanish trade lost by England, reacted in the usual way to inconvenient legislation by ignoring it whenever possible.

. . . **THE BARONS DO NOT**

Only one section of the Scots community, by the late sixteenth century, had failed completely to show any sense of developing political maturity. Not only during the minority of James VI but well into his adult reign, the nobles of Scotland made constant efforts to bolster or improve their own situations by trying to get the king's person under their control. Some, like the Gowrie conspirators of 1582, could at least claim that they were not acting for personal reasons; but even they could resort only to a medieval solution. Scotland was still a country in which the strong arm prevailed and that arm did not necessarily belong to the king (James's standing army was his bodyguard of forty men).

Parliament's importance was still held in check by the Committee of the Articles, which was packed by whoever was in power; it was also in danger of being overshadowed by the General Assembly. The burghs, who had organised themselves into a convention that replaced the long-outmoded 'Four Burghs', kept their focus firmly on trade and their own privileges and made no contribution as such to the national debate. The two men in the kingdom with the most modern ideas were the king and Andrew Melville, although it is wrong to think of them as solitary figures. Each had his aides and councillors. James was advised through the ever-present machinery of household officials, headed by Maitland of Thirlestane whose elder brother Lethington had served his mother. Andrew Melville operated through his network of presbyteries. Both had visions of a structured and unified kingdom, and both had to contend with the reality of a set of nobles whose basic attitudes had hardly shifted in two hundred and fifty years.

James must have become a source of disappointment to his more Presbyterian-minded tutors, but he had grown up into a man in whom strong will was linked to a patient temperament and a devious mind. In 1589 he made an uncontroversial marriage with Princess Anne of Denmark. The easily offended queen of England may have felt them presumptuous to call their first son Henry, but Henry had been Darnley's name. James was content to contain trouble when it was too dangerous to crush. The Catholic Earls of Atholl, Crawford, Errol and Huntly were in a state of constant unrest and rebellion between 1589 and 1595 without ever being able to make a decisive move south, though in 1594 Huntly defeated a royal army under the seventh Earl of Argyll in a pitched battle in Glenlivet. The position was complicated by the fact that James was personally attached to Huntly and perhaps unwilling to have the out-and-out confrontation with discontented Catholics that was so strongly urged on him by the Presbyterian activists.

More immediately threatening was the unstable, nominally Protestant

JAMES MELVILLE GOES TO SCHOOL

The diarist James Melville (1556–1614), nephew of the reformer Andrew Melville, was professor of Hebrew at St Andrews and minister of Kilrenny, Fife.

'My father put my eldest and onlie brother David, about a yeir and a halff in age above me, and me togidder, to a kinsman and brother in the ministerie of his to scholl, a guid, learned, kynd man, whome for thankfulness I name, Mr Wilyam Gray, minister at Logie, Montrose. He haid a sistar, a godlie and honest matron, rewlar of his hous, wha often rememberit me of my mother, and was a verie loving mother to us, indeed. Ther was a guid nomber of gentle and honest men's berns of the cowntrey about, weill treaned upe bathe in letters, godlines, and exerceise of honest geams. Ther we learned to reid the Catechisme, Prayers and Scripture, to rehers the Catechisme and Prayers par ceur . . . the Rudiments of the Latin Grammair, with the vocables in Latin and Frenche, also divers speitches in Frenche, with the reiding and right pronounciation of that toung. . . . A happie and golden tyme indeid, giff our negligence and unthankfulness haid nocht moved God to schorten it, partlie be deceying of the number, quhilk caused the maister to weirie, and partlie be a pest quhilk the Lord, for sinne and contempt of his Gospell, send upon Montrose, distant from over Logie bot twa myles; sa that scholl skalled, and we war all send for and brought hame.'

Francis Stewart, Earl of Bothwell. In 1589 he tried, with Huntly, to seize control; in 1590 he appeared to have been hatching a plot to kill King James through the agency of a coven of North Berwick witches. James had a superstitious dread of witchcraft, and his prosecution of witches had a baneful effect on Scottish life. Among the books he wrote was a *Demonologie*, revealing that in some respects his ideas were not modern at all. In 1592 Huntly engineered the murder of the Protestant Earl of Moray, and later that year Bothwell entered Holyrood Palace by night and actually did capture the king. James used his nerve and intelligence to humour the half-mad Earl until he could engineer a coalition of nobles to force him out of power.

CHURCH REFORM:
THE COUNTER-REFORMATION

During this period James was also compelled, in the 'Golden Act' of 1592, to accept the formal Presbyterian organisation of the Kirk in which the bishops he had appointed would have only a shadowy, insubstantial role. In the mid-1590s James was gaining control. Bothwell was forced to flee the country in 1595, and the northern earls finally submitted in 1596. James VI was able to make his own innovations in government and to move against the Church now with greater maturity and ease because Chancellor Maitland, architect of the 'Golden Act', had died in 1595. Eight Commissioners of the Exchequer were appointed, and these 'Octavians' were functionaries whose job it was to ensure that the royal income went to the king without being leached away by hereditary officials.

Relations with the Presbyterians came to a head in the winter of 1596–97, when the Minister of St Andrews, David Black, argued before the Privy Council that it had no power to judge him. In December 1596 a riot broke out in Edinburgh while the king was sitting with the judges in the Tolbooth. James seized the opportunity to take strong measures. The Council re-enacted the 'Black Acts' of 1584, and in a doubly shrewd move, Church courts were forbidden to meet in Edinburgh. The Court of Session was ordered to move to Perth. The king ordained a parliament and a General Assembly to meet there at the beginning of March, and this Perth Assembly was well packed with ministers from the north, less extreme in view and more respectful to their sovereign than those from Edinburgh and Glasgow.

Andrew Melville had taken James by the sleeve and reminded him that he was 'God's silly [mere] vassal', not something that the theorist of the Divine Right of Kings wanted to be told. In Perth the delegates agreed to confirm the king's supremacy and to forbid extempore criticism of the king from the pulpit. The bailies of Edinburgh were fearful that James would make Perth the capital of Scotland. They ignored the advice of their ministers and gave the king their humble apology and submission, with a peace offering of twenty thousand pounds. James made further uses of his right to convene assemblies, choosing northern towns where he could be sure of a majority. At Dundee in 1598 it was agreed that his shadowy bishops could sit in the parliament. He was making no secret of his wish to introduce a full hierarchy of bishops, but not even a partly tamed Kirk would swallow that.

In August 1600 there was a botched attempt by the third Earl of Gowrie, John Ruthven, and his brother Alexander to seize the king in their house in Perth. The motives are unclear, and their father had tried the same course and had been equally unsuccessful in 1582. The young earl was one of the few nobles to take up the Presbyterian cause, and the ministers saw in him a better Bothwell. When James VI returned from Perth with an undeniably confusing account of events and with the earl and his brother dead, the five ministers of the capital suspected a royal plot and refused to give thanks for the king's deliverance. The resulting furious row enabled James to appoint three new bishops to the northerly sees of Aberdeen, Caithness and Ross.

Bishops remained a redundant ornament on a still-Presbyterian Church, but the initiative was now with the king. He wanted a Church that did not presume to overrule his civil powers, but he also wanted a Church whose structure would make it far more amenable to royal management and a force for stability within the national structure that devolved from the king. After the upheavals of the mid-century, James VI in the 1590s embodied the counter-revolution.

THE STATE OF THE NATION
UNDER JAMES VI

Policy towards the Church was only one facet of his overall approach to royal government. With greater ease he brought reform to the law, to parliament and to the process of government. His task may have been easier because of the increasing perception of his fellow-countrymen that this busy, restless, worried, sometimes disarmingly affable figure was not 'just' King of Scots. He was going to be king of England. There was intense speculation on what this might mean. It must have made him seem to cast a longer shadow.

By comparison with the neighbouring kingdom, James was monarch of a disorderly and poverty-ridden country. The agricultural techniques of Scotland had hardly changed in centuries and they were particularly susceptible to bad weather. Wet summers and cold winters caused famine and heavy increases in food prices, which in turn caused further hardships and difficulties. Despite acts of parliament forbidding food exports, there were years in which grain had to be imported. Plague erupted sporadically in the little towns. Local warfare and feuds in the Borders and Highlands, combined with the legal depredations of the king's lieutenants in the Highlands and Islands, created a constant supply of 'broken men' who either took up cattle rustling and banditry on the Highland edges or came to join a fluctuating group of beggars, 'entertainers', fortune-tellers, messengers, torch-bearers, chair carriers, protection racketeers, muggers, prostitutes, pimps and petty thieves in the capital and any other town of any size. Their Gaelic gave them the shared private language of an urban subculture, even if it was not passed on to their children.

Luckier Highlanders became sorners, who attached themselves to a chieftain as armed retainers and were thereby entitled to sleep on his floor and consume a share of the payment in kind that he received as rental from his clansmen or tenants. The numbers of beggars were added to by Lowlanders who had fallen out with their landlords, or who could not pay a debt, or who had been excommunicated by a zealous minister, or who perhaps just abdicated from the unending dreariness of their lives. More than half-hidden behind the parade of political events, detectable often only by the acts of parliament enunciated against them and the contemptuous remarks of those who could write, these people formed perhaps a tenth of the whole population around 1600. An act of parliament of 1575 ordered that such persons should be scourged and burned on the ear with a red-hot iron. Official barbarity of this sort underlines the extent to which violence continued to be endemic throughout society.

LAW AND ORDER

In 1594 Parliament complained about the wild behaviour of university students and teachers, armed with 'suordis, pistolettis and utheris wapynnis' [swords, pistols and other weapons]. In 1595 the boys of Edinburgh High School mutinied, locked out the masters and shot a remonstrating town bailie dead. The man was one of the city's wealthiest merchants but the boy responsible got off with a light sentence. The killing of the 'bonnie' Earl of Moray in 1592 was the result of a complicated blood feud between a whole group of rival barons. Wars in Ireland and the Netherlands provided constant opportunities for mercenary soldiers, who returned, accustomed to seeing power wielded by the gun and the sword.

James VI could see there was a great need to develop the rule of law. In 1587 eight experienced judges were to be appointed to the Court of Session, which would meet regularly and would not be intimidated by shows of strength or bought off by bribes. Worthy and responsible men in the country and the towns were to be made King's Commissioners and Justices, enabled to try minor cases and to hold suspected criminals until the next circuit court. These were to be held at six-monthly intervals rather than every few years, as before. Lack of funds and management meant that these reforms were only partly applied.

GOVERNMENT ORGANISATION

The king was more successful in adapting the instruments of government. The Privy Council had a long history as the King's Council or Council of Regency, but during the reign of Mary it appears to have become a more formal body and her son developed it, with its own procedures and about thirty members, of whom around half were high officials and half hereditary nobles. It was convened by the chancellor. The Council's decisions had the force of acts of parliament, although parliament was usually required to ratify them. It developed new laws and acted as a supreme court, with torture among the sanctions it brought against suspects and witnesses. To give it some sense of embodiment within a structure of Three Estates, two ministers and two burgesses were co-opted when Church or burgh matters were discussed, but they had no vote.

As a rapid extension of the Privy Council, the Convention of the Estates could be summoned when it was clearly necessary to show an authority equivalent to that of the parliament. Such a convention, composed of ten nobles, four officers of state, ten clerics and thirteen burgesses, made the treaty with England of 1585, although parliament duly ratified it in 1586. Even as the king felt his way towards autocracy, the concept of the Community of the Realm would not quite disappear. Parliament itself was not neglected by James. The efforts of James I to make the county freeholders attend had failed; the only one they ever came to in numbers was the Reformation Parliament of 1560. In 1587 it was agreed that the freeholders worth two pounds a year or more in each shire or sheriffdom would elect two members. These members, known as 'barons', made their appearance in the 1592 Parliament.

ENGLAND BECKONS:
THE UNION OF THE CROWNS

By the time he received confirmation of the news on 28 March 1603 that he had been proclaimed king in London, the years of work that James VI had put in as king of Scotland had resulted in many changes. Both king and Reformers might claim responsibility for some of these, and certainly the establishment of the presbytery and the kirk session helped to keep much of the country in a state of relative peace, however much James deplored their potential for developing anarchy or theocracy.

Intelligent and pragmatic, for all his tendency to theorise or pontificate, James lived on for more than two decades in the enjoyment of the reward he had so anxiously awaited. The Union of the Crowns was his triumph, even though he had had to do nothing for it except stay alive and be on his best behaviour. That it was a tragedy for his family and for Scotland could not have been foreseen.

CHAPTER NINE

From 1603 to the Union

LIFE WITHOUT THE KING

In the days and weeks after James VI and his retinue had set off for London, Scotland gradually became aware of its strange new status. It was still a kingdom and still had a king, but the king was an absentee. There had been kings before, like David II, who had lived outside the kingdom. Indeed, James himself had been away for six months in 1589 at the time of his marriage to Anne of Denmark. But there had always been the expectation that the king would eventually return. Now this was not the case. So much in Scotland had devolved from the kingship, not only in terms of law and administration. The king acted as a symbol of paternal care and authority. The underlying patriarchal ethos still permeated the whole nation in sentiment and actuality. To be permanently deprived of the king was a shock to the whole of society. This was felt most keenly in Edinburgh, which also suffered the commercial loss of the court and its appetites for entertainment, loans and luxuries. The departure of the court was also a sharp indication of the difference in status between England and Scotland; it was never a serious possibility that James I of England would reign over his new kingdom from the capital of Scotland. He only ever made one return visit to Edinburgh, in 1617, fourteen years after his departure.

Governing Scotland at a distance does not seem to have been a serious problem for James. He had mastered the management of his native countrymen and, true to the principles set out in his book *Basilikon Doron*, a guide to the role of the king for his eldest son, Henry, he achieved his reign over Scotland without the appointment of a viceroy. The reins of power stretched all the way to his London power base. James now also had access to the information supplied by the substantial spy network that had long kept Elizabeth I and her ministers well informed on events throughout Scotland. Privy Council, Convention of the Estates and Parliament all continued to function in Scotland. The Council was the prime source of action and legislation in the north, and the machinery of government, law and taxation ran as smoothly as ever. The Council dealt with such matters as the arrest and execution in 1615 of the Stewart Earl of Orkney for his excessive independence and repressive rule. The focus of government was on domestic matters

NOVA SCOTIA – A FIRST
SCOTTISH ATTEMPT AT EMPIRE

By the early seventeenth century, European colonies were well established in North America, chiefly by Spain and France. Scotland, despite its openness to the West, had never displayed any interest in such expansion. But, under the aegis of James VI's 'Great Britain', Sir William Alexander obtained a royal charter in 1621, confirmed again by Charles I in 1625, for the development of a great region of North America. It had already been explored by the French and named Acadia, but was largely empty, populated by a few North American Indian tribes. In return for the supply of men and money, baronetcies were offered, but the take-up was relatively limited. A number of emigrants were shipped out, but their numbers were far too few to be viable. The French reasserted their rights to the area, and by 1632 the colonists had been forced to leave. Acadia resumed, and Nova Scotia was not renamed until the British conquest of French Canada in the eighteenth century.

Alexander himself was an enterprising figure, builder of Argyle's Lodging in Stirling. By 1631 he was Earl of Stirling, and in that year he purchased the monopoly on the production of copper farthings. He was also no mean poet.

within its borders. There was no intention that Scotland should have an independent foreign policy, even although it did have an independent foreign trade.

TRADE AND INDUSTRY
IN THE TIME OF JAMES VI

The struggles of a developing industrial base were beginning to be apparent. Serfdom had gone. In 1606, however, there was an act of parliament to establish the hereditary status of male and female serfs to work for the coal and salt industries. These industries were of growing importance because wood was in very short supply and so coal or peat were the only means of heating and cooking. Salt production was important, too, because it was a vital food preservative, used in huge amounts. Salt was used in such quantities that around 1590 it was the third most valuable import into Scotland after iron and timber. Salt-panning had long been practised on the east and west coasts of Scotland, but Lothian landowners like the Seton family were now developing the industry on a large scale. Coal heughs, or outcrops, where coal was near the surface of the ground were largely worked out by the end of the sixteenth century. New deep mines and coal shafts were now beginning to be opened. In both industries the work was hard, unpleasant and often unrewarding drudgery. Organising indentured labour was seized on as the way to keep a stable and experienced labour force in place. The workers were the property of the owners: they could not leave.

A COUNTRY OF PEASANTS

Industries were run on a local basis and the numbers of people employed in them were still relatively small. Scotland was still essentially a country of peasants, growing coarse barley (bere), oats, kail (cabbage) and flax where there was arable land and keeping cows and sheep in nearby fields. More remote uplands were pastoral areas where sheep and black cattle were bred. Bulk transport had to go by sea. Otherwise goods were carried on people's own backs, by horse pannier or by horse-drawn sledge. Little use was made of wheeled carts or carriages. The organisation of social life was on a very localised basis, with the cottar at the lower end of the social scale. Cottars worked small areas that went with their huts and their families also worked for the tenant farmer.

Tenant farmers rented their lands in turn from the 'baron', who often held the land on behalf of a greater lord or even sometimes directly of the crown. These smaller barons were cadets of the noble families or, near Edinburgh in particular, prosperous lawyers or officials. The barony functioned as a miniature state in some respects. A large barony would have its own law court where the baron interpreted the laws of the land as he understood them. The baron usually dealt with offenders or held them in confinement for the circuit court to deal with. The powers of the baron courts were sufficient for some to have gallows for their male offenders and a drowning pit or pond for female offenders. Capital punishment was not in fact very frequent, although the courts would ordain other brutal lesser punishments using whips, brands and pincers, as well as the jougs, or stocks, for the unhappy criminals. The baron would compel tenants to use his mill. If they used another mill, he would still extract the multure, or milling charge, due to himself or his miller. The thirling, or the tying of tenant farmers to a single mill, was a source of discontent among many tenants, with all the problem features of a local monopoly, inefficiency, exploitation, bullying and favouritism.

The country people of Scotland still lived in houses that were made from the materials available locally, and the general arrangement of their homes

177

varied little. The essential supporting elements of the houses were cruck timbers, and if the family moved it took its crucks too, leaving the house to crumble and return to the earth on which it had been built. Walls were made of turf, of rough stones, or of wattle and daub – a form of twig and mud construction. The houses were low, virtually windowless and would have a single smoky dwelling room for a family of up to three generations. Adjoining, under the same roof and open to it, was the byre, or stable, where cattle were kept in the winter. Conveniently by the front door was the dung heap, and by this same door was the washtub, not a vessel for washing but a tub of the family's stale urine which was an essential aid in the preparation of cloth. Water was brought from a well or stream and it was conserved with care. The country people had no privies and used defined areas close to the house for their toilet. It is not surprising that the Scots language should have developed a highly varied vocabulary for ailments such as dysentery; or for activities that involved plowtering about in foul water; or for every possible modulation of a fickle climate. The cottars were self-sufficient in food supplies to a great extent but they had to buy or barter for such vital items as salt, tar, knives and shoes. Money was scarce in the extreme. Make do and mend was a vital principle. Nothing could be wasted and before anything was thrown away it had to be utterly devoid of any kind of usefulness. The experience through generations of this vitally necessary domestic care could not fail to affect the national character and the way it was perceived and depicted.

THE HIGHLANDERS AND ISLANDERS – HALF THE POPULATION

More than half the population lived north of the River Tay. Not all the population in the Tay region and beyond were Highlanders, as the Scots-speaking culture of the Lowlands had spread right around the northeast coast almost as far as Inverness. Following the 'herschip' of Robert the Bruce, that is, his plundering of Buchan, the language of the south also ran deep into the areas beyond Aberdeen. Inverness was the seat of a sheriff with vast territorial responsibility as well as a royal castle, the main frontier town for the wild country beyond. Small centres like Nairn, Dingwall and Dornoch were tiny towns built around a castle or a little cathedral. They would characteristically have a harbour and local trading rights. Such towns served as markets, for church gatherings and as school centres for a large, dispersed population.

On the coastal strip a typical settlement would be a ferm toun, or farm town, of randomly placed cottars' houses. In the glens and on the islands, the settlement was generally the clachan, little different in constructional style or in the activities of those who lived there. Both cottars and clansfolk still practised agriculture on the run-rig system where the community shared the rigs and the work in a complex and age-old pattern that made any sort of modernisation impossible unless it was inflicted from outside. In 1600 it would be likely that some families in the Highlands still lived in crannogs. The lairds or chieftains would not yet have vacated or rebuilt their tower houses, which remained high, narrow buildings intended for defence. The lower area of a laird's tower was for storage of food, tools, planks, tar, rope, hides and other expensive necessities. Alternatively, they might also store goods ready for export at the lower level of the house. In the upper quarters the landholder would live with family, retainers and servants. The size, strength and comfort of these tower houses varied from the extremely modest to the very grand. They were vulnerable places, especially to fire and smoke. Again, there were numerous atrocities committed in and against them in the sixteenth and seventeenth centuries; such acts of arson were usually associated with feuds in which whole families were suffocated by their enemies.

Feuds in the Highland region were almost always started by disputes over territory. In the Highlands there was an uneasy blend of ancient tribal tradition and modern charter-based land-holding. Four hundred years after the Normans, Highland land-holders might still be embarrassed if asked – as they were by successive kings up to James VI – to display the title to the lands they claimed. This often unanswerable question was one of the principal weapons in the armoury of the king and his lieutenants. It was they who were always seeking to reduce the anomalous status of the *Gaeltachd*, which held about a third of the country's population.

The Highlanders had seen their Lowland-living fellow countrymen become different people, the process spreading generation by generation, in a way only perceptible by hindsight, across a set of parishes or through a barony. The gradual change of speech from Gaelic to bilingualism to monoglot Scots marked it. So did a change in the relationship between landholder and tenant. The Lowlands had changed away from the tribal structure of society, based on the family or clan who lived on and defended the ancestral territories. The Highlands and Islands retained the clan structure, partly in fact and even more in spirit. Their society was organised for warfare, and much of its poetry and song celebrated the warrior chief, his heroes and the battles they fought. The clansmen were still responsive to the war symbol of the fiery cross and to their chief's call to arms. They still regarded a slight to one as an insult to the whole clan, to be avenged at the first suitable opportunity. They still thought, or liked to think, of black cattle as a common resource that could be taken at will. Particularly in the far west and the isles there was a distinction between the men who went fighting and raiding and the men who tilled the soil. The fighting men were sorners, retainers who lived and depended on the chief and shared his rental of beef, eggs, grain and butter. Often, sorners would be hired out as mercenaries to an Irish earl or sent to fight in alliance with neighbouring clans. They would expect loot as payment for their service.

Throughout the sixteenth century, the affairs of their fellow-Gaels in Ireland, who were fighting against English overlords, were much closer to the hearts of the Highlanders and the people of the west of Scotland than the preoccupations of Edinburgh. The McDonnells of Antrim were a branch of the far-flung Clan Donald, and the alien political frontiers which crossed their traditional sea lanes were ignored. Despite English protests, the Scots authorities had little success in preventing these Gaelic alliances, but when James VI inherited the kingship of Ireland along with that of England, he took a tougher approach on these issues, although the pattern of raids and mutual support among the Gaels was by no means brought to an end.

CLANS AND LANDS

Within the clan the prestige of the warriors was very important and a boy would be far more likely to aspire to being a sword-bearer than a plough-pusher. To maintain the organisation of the clan, which was often spread over wide areas of mountain and glen, the chief would use his immediate family as sub-chiefs and would allocate lands to them. More numerous and more distantly related to him were the *duine uasal*, or gentlemen, who lived at a superior level to the common clansmen and who played a crucial part in mobilising the clan's manpower. Their lease was known as a 'tack' and themselves as 'tacksmen'. They paid and received rent and lived on the difference, supplementing their livelihood with their crops and what could be made from raiding on land and piracy at sea.

Heredity was a vital element in preserving social cohesion among the Highlanders. Particularly within the greater clans, of which the MacDonalds were the largest – it remains the most numerous Mac- surname – there were numerous hereditary roles and functions from the sennachie, or bard, to the piper, the carpenter and the boatman, where son would follow father into the same trade or function. Sometimes a surname would indicate their role, as with the name MacIntyre, which in Gaelic is *mac an t-saoir*, meaning 'son of the carpenter'.

The Highlands were by no means set in a fixed pattern of clan lands, each neatly occupied by people sharing the same name. While boundaries of lands were clear, their ownership was often in dispute and occupancy was a different matter again. The chief of the MacIntosh clan acquired the rights to some land in Lochaber from the crown, but he found it impossible to drive out the resident Camerons, the clansfolk of Lochiel, and also impossible to rid it of the MacDonalds, whose allegiance was to MacDonald of Keppoch. On the other side of the country there were many small and semi-independent communities of ancient standing on the braes of Angus. Many of them took the surname of Lyon in order to receive the protection of the Earl of Strathmore against the loose federation of Clan Chattan farther north.

More and more the legal possession of land was the main factor in Highland disputes. The problem of the MacGregor clan, relatively small, close-knit and conservative in outlook, was that they had no charter to their ancestral grounds. Caught between Campbell of Argyll and Campbell of Breadalbane, they became a group that could be compared with modern squatters. Since the MacGregors continued to feed and defend themselves, they were treated as thieves, outlawed, their name was banned and they were subjected to savage harassment. There were other clans in a similar situation and the MacGregors were unique only because of the remarkable length of their persecution.

Earlier in the sixteenth century, the Privy Council had instructed the Earl of Huntly to take steps to eradicate Clan Chattan because of persistent feuding. The rights and wrongs of Highland disputes were far beyond the capacity of the Privy Council to solve, since the Council could not accept the validity of Highland custom and practice. From the Highland point of view, their traditions and ways of life had never changed (although in fact they had to a considerable degree) and there was a widespread and real resentment of new laws that could not be reconciled with their traditional way of life. When James VI, as inheritor of the rights of the Lord of the Isles, attempted in 1597 to 'plant' the Isle of Lewis with Fife lairds and tenants, indignant Islesmen violently wrecked the experiment in social engineering within two years. Despite all their legal documents, charters and leases, the surviving Fife settlers went home again.

HIGHLANDERS, LOWLANDERS, BORDERERS

Other divergencies of usage separated the Highland and Lowland communities and in some cases differences were created within the Highlands themselves. Some eastern clans became Protestant and Presbyterian, while others, although accepting Protestantism, favoured the Episcopal system which retained the hierarchy of bishops they had been familiar with for centuries. Most central and western clans remained Catholic.

Costume diverged, particularly among men. The plaid was the outer garment of all Scots, and homespun, coarse grey cloth its basic material. The same material made petticoats and breeches for women and men which were worn until they were ragged. Fighting clansmen, however, wore linen shirts which were dyed yellow with saffron and which were long enough to be tied between the legs. In the Highlands dyes were used to give the plaid colour and pattern, although this was not at all a formalised tartan. Clans used symbols for recognition, like the MacGregor pine sprig or the Ross twig of juniper.

Men of the Highlands wore trews, which were long, tight trousers or leggings. The modern form of the kilt had not been devised, but men wore the great kilt, or belted plaid, and for speedy travel usually went bare-legged. In battle they discarded the plaid and fought in their shirts. The sixteenth-century English defenders of Irish castles called the Islesmen 'Redshanks'. Few people possessed real shoes, and those who did might keep them for special occasions.

The pastoral Highlander possessed skills long lost to the agrarian Lowlander. He was a skilled huntsman and tracker, with the geography of a vast region clearly mapped out in his mind. But both communities still had much in common. Apart from many aspects of domestic life, they shared a continuing fondness for the bagpipes long after they went out of fashion in other countries. Among the hereditary piping families of the Highlands, the continued love of the pipes resulted in the seventeenth century in the development of the classical music of the pibroch to a high art.

The Borderers had a way of life that in many ways resembled that of the Highlanders. Their society was clan-like in structure. Council decrees and legal disputes were often related to specific surnames like Armstrong or Reid. Borderers were Protestant and their language was Scots rather than Gaelic. They kept many connections with the Northumbrian and Cumbrian English-speakers on the southern side of the border. Their ancient role as frontier guards had in the past excused and supported a lifestyle of raid and rapine, normally conducted on English soil but often practised among themselves. But already, in the reign of James VI, the Border ethos had acquired vulnerability.

James VI's policy of peace and co-operation with England had no appeal to the Borderers and their occasional floutings of it caused rage and embarrassment in Edinburgh. The occasion in 1596, which has been immortalised in a Border ballad, when the 'bauld Buccleuch', the 'bold' Earl of Buccleuch, rescued his henchman Kinmont Willie from imprisonment by

BAGPIPES

In early Europe, the bagpipe was the most common musical instrument. Forms of it can be seen in many Dutch paintings. By the sixteenth century, it survived only on the farthest eastern and western fringes of the continent. In Scotland, the oral tradition undoubtedly helped to preserve the music and so the instrument. For the tradition-conscious Gaels, it was their own music; and its abandonment elsewhere would only have encouraged them to maintain it. But it was not an art form in decline. During the seventeenth century, Highland pipers elaborated the formal and classical pibroch: the *ceòl mór*, or 'great music'.

Pipe music was common throughout the country and was one of the links that united Highlands and Lowlands. Most towns had a piper, often as a hereditary post. The pipes were heard at feasts and mournings, accompanied dancing, and were an element in Highland warfare. On his deathbed in 1734, Rob Roy MacGregor listened to the lament, *I Will Return No More*. The most famous piping family were the MacCrimmons, on Skye, and many went to be taught by them. In the later eighteenth century, bagpipe music began to be published and a new interest grew. During the nineteenth century, the fiddle and then the piano-accordion took over for dances, except for exhibition dancing which is still performed to the pipes.

The bagpipe was proscribed along with other accoutrements of Gaeldom after the 1745 uprising. But soon it was resuscitated, with the creation of new Highland regiments, and the pipes and drums became strongly associated with the army. In the Indian Mutiny, the pipes of Havelock's Highlanders heralded the relief of Lucknow to the besieged British community. Each of the many new battalions recruited in the First World War had its own pipe band. In 1930 the Scottish Pipe Band Association was formed, and still promotes competition and controls standards.

Artist's impression of a modern piper and bagpipes

the English border warden Lord Scrope is the most notable. But after 1603 the Borders were caught between the hammer and the anvil. The 'Great Britain' of King James no longer needed frontiersmen, and from north and south the royal lieutenants attacked the Border keeps and broke the military power strongholds of the barons. The greater lords from the borders became courtiers; the lesser nobles and their families led diminished but fairly peaceable lives as rural lairds. But many ordinary people left the area or were driven out by the fact that the land alone could not support them. A great number of Border families emigrated to Ulster when the 'plantation' of the province was begun in 1608. This 'plantation', much larger than the failed efforts to colonise the Island of Lewis, was the second of the three significant population movements between Scotland and Ireland, the only east-west one, and its consequences loom large in the modern history of Ireland.

THE BURGHS AND
FOREIGN TRADE

The Scottish burghs had not changed greatly in the sixteenth century and, apart from Edinburgh, the Fife coal-exporting towns and Dundee with its cloth industry, had not advanced much. The number of royal burghs changed little, but the number of baronial burghs increased considerably. Between 1560 and 1660 nineteen royal burghs were either newly created or promoted, and seventy-five burghs of barony were established. This was caused less by an overall expansion of trade than by the urge of the barons to create their own market centres. The royal burghs clung to their privileges, especially to their rights relating to foreign trade and levying customs on exported goods. Many did their utmost to prevent other burghs, which were potential rivals, from being established at all. Fierce local rivalries developed, and Rutherglen, for example, prevented Glasgow – a burgh of barony established by its bishop – from acquiring any additional trading rights for a long time. Such protectionism was typical of the age, when more energy was devoted to preserving what little commerce the burghs might have than to expanding it.

Manufacturing activity was on a domestic scale. Within the family of a typical burgess, the father might be a metal worker who employed one journeyman and a couple of apprentices; the mother might brew ale; and the children might work at carding flax and spinning threads. Brewing was very much a female preserve until the Society of Brewers banded together in Edinburgh in 1590, depriving many wives and widows of their livelihood.

During the sixteenth century, the Convention of Royal Burghs became a significant part of the social structure. It was committed to regulating disputes between burghs and to maintaining their rights and privileges. There were many arguments with the king over the maintenance of a Scottish staple port on the Continent. Some merchants liked the idea of free trading, which allowed them to pick their opportunities wherever they thought fit among the ports of northern Europe. Other merchants wanted the security of one staple port from which to trade as a fixed base. The king himself preferred a staple port for two main reasons. Firstly, a staple port ensured a clear and full control on trade. There was a Conservator of Privileges of Scots Merchants who would report back on all shipments, trading deals and on the behaviour of the Scots. Secondly, there was the matter of the king's revenue. A modest town like Campveere would find it worthwhile to have the role of a Scottish staple port and would be prepared to give handsome gifts to the king for the privilege. In 1531 a bribe paid by Middelburg to James V to relocate his staple port had to be repaid when the burghs objected to moving their base; shortly afterwards the king received one thousand merks from Campveere instead.

Foreign trade was recorded as the 'Wild Adventure' in the minutes of Edinburgh Town Council. Apart from the natural hazards of travel, it was subject to outbreaks of war even when Scotland was not directly involved. Piracy was also a problem that the merchant fleets had to face. In 1581 the island of Inchcolm in the Firth of Forth was described as a 'receptacle of pirates', and these were fellow Scots. English and Dutch pirates also menaced the shipping lanes, and many small naval battles were fought off the coasts of Fife and Lothian. Shared ownership of cargoes was one way of minimising possible losses. As many as forty merchants from different burghs might combine in purchasing and despatching a single shipload. Such shared ventures were a prime reason for the tight controls exercised on foreign trade: everyone involved wanted to minimise risk and maximise profit, and get their share.

The burgh of Edinburgh in association with the independent harbour town of Leith was now by far the predominant town in Scotland in terms of population, wealth and trade. In the sixteenth century it was common for other burghs to look to Edinburgh for leadership. In 1500 the Court of the Four Burghs instructed Edinburgh to maintain merchants' privileges in all burghs. Edinburgh was also a frequent model for the rules and regulations imposed elsewhere. When, in 1585, a special tax was levied on all burghs to raise money for the wedding expenses of James VI, Edinburgh paid forty thousand pounds out of the total of ninety-eight thousand pounds required.

It was in Edinburgh that the rise of the craftsmen in municipal affairs had begun. Until the late fifteenth century, towns were governed mainly by merchants and there were laws in place to prevent anyone other than a merchant becoming a burgess. But as Edinburgh grew larger, the demand for skilled craftsmen grew greater. Different crafts began to grow and become more diverse, despite resistance, and the craftsmen organised themselves into associations of guilds. In Glasgow, a growing town but still far smaller than Edinburgh, the idea that craftsmen should play a part in local government was not such a problem, but in many burghs deep suspicion as to the motives of the craftsmen often remained. Craftsmen were always suspected of rigging prices and were snobbishly despised by the more pretentious merchants and by court circles as people who got their hands dirty at the shoe last, in the tannery, at the forge or at the butcher's block.

Scottish trade was still a matter of exporting primary products such as coal, wool and hides, and importing not only luxury items but almost any kind of manufactured article, from cutlery to drinking glasses and playing cards. In addition, timber and iron had to be imported. At the end of the sixteenth century, there were still extensive forested lands in the west but it was easier and cheaper to import timber to the east coast from Norway where the lumber trade was efficiently organised. Self-sufficiency in cereals was always precarious and a bad harvest would lead to a substantial increase in grain imports from Europe, which put a heavy strain on Scottish gold reserves.

Gold had been found at a number of places in Scotland, and in 1526 a combined Dutch and German group had been given the lease of all the gold

---

THE DOUNE PISTOL

One interesting exception to the lack of sophisticated manufacturing in Scotland was the pistol-making industry. This no doubt makes its own comment on conditions at the time. The country was swarming with vagrants and there were nests of out-and-out bandits just beyond the Highland Line. No one was likely to go travelling unless he was armed. Every man carried a weapon, and the quality of his weapons was a mark of his status. In a string of places close to the Highland-Lowland divide, pistols of high quality were made during the seventeenth century. Perhaps the best were made at Doune, in the workshop of Thomas Cadell, established in 1646. Beautifully made and ornamented with engravings, they could cost up to twenty guineas a pair, and were often presented to foreign princes, including one set to the king of France.

and silver mines in the country. Hopeful attention was focused on gold-mining for a time, but the venture did not produce sufficient quantities of gold to enable the kings of Scots to escape their perennial, if highly relative, poverty. In 1597 a general import levy of a shilling in the pound was introduced for the first time. At the same time, the import of cloth from England was prohibited. Underlying such acts was the perceived need to expand the home market and productivity in Scotland. Specialist craftsmen were brought into the country, usually from Flanders. They were often given the name Fleming, and although they were given special privileges in return for teaching their skills, the impact of their participation was small.

'A ROUGH COUNTRY'

Scotland seen through English and Continental eyes in the early 1600s remained a rough and somewhat primitive country. Its currency was of dubious value and its internal economy ran largely on a barter system of payment in kind. It had few amenities, and although James IV and James V had encouraged the setting-up of inns in the towns, these were places where a traveller would put up his horse and look elsewhere for a bed. The cynical visitor might suppose that the High Kirk of Edinburgh was aptly dedicated to the patron saint of beggars. Beggars and near-beggars were a constant harassment in towns and in the countryside. On the mainland of Europe, Scotland was chiefly known as a source of itinerant pedlars and of mercenary soldiers.

Its cultural contribution in the age of the high Renaissance was not negligible, but was not widely known beyond the boundaries of Scotland, and in the case of Gaelic verse and music, little knowledge of it travelled beyond the Highlands. The hard fingers of religious obsession were soon to grip the windpipe of the Scottish muse. William Drummond of Hawthornden, who died in 1649, was the last Scottish poet in the Renaissance tradition, and a lone figure. *The Gude and Godlie Ballatis*, published around 1640 by the Wedderburn brothers and then in many subsequent editions, were more in tune with the wishes of the Kirk. They were crude distortions of traditional songs and verses, wrenching the unselfconscious lyrics of the people into an artificial and trite religiosity. The fine arts of the period, particularly in gold and silver work, did not entirely pass by. There were some finely crafted pieces made in the late sixteenth century that reflected the availability of these materials and their workability in tiny workshops by a handful of skilled people. Painting, sculpture, architecture and tapestry work are hardly in evidence at this time. Scotland did not have the patrons, the wealth or the cultural base to support these activities on a large scale. The

THE 'KING JAMES' BIBLE AND SCOTLAND

Although dedicated to James VI, the Authorized Version of the Bible, first published in 1611, was a wholly English undertaking. Its importance to Scotland was, however, great, and its influence was very strong in three respects. The first was religious. From now on, whatever the disputes about bishops and liturgy, the words of Scripture were there in approved form for everyone to read. The second was stylistic: in Scotland, as elsewhere, the majestic cadence of its Jacobean prose had an enduring effect on writing. The third was linguistic: its language was unquestionably the King's English and not the King's Scots. Tyndale's translation of the New Testament had been rendered into Scots by Murdoch Nisbet as early as 1520, but never published, and although Parliament in 1543 passed an act for a Bible to be published 'in Inglis or in Scottis', this was never done. As the language of the Bible, English was seen as right for solemn and formal use. As a result, the Authorized Version, by its very popularity, played a part in the marginalising of Scots as a literary language.

Catholic Church, which might have played a role, had become a fugitive cult. Presbyterians were still imbued with the guilty fervour of their iconoclasm which had hacked away beauty as well as graven images from inside and outside the churches. The twentieth-century poet Edwin Muir accused John Knox, with rather unfair particularity, of robbing Scotland of all the benefits of the Renaissance.

ENGLAND SAYS NO

Once established at Whitehall, James VI began to campaign for the full union of Scotland and England as Great Britain. He commissioned a design which was the prototype of what was to be the Union flag. There was more than administrative convenience in this; James VI was a shrewd and far-sighted protector of the interests of the house of Stewart. He knew that two kingdoms could revert to having two kings.

The Scottish parliament obediently approved a Treaty of Union in 1607, which was suspended until it was also passed by the English parliament. But the English parliament rejected the proposal. 'Suppose one man is the owner of two pastures,' said one member, '. . . with one hedge to divide them, the one pasture bare; the other fertile and good; a wise owner will not quite pull down the hedge.'

It seems ironic that, after the painful centuries of English possessiveness, they found the union of the two countries undesirable. On the other hand, the logic of the English members seemed sound. Impoverished Scotland would press for English subsidy. More Scots would come south seeking office from 'their' king. Above all, they were sure that the Scottish sting had already been drawn. The Old Alliance between the Scots and French was dead. It would have been a wild dream in 1607 that Scotland and England should go to war with each other again. The best that James VI was able to achieve was to grant common citizenship to those born on both sides of the Border after the union of the crowns. The trading policy of England did not change, and for the Scots merchant nothing changed.

'This I must say for Scotland,' declared James VI to his English Parliament, 'and may truly vaunt it: here I sit and govern with my pen: I write and it is done; and by a Clerk of the Council I govern Scotland now, which others could not do with the sword.' The boast held good during his lifetime. He reformed the Scots parliament into a complaisant body, wholly dominated by the Lords of the Articles. To this body the nobles elected eight bishops, who would then elect eight nobles to join them. The chosen bishops and nobles elected eight shire members, or barons, and eight burgesses. As the king had nominated the bishops in the first place, he was in a position to control everything that followed. The most distinguished of James's bishops was Andrew Knox of the Isles, who presided over a gathering of Western chiefs on Iona in 1609. He combined force, guile and persuasion to obtain the agreement of the chiefs to the 'Statutes of Icolmkill', in which they pledged to respect the king's law.

SIXTY YEARS OF
CALVINISM

Within the Kirk of Scotland, James progressively improved the status of his bishops until, by the end of 1609, they were effectively in charge of Church government as moderators of the synod of each diocese. The word 'presbytery' was abolished as 'odious to His Majesty'. The more extreme Presbyterians left the country or stayed silent. Despite the change in administration, the liturgy of church services remained that of Knox and Melville, but James VI used his brief return visit to Scotland in the summer of 1616 to urge changes to this. A General Assembly at Perth in August 1618 finally passed the Five Articles requested by the king. These included such matters as enforcing the observance of Church festivals, of kneeling to take communion, and the allowance of private communion. The Five Articles were all examples of the 'Popery' that had been denounced now for longer than the average lifetime. Opposition to the changes was widespread but muted. Nevertheless, it took James three years to obtain ratification from the Scottish parliament of his reforms, and they were largely ignored by ministers and churchgoers alike. The bishops, themselves not the sponsors of the Five Articles, did not seriously try to enforce them.

Sixty years of Calvinist theology had made a difference to the Scots. Living as they did in a tightly knit society that often seemed only one step away from chaos and bloodshed, they perhaps felt protected rather than oppressed by the noseyness of the kirk session, with its opportunities for victimisation and humiliation. Such judgments began to seem much more intrusive and objectionable in the eighteenth century. The Scots relished the Calvinist insistence on the direct relationship of the individual to God, which appealed to a very Scottish combination of personal pride and ingrained respect for patriarchal law. To people who did not expect, or receive, material reward from life, the Protestant religion offered infinite riches, not through the unaffordable purchase of prayers and masses but through a personal act of faith. Calvinist doctrines of predestination and the assurance of the Kingdom of Heaven to the righteous people of God struck a responsive chord in the Scottish mind. Through its Presbyterian structure, reformed religion offered the possibility of participation, if only to men. It was their religion by choice, shaped and formulated in the lifetime of their fathers. They were also getting it very cheaply, as it happens: the Kirk's share of the old Church revenues was greatly eroded and many parish ministers were desperately poor. An act of parliament of 1617 set the minimum stipend of a Presbyterian cleric at five hundred merks, to be paid by the recipient of the teinds, or tithes, but it was unenforceable. The Kirk and its congregations were still a mingled group, ranging from the keenly Episcopal to the keenly Presbyterian. But even among those who wanted bishops, very few also wished to see the Five Articles enforced.

It is impossible to detach religious questions from the political events of the seventeenth century in Scotland. Religious issues lay at the core of life- or death-determining events. And yet the Scots had never been demonstratively religious as a people. The old Church had latterly neglected the people, and there is no evidence that the Scots had a strong taste for doctrine or an especially passionate attachment to ritual. The saints unearthed by Bishop Elphinstone's researches had long been forgotten by the faithful. And yet, in 1640 the Scots were ready to defy the king and go to war in order to defend their own form of religious observance. In 1314 at Bannockburn, they knelt to ask the help of God in the struggle for the national cause. In 1640 they risked their lives to defend their conception of God. It was a remarkable change of attitude.

CHARLES BECOMES KING

Charles I was born in Dunfermline but had left Scotland at the age of three. His promising brother, Henry, heir to the throne, died when his younger brother was still twelve. Thus in 1625 Charles became king at the ripe old age, for a Stewart, of twenty-five. In the same year as his coronation in Westminster Abbey, he married the young, Catholic, French Princess Henrietta Maria.

His father, the theorist of the Divine Right of Kings to rule unchallenged, had cloaked his autocracy in informality and humour. Charles did not inherit the latter qualities, and his public manner was coldly imperious. In 1625 he issued an Act of Revocation, intended to secure all former Church property to the crown. As most Church property was now in the hands of the Scottish nobility, this aroused considerable hostility among the lords. Between 1625 and 1629 the Act was amended to leave present possessors with the right to gather the revenues of estates until the crown should buy them. With this legislation an obligation to pay each parish minister eight hundred merks from the teinds of the estates was also included.

In 1633 Charles came to Edinburgh for a somewhat belated Scottish coronation in Holyrood and with plans for further reformation of the Kirk. His aim was to continue what his father had begun, and bring the two Churches of which he was head into a single community modelled on the Anglican scheme of Archbishop Laud of Canterbury. Educated in line with his father's principles but without his father's pragmatism and with none of James's hard-acquired personal knowledge of the Scots, Charles published the *Code of Canons* in 1636 and a *Book of Common Prayer* in 1637, without troubling to call a General Assembly. The newly appointed Bishop of Edinburgh announced that the new service book must be used on Sunday 23 July 1637. The result was an uproar in St Giles, which had been promoted, for the time being, to the status of a cathedral, and in all other churches where the ministers obeyed the Bishop's order.

THE NATIONAL COVENANT

The king's reaction was simply to restate his command to the Privy Council to ensure that every minister bought and used the new prayer book. The Council temporised, and said the book must be bought but need not be read. When disturbances continued in churches throughout the country, the king responded to a petition signed by nobles, lairds and burgesses by proclaiming that the Privy Council should be removed from Edinburgh to Dundee. In October 1637 a second petition was drafted to demand that the bishops should leave the Privy Council altogether until the dispute could be settled. While the citizens of Edinburgh stormed in the streets, the Lord Advocate asked the complainers to form a representative committee to confer with the Council. They did so with alacrity, and four nobles, four lairds, four ministers and four burgesses were elected. The committee became known as 'the Tables' because its members sat at separate tables in Parliament House. 'A troop of horse and a regiment of foot had prevented all that followed,' wrote Bishop Burnet in his memoirs. But Charles I had no armed forces to assert his authority. When the Lord Treasurer went to London to tell him that forty thousand men would be needed to impose the Liturgy, the king proclaimed that he himself was responsible for the Liturgy and that to refuse it was treason. When this was read out in Edinburgh, 'the Tables' decided it was time to act, and drew up the National Covenant. This document presented a résumé of all previous attacks on Catholicism and a protest against 'manifold innovations and evils', together with a solemn promise to maintain '. . . the true religion and his Majesty's authority . . . against all sorts of persons whatsoever.' This disingenuous phrasing glossed over the fact that 'the true religion' and the king's authority were incompatible.

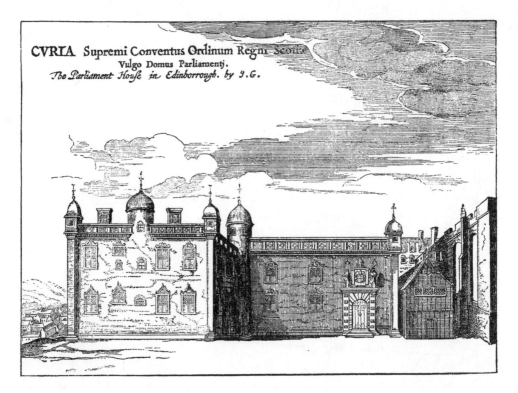

A contemporary engraving of Parliament House, Edinburgh, at the time of Charles I

The National Covenant was displayed in the Church of the Greyfriars on Sunday 28 February 1638, and copies were distributed throughout the country. Many thousands signed the petition, some with their own blood, others for fear of reprisal if they did not. Some towns, notably Aberdeen where the influence of the Marquis of Huntly was strong, showed little enthusiasm, but even Episcopalians signed the Covenant, the content of which was carefully unspecific about bishops. Other than the Catholic clans, Scotland had become a nation of Covenanters.

Late in 1638 a General Assembly was held in Glasgow, convened by the Marquis of Hamilton on behalf of the king. The gathering was of an altogether different stamp from previous assemblies. Its Moderator, who had helped to draw up the National Covenant, was Alexander Henderson, Minister of Leuchars, and its Clerk, Archibald Johnston of Warriston. Seeing that it was out to abolish the bishoprics, Hamilton formally dissolved the Assembly on 25 November, but it ignored his decision and sat on for three more weeks. The only Privy Councillor to remain at the Assembly was the Earl of Argyll. At the end of their discussions, the Assembly had abolished all bishops, excommunicated eight of them, proscribed the use of the Code of Canons and the Book of Common Prayer, and condemned the Five Articles of Perth. A permanent commission was set up to ensure that non-Presbyterian views would not be allowed to exist. It was an invitation to war.

In the spring of 1639, a Scottish army was mustered and marched south. It was an extraordinary situation. No war had been declared and there was certainly no intention of making war on England. The Scots knew it was the policy of Charles, not that of England, that they were opposing. Their actions resembled in some ways the rising against James III, except that now to reach the king their forces had to travel through England. What made this different from previous occasions was the depth and force of popular feeling. The National Covenant had become a national cause, uniting the community. It was not a reluctantly driven levy that set out but an army of enthusiastic recruits, many of whom were veterans of foreign wars. Their general, Alexander Leslie, had been one of the successful commanders in the Thirty Years' War and was a military leader of ability and experience. Their confidence was reinforced by the knowledge that the king could not raise an army in England without calling a parliament, and that a parliament would be most unlikely to grant the king funds without extorting concessions that the autocratic Charles would find unacceptable.

The campaign, called the first 'Bishops' War', ended as little more than a brief show of force. The king's allies in Scotland, the Marquis of Huntly and the Marquis of Hamilton, were to join forces in Aberdeen and march south.

The Earl of Montrose wrecked their plans by swiftly leading a Covenanting army to Aberdeen, where he took Huntly prisoner. On 18 June 1639, the Pacification of Berwick was signed, providing for a new General Assembly and a new parliament. The king used this pact as a delaying tactic that lasted little more than a year. In the parliament of June 1640, which Charles I tried unsuccessfully to postpone, the abolition of episcopacy and the supremacy of the Covenant were confirmed. The power of the Lords of the Articles was now substantially reduced. For the first time the Scottish parliament could freely discuss any matter it chose. This was not a step towards democratic debate but simply a device to break the royal management of proceedings. A fiercely determined Presbyterian orthodoxy prevailed, and no member was likely to express any sort of contrary opinion. As a deterrent to neutralism, the Earl of Argyll was entrusted with a savage campaign of fire and sword across the southern Highlands in which he ravaged the lands of Atholl and Airlie.

'KING CAMPBELL'

Rumours that Archibald Campbell, the Earl of Argyll, had ambitions of his own were rife. There was dark talk about 'King Campbell'. A proposal was made to put the country on a war footing by placing one man – Argyll – in charge north of the Forth, and two men in the south. Montrose protested in public, and in private made the 'Cumbernauld Band' with a number of moderately minded associates 'to uphold the letter and spirit of the National Covenant'. In his view Argyll was trying to hi-jack the Covenant for his own aggrandisement.

The stand-off between king and Covenanters continued. In the second Bishops' War in August 1640, Charles I assembled a motley army, the Scots army formed again and this time crossed the border, drove back the royal forces at Newburn and occupied Durham and Newcastle. By a mixture of chance and collusion with the English parliamentarians, the invasion drove forward political events in England. The king was forced to call the Long Parliament. The invading Scots were granted £300,000 by this Parliament and the king, cornered, promised to ratify the acts of the Scots parliament. The motive of the Scots was never to kill or depose the king but to make him change his policy. The discussions that Charles had had with nobles such as Montrose showed him that he had potentially powerful friends in Scotland, and his own observation revealed that Scotland had the only effective army on the mainland of Britain.

In August 1641 Charles went to Edinburgh to find friends and allies. But Montrose was in prison, having unsuccessfully challenged Argyll with planning to make himself master, or even king, of Scotland. The king negotiated his release. The Presbyterian party was in full control, and having made even more concessions to his opponents, Charles went back to London with nothing to show for his visit. Almost exactly one year later, in August 1642, the English Civil War began. Scotland declared itself officially neutral. The Privy Council, led by the Marquis of Hamilton, inclined towards the king, so long as he would guarantee Presbyterianism in Scotland. The Presbyterian party, with Argyll – who had been made a marquis by Charles during his time in Edinburgh the previous year – as an important member, wanted to give support to the English parliamentarians and despised Hamilton's approach. Having seized on the essential fact that two religions under one king were incompatible, the Presbyterians were determined that the one common religion should be theirs. In this way they would not only secure the future of the Scottish Church but bring enlightenment to the English. They were right to distrust the king, but their assessment of England as a mission field was hopelessly wrongheaded.

The Marquis of Argyll had other reasons for opposing the king. He knew that Charles was in touch with the Catholic Earl of Antrim about an invasion of western Scotland, with Kintyre as a reward. In September 1643, the English parliament finally made its bargain. In return for Scottish support, the Solemn League and Covenant was agreed. The signatories bound themselves to 'bring the churches of God in the three kingdoms to the nearest conjunction and uniformity in religion, according to the Word of God and the example of the best reformed Churches'. In January 1644 Alexander Leslie, whom Charles had made Earl of Leven three years earlier, led an army of twenty-one thousand soldiers into England, laid siege to Newcastle and helped win the Battle of Marston Moor in July. Their presence with Cromwell's New Model Army tipped the scales against royal dominance and decisively towards parliamentary victory.

MONTROSE IN THE HIGHLANDS

Montrose took the view that the king had made all the necessary commitments to the Covenanters' demands and that it was now the duty of a loyal subject to support him. In February 1644 Charles made him a marquis and King's Lieutenant in Scotland, and with no resources other than his commission he raised an army in the Highlands. The main body of this army was from Ulster, under the command of Alasdair MacDonald of Colonsay, known by his father's by-name of Coll Keitach. Unable to attract the Scottish clans, it had been marauding somewhat aimlessly through Argyll to Atholl, and Montrose caught up with it just in time to save it from being cut to pieces by hostile Highlanders. Montrose's gifts as a soldier were speed, surprise and leadership. He used them all to brilliant effect through the autumn of 1644 and through 1645. In a campaign that swept across the Highlands in a series of battles and rapid marches, he beat a Covenanting army at Tippermuir, took Perth and Aberdeen, captured the Campbell capital of Inveraray, defeated a Campbell army at Inverlochy, captured and evacuated Dundee, and won brilliant victories at Auldearn, Alford and Kilsyth. On 17 August he occupied Glasgow, and soon after that entered a submissive Edinburgh although the Covenanters still held the Castle.

Argyll had fled to Berwick. Montrose set about forming a government in the king's name. The poet William Drummond of Hawthornden wrote, 'the Golden Age is returned'. By 12 September, however, the dream was over. The news of Kilsyth had brought back to Scotland the Covenanters' ablest general, David Leslie, with four thousand men. Montrose's forces were depleted. They had lost many Highlanders with the departure of Coll Keitach and half his men, and Lord Aboyne with the Gordon clansmen had defected. Those who remained were caught by surprise and defeated at Philiphaugh, near Selkirk. The Covenanters, more than somewhat discountenanced, were restored to power and took bloody revenge on those who had fought for, or temporised with, the royalists. Montrose escaped to the Highlands and continued to carry out small-scale guerrilla warfare, but on the orders of Charles I, who was already a prisoner by now, he gave up the hopeless struggle in the summer of 1646 and fled to France. Brilliant as the campaign of Montrose had been, it was ultimately a sideshow which had little lasting effect on the action taking place in England where the parliamentary army of England and the Covenanting army of Scotland were settling matters, in a way which would have enormous repercussions in both kingdoms.

DISUNION AMONG
THE COVENANTERS

Charles had surrendered himself to the Scots army at Southwell near Newark on Trent on 5 May 1646. Optimistically, he had hoped that they might take his side, as it was plain that there was little chance of the grand Presbyterian ambition being achieved in England where Cromwell and the Independents were becoming dominant. But the Scots would do nothing unless he signed the Covenant, and although Charles spent several months being instructed in Presbyterianism by Alexander Henderson, it was to no avail. The Scots handed him over to the English parliamentarians on 30

January 1647, accepted half of the four hundred thousand pounds they were owed as back pay, and went home. The king, now in the hands of the English army, made another of his belated compromises. This was the 'Engagement', made with the Earl of Loudoun as chancellor, the Earl of Lauderdale and the Earl of Lanark, and by it the king made an undertaking to establish Presbyterianism in England for three years and to confirm the Covenant; the Scots in return were to fight on his behalf. It was a deeply controversial move and was heavily resisted by the Presbyterian party. The Covenanters were no longer united. Nevertheless, the Duke of Hamilton led an army south to join up with English royalists, and between 17 and 19 July 1648, in a three-day running battle of skirmishes and occasional heavy fighting, between Preston and Warrington, they were defeated by Cromwell. Hamilton was captured and executed in London. The Engagers were left helpless.

The Galloway Covenanters, known as Whiggamores or Whigs, subsequently marched on Edinburgh, and the Committee of the Estates capitulated. Supported by Cromwell's cavalry, the new rulers published a manifesto 'against Toleration', followed by the vicious legislation of the Act of Classes. The act divided all those who had supported the royalist cause or the Engagement or who had merely 'neglected to protest' into three groups, the first of whom were deprived of holding any office for life, the second for ten years, the third for five years.

On January 30th, 1649, after trial, Charles I was executed in London. By killing their king, the English also killed the king of Scots.

CHARLES II AND MONTROSE

The son of Charles I, in exile, was immediately proclaimed king in Edinburgh, although an act of parliament provided that he should have no authority until he had subscribed to the Solemn League and Covenant. But Charles II was chary about acceding to the Covenant. In the spring of 1650 he sent the Marquis of Montrose to Scotland to promote a royalist rising in the Highlands. It was a forlorn venture. Montrose landed in Orkney, where he recruited a few hundred men, but found no support on the mainland. At Carbisdale on the Oykell he was defeated, and shortly afterwards was captured and handed over to the authorities by MacLeod of Assynt. On 21 May he was hanged in Edinburgh. His last words were 'God have mercy on this afflicted country'. After his death he was dismembered. His head was placed on a spike on the Tolbooth of Edinburgh and his limbs taken to Stirling, Perth, Aberdeen and Glasgow. Charles II, who was capable of any sort of dissimulation in order to further his own cause, had disowned him.

OLIVER CROMWELL IN SCOTLAND

A month after the execution of Montrose, Charles, having signed his name to the National Covenant and the Solemn League and Covenant, appeared in Scotland. Oliver Cromwell invaded with the English army in July 1650. The new king was very far from being in charge of affairs. Extreme Presbyterians were in control and continued their purging exercises, excluding those who had fought for Montrose or the Engagement and thus greatly reducing the strength and quality of their army. After weeks of advance and counter-advance, on 3 September 1650 Cromwell defeated David Leslie and his army at Dunbar, aided not a little by the committee of divines who, 'weary of lying in the fields', prevailed upon Leslie to abandon his strong military position on Doon Hill and advance down towards the English. According to Cromwell's estimates, three thousand Scots were slaughtered and ten thousand were taken prisoner. Nevertheless, Dunbar was not a decisive battle, although it allowed Cromwell to hold Edinburgh Castle and Lothian. The Scots regrouped around Stirling Castle. Far from losing resolve, the extreme Presbyterians felt that Dunbar was God's retribution for their laxity.

They disowned Charles II and organised a new army, but Cromwell's Lieutenant, John Lambert, dispersed it at Hamilton. The 'Protesters' or 'Remonstrants' were reduced to a vocal minority centred in the southwest. A more moderate faction, the 'Resolutioners', who had been ready to co-operate with the terms of the Engagement, took control. Charles II was crowned on 1 January 1651 at Scone, in a deliberately traditional ceremony; tempers cooled, and the Act of Classes was disregarded and eventually repealed by June of that year. David Leslie regrouped his army into a strong fighting force. Cromwell attempted to attack Leslie from the rear, by crossing the Firth of Forth, marching through Fife and taking Perth. But the Scots marched south into England, hoping vainly to raise more support for Charles II. Cromwell pursued them to Worcester, and there, in what he called 'the crowning mercy', he destroyed them.

Charles II fled to France, and General George Monk completed the subjugation of Scotland on Cromwell's behalf. Scotland, which in 1639 had commanded events, was in 1651 a nation without a king, an army, or a government. Agriculture and trade had been severely disrupted. Throughout the country there was hunger and destitution. The last vestige of home rule went in 1653 when the General Assembly was done away with. Scotland was integrated into the Commonwealth, with thirty members in the Protector's Parliament. Garrisons at Ayr, Inverlochy, Inverness, Leith and Perth maintained the peace, and a royalist uprising in the Highlands in 1654, led by the Earl of Glencairn and the ex-Parliamentary General Middleton, was quickly put down. A seven-man Council of State, of whom six were English, replaced the Privy Council, and seven incorruptible Commissioners dispensed justice. The Cromwellian period was one of peace, enforced for the first time by a standing army.

The Scottish nobility, for the first time in history, played no part in the government of the country. Officially Scots merchants were allowed freedom to trade with England and its colonies but the practice was different. The war between the English and the Dutch in 1652–54 cut off their major foreign trading partners in Holland. Scotland was taxed heavily to pay for the occupying army, although the collection of taxes was much fairer. To the horror of the Remonstrants, religious toleration was enforced. They were allowed to preach – but so were Quakers, Anabaptists and all sorts of Independents. Cromwell had succeeded in Scotland where previous English leaders had failed, but his system of government and his union put down no roots.

'NOT A RELIGION FOR GENTLEMEN'

The eight years of enforced union came to an end with the restoration of the Stuarts in 1660. Bishop Burnet noted, 'The herd of the cavalier party were now very fierce and full of courage in their cups, though they had been very discreet managers of it in the field.' Sir Thomas Urquhart of Cromarty, the

---

A PRESBYTERIAN LAIRD – ALEXANDER BRODIE OF BRODIE

The laird of Brodie was born in 1617 and grew up a keen Presbyterian. In 1640 he helped to destroy the carved woodwork of Elgin Cathedral. He was a ruling elder of the Kirk, the member of parliament for Moray, and a lord of the Court of Session. Under the Cromwellian rule he retired to his estate, and was saved by attack in Glencairn's rising by a spate in the River Findhorn. He thanked God for a deliverance, but his neighbour, the Laird of Leathin, was less lucky. Brodie went to pray with him and his people, and brought them a supply of oats. In 1658, he was 'sinfully inclined' to accept a judgeship. On a visit to London in 1651, he bought history books but no divinity, noting 'this feared me I was withering'. He read the *Koran*, but found 'nothing to seduce or stagger me'. Greatly excited by a witch trial at Inverness, he was disappointed by their acquittal.

writer and translator, is said to have died of joy. Even the Presbyterians may have felt secure with a king who had signed the Covenants. But Charles II who, during his sojourn in Scotland, had listened to endless sermons and had, under pressure, allowed himself to affirm that his mother was an idolatress, had no liking for Scotland and a loathing for the Presbyterians who had patronised and lectured him. He appointed John Middleton – created an earl in 1656 – as his Royal Commissioner to Scotland to manage matters in Edinburgh. The Earl of Lauderdale, nicknamed 'The King of Scotland', was made his Secretary of State to advise him, largely at Westminster.

Although Lauderdale assured him that a contented Scotland would be a guarantee of peace, Charles had already found that Scotland was neither comfortable nor sure. His safety was rooted in England, and he saw no reason not to pursue the policies of his father and grandfather. He found an ally in James Sharp, the minister of Crail, sent to London to represent the moderate Presbyterian interest. Sharp soon developed an enthusiasm for episcopacy, and drifted away from his commitment to the Covenant. Lauderdale, too, informed by the king that Presbyterianism was 'not a religion for gentlemen', gradually abandoned his earlier attachment to the principles of the Covenant, whilst Middleton was already a committed royalist.

The Restoration Parliament met on 1 January 1661 and earned the sobriquet of the 'Drunken Parliament'. Drunk or sober, it treated the previous three decades as though they had never been. All legislation later than 1633 was cancelled out by an Act Rescissory. At a stroke, everything that had been argued over, schemed and fought for, was wiped out. Back came the Committee of the Articles with all its powers of suppression and management. The Privy Council was reinstated and announced that the Kirk in Scotland was to take the form it had in 1633, with bishops as part of the organisation. By the end of 1661, James Sharp was Archbishop of St Andrews; by the summer of 1662 parliament had declared the Covenant to be illegal. An Act of Indemnity to pardon Presbyterian campaigners was passed, but there were acts of revenge. The Marquis of Argyll and Johnston of Warriston, arch-plotters of Presbyterianism, were executed and some eight hundred others were heavily fined. The head of the Marquis of Argyll replaced the skull of Montrose on the Tolbooth of Edinburgh.

The recent past could not be entirely suppressed, and the Scots nobility, many of whom had become impoverished from high spending and the neglect of their estates, did not regain their dominance in public affairs, although their rights and prestige in their own territories were restored and regained. The leaders of the Privy Council, the Earls of Glencairn, Middleton, and Rothes, were military types who owed their status to the king rather than dynasts who felt the blood of Bruce flow through their veins. The lairds and country gentry gradually became stronger politically, in response to the opportunities offered by the changes in religion and politics. Already profitably involved in the affairs of many burghs, the lairds were becoming a distinct group with their own economic interests, and they now also often possessed a legal training. They saw their attendance at Parliament as natural, rather than the tiresome burden it had seemed to earlier lairds.

The Cromwellian administration had left a more efficient tax-gathering system which the new managers of the state adopted. Above all, it had also maintained a level of law and order that Scotland had not known before. With these advantages, the new Parliament's restoration of the monarchy might have been relatively trouble-free had it not been for the restoration of lay patronage of the ministry. Presbyterian congregations in the past had chosen their own ministers. Now all ministers had to have their positions reconfirmed by the lay patron of the local kirk and by the bishop. Ministers were given until 13 February 1663 to conform to the new conditions.

THE YEARS OF THE
CONVENTICLES

On the day of the appointed deadline, some two hundred and sixty of the clergy resigned their charges. The 'outed' ministers were chiefly from the southwest and Fife. The raw Episcopalian 'curates' drafted in to replace them were treated with contempt.

The faithful began to attend meetings on the open moors where the outed ministers preached a gospel of divine wrath and judgments to come against their oppressors. The Privy Council fined those who attended these meetings, or conventicles, and fined them again for not attending church. The authorities used dragoons to hunt out the illegal gatherings and extort the fines. This led to an uprising in Galloway, and in November 1666 between two and three thousand protesters marched on Edinburgh, lost their nerve, and turned to go home. At Rullion Green they were overtaken by regular troops and dispersed. About thirty were executed, others were transported to Barbados, while at least two were tortured to death. The zeal that the two churchmen, Archbishop Sharp of St Andrews and Professor Burnet of Glasgow, showed for the hunting down of the Whigs put them in bad odour with many who did not share the extreme views of the victims. The Whigs would gladly have re-established the religious tyranny which briefly flourished after the collapse of the Engagement: they suffered martyrdoms but they would have willingly martyred others who did not share their opinions. For two decades such scenes were to be repeated, despite occasional attempts to compromise on the government side.

In 1669 Lauderdale persuaded the king to issue a Letter of Indulgence, allowing outed ministers to return to their parishes if they had lived peaceably. Only forty-two responded to the offer. By 1670 attendance at a conventicle was equated with treason and preaching at one was a capital offence. In 1672 a second Letter of Indulgence offered the absurd compromise of placing two outed ministers who were not in conflict with government orders in each of fifty-eight parishes. Every effort was made to stamp out conventicles, with pressure on landowners and employers to prevent the meetings on their lands increasing year by year.

In 1678 an army of six thousand Highlanders and three thousand Lowland militia was quartered in Galloway and the southwest, both as a punitive infliction on the population and as a police force to supervise their actions. Archbishop Sharp, viewed as a prime instigator of the repression, was dragged out of his coach and hacked to death near St Andrews in May 1679. In that same month, at Drumclog, a strategically placed group of Covenanters defeated a government troop under Graham of Claverhouse and went on to take Glasgow by storm. On 22 June, James, Duke of Monmouth, illegitimate son of Charles II, arrived in Scotland with a royal army, and the Whigs, riven by factions and perhaps over-comforted by a misguided sense of destiny, were defeated at the Battle of Bothwell Brig. A thousand were taken prisoner and penned up in the Greyfriars' Churchyard in Edinburgh, where so many had once queued to sign the now illegal Covenant. Four hundred were shipped to the West Indies, the others were set free on a promise of keeping the peace. Seven leaders were hanged. Only a tiny sect known as the Cameronians, preaching complete civil disobedience, now remained in arms. They published manifestos that were widely read, including the *Apologetical Declaration*, declaring war on all 'enemies to God and the covenanted work of reformation'. But the policy of heavy repression remained, and when, at the end of 1679, the king's Catholic brother, James Stewart, Duke of York and Albany, was sent to Edinburgh as Commissioner, it was a sign that there would be no compromise on government policy.

In 1681 Parliament declared that the sovereign need not be a Protestant and passed the Test Act. The new legislation was imposed on all who held any public office, including ministers and teachers, requiring each signatory to remain faithful to the Protestant religion, as defined in the first Confession of Faith, to renounce the Covenant, to defend all the king's rights and prerogatives, and to treat of no matters, whether secular or sacred, without his consent. Since the Confession of Faith pledged loyalty to God, it could not be reconciled with a promise of such absolute obedience to the king. The Test was flawed. It was realised that the king placed more emphasis on obedience to him than on the faith. Archibald Campbell, the ninth Earl of Argyll, declared that he took the Test 'so far as it was consistent with itself', was put on trial for treason, escaped and fled to Holland. Eighty ministers, including many Episcopalians, refused to take the Test and were 'outed'. Ministers were now required to provide lists of those men who did not attend church. Never had the churches been so packed, but the enforced attenders did not come to worship. They talked loudly, slept ostentatiously and generally spoiled proceedings for the sincerely religious.

The Rye House Plot of 1683, which involved threats of kidnap or even death to the royal house, frightened the king and his brother, James. Although it was an English conspiracy, it had links with some prominent Scots, including the Earl of Argyll. Those who could be detected were sent to Scotland for trial, among them William Carstares, a Presbyterian minister who was subjected to the torture of the 'thumbikins' but gave nothing away.

Repression continued, and anyone who refused to reject the *Apologetical*

Entrance to the Covenanters' prison, Greyfriars' Churchyard, Edinburgh

Declaration could now be shot out of hand, so that this period passed into Presbyterian history as the 'killing time'. The number of arbitrary deaths may not have exceeded one hundred, but the fact that the propaganda name stuck shows the strength of feeling. The power of central government in Scotland had never been so great, and it had a widespread police system. In 1685, the year that Charles II died, it was still hunting down those suspected of having fought for the Whigs at Bothwell Brig six years before. In May of that year, the Earl of Argyll

Artist's impression of 'thumbikins' or thumbscrews, similar to the ones used by the Scottish Privy Council for extorting confessions from prisoners. These ones were used by the civic authorities of Montrose

landed in his own territory with a few hundred men in an attempt to raise a rebellion against the openly Catholic James VII and to install the Duke of Monmouth as king. But his campaign collapsed and he was taken and executed by the guillotine.

THE CATHOLIC INTERLUDE AND ITS END

The second son of Charles I became James VII at fifty-one years of age. It is hard to say how many Scots were closet Catholics or retained Catholic sympathies, a hundred and twenty years after the Reformation. The Roman Church had never stopped training Scots for the priesthood in its Scots College, and its priests, more or less undercover, moved from castle to castle under the protection of families like the Douglases, the Setons and the Maxwells. Under James VII, it suddenly became possible to be openly Catholic, although penal acts against Catholicism were still in force.

Few people took the opportunity to convert openly to the Catholic Church, but among those who did were the Earl of Perth, who became Commissioner, and his brother Lord Melfort, who became Secretary of State to Scotland. When parliament refused to repeal the anti-Catholic acts, James issued a Letter of Indulgence in 1687 which allowed Roman Catholics and Quakers to hold meetings in private houses, and another royal decree extended these rights to Presbyterians in June 1688. Open meetings, or conventicles, remained illegal. The Presbyterian Church now regrouped, with factions of Moderates, Indulged and Outed members now largely reconciled. Their reunification was assisted by the execution of James Renwick, last leader of the irreconcilable Covenanters, who had been vocal in dividing the different groups against each other. The Episcopalians, for the first time without support from the king and government, were left in limbo, and bishops disappeared from the Council. James VII received little gratitude for his toleration, which was generally interpreted as a transition towards the reimposition of Catholicism.

But Scotland played no part in the revolution of November 1688 that brought William of Orange and his wife Mary to England and sent James VII in flight to France. The political situation was confused and dangerous. James VII was still technically the king. In December 1688, a mob broke in and stripped the Chapel Royal of Holyrood, which had been restored for the purposes of conducting Catholic rites. The Chancellor was put in prison. The imposed 'curates' of the southwest were ignominiously hounded out of their parishes. But the garrison of Edinburgh Castle remained loyal to the not-yet deposed king. A Convention of the Estates met in March 1689, and although it received messages from both James and William, there was no doubt about its intentions. It set out a Claim of Right in which it assumed the power to depose the sovereign. It listed the crimes of James VII and offered the crown of Scotland to William and Mary. She as a daughter of James VII and he as a grandson of Charles I, both offered an element of Stewart legitimacy, but William was the dominant figure in their joint sovereignty. A key condition was attached to their accession: the new monarchs must abolish episcopacy. William agreed to do this on condition that there would be no religious persecution. It was now the turn of the episcopal clergy to step into a proud uncertainty. Despite their neglect by James VII, they could see only a bleak future ahead under the new regime. Almost two hundred refused to renounce their oath of allegiance to James VII and were turned out of their churches.

EMERGENCE OF THE JACOBITES

In the course of the seventeenth century, the government of Scotland, with its inseparable components of religion, the royal interest and the effort to maintain stability as well as sustain the economy, had swung wildly from out-and-out Presbyterianism to a draconian Episcopacy. Such a fluctuating state of affairs reflected the primitive political make-up of the country and did not necessarily represent public opinion at any stage. The mass of the population had no say in political affairs and did not yet expect one, but the times provided a rich seed bed for future political thinking. Just as James VII and his agents had sought to manipulate the very restricted burgh electorates with his supporters, so the Convention of March 1689 was packed with his opponents. Those who were on the side of James, already called Jacobites, stayed away for their own safety. It is possible that they formed a majority in the country, since the Scottish respect for Stewart legitimacy remained strong and could transcend the religious divide. The Judge of Session, Lord Tarbat, noted that 'The Presbyterians are the more zealous and hotter; the other more numerous and powerful.' But there was no means by which the 'other' could translate that superiority into effective control. Except for the old remedy of brute force, duly tried by the energetic Claverhouse, who was by now Viscount Dundee and had been lately the scourge of the southwestern Whigs. Between March and June he was in the Highlands parleying and bargaining with mutually suspicious chiefs, uniting them, and forging an army. A government army under Hugh MacKay of Scourie was sent out to meet him, and on 27 July 1689, in the steep-sided Pass of Killiecrankie, the Highlanders routed it in a single charge. But Dundee was killed in the battle and without his leadership the cause was lost. Three weeks later, under his successor appointed by James VII, General Cannon, the Highlanders were driven back from Dunkeld by a regiment of Cameronians, formerly persecuted figures and now heroes of the new order. The new monarchy was safe, although the Jacobites had not gone away.

Artist's impression of the Battle of Killiecrankie. Among those who fought with the Highlanders under Viscount Dundee was the eighteen-year-old Rob Roy MacGregor, whose later exploits as an outlaw were to become legendary

SIR GEORGE MACKENZIE OF ROSEHAUGH

As Lord Advocate, Mackenzie was crown prosecutor against the Covenanters, who rewarded him with the name 'Bluidy Mackenzie'. He was born in Dundee in 1636 and studied at St Andrews, Aberdeen and Bourges. His first major case was in defence of the Marquis of Argyll in 1661, which he lost, and his client lost his head. It did not put him at odds with the king, and he became Lord Advocate in 1677. In Parliament he represented the Mackenzie homeland of Ross-shire. He was a keen writer on many subjects, interested in literature, and was a friend of the English poet John Dryden. His great legacy was the Advocates' Library, which he founded in 1682 and to which he presented his own books: it developed into the National Library. Mackenzie died in London in 1691, but was buried in Greyfriars Churchyard. Robert Louis Stevenson recorded how, much later, the town urchins used to knock on the door of his vault, crying,
'Bluidy Mackenzie, come oot if ye daur!'

THE ANOMALOUS KINGDOM
OF WILLIAM AND MARY

William of Orange, although a Calvinist, believed in religious toleration. He had little interest in Scotland, whose governmental independence seemed to him anomalous. He wanted to operate on a European stage. In his immediate retinue had been such men as William Carstares, a moderate Presbyterian with first-hand experience of government oppression, but he still needed men of acknowledged rank and status to form his government.

Many of the nobility drew back from joining his government, put off by the Presbyterian vigour of the new parliament and also because of the old claims of loyalty made on them by James VII. Nevertheless, the Campbells and Hamiltons embraced the new order, and other families with a professional, legal or landed base, like the Dalrymples and Primroses, supplied men to operate the government. Parliamentary opposition came from the more extreme Presbyterian side rather than from Jacobites. Calling themselves 'The Club', they were serious anti-monarchists and harked back to the cuts in royal power made by parliament in the 1640s. They engineered the abolition of the Committee of the Articles and blocked the appointment of judges by the king. As the king became more firmly established, he was able to ignore the Club, which soon split into rival groups.

The future of the Kirk was decided under this new regime. In 1690 royal supremacy over it was abolished, and all ministers deposed since 1661 were reinstated. The Confession of Faith, formulated at Westminster in 1647, was adopted as the standard. Parishes from which Episcopalian clergy had been expelled were declared vacant, and lay patronage was abolished. The Cameronians were accepted into the body of the Kirk and moderated their militarism, if not their fervour. Despite the anxiety of the king to avoid persecution of any religious group, the revived Kirk promptly set up a commission to investigate its ministers. This was done to such effect that six hundred and fifty ministers were removed, mainly from parishes in the south of Scotland since a Presbyterian structure did not exist or had long collapsed in great parts of the north. To avoid the charge of religious persecution, Episcopalian ministers were accused of drunkenness, immorality or negligence, often on flimsy or fabricated evidence. Parallel to all this went the daily work of the local kirk sessions which were keen to investigate, publish, condemn and punish the misdeeds of the parishioners. The Presbyterian Church was fully restored as the national Church, but it had paid a price. Church and state were now distinct entities, and no longer could the Kirk claim that its rule transcended the 'carnal' business of state government.

Disturbed by the narrow squeak of Killiecrankie and aware that the clans had sworn to maintain the Jacobite cause, the regime of William of Orange gave much thought to the pacification of the Highlands. Men like Tarbat and the Lord Advocate, Sir George Mackenzie, knew that much of the unrest in the Highlands resulted from resentment of Campbell encroachment, and indeed also of Mackenzie imperialism in the northwest. But with the tenth Earl of Argyll in high favour at court, it was unlikely that the Campbell coat would be clipped.

Sir John Dalrymple of Stair, as joint Secretary of State, operated a policy of carrot and stick as he felt necessary. One incentive offered was a sum of twelve thousand pounds, to be dispensed by the Earl of Breadalbane on behalf of the government to clan chiefs who pledged loyalty to the crown. The stick was flourished at all who had borne arms against William. They must sign an oath of allegiance before 1 January 1692. By doing so, they would be pardoned and indemnified; if they failed, they would be pursued by force. The chiefs sent emissaries to James VII to ask what his will was. Tardily, he gave them his permission to take the oath. Breadalbane's twelve thousand pounds was never accounted for, but the chiefs all signed. The last of the mainland chiefs to sign the oath, five days late, was Alexander MacDonald of Glencoe, whose small clan was a source of trouble to Breadalbane. With Stair keen to make an example of someone just to show the length of the government's arm, and with Breadalbane keen to pay off old injuries, a plot was hatched. The Privy Council was not informed that MacDonald had taken the oath, and Stair, who knew that he had, ignored the fact and procured the king's signature on a warrant for the extirpation of the MacDonalds. A detachment of Campbell troops was sent to Glencoe early in February 1692, apparently to be lodged by the MacDonalds, and were hospitably received. On the night of 13 February, they turned on their hosts, killed thirty-eight, and the rest fled into the snowy wastes. Internecine strife in the Highlands had seen worse deeds than this, but the Glencoe massacre was different, in its breach of an ancient law of hospitality and in the authorisation by a government that was supposed to be dedicated to justice. Despite efforts to hush the matter up, the Glencoe massacre became even more of a scandal by the lack of reprisal against its instigators. Jacobite politicians made the most of it in pamphlet after pamphlet, but Stair was not removed from office until 1695. The Jacobite Highlanders remained in a state of uneasy peace, suspicious and unreconciled.

AN ECONOMY IN TRANSITION

In 1695 the population of Scotland numbered approximately a million people. That of England was approximately six million. Scotland's annual revenue was around one fortieth of England's. Scotland was still one of the poor countries of Europe, and the average income of its citizens was very low. At this time perhaps a fifth of the population owned virtually nothing at all and were destitutes and beggars. The Scots pound was worth only a twelfth of the English one. The economic record of Scotland in the seventeenth century was very far from being all bad, but the union of the crowns and the consequent shackling to English policy had produced no benefits for the development of Scottish economic life, and through continuing anti-Scottish discrimination and Continental war had often hindered it. Common citizenship was meaningless without common rights. With its very restricted domestic manufacturing base, Scotland had to export or live at a very basic subsistence level. As at the beginning of the century, the country was primarily agrarian. In a good year grain could be exported in substantial quantities; in a bad one the trade was all the other way.

The chief overseas markets were Norway and Sweden, from where ships could return with timber and iron. East coast exports of grain in 1685 were reckoned to be worth around a quarter of a million pounds in Scots currency. In most forms of activity, there had been little successful growth. The exceptions were in the production of coal and salt. Here the export trade had grown, and the harbours of towns like Saltcoats, Port Seton and Methil were enlarged to cope. By 1670 there were fifteen coal mines in the Forth area. At Culross Sir George Carnock sunk a coal pit under the sea and drained it by a water-driven bucket chain. Much of the coal was used to boil off the water from the salt pans, whose product, though of inferior quality, found a sale at home and in cheaper foreign markets. Lead mining, based on Leadhills and Wanlockhead, was a variable source of revenue, but in a good year it could rival the earnings of the coal export trade.

Fishing, despite efforts to promote it, including a grandiosely named but ineffectual Royal Company for the Fishery of Scotland in 1670, remained a modest industry, pursued by small inshore boats. The highly organised Dutch industry, by comparison, fished the whole North Sea and often came right into the inshore Scottish grounds, causing confrontation and protest. Exports of salted fish, like other commodities, were vulnerable to tariffs and import bans. There was a crisis for the fishing industry in 1689 when France banned the import of salt herring.

In the latter part of the century, the export of cattle on the hoof to England was becoming important. This was the primary economic activity of the Highlands, which raised thousands of black cattle each year to be sold to the drovers. This business was usually funded by a magnate, like the Duke of Montrose, who for some years bankrolled Rob Roy MacGregor. The animals were driven south in great herds and sold again for fattening on English grasslands, so that the sponsor and the drover would recoup their investment. Sheep hides and other animal skins, including fox and goat, were exported, chiefly to the Baltic lands. The days when bears had roamed the Scottish woodlands were long gone and by now the wolf was virtually extinct. Surprisingly perhaps, deer skins do not seem to have been a significant export item, but at that time the Highlands were extensively populated and the concept of the deer forest had not arisen. The shy and elusive red deer could not be turned into a cash crop like the cow.

Wool was a significant export item to France and the Netherlands, although, like most other Scottish products, it was not of the best quality. Textile production continued to be carried on throughout the country, mainly as a cottage industry and mostly to meet a family's own needs. In the towns, however, weaving was organised into a craft guild, and woollen and linen cloth was produced on handlooms for internal and export sale. Despite its preservative qualities, whisky does not appear to have been exported. Its production was home-based, rural and on a small scale. The barber-surgeons' monopoly would not have extended far into the countryside. The drink itself probably resembled fire water more than the modern product.

Against this export trade was set an import trade, the bulk items of which remained timber and iron. Substantial amounts of air-evaporated Biscay salt were imported as it was a better preservative than the boiled-out Scottish salt. Tobacco and sugar were coming to Scotland in bulk. From the 1660s

THE CAPITAL CITY

There is no single moment in its history at which it can be said that Edinburgh became the capital. The concept of the capital city is not an old one. The Scottish government, until the sixteenth century, was centred with the king and his court, wherever they happened to be. Parliaments were called at different places, including Perth and St Andrews, to suit the royal convenience or purpose. The principal fortress was Stirling Castle. With the decline and periodic loss of Berwick, Edinburgh-Leith became the principal centre of trade from the fourteenth century onwards. Increasingly, Edinburgh set the rules that the other burghs followed. Key dates in the political importance of the city are 1501, when James IV began to build the palace of Holyroodhouse; 1508, when Edinburgh became the centre for the annual royal audit; 1532 with the establishment of the Court of Session; and 1552, when the Convention of Royal Burghs instructed all burghs to model their constitutions on that of Edinburgh. By the arrival of Mary, Queen of Scots in 1561, it was unquestionably the centre of affairs, and James VI's proposal to move his government to Perth caused panic among the Edinburgh magistrates. The building of Parliament House in 1632–40 finally confirmed the status of Edinburgh. Charles I's charter for the bishopric specifically calls it the principal and capital city.

Artist's impression of Edinburgh Castle in the sixteenth century

tea and coffee began to arrive from Holland and England, at first in very modest quantities for medicinal use, and they did not displace the traditional breakfast ale. Drinking chocolate began to arrive from South America. An immensely long list of manufactured items was brought in, substantially greater than in earlier centuries, showing the extent to which the Scots with any money were keen to stay up-to-date with the rest of the world, and also how little was made at home. For the new Holyrood Palace, Sir William Bruce brought in Delft tiles, linseed oil, marble fireplaces and ready-carved woodwork.

THE TAMING OF THE ROYAL BURGHS

The towns remained very much trading centres. Their merchants still formed a ruling class in their little communities. In any larger town the craftsmen outnumbered the merchants; the craft guilds were larger and, though varying in status, did not have the prestige of the merchant guilds, which took precedence at all parades and other occasions. But both merchants and craftsmen ran a relatively closed system which supplied their own town itself and its hinterland with necessary articles. Sir George Mackenzie noted, 'Our people are forc'd to buy all things abroad, because our Deacons and Trades here will allow no expert tradesmen to live among them.'

Around 1690 Edinburgh had thirty thousand inhabitants while the fast-growing Glasgow had maybe half that number, and Aberdeen and Dundee each had a population of ten thousand. Of the rest, only Perth had as many as five thousand inhabitants. Many other smaller towns had only a hundred or so people. One of the reasons for Glasgow's growth was its encouragement of manufacturing. In the later seventeenth century its people began to make soap, to refine sugar and to produce woollen cloth; in 1690 the first rope works in Scotland was established there. Another reason was the increasing volume of Atlantic trade. In 1667 the town council began the construction of a deep-water harbour at Port Glasgow. Trading rights jealously guarded by old royal burghs like Dumbarton, Renfrew and Rutherglen nearby spurred the Glaswegians on in their enterprises, although their city had already grown far larger than its neighbours.

Those who took a national view, like the competent Lauderdale administration of the 1670s, could sense how the conservatism of the burghs was damping down the chances of Scottish expansion. The complacency and pride of all the royal burgh merchants was shaken in 1672 when the Privy Council broke their monopolies. Markets and fairs were licensed to operate outside the burghs. Any burgh could now trade for export and import except in certain categories. The royal burghs still kept their monopoly on luxury items like wine, silk, spices and dyes, but these were low-volume imports. Ironically, the Convention of Royal Burghs had been paying the Duke of Lauderdale sixteen hundred pounds a year for his good services. This subsidy was promptly withdrawn, but Lauderdale more than restored it from the new earnings of his own baronial burgh of Musselburgh.

This relaxation of trade drove on the growth of newer burghs like Greenock and Bo'ness. Another significant act of 1681 established a policy of economic protection for Scottish industries. Such policies, borrowed from the French, were becoming common throughout northern Europe. New 'manufactories' were given special privileges of monopoly sale and freedom from taxation. In some cases, export of the necessary raw materials and import of goods that rivalled home-produced goods were banned. This was a rough-and-ready economic tool that gave rise to reciprocal bans in some cases. Protection did not always work to the benefit of the early Scots capitalists, but the overall policy demonstrated a new and positive approach and helped to sustain the growing perception that progress and improvement were a real possibility.

The 1670s and 1680s were a time of substantial enterprise and development, still small in scale and halting in their progress. The 1690s, by contrast, were christened by Jacobite propagandists 'King William's ill years'. From 1695 to 1699, wet autumns and a lack of seed corn ensured a series of disastrously bad harvests. Overseas trade was disrupted by war between England and France, and most countries to which Scotland exported were now creating tariff barriers. This included England, which imposed tariffs on Scottish coal and salt. The Netherlands, a prime customer for Scottish coal, raised the import duty to such a point that the trade was killed off. The English Parliament passed Acts of Trade and Navigation that were designed to keep the colonial trade for English vessels only. While few of these bans and impositions were completely enforceable, life for traders was made extremely difficult and risky, and many simply gave up or went bankrupt. The Scottish economy went into steep decline. Many people left the country, a high proportion making for Poland and the Baltic states. Large numbers of men joined the English army or the forces of England's enemies. The ever-present underworld of the dispossessed, disabled, deformed, maimed and diseased continued to grow, despite the inevitable increase in the death rate that accompanied the famine.

'THE COMPANY OF SCOTLAND'

From this half-collapsed economic base the Darien Scheme was erected. It began in May 1695, when an act of parliament was passed to establish 'the

Company of Scotland Trading to Africa and the Indies'. This enterprise was the brainchild of the effervescently intelligent William Paterson, the Scots founder of the Bank of England. Modelled on the English and Dutch companies, it was to have a monopoly of the Scots trade with Asia, Africa and America. When the subscription lists for those who wished to buy shares in the venture were opened in London, English investors rapidly subscribed their allocated half of £300,000. Then the storm broke. English commercial interests were being attacked. The two houses of parliament protested to the king. The king dismissed the Commissioner for Scotland, the Earl of Tweeddale. Around £285,000 of investment was withdrawn. The Scots proceeded to invest £400,000, but their efforts to raise further funds in Holland and Hamburg were spiked by the Dutch East India Company and the English Resident respectively, who pointed out that they had no authority from the king to raise the money outside the English realm.

The East Indies project was abandoned, but Paterson put forward a grander scheme. This was for a Scottish colony on the Isthmus of Darien, now the site of the Panama Canal. It would be an exchanging point for the world's trade. Ships would unload and reload on the Pacific and Caribbean coasts, with the trans-shipped goods borne across the narrow isthmus. No longer would ships have to double the notorious Cape of Good Hope or Cape Horn. There was, he insisted, fertile soil, a good climate, and gold waiting to be found. The whole country shared in his enthusiasm, and three new ships, built on the Continent, *Caledonia*, *St Andrew* and *Unicorn*, left Leith on 17 July 1698, bound for Darien with twelve hundred eager colonists. Within a year, hunger, disease, dissension and an absolute lack of trade made them abandon the colony. Two further ships arrived to find the site deserted. One was destroyed by fire; the other made for Jamaica. A third expedition of four ships with thirteen hundred colonists left Scotland despite the rumours of disaster, and re-established the deserted colony, only to be besieged by Spanish forces. Allowed to leave on honourable terms, the survivors set sail for Jamaica, but three of the vessels were lost on the way. Two thousand people had died. The vast investment, to which so many people had contributed, had evaporated. It was an irretrievable disaster. In Scotland there was no hesitation in blaming the king for the whole thing. William had certainly proved to be no king of Scots at all, but the failure of Darien lay in the over-optimism, bad planning, ignorance and pride of the venture. Just as in the last years of James IV, the Scots could not withstand the urge to measure themselves against the greater neighbour-state, and seem more grand and powerful than they were. Nemesis was again waiting. This time, for the investors though not for the unlucky colonists, it was a financial reckoning. The

THE DIET OF THE SCOTS

An interesting study by A. Gibson and T. C. Smout, published in 1989, sheds light on what the Scots ate, and on the gradual change in the people's diet between the fifteenth and the eighteenth centuries. In the later Middle Ages, the Scots ate a varied diet of meat, fish (both in salted form for at least five months of the year), fowl, cheese and barley meal. They drank ale, normally rather weak and watery. Wine was an expensive import; whisky was a monopoly, first of certain monasteries, then of the barber-surgeons' guild of Edinburgh. The French historian Jean Froissart, who visited Scotland in the later fourteenth century, recorded the cooking practice of the Scots soldier on the march. As well as 'sodden flesh', they ate oatcakes which they cooked themselves, on girdles carried in a flap of the saddle. In the sixteenth century, by which time the population had grown considerably, there is much evidence of shortages of meat. The Scots method of winter care, practised until well into the eighteenth century, was to keep the animals indoors on a short diet. This meant that many of them died, and any lack of fodder reduced the herd drastically. In times of hardship, Highlanders would draw blood from their cattle to mix with the scanty supplies of oats or rye. The surviving small cows had to be literally carried out in the spring to graze and regain their strength. Through the seventeenth century there was a shift towards a diet based mainly on oats and other cereal food. Even when the country was raising cattle in unprecedented numbers, these were for the export trade, and meat became a luxury food in Scotland. For most, it was reserved for special feasts, like weddings, the New Year and Shrove Tuesday. The resulting diet, summed up in the refrain of a nineteenth century bothy ballad, 'Brose for my breakfast, my dinner, my tea', although highly monotonous, was not lacking in nutrition, especially if supplemented by milk and cheese. Kail, peas and beans eked it out in season. From the later eighteenth century, the potato made up a very high proportion of the Highland diet, leading to disastrous famines when the crop failed in the 1840s.

disaster left many families in straits and absorbed a substantial proportion of the country's capital wealth.

STANDARDS IMPROVE – FOR SOME

The countryside of Scotland did not appear to change greatly throughout the seventeenth century but real changes did take place. In the fertile eastern areas, more land was taken in for grain cultivation and the ferm touns, or farm settlements, became larger. Agricultural methods were still primitive and labour-intensive – it could take ten oxen and as many people to drive a plough. The Scottish landscape was still open and bare of trees. Largely undrained, the land held far more lochans, bogs and reedy marshland than would be the case a hundred years later, even in the fertile districts. An awareness of the desirability of fertilising was growing. Edinburgh gathered its publicly deposited excrement from both humans and animals and sold it as manure, while most other towns dumped their ordure on the adjacent common fields. There was a new interest in tree-planting. New species of trees, such as the lime, the maple and the walnut, were introduced, although the primary aim was to ornament the policies, or lands, of big houses. John Reid published the first Scottish book on cultivation, *The Scots Gardiner*, in 1683.

The dwellings of the peasantry in the Highlands and Lowlands did not change and were as scantily equipped and furnished as before. Landowners still lived in tower houses, but these now began to become more elaborate in style, with their machicolations and turrets aimed more at decoration than at defence. Larger windows were cut into ancient walls, and inside grander homes there was far more in the way of panelling, carving and decorative plasterwork. The main developments came after the restoration of Charles II, when there was an aesthetic as well as a political reaction to the austerity of the Commonwealth period. Domestic furniture became more elaborate in construction and more intricately carved. The day-bed appeared as an item of drawing-room furniture. Cane furniture was introduced, and other products of colonial trade appeared in ornaments: ebony, mother-of-pearl and ivory. The growing practice of tea-drinking led to the acquisition of various associated items, including fine china. The practice of strewing floors with rushes gradually ceased, giving way to polished wood and even carpets. The houses of the well-to-do became places of comfort inside while still retaining, through conservatism, lack of capital and a prudent appreciation of the temper of the times, a sternly military air on the exterior. But the tower houses were becoming obsolescent. The shape of grander houses to come was displayed by the work of Sir William Bruce, who was made King's Surveyor and Master of Works in 1671. He brought the new, expansive, open Palladian style to Scotland in his rebuilding of the much knocked-about Holyrood Palace, and the new Auchendinny and Hopetoun Houses.

Change to the towns was much more apparent. In the more substantial or successful burghs, the huddle of low thatched houses around the church tower and market cross, typical of previous centuries, was changing from the town centre outwards. Houses became taller, of two or more storeys, built of cut stone and roofed with tiles. In towns like Stirling, Banff and Dumbarton, wealthier lairds built town houses for themselves. This reflected the interaction between the town and the country beyond. The lairds took a close interest in burgh affairs and often took office in royal burghs. There was advantage in this. Tain, for example, had three thousand acres of moorland that were used for pasturing and peat-cutting and were feued to councillors or their friends at a low rental.

There were many other ways of transforming public property into private gain. In 1672, the provost of Edinburgh, Sir Andrew Ramsay, was accused in a court case of 'having govern'd most tyrannically for ten years, applying the common good to himself and his friends.' The handsome mansions were often paid for by the diversion of public funds. In the busier seaports like those of the Fife coast, stone houses rose up around the harbours, built for merchant traders and often showing the influence of Flemish style. Workshops and stores might back on to the new buildings, but their interiors would be as well appointed as those of the country barons. Beyond the central nucleus of the town, rows of low cottages remained, each keeping its field at the back and an open space in front, the midden heap still prominent and the rough-surfaced causey, or roadway, running equidistantly between the dwellings.

INTELLECTUAL ACTIVITY

The intellectual life of Scotland had showed signs of vivacity from early in the century. John Napier of Merchiston, mathematician, economist and religious thinker, published *Mirifici Logarithmorum Canonis Descriptio* in 1614, introducing the concept of logarithms to the world (and titled in the language of universal learning). Sir Thomas Urquhart, duellist and royalist, dabbled in trigonometry and the concept of a universal language but is renowned for his translations of *The Works of Mr Francis Rabelais*, published in 1653. The laws of Scotland were at last organised and codified in 1679 into *The Institutions of the Law of Scotland* by James Dalrymple, later created first Viscount Stair, a magisterial work which remains at the foundation of modern Scottish law. George Jamesone, who was at work in Aberdeen in the 1620s before transferring his studio to Edinburgh, was the first of a distinguished line of Scots portrait painters. In 1662, Forbes's *Songs and Fancies* was published in Aberdeen — a town notably lukewarm to Presbyterianism — the first collection of such songs from the popular tradition. Such different activities indicate a climate of thought that was far from being suppressed by oppressive religious fervour. The 'Enlightenment' of the eighteenth century falsely suggests a darkness in the intellectual life of Scotland before. It only happened because the lamps had been lit in the preceding century. The cultural and economic progress of the seventeenth century has been drastically and unfairly overshadowed by a past tendency to concentrate on the religious struggle, as if nothing else was happening.

Literature was the chief sufferer in the seventeenth century. Theology was undoubtedly the biggest intellectual industry of the century, both expounding and analysing. Calderwood's *History of the Church of Scotland* was published in 1678 and remains an important source for many debates within the Church at that time and later. It cites material from many documents that have been lost, and was one of the many works used to set out the Kirk's self-justification. Unfortunately, the prose of the theologians is too turgid to reach the level of literature. Among secular writing of the time, mostly memoirs and guidebooks have survived. Some are written in Scots and others in English. This may be partly explained by a desire to reach the English market, as with the traveller William Lithgow and his *Totall Discourse of Rare Adventures and Painfull Peregrinations* of 1632, but already there are signs of the adaptation to English ways that would be such a feature of the eighteenth century.

THE ILL-WILLED UNION

Despite these hints of English-ward leanings many things that happened in the last years of the seventeenth century served to convince the Scots that separation from England was the only hope for their nation. A trading nation without the freedom to operate its own foreign policy was a nonsense, and to many Scots the Darien Scheme was only the most expensive illustration of how completely un-free Scottish foreign policy was. The English parliament passed acts that were implacably opposed to Scottish trading interests. The monarch, too, appeared to regard Scotland as a disagreeable distraction. There seemed to be no prospect for a new policy short of a new king or a complete union.

This was the unambiguous political legacy of 1603, a possibility foreseen by James VI but beyond his ability to prevent. Separation of the crowns appeared a serious likelihood, and in London a growing body of opinion recognised that partition might happen. With every dynast's care to preserve and consolidate what power he has, even on his deathbed in 1702, William of Orange urged that a complete union should be formed. His sister-in-law, Anne, the younger daughter of James VII, (who had died in 1701), inherited the thrones of Scotland, England and Ireland without controversy. The second Stuart queen to rule in her own right, she lacked the wilful glamour of Mary Queen of Scots and took no more interest in Scotland than William had. Like him, and for the same reason, she was very much in favour of a parliamentary union. In November 1702 she brought twenty-three English and twenty-three Scots Commissioners together at Whitehall in order to draft a treaty of union. The discussions were wrecked by the intransigent attitude of the English members. Despite agreement in principle, both on union and on the dual monarchy passing to the house of Hanover, the English side would make no concessions at all on the question of trading rights to Scotland and therefore made a nonsense of the whole issue. Queen Anne was already forty-seven years old and had outlived all her seventeen children, so the question of the succession was a fairly urgent one.

The English parliament had already decided to choose a monarch from the house of Hanover. The Scots were aware that their freedom to choose a king, which their parliament had taken to itself in 1689, was one of their few assets and deliberately stalled on the issue. James Stewart, the Pretender, son of James VII, was to many the legitimate king. The Pretender was in active contact with friends and possible friends on both sides of the Border. The English government had no political will for a union of parliaments, but it had no desire to have the Pretender set up as king in Scotland. It was well known that James would not be satisfied until he was king of England and Ireland as well. Jacobite support for the Pretender in England had not been tested: there might be civil war as well as war with Scotland. Nor could the English side see any economic benefits from union. Scotland already imported a high proportion of its needs from England, and the strong protectionist lobby that had seen off Paterson's Company of Scotland remained deeply hostile to the idea of equal trading rights.

The economic argument within Scotland for union was stronger. The country was chronically short of cash, and most official salaries and payments were deep in arrears. Nevertheless, the most enterprising people in the country, whether they were Glasgow traders or country landowners like Andrew Fletcher of Saltoun, saw plenty of opportunity for economic growth in a truly independent Scotland whose trading would not be confined or stifled by England's embargoes or imperialistic wars.

In the governing of Scotland there was an extraordinary level of discordance between the government, as represented by the queen and her Commissioner, the Duke of Queensberry, and the Scots parliament itself. A new parliament met in 1703 while England was deeply engaged in war between Spain and France, and passed an act that reserved to it the exclusive right to make war or foreign alliances on Scotland's behalf. Other acts were passed to enable trade to continue with France. In 1704, an Act of Security was passed, stating that the Scottish crown was not to pass to the successor to the crown of England unless Scottish trading rights, independence and religion were guaranteed. The English parliament replied with the Aliens Act of March of the same year. Under this act, the Scots were given the choice of negotiating parliamentary union or accepting the Hanoverian monarchy but otherwise leaving matters unchanged. If the Scots were to put the Act of Security into practice, they would lose the common citizenship and suffer a ban on all trade of coal, cattle and linen. A deadline for the Scots to accept English terms was set for Christmas Day in 1705. Whitehall had revealed its big stick. Cunningly, it was pointed at the nobility and wealthy. At the same time, and much more discreetly, the English government was distributing its carrots. Hostility between both countries was inflamed almost to the point of war by the *Worcester* incident, early in 1705, when the Scots hanged, on doubtful evidence, three men from an English ship for alleged piracy against one of the Darien ships. This was the lowest point. There was no war party on either side, despite a great deal of mud-slinging, and a mutual realisation arose that an accommodation of some sort had to be reached.

Artist's impression of Parliament Square, Edinburgh. On 16 January 1707 the Act of Union was passed and, by the time it became a law on 1 May, the old Scots Parliament had held its last session.

Within the Scottish parliament there was no consensus on what the accommodation should be. There was a Court party, naturally in favour of union and now led by the Duke of Argyll. There were the Jacobites, wholly opposed to union; and there was the Country party, notionally against union, which was led by the Duke of Hamilton and from which emerged an independent group called the 'Squadrone Volante', favouring some form of union. After furious debate, it was agreed to send commissioners to London to draw up a treaty. Hamilton, no doubt for a substantial reward, proposed that the Scots commissioners should be chosen by the queen. Parliament's agreement to this was a body-blow to the anti-unionists. The London parliament duly abrogated the Aliens Act, and the English-approved commissioners departed for London.

Negotiations began on 16 April 1706. Outside parliament, intense discussion went on throughout the country, and a war of pamphlets was waged between pro-unionists and anti-unionists. Presbyterian clergy were fearful for the future of the Kirk in a unified state and preached against union. The voteless population's views were expressed by mob riots against union in Edinburgh, Glasgow, Dumfries and other towns. Despite the attractions of equal trading rights, the traders of Glasgow were anti-union. The councils of the royal burghs were against union. Among those who were in favour of union, a federal solution was preferred, although no coherent case for federation was ever put forward in the negotiations. When the draft treaty came back, it was for a full incorporating Union. Scotland and England would become a single country, except that Scotland would retain its Church and its legal system. In September 1706, the Duke of Queensberry, again Commissioner, set about getting a majority of the two hundred members of parliament to agree the treaty. Through October and November the debates went on. Queensberry's expert management, combined with Hamilton's vacillation, ensured that despite uproar in the streets, the Act of Union was carried, clause by clause, with no significant amendments. However vocal, articulate and passionate the opponents of union were, they could not agree on a united programme of alternatives. Many who opposed union had no wish to see the Stewarts back; the Jacobites were divided between those who wanted a king for Scotland and those who shared the Pretender's aspiration to the United Kingdom. Many members of Parliament felt that they must take what was on offer, remembering the dangerous time of the *Worcester* incident. Any alternative was uncertain, and time was passing. To throw out the Treaty would have an incalculable, perhaps devastating effect. The way in which it had been framed scarcely gave room for significant amendment without wrecking the whole. Delay felt increasingly pointless and intolerable. On 16 January 1707, the act was finally passed, and Queensberry touched the document with the sceptre of Scotland, the confirming sign for all Acts of Parliament. On 1 May 1707, it became law, and by then the old Scots parliament had held its last session. The last Chancellor, the Earl of Seafield, remarked that it was 'ane end of ane auld sang'. A new song, admittedly written much later, said, 'We're bought and sold for English gold; Such a parcel of rogues in a nation.' English gold played a significant part, but even without the carrots, it is likely that the union would have been approved. The only figure of enough standing to rally and unite the opposition was the Duke of Hamilton, who lacked the backbone to do it, even if unbribed.

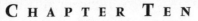

CHAPTER TEN

From Union to Empire, 1707–1799

THE GREAT DEBATE

With the exception of the heady days of 1560, the Scottish parliament had never been so vocal, so important, so much a focus of the national spirit as in the three years before it voted itself out of existence. The intense debate that raged throughout the country did much to define and intensify a spirit of national identity even as the nation of Scotland itself became part of a Great Britain that was inevitably dominated by England. Compared to the two hundred members of the Edinburgh parliament, only forty-five Scottish commoners and sixteen peers were to join the Westminster parliament. The rest returned to their estates, baronies and burghs to pursue life and business within the new order of things. The focus of attention grew narrower. So many words had been expended on what Scotland was, and on what it might be. Now, for better or worse, the conduct of the state was out of their hands. There were few opportunities open for Scots in the affairs of state, now conducted from four hundred miles from Edinburgh, in what most Scots still considered a foreign capital.

SCOTLAND AFTER THE TREATY OF UNION

But the minds of all thinking people had been thoroughly stirred up, and though some of the new ideas were made impossible by the union, others remained feasible. Throughout society there was an urge towards economic growth, beginning at a purely domestic level. The new comforts of life, like tobacco, tea and coffee were expensive and had to be paid for, even when they were smuggled into the country. Old standards of household life were being rejected by people who wanted windows with glass in them, curtains, carpets, teacups and more furniture. All these things had to be paid for in cash. But now there was a wider market to operate in. Access to England and the English colonies meant that Scottish merchants might have better prospects in these new trading areas. Despite the hopes expressed in the Treaty of Union, however, there was not an immediate improvement in the economy. The base of industrial and commercial activity was very narrow and standards of production sometimes low. Scotland had long traded as one of Europe's cheap sources of supply. Its coal and woollens, and linens and salt were never the best available. The English preferred, and could afford, better quality. Even Scots cattle went out cheap, to be resold by English dealers at vastly higher prices when fattened for the London market. Despite freedom of trade, English merchants and their overseas agents were

---

SCOTTISH CURRENCY

The first Scottish coins were minted in the reign of David I. Mints were established at Berwick and Roxburgh, on a small scale. The coins were silver, of equivalent value and similar design to the English noble. As long as they were made of pure metal, the intrinsic value of different currencies remained the same, although the value of the metal itself might fluctuate. debasement and consequent devaluing of the Scottish currency began in the reign of David II and went on throughout successive reigns. In 1466 an attempt was made to put low-value copper coins into circulation, to bring the poor into the monetary system, but this 'black money' was widely unpopular. Nevertheless, low-value coins were needed, and the energetic Sir William Alexander, of Nova Scotia fame, had the monopoly on the production of copper placks. By 1707 a Scots pound was equivalent to an English shilling. Silver coins were never in wide circulation within Scotland, and in order to enable cash transactions to be made, coins of lower value had to be introduced. The lowest was the Scotch penny, or doit; then came the bodle (called after the coiner Bothwell) of two pence; the plack (French *plaque*) of three pence; and the bawbee (French *bas billon*) of six pence. A bawbee was a considerable sum. At all times a variety of low-value English, Dutch and Irish coins also circulated. At the time of the Union, the currency was standardised, and the Scottish silver coins

Artist's impression of the currency of the seventeenth century

were called in for exchange. The copper and base metal coins continued to circulate within the country until at least the 1760s.

SMUGGLING

Smuggling was rife in Scotland throughout the period from the Union of 1707 until around 1830. The Licensing Act of 1823 was responsible for its demise. During its long heyday, its contribution to an unmeasurable 'black economy' must have been very large. Centred on wine, gin and tobacco, it also involved tea and coffee, in a mixture of goods bought duty-free on the continent and stolen from warehouses. The resistance of the Scots to the new import duties after 1707 was so fierce that smuggling was often scarcely concealed. A folklore of smuggling grew up, in which the clumsy Revenue were always outwitted by the crafty smuggler, typified by the Orcadian Mansie Eunson. But throughout the country, the business was normally organised by the leaders of local society, lairds and merchants, who made substantial profits whilst the dirty work was done by others, who understood that, if caught, they ran the risk of being hanged.

the opposite of accommodating to their Scottish competitors. The harvest of 1709 was a poor one and grain could not be exported. Although part of the Union settlement involved a scheme to compensate the Darien investors, people were cautious with their capital. The Bank of Scotland, which had been established in 1695 and had been given a monopoly position for its first twenty-one years, had very limited funds and would lend only against strong security. There was no post-Union boom, and it became clear that the Scots were going to have to haul themselves up by thier own bootlaces. The chagrin of this awareness was sharpened by the imperial parliament's breaches of the Treaty of Union in both letter and spirit. The Scottish Privy Council was abolished in 1708. The abolition of the Scots currency proved a slow and painful process. Article 14 of the Treaty had prohibited an increase in the tax on malt, which was vital in making ale, 'during the present war'. But parliament tried in 1712 to increase it and was stopped only by united and furious Scottish protest. The Scots could not prevent an export duty being imposed on linen in 1711. Resentment was again caused on both sides of the border when the customs system of England was extended to Scotland, which up to this point had taxed most imports lightly if at all. To the English it was intolerable that duty-free goods should be brought in from the north. The Scots responded by setting up smuggling ventures that often worked quite openly, and doing their utmost to frustrate the new customs officials, many of whom were English and many of whom were open to bribery. Despite the provision made for the Church of Scotland in the Treaty, parliament passed the Patronage Act in 1712, which restored lay patronage, thereby attacking one of the fundamental principles of the freedom of the Kirk.

GEORGE I IN ENGLAND

As a result, feelings against the Union ran high through all sections of society. When George I was speedily installed as king in 1714 on the death of Queen Anne, Jacobite sympathisers were outraged and their leaders felt sufficiently confident to mount an armed rebellion. The fulcrum of revolt, the stone in the catapult, just as it had been for Dundee in 1689, and would be again in 1719 and 1745, was the Highlands, particularly the clans of the Central and Western Highlands where Catholic and Episcopalian sympathies were strong.

By 1714 Newcomen had built his first steam engines, Newton had published his greatest discoveries, Locke and Leibniz had opened new fields of philosophy: a new world was forming which a generation of Scotsmen still in their cradles would soon help to shape. The Highlands and Islands remained a vast enclave of the old world. But they were by no means unaffected by change. Their magnates, like the Earl of Mar, who led the rising of 1715, and the Duke of Argyll, who led the government forces against it, presented two faces to the world. One was the London-based courtier, a man of the modern world. The other was that of the patriarchal chief, a man of the ancient world, who spoke to his people in their ancient language, administered his own law and that of the king, and maintained, as far as he could, their ancient traditions. There was a tension between these roles.

In London it lent a certain cachet to the Duke of Argyll that he could call out a private army of five thousand devoted clansmen by sending around the fiery cross. But he also had to answer to the government in person for their good order. To keep himself in ducal style both in London and in Inveraray, he needed money, which had to be provided by the same clansmen. Perhaps a third of the country's population, around three hundred and fifty thousand people, lived in the Highland area. For a long time the greatness of a chief had been measured by the number of people he commanded. Now this attitude was changing as chiefs found that numbers did not equate to wealth, and wealth became increasingly important to them. More and more, the heads of the Highland clans perceived themselves to be landowners rather than chiefs. They preserved the Celtic panoply of former days, but their minds, and those of their chamberlains and tacksmen, were increasingly focused on the business of making the estates pay their way in an era of mercantile capitalism.

THE LEGACY OF THE GAELS

Except in the frontier areas, the only language of the great mass of the Highlanders remained Gaelic. This was a further source of irritation to the central government which had never throughout Scottish history attempted to set up a Gaelic-speaking office. The language barrier was a major hindrance to understanding, and it was accompanied by a whole range of cultural differences. Not only the government found this irksome. In 1709 the Kirk set up the Society for the Propagation of Christian Knowledge, to support education, of a Presbyterian variety, in the Highlands and Islands. Education was much needed, but this began two centuries of resolute campaigning in the Highlands and Islands against the use of Gaelic. Gaelic was hampered by its oral culture: although it had been a written language for centuries, a largely illiterate population meant that there was little printed material available, even after printing became widespread. A Gaelic version of the Bible was published in 1690 by the Rev. Robert Kirk, minister of Aberfoyle, who also wrote the remarkable *Secret Commonwealth of Elves, Faunes and Fairies*, but it was not widely circulated. Even a fine lyrical poet like Duncan Bàn MacIntyre could not write down his own verses but had to have them transcribed.

The Highlanders did not live in a state of complete ignorance of the world beyond their homes, and news passed rapidly from clachan to clachan, but they had to make special efforts to obtain education of any kind. Trade was vital to their existence, and in the early years after the Union the cattle trade was strong. But to a large extent they lived in their own world, looking to their own chiefs, aware of the many divisions among themselves caused by land rivalry, old feuds, different religions; and among smaller clans, the deliberate manipulations of the greater chiefs, always looking for aggrandisement. The immediate world of the Highlanders and Islanders was still one of intense loyalty, a loyalty based on the principle of care and support given in return for loyalty and regular tribute, established on a mutual basis from the humblest clansman to the chief and beyond the chief to the king. But the king, as they well knew, was now a German who knew little and cared less about matters sacred to the Highlanders. The clanspeople were uneasy on many accounts. The agents of Jacobitism could point to many things that would be improved if the Stewarts came back.

THE JACOBITE UPRISING OF 1715

The Earl of Mar had been chief lieutenant to Queensberry in pushing through the Act of Union. On 6 September 1715, he raised the standard of

James VIII on the Braes of Mar and rapidly assembled an army of around ten thousand men. Nicknamed 'Bobbing John', he was not a man of swift decision and not a military leader. By the end of the month he was master of Scotland north of Perth without having had to fight. But the death of Louis XIV of France deprived James, the 'Old Pretender', of the massive support of men and munitions he had expected. Despite their hostility to the Union, the leaders of the Kirk observed that Mar was installing Episcopalian ministers in the north, and as a result the Jacobite rising was preached against from every pulpit. A government army was mustered under the Duke of Argyll, who had been one of Marlborough's generals. A smaller rising took place in the southwest under Viscount Kenmure but he never linked up with the forces of Mar in the north. While Mar remained somewhat irresolutely in Perth, waiting for the Pretender to arrive, Brigadier William Mackintosh of Borlum moved south with a smaller force, crossed the Forth and almost captured Edinburgh before Argyll and his troops pre-empted him. Mackintosh then went south to join up with an ineffectual Jacobite rising in northwest England, and was defeated with them at Preston. Shortly before, the Jacobites and the government forces had met on Sheriffmuir above Dunblane. In a confused and uncertain battle fought over undulating ground, the left wing of each army was broken by the right wing of the other. Both sides claimed victory, but the tactical advantage was left with the government side and public opinion mocked both:

> 'There's some say that we wan,
> Some say that they wan,
> Some say that nane wan at a', man;
> But o' ae thing I'm sure,
> That at Sheriffmuir
> A battle there was that I saw, man.'

Mar retreated to Perth while the government army gathered together a further six thousand seasoned troops from Holland. On 9 January 1716, James finally landed at Peterhead. By now Argyll was advancing and it was clear that the cause was lost. On 4 February, the Old Pretender and Mar fled by ship from Montrose, leaving a depleted and demoralised army to sort itself out as best it could. In fact reprisals were relatively mild, although Kenmure was executed and a number of Jacobite landowners had to forfeit their estates.

Although the Jacobite rising had failed, it left open the possibility of further action. Mar's incompetence had been apparent, and Sheriffmuir had been inconclusive. The late arrival and furtive departure of the Pretender had done him little good, and although his cause was still alive, the Highlanders were realistically doubtful about their ability to achieve success without more support. In 1716, the first of several Disarming Acts was passed, requiring the clans to give up their weapons in return for indemnity against prosecution and imprisonment. This merely took away the weapons of the clans loyal to the government. Those clans who harboured anti-government sentiments surrendered only obsolete muskets and rusty weapons. George Keith, the Earl Marischal, made a futile attempt to start another rising in 1719, landing in Kintail with a variety of foreign mercenaries, including three hundred Spanish troops. The rest of his foreign support, still at sea, was scattered by the 'Protestant winds'. Barely a thousand Highlanders joined this uprising, the ageing Rob Roy MacGregor among them, and General Wightman and his government army had little trouble in defeating them in the Battle of Glenshiel.

WADE'S NEW ROADS
AND OTHER DEVELOPMENTS

General Wade, appointed military commander in the Highlands, set about the construction of roads that would divide the Highlands into manageable sectors and enable armies to march at speed from point to point. By 1736, two hundred and fifty miles of narrow road, but specifically built for

'wheeled carriages', and forty bridges had been built. Strategic garrison centres at Fort George and Fort Augustus were also constructed at this time. Ironically, the chief beneficiary of the military road improvements was to be the 'Young Pretender', Prince Charles Edward Stewart, in 1745.

To-ing and fro-ing between committed Jacobites and the exiled court, now removed to Rome, continued. The government spied diligently on all this activity, latterly aided by the Earl of Mar, who turned informer in the hope of working his passage home from France. The Stewart cause was a convenient pawn in

Artist's impression of the young Charles Edward Stewart, based on a portrait by Antonio David, 1732

European affairs when any state wanted to move against Great Britain. France, Spain and even the Russia of Peter the Great supported the Jacobites at different times, but only for their own convenience and advantage. No country seriously backed the Stewarts for their own sake.

Outside the Highland time-warp, new developments were taking place and the watchword was 'Improvement'. In agriculture and manufacturing particularly, the more intelligent practitioners, were anxious to improve their methods, efficiency, products and profits. Rather than bringing in experts from abroad, as in the past, they looked for knowledge from the increasing number and range of books that were being published, by experimentation and by sharing ideas among themselves. They also borrowed heavily from their knowledge of modern English agricultural practice. In 1723, the Society for the Improvement in the Knowledge of Agriculture was founded in Edinburgh. The location was significant: almost every advocate and Lord of Session had his country estate somewhere not far from the capital. Whatever else they were, they were farmers too. In Aberdeen and other centres similar bodies were established.

DEVELOPMENTS IN AGRICULTURE

Improved equipment, like the horse-drawn seed drill designed by the English lawyer and farmer Jethro Tull, was becoming available. Often the profits made from these improvements and experiments were the last thing to flourish, and some of the most enterprising Improvers, like John Cockburn who created the model village of Ormiston in 1734, ultimately went bankrupt. Others, however, like Sir Archibald Grant of Monymusk, who concentrated more on farming and less on social engineering, prospered. In time, progressive ideas gradually became normal practice. The Improvers' encouragement of a new state of mind, as well as their sponsoring of new vegetables like turnips or potatoes, was of enormous importance.

Progress was not confined to arable farming. That the price of improvement would not just be paid by pioneers like Cockburn was made clear in Galloway. Here was a strongly agrarian area, where cattle, oats and barley were farmed on the grasslands, and sheep and rye on the higher ground adjoining, and often taken in from, the moors. Galloway was also ideally placed for importing and reselling Irish cattle brought across the North Channel to Portpatrick or the Solway shore. With its proximity to England, the region had a natural commercial advantage, and in the 1720s the Galloway lairds began systematically to exploit their position by combining and enclosing large tracts of land in the shires of Kirkcudbright and Wigtown behind dry-stone dykes and the half-stone, half-thorny-hedged 'Galloway hedges'. Within these enclosures they fattened black cattle in great numbers. To accomplish this, they evicted large numbers of tenants who, often through many generations, had occupied smallholdings.

THE GALLOWAY LEVELLERS

The tenants who were thus dispossessed or under threat of eviction formed themselves into bands to destroy the enclosing walls and hedges and became known as the 'Galloway Levellers'. Theirs was a popular protest on a substantial scale, the first of its kind in rural Scotland since the Presbyterian conventicles. It delivered a similar shock to the authorities, who duly reacted by bringing in troops and suppressing the Levellers by force. There were outbreaks of serious unrest from 1723 which died away gradually in 1725 after the ringleaders were deported, imprisoned or heavily fined.

The dry-stone dyke, first used in Kirkcudbright around 1710, soon became a typical feature of the Scottish agricultural landscape, and would eventually spread throughout the land. Daniel Defoe noted in his *Tour Through Britain* (1724–26) that a Galloway nobleman might easily send four thousand sheep and four thousand cattle to England in a season. Such volumes of traffic generated considerable wealth, displayed in the fine country houses and tree-clad estates of the gentry.

POPULAR UNREST
IN THE TOWNS

Early efforts towards Improvement did little to alleviate the problems of farming. There were still serious food shortages, and when the harvest failed in successive years as it did in 1739 and 1740, the price of food rose sharply and led to riots in the towns. As long as the Union seemed to have brought no benefit, the townsfolk remained volatile. In 1725 a new effort to impose a tax on malt set off violent protests in Glasgow, known as the Shawfield Riots, in which the house of the Whig member of parliament, Daniel Campbell of Shawfield, was set on fire. Hatred of the new customs authorities was shown in the Porteous Riot of Edinburgh in 1736, when a town mob rescued a convicted smuggler, Andrew Wilson. In trying to quell the riot, John Porteous, Captain of the Town Guard, fired on the rioters and wounded thirty or so among them. The citizens called for Porteous to be tried and hanged, and when the authorities hesitated, the mob burned down the doors of the Tolbooth and lynched him.

The effects of food shortages in the 1740s were not so dire as in the 1690s and previous famines, partly because of imports of grain on an unprecedented scale. This was made possible by an increase in overall national wealth. The bootstrap operation was beginning to have positive results.

Until the eighteenth century, virtually no paved roads had been laid since the time of the Romans, except for stretches from Edinburgh to Glasgow, and between Edinburgh and the strategic lead-mining centre at Leadhills. From 1713, Turnpike Trusts were established, and those who wished to improve roads were allowed to levy tolls, although little was done until the second half of the century. Sea-borne traffic was still far more important to communications and trade routes. Any development that required bulk haulage was likely to be close to a harbour. Iron-smelting, which used charcoal from the surrounding forests, began at Invergarry around 1725, with the building of the Great Glen road, and was established around 1750 at Furnace and Bonawe, places virtually inaccessible by road — but which could be reached by sea.

TOWNS AND VILLAGES –
IN WITH THE NEW

One of the most notable developments in the wake of John Cockburn's experimental village at Ormiston was the establishment of villages that were neither the old ferm touns of cottars and labourers, nor the clachans of Highland peasants, but planned communities of stone houses built along a main street or grouped around a market square. In the eighteenth century, more than a hundred were established, either by enlarging the existing nucleus of homes or by building on a 'green-field' site. They ranged geographically from Lybster and Sarclet in Caithness, which were established as fishing stations late in the century, to Cromarty which was planned as a renovated town in 1772, Tomintoul, the highest village in the country (1779), Thornliebank, now a suburb of Glasgow (1778), Moffat (late eighteenth century) and Port William in Wigtown (1770). Most were on the eastern side of the country, but there were some twenty or so in the area around Glasgow and a dozen in the southwest between Port William and Newcastleton on the border (1793). A few new villages were also created on the west coast, at Ullapool and Tobermory (1788), while Oban and Bowmore were built in the mid-century and Millport dates from late in the century. The process went on into the next century, with one of the last to be established being Edzell in 1839. Most remain today and the majority, despite later alterations and accretions, still have a touch of the eighteenth century about them.

Sometimes the new communities were established by landowners who wanted to create centres of consumption for local produce. Some landowners were concerned by the need to provide both accommodation and work for tenants who had been displaced by reorganisation of land-use from run-rig to the more efficient enclosed-field system. To provide suitable work was more difficult, and some villages were wretchedly poor. Others, like Fife Keith in Aberdeenshire, made linen or, especially in the south and the Perth-Angus area, became prosperous on cottage industries such as weaving. Some of the coastal settlements were built by the new British Fisheries Society to promote the fishing industry.

Landowners or official bodies were not the only developers. Communities such as New Lanark were set up, in this case by the Glasgow businessman David Dale with the acquiescence of the landowner, the notorious judge, Lord Braxfield, to take advantage of the water power generated by the River Clyde. Places like this became integrated industrial communities rather than rural villages. Much thought was given to the appearance of these villages. The Improvers were not impressed by the legacy of cottage-building in Scotland. Although each house in a new village still had an ample back garden, the front doors opened directly onto the pavement. The midden heap now had to go out of sight, along with the poultry. Cockburn, writing of Ormiston, shrewdly put his finger on a national trait: 'I can give my consent to no houses being built in the Main street of the town but what are two storys [sic] high . . . It is a common wise practice which proceeds from their wise heads and noble way of thinking in Scotland that if anything is made to look ugly, or if neat, is spoiled in dressing, it is thrift.' ['I insist that houses should be two storeys high if they are built in the main street of a town . . . The Scottish way of thinking is that if anything looks ugly, or is spoiled by skimpy work, it is praiseworthy thrift.']

Artist's impression of William Burnes and his family outside his cottage in Alloway, 1761. The building was typical of many one-storey dwellings of the time

The least successful villages were hamlets built in the 1760s by the Commissioners of the Forfeited Estates to house veteran soldiers. Of these, only Callander and Kinloch Rannoch survive. The substantial architecture of the new model villages did not displace more traditional styles. When people built their own houses, as they often did, they used cheap traditional materials and the buildings followed the plan of a traditional long, low, one-storey construction with byre and dwelling under the same roof. The house built by William Burnes in Alloway, in which his son Robert Burns was born in 1759, is typical of its kind.

THE JACOBITE UPRISING OF 1745

Against this background of change, development and improvement, the strange, tragic drama of the 1745 rising was played out. Jacobitism continued to be a diplomatic game played between the courts of Europe, useful to tweak the British government's tail. For the French at least, there was the

---

JACOBITE AND ANTI-JACOBITE ATTITUDES

Clan chiefs were often accused of ambivalence in their support of Jacobitism, and some, like Lord Lovat, had supported both sides in their time. Others were reputed to send one son to fight for King James and another to fight for King George. But sometimes the chief could not help himself. In 1715 the Duke of Atholl called up his men to fight for the Hanoverian government, and had to watch them march away under his son, the Marquis of Tullibardine, to fight for the Jacobites. Tullibardine returned for the campaigns of '19 and '45. His younger brother, James, became duke in 1724, and supported the government in the '45. His brother Lord George was the Prince's best commander. George's own son, John, was a captain in a government regiment, the 43rd Highlanders. Many other families were as divided as the Murrays.

There is no doubt that even pro-Hanoverian Scots were rather discomfited by finding a prince of the house of Stewart in their midst, especially one who promised to honour the status of the Presbyterian Church. They may have reflected that similar promises had been made, and broken, by his great-uncle to their great-grandfathers. But if they did not join the prince, they gave him a remarkably trouble-free passage through the country, and a pleasant sojourn in Edinburgh – a city unvisited by George I or George II.

implicit promise of the kind of support once given by the Auld Alliance, if they should choose to invade England. In 1744 it seemed that that might indeed happen, and Prince Charles Edward, son of the Old Pretender, was ready to land with ten thousand French troops. Bad weather and the presence of the Royal Navy in the English Channel prevented the expedition.

In August 1745 the Jacobite chiefs were horrified to discover that the Prince had landed near Arisaig with only seven companions, four thousand gold pieces and a modest quantity of weapons. They had always said that a rising would require six thousand troops, arms for four thousand more, and thirty thousand gold louis. Charles had first landed on the island of Eriskay where Macdonald of Boisdale advised him to go home. 'I am home,' said the Prince. Despite his charm and the romantic challenge of his arrival, the chiefs of Macdonald and MacLeod were not lured into the rising. But Donald Cameron of Lochiel was blandished into putting ancestral loyalty into effect. In front of seven hundred Camerons and two hundred others, the standard was raised at Glenfinnan on the Scottish mainland on 19 August 1745.

The Prince's impulse had taken the British government by surprise. In Scotland there were based scarcely fifteen hundred regular troops. With no Privy Council to provide an immediate response, the government reaction was slow and confused. Meanwhile, the Jacobite army marched smartly over Wade's military roads, through the Pass of Corrieyairack in Inverness-shire and on to the main route south to Perth. By 17 September, the Prince had entered a defenceless Edinburgh, although the castle was held by its Hanoverian garrison. A few days later, the Jacobites routed the government forces, a small army incompetently commanded by Sir John Cope, at Prestonpans. The Prince had by now gathered a formidable force, swelled by clansmen from Atholl and with an effective general in Lord George Murray. But even with Scotland apparently in his power, few joined him from south of the Highlands. And in the north, Duncan Forbes of Culloden, the Lord President of the Court of Session, had hurried back to his home and was spending his considerable influence successfully to keep the uncommitted northern clans out of the action. The Prince had published two manifestos; one for England ran, 'I am an Englishman and that is the first title I claim'; and one for Scotland declared, 'The Act of Union has reduced Scotland to being no more than an English province.' Neither convinced the uncommitted. As prosperity grew, hostility to the Union had been slipping from the Scottish agenda, and the tartan-clad Prince with his Gaelic-speaking army, clad in belted plaids (and behaving with considerable tact and discipline amid the temptations of the capital) was not merely unwelcome. Much worse than that, he was irrelevant.

Artist's impression of the Battle of Prestonpans in 1745

Knowing that the bulk of the English army was fighting on the Continent, the Jacobite commanders agreed to the Prince's demand to make a strike for England. He was confident of gathering support along the way and had written to his father promising that London would be in his hands by Christmas. By the time the army had reached Manchester, supposedly a centre of Jacobite enthusiasm, it was clear that there was virtually no active support to be had in England. The clan chiefs had never supposed that they alone would, or could, place the Stewarts back on the throne of England. They knew that two government armies were being prepared and that the Londoners, if panic-stricken, were also preparing a defence rather than a welcome. At Derby on 6 December, the furiously reluctant Prince was compelled to begin a retreat. Now the army of the Duke of Cumberland was in pursuit, but in a minor engagement at Clifton in the Lake District the Highlanders held them off. In a more serious battle outside Falkirk on 17 January 1746, General Hawley's army was defeated and fled, leaving their baggage and artillery to the victors. Again to the dismay of the Prince, the chiefs insisted on retreating farther into the Highlands. They promised to resume the campaign later, but their men wanted to get home with what they had by way of loot. With inexorable patience, the Hanoverian army plodded on after them. By April the Prince was in Inverness when news came that Cumberland was approaching with nine thousand men.

CULLODEN

The Jacobite army of five thousand men, tired and hungry, was drawn up on Drumossie Moor near Culloden House. At a late stage the Prince ordered a night attack on the government army, now encamped at Nairn, and celebrating Cumberland's twenty-fifth birthday. They failed to reach it before dawn, and the tired clansmen were led back up on to the moor. Lord George Murray, no longer in command following his dismissal by an imperious Charles Edward, later condemned this site as a hopeless place for a Highland battle. The chief adviser to the Prince was now his quartermaster, Colonel O'Sullivan.

On the bare moor the clansmen stood in ranks, their ardour cooling as the government cannon struck many of them down, before being ordered to charge on the rising slope. Poor tactics, the devastation of the cannonade and disciplined musketry ensured the defeat of the Highlanders. A sizeable body of clansmen escaped in the direction of Badenoch, but those who fled in the direction of Inverness and the west were caught and cut down.

Artist's impression of the aftermath of the Battle of Culloden, 1746

The aftermath of Culloden was very different from the relatively mild consequences of the 1715 rising. A large and victorious government army was in the heart of the Highlands and determined to make its presence felt. Those like Duncan Forbes of Culloden, who argued for clemency and restraint in the treatment of the defeated Highlanders, were given short shrift by the Duke of Cumberland and his advisers. The ferocity of the pursuit frightened some chiefs, like Glengarry, into blaming their clansmen; others, like Grant, handed their men over to the dragoons. The Prince was on the run through the West Highlands and the Isles for five months. He was closely protected, despite the huge reward on offer, and a bold French captain eventually managed to take him to safety. Even so, Prince Charles had some close shaves, including the episode when he dressed as the Irish maid of Flora MacDonald, the daughter of a government loyalist. Many of his followers were informed on or otherwise identified, arrested and imprisoned or shipped out to the colonies. One hundred and twenty men were executed after some form of trial; more were shot out of hand. It was not entirely English or German troops who carried out the orders to shoot and destroy. The Presbyterian and pro-Hanoverian clans played their part, as did many Scots from south of the Highland line.

THE HIGHLAND PROBLEM

London had been given a bad fright and had had enough of Jacobitism. To have the Highlands as a large redoubt of people with a separate language and culture was tiresome enough but for them to be a continuing military threat was intolerable. Cumberland's policy was analagous to that carried out in earlier centuries by English kings who saw the whole of Scotland in the same way that he viewed Gaeldom. But now many in the south of Scotland also saw with his eyes. Disarming the Highlands was only part of the intention. Clanship was to be stamped out. Visible evidence in the costume of the people was forbidden. The Gaelic language was now outlawed. The people were harried, bullied and victimised. The government took the opportunity to bring not only the Highland chiefs but also the Lowland lairds into the eighteenth century by passing the Act for Abolishing Heritable Jurisdictions. By this, the long-established Scottish institutions of the baron court and hereditary sheriffdom were stripped of their legal function and authority. What power a chief retained was determined purely by his own personal qualities, the inertia of tradition and, by no means least, the rights and status of a landowner. All this activity at many levels galvanised a process that was already under way.

Even before the 1745 rising, many clan chiefs had been moving more towards the role of landlord. The best-documented example – because the Dukes were largely absentee and had to communicate with their factors and agents by letter – was MacCailein Mòr, as the Duke of Argyll was known in the Highlands. His predecessors had greatly enlarged the original territory of the Campbells, to the detriment and long hostility of their neighbours. To guarantee security, Campbells were given tacks, that is, large tracts, of land in areas like Kintyre, Mull and Morvern, though sometimes they had to fight to hold them. From 1710 onwards, the second Duke of Argyll adopted a policy of selling tacks to the highest bidder. These were new leases rather than the traditional tack, with its provision for military service, and now carried with them instead the requirement to improve the land. The rents were raised considerably. New tenants concentrated on the rearing of cattle and sheep, which generated cash and required less work than cultivation. Sub-tenants or traditional inhabitants were moved out. Some other chiefs pursuing the same course sold their people as indentured labourers to the West Indies. Argyll's policy succeeded in raising money. But when the crisis of 1744 to 1746 arose, the Duke could no longer count on raising a Campbell army of its old size. His West Highland empire felt vulnerable. The third Duke, who became the political master of Scotland after the rising, reduced the rents in some cases to ensure that his main tenants were still 'people well-disposed to my interest'.

Farther north, the chief of MacKenzie, whose father, the fifth Earl of Seaforth, had forfeited his lands and title to the crown after the uprising of 1715 (his loyal tenants paying their rent to the exile as well as to the Commissioners of Forfeited Estates), was practising similar policies. MacKenzie stayed well clear of personal involvement in the uprising of 1745. In different ways, the Union drove these changes on. Even chiefs who did not feel the need to cut a figure in London still felt part of a changed world, one that ran on cash and bank drafts rather than on men and farm produce. Consequently there was already a drift of people from the Highlands, both voluntary and enforced. Many went overseas and others joined the host of beggars in Scotland. Only when the kelp industry began to become important and needed labour did the chiefs take an opposite view and begin to stem the departure of potential kelp gatherers and burners. When the kelp industry became obsolete in the following century, the chiefs reverted to former policy.

Many Jacobite leaders, like William Mackintosh of Borlum, who wrote a book on estate management while he was imprisoned in Edinburgh Castle, were involved in the process of Improvement. The Earl of Mar was an active manager of his coal mines and set up the glass industry in Alloa. Atavistic as their political and dynastic views might have been, the leaders of the rebellion shared the same expectations and economic ambitions as their fellow-countrymen. No one, other than the dream-court of the Pretender, gave much thought to matters like the Divine Right of Kings. Divested of sovereignty and, to a large extent, of participation in the political nation and possibly suffering a psychological wound which has never been fully articulated or explored, the non-Jacobite Scots in the post-Union period settled down to adopt a pragmatic, resolutely down-to-earth approach in all their undertakings, from philosophy to farming, from medicine to economics.

EDUCATIONAL REFORM

The result of this was a surge of intellectual energy. The universities began to reform their approach to teaching. The first Scottish university to change its approach to the traditional subjects was Edinburgh, guided by its reforming principal, William Carstares. Until now the system of regents had meant that one teacher taught a whole range of subjects to a group of pupils, often dealing with matters far beyond his own knowledge or competence. The importance of specialisation was now accepted, although change took place in a gradual manner throughout the century. Individual teachers, like Francis Hutcheson, professor of moral philosophy at Glasgow from 1730, imparted a questioning intelligence to their students. Theology was still supreme and the influence of the clergy was pervasive.

It prevented David Hume, Scotland's greatest philosopher, from occupying a professorial chair because he was an atheist, although it could not prevent him publishing his work. As Hume himself remarked, his *Treatise of Human Nature* 'fell deadborn from the Press' in 1739, but in the end its influence was to change the course of European philosophy. His *Essays, Moral and Political* and his *History of England* brought him fame in his own time. In Edinburgh also, the polymath Sir Robert Sibbald had established the College of Physicians in 1685 and the medical school grew strong with further finances provided by the city council (the university had after all had begun as the 'Toun's College'). The University of Glasgow also established a reputation for medicine, as well as doing pioneering work in physics and chemistry. It was the university that provided a haven for the young and gifted James Watt by appointing him its official instrument-maker when the Hammermen of Glasgow refused him admission to their guild.

Professors augmented their incomes by private teaching beyond the light requirements of their official posts. Latin was still an obligatory subject, and lectures in the humanities were given in Latin. The keenest proponents of the new pragmatism objected to this. The minister of Govan, William Thom, protested to Glasgow University in 1762 about the pointlessness of a classical education for 'a commercial people'. Such attitudes helped in the founding of the academies in provincial towns, of which Perth's was the first, in 1760. Perth already had its grammar school; the academy was intended as a substitute for the universities, providing a strong emphasis on science and commerce. Agitation for a similar institution in Glasgow and elsewhere prompted the universities to speed up development of their curriculum. Nevertheless, by the end of the century Anderson's University, with its focus on technical and practical subjects, had been founded in Glasgow. Other academies tended to merge with, as well as grow from, existing burgh grammar schools and did not compete with the centres of higher education.

Ever since the Reformation, and indeed before, the Scottish government had shown an interest in education. In the fifteenth century it was in order to develop a cadre who knew and could administer the law, in the families of the nobility. In the sixteenth century, the scope widened, partly because of the influence of Presbyterian theology – the intention was to make every man capable of reading the Bible. The ambition of establishing a school in every parish, often reiterated, lastly in 1689, was never achieved. Many parishes were too poor, or the laird too mean, to provide the necessary funds for a schoolhouse and schoolteacher, and the ambition had to be carried on into the eighteenth century to be achieved.

The basic salary of a teacher was low, although he might hope to supplement it by giving private lessons, and his status was not very high. A pre-Union pamphleteer made the point in 1704: 'There are in the kingdom near to one thousand parishes and in most of them Latine is pretended to be taught, though not one of fifty of the School-masters is capable to teach it:

SIR JOHN SINCLAIR AND
THE STATISTICAL ACCOUNT OF SCOTLAND

Sir John Sinclair of Ulbster (1754–1835) was born in Thurso Castle, and grew up to be one of the many eminent men of his time who saw no difficulty in reconciling their Scottish and British identities. He studied at Edinburgh, Glasgow and Oxford, was MP for Caithness in 1780, and for Lostwithiel in Cornwall from 1784 to 1811. He qualified in law in both Scotland and England. An ardent advocate of progress, he was the first President of the Board of Agriculture, from 1793 to 1798 and again from 1803 to 1816, and initiated new methods of tillage, sheep-shearing and new livestock breeds. He was the moving spirit and supervisor of the many volumed *Statistical Account of Scotland*, produced from 1791 to 1799, a more or less detailed account of every parish, compiled with the help of parish ministers, and an immensely rich source of information on the period. His many interests extended to economics – he wrote in 1784 *A History of the Revenue of the British Empire* – and town planning, which he put into practice by laying out the town of Thurso. An imposing full-length portrait of him was made by Sir Henry Raeburn.

And no wonder, for not one of fifty of them was tolerably taught it.' Later in the century, Robert Burns commented critically on university graduates – perhaps with a hint of jealousy for the college education his poverty had denied him:

> 'A set o' dull, conceited hashes
> Confuse their brains in college classes;
> They gang in stirks [calves], and come out asses,
> Plain truth to speak . . .'

However patchy the education was in places and however incompetent the teachers, Scotland, although not a rich country, was one of the very few countries in Europe to have, by the eighteenth century, a complete educational structure that extended from the village school to the university. At the elementary stage, it was open to all. Its openness, even in the higher stages, is attested by the pamphlet already quoted, which protests that it is easier for 'Mechanicks and the poorer sort of people' to put their sons to the university than to apprentice them to a worthwhile trade.

Education, although it had to be paid for, was relatively cheap, and a bag of oatmeal was the staple diet for a term for many students from the country. The age of entering university was still very young; the age group of the undergraduates was from fourteen to eighteen. Entry to the university was a relatively democratic affair, but some of the faculties could be more exclusive. Law and medicine were difficult, if not impossible, for those who had not some claim to be of the gentry, because of professional closed-shop practices. The Church and schoolmastering were more open. And none of this, of course, was for women. The daughters of the poor learned what they might from brothers or relatives; those who had wealthier parents had to be taught privately.

At all levels there was a new thirst for learning. Improved typesetting and printing made books cheaper and more readable, and they were being published in great numbers. By the 1760s even small country towns like Irvine had a bookshop, and by the mid-1780s it was possible for a rural poet such as Robert Burns to arrange for the publication of his own book in Kilmarnock. The greatest demand was for information and practical guidance, especially on gardening, medicine, science, religion and history. There were many other topics of popular interest, such as *The Oeconomy of Love*, published in London by Dr John Armstrong in 1736, which was a manual for newly-weds written in verse. In 1768 William Smellie began publication of the *Encyclopaedia Britannica* in Edinburgh; its aim, borrowed from France, was to provide a conspectus of all knowledge on all subjects.

POPULATION GROWTH AND ITS EFFECTS

In the course of the eighteenth century, the Scottish population grew rapidly. It was a young country. A succession of new, larger, more youthful and zestful generations served to expand the domestic market and to keep up the momentum for doing things better and differently. In 1755 Dr Alexander Webster published the first attempt to make a scientific census of the population and estimated it at 1,265,000 – perhaps a quarter more than at the Union. The first official census of 1801 put the Scottish population at 1,608,000.

The growth in numbers helped to drive the efficiency of agriculture forward, and perhaps also explains why, among the majority of the population, meat-eating was a rarity. Cereals were the staple food. The work of the early eighteenth-century Improvers now paid off handsomely for their sons and grandsons. Not without reluctance and local resistance, tenants were persuaded or compelled to abandon the old companionable but restrictive co-operation of run-rig farming and to sign leases for longer term use of land. Enclosed by dry-stone dykes and managed according to the best scientific advice, the new fields produced a greater return per acre and crops that were of a better quality. Vegetables that had once been a luxury, such as turnips and potatoes – one visitor to Scotland had claimed that turnip was served as a dessert – were now major crops to be found everywhere, including the Western Isles. The majority of Scottish farms remained small family concerns that preserved a tradition of mutual assistance at harvest time. In Lothian and the Merse of Tweed, larger farms began to depend on seasonal migrant labour – often girls from the Highlands. Work of this kind also of-

---

SCOTTISH SLAVE-TRADERS

S lave-trading was a major industry through the late seventeenth and all of the eighteenth century. Slaves were transported and sold from Africa to the West Indies, and as the southern cotton industry of the United States grew, often sold on from Jamaica and other Caribbean islands to Georgia. The major centre was Bristol, but Glasgow and Greenock both engaged in the slave trade in a minor way. As early as 1710, Negro slaves were imported into Virginia by vessels like the *George* of Glasgow and the *Isabella* of Greenock. There is no record of Scots families having black slaves, as was common in Bristol and London. During the early 1740s, at a time of famine, with many people on the roads, boys and young men were snatched up by slaving gangs, shipped off and sold to North American plantation owners.

---

fered periodic earnings to the nomadic semi-gypsy communities of the Borders, composed of dispossessed, disadvantaged and professionally vagrant Scots. The number of true Romanies was very small. Despite the better yields, food prices rose steadily through the later decades of the century. Even on the farms, few people ate meat unless it came from an animal that had dropped dead of old age or disease. Meat was for export and for the wealthy.

Growing numbers of children, although fewer than half of them were eligible for education, meant that the burgh councils expanded their grammar schools and looked around for more teachers. Councils were increasingly conscious of the need to have a working population of people who could count, who could write clearly and who could write in foreign languages, and who could acquire the new skills of navigation and engine-maintenance. Only by this could growth be assured. If the Scottish burghs could afford to pay for this knowledge, it was because their own commerce was growing quickly. In turn, business attracted more people – economic migrants from the fading, unprogressive burghs or from the ever more enclosed and intensively farmed countryside.

GLASGOW'S INFLUENCE ON ADAM SMITH

Glasgow was expanding at a great rate and was already the main centre of trade and industry. Cotton and tobacco were basic to the economy. They were imported raw, processed and re-exported at a profit to all involved. Tobacco imports tripled between 1755 and 1771, and in the latter year accounted for just over half of Scotland's total export value. Tobacco money financed the growth of merchant banking, which in turn sustained new and growing industries. The British Linen Company was established in 1746 to help finance the linen industry. Smaller country towns like Perth and Ayr also set up banks. The bank in Ayr collapsed in 1772 but was finally able to pay off its obligations. Scottish entrepreneurs were moving into uncharted waters. The 'tobacco lords' of Glasgow became very rich very fast, and when the American War of Independence came, cutting off the flow of tobacco, they faced collapse. But many were also dealing in cotton and sugar and exporting coal, linens, ale and coarse cloth and the city's growth triumphed over the catastrophe. Amidst the fever of this active business practice, a great theorist was making observations and deductions.

Adam Smith, born in Kirkcaldy, had been a student of Hutcheson at Glasgow University and wrote on logic and morality as a philosopher. From 1751 to 1764 he was a professor at Glasgow, first of logic then of moral philosophy, and his great work was intended as the first part of a massive treatise encom-

THE METAMORPHOSIS OF GLASGOW

Well into the eighteenth century, and even although it was already a manufacturing town, Glasgow won the praise of visitors for its beauty and cleanliness. Its orderly and regular layout, around the main cross-roads, and dominated by its spired cathedral, pleased the eye. Around 1700, Daniel Defoe described it as 'the cleanest and beautifulest city in Britain, London excepted.' A few years later, his fellow-Englishman Burt called it 'the prettiest and most uniform town I ever saw, and I believe there is nothing like it in Britain.' Smollett's character Jerry Melford, in *Humphrey Clinker*, writes 'Glasgow is the pride of Scotland, and indeed it might well pass for an elegant and flourishing city in any part of Christendom.' That was published in 1771. Such comments make a stark contrast with the remarks made on the state of the city centre by the 1840s, by which time it was the most notorious slum in Great Britain.

passing philosophy, politics and law, all as elements of moral philosophy. His first lectures, *The Theory of Moral Sentiments*, which were published in 1759, underlie his later economic theories. With the publication of *The Wealth of Nations* in 1776, Adam Smith established the modern science of political economy. Smith and Hume were the two figures of world stature who emerged in the Scottish Enlightenment of the mid-eighteenth century.

CITIES AND INDUSTRY

The two main cities developed rapidly, particularly in the second half of the century. The Edinburgh occupied by the Highlanders in 1745 was still the Old Town, its tenements clinging to the spine of the Castle Hill and surrounded by a clutch of subordinate townships. In 1767 a master plan for a completely new section of Edinburgh was begun. This was the New Town, a regularly planned grid of streets, squares and circuses to the north of the Castle Rock. Fashionable Edinburgh decamped there as soon as the houses were built, leaving the old social mix, the odours and the intimacies of tenement life for ever. The Old Town fell into decay, its rents went down, its buildings were neglected and it became the home of the poor. Lawyers still went to the Old Town to conduct their business in Parliament House, and the area of the High Street, with the Town Cross and St Giles, remained the heart of the city, but the character of the city was dramatically changed.

Glasgow by the 1760s was no longer a country town but a centre of indus-

When the inhabitants of the Old Town of Edinburgh wanted to expel waste from their homes they would shout 'Gardy Loo!' (taken euphemistically from the French, gardez l'eau) and throw it out of the window on to the street below. This goes some way to explain the noxious contents of the Nor Loch (later drained to become Princes Street Gardens).

Illustration by William Hole from the Book of Old Edinburgh, 1886

try growing at a rate that would bring its population to rival Edinburgh by the end of the century. Changes in Glasgow were not the result of mere growth; the community transformed itself in the face of completely new conditions. There was no yardstick to measure by. In 1750 it was a matter of note that a silversmith and a haberdasher had set up in new buildings by Glasgow Cross. Such sophistication was breathtakingly new. Twenty-five years later, Glasgow was one of the most opulent cities in Great Britain, with any number of shops, and streets of handsome new houses to rival those of Edinburgh. The River Clyde had been dredged and made deep enough to bring seagoing vessels right up to the first bridge. In and around the city were the works, the bleaching greens and the mines that fuelled their growth. Glasgow employers advertised widely for workers, and every day they arrived, trudging in from the country, wearing their peasant greys, with blue Scotch bonnets, packs on their backs, looking in apprehension or wonder at the future.

Yet industry, by now widespread throughout urban and rural Scotland, was still on a small and mostly domestic scale. The New Lanark mills, which had been preceded by a water-powered mill established at Rothesay in 1779, were an indication of the growing demand for power generation of the later eighteenth century. The pace of invention and adaptation of inventions was increasing rapidly. Carron Ironworks were established at Falkirk in 1759 and were among the first large factories of their kind in Europe. The sight of their steams and smokes suggested to Robert Burns a vision of Hell.

The cotton industry, well established by the time that the crisis in the tobacco trade came, was built on the experience and skills gained in making good-quality linens. The spinning and weaving of cotton in large quantities were improved by importing technology already developed in Lancashire, and also in France, into Glasgow and Dunfermline. The new technology could be applied in large-scale and cottage-scale work. By 1795, nearly thirty-nine thousand handloom weavers were at work in Scotland. The industry grew even more in the nineteenth century, when steam power increased output and reduced the work force. But by then cottons were just one sector of a wide variety of industrial activities which even in 1795 could scarcely have been anticipated.

THE LEGACY OF THE UNION

In the later eighteenth century, nobody argued that the Union of Parliaments had brought no advantages to Scotland. Prince Charles Edward Stewart died in 1788, his only child an illegitimate daughter. His brother, though he took the title of Henry IX, was a cardinal in the Roman Catholic Church and had no conceivable chance of supplanting even such a peculiar king as George III. Jacobitism was dead and would soon be a safe subject for nostalgia.

For many leaders of opinion in Scotland, the encouraged trend was assimilation, to English speech, English practices and English ideas. Prejudices and attitudes formed in England over many centuries had not gone away in 1707, and for many years Scots arriving in London found that they were regarded as members of a rough and even semi-barbaric community, something the alarm and the fright generated in 1745 did nothing to dispel. The reaction of the Scots was to seek conformity. Elocution teachers taught the niceties of English diction. In the *Edinburgh Review*, Alexander Wedderburn wrote: 'The memory of our ancient state is not so much obliterated, but that, by comparing the past with the present, we may clearly see the superior advantages we now enjoy, and readily discern from what source they flow.' Although mocked and resisted by many, this subservience and sense of apology for being Scottish, so well summed up in the first exchange between James Boswell of Auchinleck and Dr Samuel Johnson –

Boswell: 'I do indeed come from Scotland, but I cannot help it.'
Johnson: 'That, sir, I find is what a very great many of your fellow-countrymen cannot help.'

– was to sap and shrink the self-confidence of Scotland's ruling class even as the country grew wealthier than it had ever been.

The nobility and country gentry became firmly Unionist in their sympathies, and since they still exercised not merely influence but a degree of power, their attitudes were widely imitated, even by those who could not afford to send their sons to be educated in England or aspire to marry into the English nobility. The power of the gentry was expressed chiefly by their monopoly of the parliamentary vote in landward (non-burgh) areas, and their local responsibilities as Commissioners of Supply, a function established in 1667 with the prime purpose of raising and distributing the land tax or 'cess'.

POWER AND PATRONAGE

The third Duke of Argyll's management of Scottish affairs on behalf of the London government ended with his death, in 1761. His dominance was emulated ten years later when the role was taken over by Henry Dundas, member of parliament for Midlothian from 1790 and a member of a prominent legal family. Suave and clever, Dundas was not a political thinker but an expert fixer, and he ran Scotland smoothly in the Tory interest for three decades. At the age of twenty-four, in 1766, he was Solicitor-General for Scotland. The role of Secretary of State had been abolished after 1745, and his position was that of Lord Advocate, then Lord President of the Board of Control of the East India Company. Dundas held this position between 1775 and 1783. He took other official roles besides, as Keeper of the Signet (1782) and Keeper of the Privy Seal (1800), and after his retirement he was impeached for 'gross malversation and breach of duty' as treasurer of the Royal Navy.

Dundas's great weapon in the mangement of Scotland was patronage. He had the responsibility of appointing men to public office. These positions were often sinecures, such as that of Controller of Customs, a position given to Adam Smith, but even arduous minor posts, like the Excise job of Robert Burns, were part of the system. The radically minded Burns had to grovel to his superiors in order to keep his position in the witch-hunting atmosphere of 1792. Posts in the East India Company, so useful for younger sons, were also handed out by Dundas. Far more 'Henry the Ninth' than the Stewart cardinal in far-off Rome, Dundas presided over a network of political jobbery.

THE ELECTORAL SYSTEM

The entire country had only two thousand or so voters to choose its forty-five representatives to parliament in Westminster. In the counties, where the criterion to obtain a vote was to own property worth forty shillings in the days of Alexander II (worth around £130 by this time), electors were almost always landowners or their selected supporters, who were given artificial feudal superiorities, or titles to land ownership, to enable them to vote. Apart from Edinburgh, which elected its own member of parliament, burghs were grouped together to elect their members. Each town council appointed a delegate, and the four or five delegates met to elect their candidate. Since town councils were formed on the principle that the retiring council could choose the next, any element of popular democracy in the whole system was purely accidental.

Under the Duke of Argyll, the Scottish members of parliament had been Whig to a man; under Dundas, forty-three out of forty-five were Tories. Political appointees included jurymen, and Whig plaintiffs or advocates tended to lose a high proportion of their cases. The most vocal political opponents of Dundas were the Whig lawyers, led by Henry Erskine, Dean of the Faculty of Advocates, who in 1796 lost his office for attending a Whig demonstration. It showed the degree of firmness with which Dundas controlled the country in a time when the authorities were fearful of the French Revolution and its possible repercussions. It was a time in the wider world when the most extreme political ideas were not only discussed but put into effect – but there was very little unrest in Scotland. America fought for and won its independence. Ireland agitated furiously for its own parliament. Sir Horace Walpole voiced the fear, 'I shall not be surprised if our whole trinity is dissolved, and if Scotland should demand a dissolution of the Union. Strange if she alone does not profit of our distress.' Walpole underestimated the degree to which assimilation had sunk in. In fact, the crack-down imposed on radical ideas was aided by a general fear of revolution that silenced even those who knew the system was rotten. Lord Cockburn recorded, 'Even in private society, a Whig was viewed somewhat as a Papist was in the days of Titus Oates.'

In the first years of the 1790s, anyone who ventured to utter criticism of the government or to suggest radical views could be arrested, imprisoned, possibly deported to the colonies or sentenced with an unjudicial relish by Lord Braxfield: 'Ye're a fine chiel, but ye'll be nane the waur o' a hanging'. A memorial on Calton Hill in Edinburgh was erected in memory of the political martyrs of 1793 and 1794. It still looks down towards the fine Roman-style column in St Andrew's Square, erected by a grateful nation to Henry Dundas, first Lord Melville.

THE CHURCH AND ITS RESPONSIBILITIES

The Church of Scotland, the affairs of which had preoccupied the country for most of the previous century and the status of which was guaranteed by the Treaty of Union, was no longer the storm-centre of national life. Its status was assured, and although Presbyterians were angry when the government reintroduced lay patronage in 1712, another breach of the Treaty and contributing to the general sense of dissatisfaction surrounding the 1715 uprising, opposition became no more than a ritualised protest at successive General Assemblies. The Kirk still remained a dominant element in national life. It was an adjunct to the civil government and took its responsibilities in the sphere of morality seriously. The kirk session still judged the morals of its parishioners and despite two centuries of Presbyterianism still managed to find much to condemn. As the body responsible for education in Scotland, the Kirk took a strong supervisory stance at every level.

Another significant responsibility was the administration of charity. The demise of the Catholic Church and the accompanying devaluation of the concept of good works meant that the Scottish kingdom had no one to rely on for necessary acts of charity and support for the destitute. Even before the Reformation there had been efforts to restrict the definition of beggars, for example, by disallowing anyone between the age of fourteen and seventy. Attempts were also made to confine the poor to their native parishes. The determinism – the idea that all events were the will of God – of Calvinism did not necessarily encourage people to give charity to the unfortunate, but in Scotland the poor had always existed and there was a tradition of rudimentary care to those in need, linked to punishment and violent assault on those who appeared to abuse that care.

In 1579 an act had been passed that placed responsibility for the administration of the care of beggars on municipal officials in the burghs, and on King's Justices who were to oversee the welfare of beggars in country areas. These latter did not exist, and when appointed thirty years later, did not attempt to fulfil the act of 1579. All those in need were forced back on the resources of their own families or on to the charity of others, who were often hard-pressed themselves. During periods of famine in the seventeenth century, the Privy Council had tried with very limited success to tax burghs and parishes to support beggars. The destitute were to be kept in jails wherever possible, but many burghs and parishes did not have jails, while others had jails that were far too small to cope with the victims of poverty. In the eighteenth century it remained a local responsibility to deal with beggary, destitution, orphaned children, foundlings and lunatics. Records are sparse, but it is clear that some parishes behaved with greater generosity or had greater resources than others. Most kirk sessions had some funds to assist travelling beggars and to speed them on their way to someone else. More concern was shown to those of their own who fell into hardship. The power of the session may have had some beneficial results in compelling accidental fathers to pay for the upkeep of their illegitimate children. The central authorities continued to issue orders and advice, but not assistance, on issues of charity. For all the efforts at organisation, the care of the very poor was a matter of chance. Into the nineteenth century, vagrant bands preferred to live outside the system, on the proceeds of begging, seasonal labour, poaching and the lifting of movable objects.

Opposition to patronage kept the Kirk in an apparent anti-government stance, which concealed the extent to which patronage was actually used by the government to keep control, and prevent the Assembly debating subjects unwelcome to it, whether the need for higher stipends or some political topic. In the 1750s, the influence of a 'Moderate' party began to assert itself against such interference by government. Efforts of the Moderate party to treat with the government on equal terms brought the Kirk into varying degrees of accord with the 'governments' of Argyll and Dundas. These set them against a 'Popular' party in the Kirk, which was more aligned politically with the Whigs. The leaders of the Moderates, like Hugh Blair, one of the most popular preachers of the time, and William Robertson, a widely read historian and principal of Edinburgh University, were associated with the Enlightenment. They were also familiar with the English scene, where the established Church was a torpid, comfortable refuge for many a cleric more interested in the world than in the niceties of doctrine. The Moderates sought to tone down some of the severer aspects of Calvinist moral doctrine, if only by their example. Some of them openly attended the theatre, which was not an activity approved by the Kirk.

Even in the earlier part of the eighteenth century, the Kirk had endured the opening of a purpose-built theatre in Edinburgh, and the opening of the first circulating library by Allan Ramsay, whose collection of books by no means stopped at the good and godly. There was a strong censorial element among the ministers, who sensed that a trend in society for the enjoyment of secular, not to say profane, culture would in time erode the hold of the Kirk on the Scottish people. Tensions remained within the Kirk, both political and doctrinal, sharpened by further disputes on the subject of patronage. Increasingly, however, the Kirk was becoming an observer of events and not an active participant.

THE REVIVAL OF LITERATURE

An independent literary culture, which had been almost eradicated in the seventeenth century, gradually crept back. Creative writing played a very secondary part in terms output to the torrent of information. The level of achievement in poetry was not high. Those who wrote in Scots were rustic and provincial, those who wrote in English were frankly artificial. Nevertheless, Allan Ramsay, himself a poet of talent, reintroduced some of the great poets of earlier centuries in *The Evergreen* of 1724. Another most useful service was performed by those who, like David Herd, collected and published songs from the oval tradition. His *Scots Songs* was published in 1776. Tobias Smollett, trained as a doctor in Glasgow, where he graduated in 1739, moved to England and became a celebrated novelist. His work, though influential in the development of the English novel, has little connection with Scotland, except for some interesting descriptions of Glasgow in *The Expedition of Humphrey Clinker* (1771).

Between 1760 and 1763 a great stir was caused in literary circles by the publication of *Fragments of Ancient Poetry Collected in the Highlands*, purporting to be ancient Gaelic poems by the legendary hero Ossian, translated into English. The 'translator', who claimed to have discovered the poems, was James Macpherson, from Kingussie. The poems were to some extent based on Gaelic ballads, with considerable additions of what the eighteenth-century mind felt to be authentic Celtic sentiments and characters. Macpherson was widely suspected to be a forger, but the impact of his poems in Europe helped to create the Romantic movement, and also led to changes in perception of the Highlands, as a well from which the country's ancient traditions could be extracted, like pure water. Controversy raged about the authenticity of Ossian, but within Scotland the most influential imaginative writer was Henry Mackenzie, whose sentimental novel *The Man of Feeling* (1771) had an enormous impact, making a whole generation of readers reach for their handkerchiefs, and made him the leader of literary Edinburgh.

THE TWO ALLAN RAMSAYS

Ramsay senior (1686–1758) was brought up at Leadhills, where his father was supervisor for the landowner. He was first apprenticed to an Edinburgh wig-maker, but set up a bookshop in 1719 and opened his library in 1728. His establishments were centres of liberated thought after the somewhat arid cultural life of seventeenth-century Edinburgh. The orthodox, of course, regarded them as snake pits, but Ramsay had many customers and supporters. Edinburgh was already a clubbable place, and the Easy Club not only provided him with a group of like-minded people but also published Ramsay's poems, both original and collected. His pastoral drama, *The Gentle Shepherd*, was very successful, and Ramsay added to the new genres of poetry as well as resuscitating the poets of the past. Allan Ramsay senior played a part in most of Edinburgh's developing cultural life; he attempted to set up the first theatre, and was one of the founders of the Academy of St Luke, dedicated to improving the art of painting. His son, Allan (1713–1784), showed early promise as an artist, and his father was able to send him to London, Rome and Naples to perfect his technique. From 1738 Ramsay junior established himself in London and became a celebrated and influential portrait painter, but he did not abandon his links with Edinburgh, where in 1754 he founded the Select Society, a debating club of the choicer intellects of the Edinburgh Enlightenment.

*Sketch of Robert Burns
based on the portrait by Alexander Nasmyth*

*Artist's impression of the Kilmarnock Edition
of Burns poems, published in July 1786*

The creative genius of the century, Robert Burns, owed nothing to the literary views of Edinburgh. His range of poetic expression, extending from tender lyricism to patriotic fervour and from humour to biting satire, fully entitled him to the appellation of National Bard, which was awarded by popular acclaim after his death in debt and poverty in 1796. Burns's work had a powerful impact in different ways. After the publication of *Holy Willie's Prayer*, there were many, apart from the poem's highly identifiable victim, whose extravagant piety was played in a lower key. People could pick on various themes from his verse, but two of the most distinctive were his passionate feeling for Scotland and his political radicalism. Burns also contributed to the tradition of David Herd by not only gathering but recasting traditional songs which, often fragmentary in the original, he would restore with his own version, in a rare instance of restoration becoming a major improvement on the original.

ARTISTS AND ARCHITECTS

The eighteenth century, and the early years of the nineteenth, revealed a new facet of Scottish creativity in the work of some remarkable painters and architects. The painting tradition was not of long standing, and the artists could look back to no Scottish equivalent of the 'makars' in poetry. George Jamesone, who began work in Aberdeen before transferring to Edinburgh, in the 1620s, is the starting point. The roots of Scottish painting are to be found in Holland, and a Dutch influence predominates in works of the seventeenth and early eighteenth centuries. When Holyrood Palace was redecorated, a Dutch artist, Jan de Witt, had been brought in to paint his notion of the Scottish kings. In 1729 Scotland's first art institution, the Academy of St Luke, was established in Edinburgh by a group of artists. From this circle emerged Scotland's first great painter, Allan Ramsay, son of the poet-librarian of the same name and a portraitist of exceptional quality. His contemporary, Gavin Hamilton, who lived mostly in Rome, widened the Scots artists' field of vision while often depicting Scottish themes, including a cycle of paintings inspired by the Ossian poems for Penicuik House in 1772, which have since been destroyed. Ramsay left Edinburgh for the richer clients of London, but a strong school of painters was now established, among them Ramsay's pupil Alexander Nasmyth, who eventually abandoned portraits for landscape painting.

A new portrait painter of genius appeared in Henry Raeburn who, though tempted to leave Scotland, decided to remain in Edinburgh and spent his working life there. He left a magnificent series of portraits of Scottish society — intellectual, military and clerical personages and members of the landed gentry. Raeburn worked on until his death in 1823, and his later work prefigures Romantic painting. But the work of his maturity, bright, clear, precise in its detail of satins and tartans, genial and profound in its vision, exemplifies the best of the Scottish Enlightenment, as does the work of Robert and James Adam.

The Adam brothers were innovators in architecture. Their father, William Adam, had already established the family name in building design and held official positions as Clerk of Works and Mason to the Board of Ordnance in North Britain, which gave him contracts to build fortifications after the rising of 1745. He designed and built Haddo House in 1732, influenced by

---

FIRST THEATRE IN EDINBURGH

Allan Ramsay opened the first play-house in 1736, in Carrubber's Close, which was immediately closed down by the city magistrates. Plays were put on in the Taylor's Hall, and to get round the lack of a licence, were advertised as being given free after a concert. Music would begin and end the evening, and the play would be performed in between. Many Presbyterians were scandalised in 1756 when the minister of Athelstaneford, John Home, had his tragedy of *Douglas* performed, with several brother ministers in the audience. Home later resigned from the pulpit in order to become a full-time author. It was 1764 before the authorities, encouraged by the 'Moderates' in the Church of Scotland, accepted that people would not be deterred from playgoing and gave a licence for a theatre.

SCEPTICISM v COMMON SENSE

It is an irony of Scottish intellectual history that, after the millions of words expended on theology, the country's greatest philosopher should have been a convinced and open atheist. David Hume (1711–76) developed the ideas of Francis Hutcheson (1694–1746) and the English philosophers Locke and Berkeley to a point which, in the view of some, brought philosophy virtually to an end. He did not share the common belief that the universe could be understood by reasoning, and demonstrated in his *Treatise of Human Nature* (1739–40) that the senses and the imagination are the only, though imperfect, tools we have to make sense of our existence. The *Treatise* was slow to achieve recognition. Hume achieved more fame with his *History of England*, and more notoriety with his *Dialogues Concerning Natural Religion*. In this he demonstrated that the concept of divinity is beyond human proof and criticised the notion of 'blind faith'. Hume's 'Science of Man' was intended to provide a basis for an ethical and progressive society, and its ideas were further developed by Adam Smith (1723–90) in *The Wealth of Nations* and the *Theory of Moral Sentiments*. The scepticism of Hume seemed extreme and alarming to the eighteenth century. Within Scotland a 'Common Sense' school of philosophy developed in reaction, led by Thomas Reid (1710–1796) and maintained in Edinburgh by Dugald Stewart (1753–1828). This sought to rescue God and the traditional values from the Sceptics. It lacked the rigour of Hume's thought, but was seized on, with relief, in the universities of Scotland, as well as becoming influential in England and the United States. Hume's ideas were diluted or ignored in his own country. They were seized on, analysed and developed outside Scotland, most notably by the German philosopher Immanuel Kant, who was himself descended from Scottish immigrants.

designs from James Gibbs' *Book of Architecture*, published some four years earlier. Robert and James generated a style of architecture that was classical and European, bringing a more romantic and decorative touch to the Palladian style and with as much attention to decoration of the interior as the outside appearance. The oval shape characterises many aspects of their work, as in the oval staircase at Culzean Castle. Buildings like Register House in Edinburgh testify to their ability.

At the same time, the Jacobite expatriate Charles Cameron was designing similar buildings of exquisite charm for the Russian Empress Catherine, the most famous of which was the palace of Tsarskoye Selo near St Petersburg. In a whole range of intellectual and artistic fields, Scotland was showing itself to be no longer an importer but a creator and innovative adapter and exporter of ideas within the mainstream of European art and thought.

The Nineteenth Century: Part 1

EMPIRE AND REFORM

The era of assimilation to the Union merged gradually with a period when Union and Empire were accomplished facts. Throughout the nineteenth century, the great majority of Scots were enthusiastic makers and maintainers of the British Empire. Assimilation had been led by the aristocracy, and did not spread down the social scale. Yet imperialism was widespread at every level and was not necessarily related to any urge to imitate the manners or mores of the English. It was a thoroughly Scottish imperialism, founded on three main bases.

SCOTS IMPERIALISM

The first basis of Scottish imperialism was trade. With North America and the West Indies already major trading partners, Scottish merchants also now turned their attention to Africa and the Far East. Trading links with the Empire were established early, during the time of Henry Dundas as chairman of a committee on Indian Affairs in 1781. This led to his responsibility for drafting the India Bill in 1784, which confirmed British government in India. Subsequently he was appointed president of the Board of Control in 1793, which supervised trade to India. India became an area to which younger sons of trusty Tory land-owning and merchant families were sent to maintain British interests.

Then there was the army. Scotland, especially Highland Scotland, which was still quite densely populated, had become a prime recruiting ground for the British army. Many new regiments were raised. From the time of the American War of Independence (1765–88), Scots troops were in the front line of extension and defence of Empire.

Emigration on a large scale also extended the scope of Scottish imperialism although its effect became more apparent later. Although much of this was to the already independent USA, at least half of the emigrant Scots

RECRUITMENT IN THE HIGHLANDS

The resentments and evil memories of the immediate post-Culloden period took some time to dwindle away, and, indeed, still colour Scots thinking. But by the 1780s a new generation had grown up. Protestant clans had long provided soldiers, and now the ex-Jacobite clans joined. Even before the restoration of Highland dress in 1782 and the return of forfeited estates in 1784, the process of recruiting Highlanders in large numbers for the British army had begun. The American War of Independence and the French wars which followed created a continuing demand for infantry soldiers. The dukes of Argyll, Atholl, and Gordon raised regiments, as did the earl of Seaforth and Cameron of Lochiel. The naval press gangs also took their share, round the coast and in the islands, in collaboration with lairds who received a bounty on each man supplied. Many thousands joined the colours each year, over a period of some thirty years. Often part of the inducement was that land-holdings would be made available to returning servicemen. The frequent dishonouring of such promises added to the bitterness of the clearance years that were to come.

sailed for places which still flew the British flag. By the end of the nineteenth century, there were few families who did not possess relatives in Canada, South Africa or New Zealand. All this made the empire seem an extension of the homeland. Scots participated in the pomp and ceremony of Empire. Durbars and processions, victory parades and festivities for the birthday of Queen Victoria rarely took place without the sound of Highland bagpipes. But the Empire's most immediate significance to most people was a great diaspora of ordinary Scots, willing and unwilling, uprooted from their native soil, who brought their Scottishness to new lands, and in the first generations at least, preserved contact with their relatives at home.

There was also an important fourth dimension to Scottish imperialism. The awareness of vast land areas inhabited by peoples who knew nothing of Christianity reawakened a strong Presbyterian missionary zeal that had lain dormant or frustrated since the failure of the Solemn League and Covenant to convert the English. Now the process of combined exploration and evangelisation began which was to culminate in a strong Scottish emphasis on religion and education in East Central Africa, and in twentieth-century Presidents of newly independent African states, like Kenneth Kaunda and Hastings Banda, being elders of the Church of Scotland. Many Scots in the nineteenth century contributed funds to the missionary effort and followed its progress with keen interest.

THE WORKING POPULATION

In 1801 the first government census of Scotland took place and established a population figure of 1,608,000. This was a great increase on earlier estimates and the rate of population growth was surging up ever faster. The distribution of population was changing, with a shift towards the central area caused by inward migration from the Highlands and Islands, and from Ireland. The population of Glasgow at the turn of the century was in the region of one hundred thousand people and was for the first time greater than that of Edinburgh – and the city was still expanding. By 1911, Glasgow's population, 101,000 in 1811, would exceed a million. This growth inaugurated the half-friendly rivalry between the two main cities. Edinburgh had dominated Scotland in every way for so long, that for it to be toppled from its supremacy both in population and industry, was something of a shock.

In 1811 nearly twenty per cent of the population of Scotland lived in the eight largest towns. The population of the Highlands and Islands was still rising, sustained by the annual potato crops, the kelp industry, soldier's pay and by seasonal migratory labour, often from farm-girls, in the south, especially Lothian. At this time, Highland landowners discouraged emigration if they had coastal estates where labour was needed to cut the seaweed or kelp. The surplus of young men was absorbed by the army, and the landowner, who received a bounty for each man supplied, ensured that they went.

The growing demand for more power to operate larger and more complex machinery resulted in great efforts to improve the power and efficiency of steam engines. The booming economy during the Napoleonic Wars of 1800 to 1815 required many goods that Scotland could supply, from cloth for uniforms to ropes, from coal and pig iron to manpower. The transition to an

---

THOMAS TELFORD, CIVIL ENGINEER

In his autobiography, Telford wrote: 'In the year 1782 after having acquired the rudiments of my profession, I considered that my native country offered few opportunities of practising it to any extent and therefore judged it advisable (like many of my countrymen) to proceed southward, where industry might find more employment and be better rewarded.'

Installed in London, Telford made a point of keeping one or two promising young 'raw Scotchmen' in his office, one of whom was Joseph Mitchell, who later became the projector and engineer of the Highland Railway.

industry-based economy, largely accomplished by the end of the eighteenth century, developed into factory-based industry. The new manufactories were much bigger than before. They were carefully sited so that they could take advantage of the convenient delivery of coal from new routes such as the Monkland Canal, which was opened in 1792. Factories were also strategically sited close to working populations.

Despite the cheap running costs of water power, the mill-wheels could not compete with the efficiency of a new generation of steam engines. These were constantly being adapted by new patented improvements on a regular basis. Linen and cotton were the chief manufactures, still spread throughout the whole country, with works in Aberdeen, Perth and Dundee as well as in the Clyde area. Finished products like gloves and stockings were made in thousands of cottages from wool supplied by merchants. Other expanding industries were chemicals, paper and dyeing.

After a long, unsuccessful war of attrition against smuggled and illegally home-distilled alcohol, an act of parliament was passed in 1822, reducing the licence fee on distilling to a ten pound charge, and the duty on whisky. From then, whisky distilling began to develop as an industry. By the following year, in 1823, distilleries as remote as Highland Park in Kirkwall, Orkney, were setting up sales outlets in London. Smuggling, which had flourished ever since the Union, died away within a few years, although illicit whisky-making, on a local rather than a commercial basis, still carried on.

A major setback to industrial growth happened with the slump in trade that followed the end of the Napoleonic Wars. Warships were paid off, soldiers returned from disbanded regiments, demand for manufactured goods fell badly. At the same time, mechanisation in factories was beginning to have an effect on the labour force. In the biggest industries, like cotton, the demand for workers was falling sharply. Those thrown out of work did not have anywhere else to turn. Many of them now lived in purpose-built tenements or back-to-back one- or two-room cottages built close to the factory. Working conditions were imposed by mill-owners, who based them on the maximum amount of effort that could be extracted from the workers. The worst aspects of human exploitation had ended with the emancipation of colliery and salt workers in 1799, but workers had few rights. Generally, it was accepted that the man who paid the wages called the tune; but this state of affairs began to be challenged before the 1820s.

REACTIONARIES AND RADICALS

Radical beliefs had been expressed in Scotland since the 1790s. Since the Friends of the People drew up their agenda for parliamentary reform in

1792, there had been voices to oppose a system based on the corruption of the Dundas regime. Deportation of their leader, the advocate Thomas Muir, to Botany Bay did not kill off their ideas, particularly as the Dundas family retained their controlling position even after the retirement of Henry Dundas himself. The new problems of an industrial economy in decline gave further impetus to other radical thinking. The temporary nature of the recession was not apparent at the time, and would have been no consolation to those affected by it. The economic background of protest in the early nineteenth century is underlined by the fact that the leaders of the Radical War, sometimes exaggeratedly known as 'the Scottish Insurrection', of 1820, were workmen rather than intellectuals like Muir. Between 1811 and 1813, handloom weavers, mainly in Glasgow and Paisley, who realised that their jobs were increasingly under threat, had attempted to form a union to protect their interests; predictably, their efforts were thwarted by the employers. When the Corn Laws of 1815 pushed up the price of grain and there was a great deal of hardship, protests and demonstrations over several years culminated in a march in 1820 from Glasgow to Falkirk, which was stopped by the militia in the 'skirmish' of Bonnymuir. Following this episode, fifty people were tried, three men were hanged and nineteen sentenced to deportation. Official repression included a tax of four pence on newspapers and magazines, intended to suppress the many new publications which sympathised with or promoted radical thinking. The founding of *The Scotsman* in 1817 helped to give a voice to the reformers, but there was also a vigorous press to support the government and point to the dangers of workers' power.

TECHNICAL INNOVATIONS

In the 1830s significant new commercial developments were in progress. Most crucially, as a nation that long used to import iron, Scotland now had its own iron industry. The hot-blast process devised and patented by James Neilson, manager of the Glasgow Gas Company, in 1828 made it possible to use the layered 'black bands' of low-grade coal and iron ore of Lanarkshire to smelt iron. With various practical improvements, the new smelting process drove up the productivity and efficiency of ironworks like those of Gartsherrie, Clyde and Calder. Scottish pig-iron was by 1835 in plentiful supply and the cheapest in Britain. Coal production went up in proportion, aided by demand from other new or developing industries, as well as for domestic use as the number of tenements and houses grew. New shapes on the skyline appeared around ordinary homes as the pit bings of colliery shale rose up around the pit-heads. The shale-oil industry, which gave the world paraffin, likewise reshaped parts of the landscape as well as doubling the population of West Lothian.

TEXTILES

The Border towns, where local flocks of sheep, and water power, were plentiful, formed a centre for a woollen industry producing coarse cloth at an early stage in Scotland's history. Now the industry began to produce better quality cloth, a twill whose Scots spelling of 'tweel', helped by a mistaken association with the River Tweed, caused Londoners to misread it as 'tweed'. The new tweed cloth quickly became a fashionable clothing material in England and Scotland.

The salt industry had almost been killed off in 1825 by the lifting of import duties on better quality rock salt from England and sea salt from the Bay of Biscay, but the already established chemicals and dyeing industries were growing fast. These were new-technology industries: Charles Macintosh had built a wall around his Glasgow dye-works and had employed Gaelic-speaking workers from his own home area to prevent his trade secrets being stolen. Bleaching textiles, which had taken up days of labour and valuable space, could now be accomplished inside a factory within hours with the use of acid. The vitriol factory established at Prestonpans in 1749 was the largest in Great Britain by the end of the eighteenth century. By the 1830s, the chemical works established by Tennant and Macintosh in the St Rollox district of Glasgow were the largest in the world. To work there or to live nearby was a serious danger to health, but such matters were scarcely considered. Local authorities in Scotland had neither the resources nor the will to tackle the problems that ultra-rapid urban growth and industrialisation were bringing every day. Factories and housing were being built in many places beyond the limits of the burghs and burgh control, in villages and on open 'green-field' sites.

THE COMING OF THE RAILWAYS

The construction of a viable steam locomotive in 1829 by Robert Stephenson, whose Scots descent did not go unremarked in a country increasingly keen to list its achievements and its 'famous sons', was quickly taken up in Scotland. Already there were some networks of horse-drawn or gravity trackways linking coal mines and harbours, and a horse-drawn passenger railway had been established between Edinburgh and Dalkeith in 1826. In 1831 the first effective steam-hauled railway in Scotland, the Glasgow and

Garnkirk Railway, was opened. From then on the growth of a railway network was rapid, paralleling developments in England.

The burgeoning railway system created its own industry of locomotive-building, carriage-works, signalling equipment; and civil engineering on a scale that Scotland had never before seen. The building industry boomed on the demand for stations and sheds, although few Scottish stations were of architectural distinction until the end of the century. In 1842 Glasgow and Edinburgh were linked by railway. Both cities were linked by rail to London by 1848. Inter-company rivalry and the desire of every community to ensure its own future by being linked to the railway network, produced the railway 'mania' of the 1840s. It resulted in many bankruptcies, the devaluation of railway shares and a recession in trade.

As the railways spread, virtually all mainland Scotland set its clocks by railway time, bringing about a standardisation where previously each town had set its own common clock. Until this time, many outlying districts had simply followed the hours of daylight in a manner as old as their history. The ease and speed of railway transport delayed further road improvement and the Turnpike Trusts fell into abeyance. The road system outside the towns decayed steadily until the spread of the motor after the First World War.

GOVERNMENT AND REFORM

In 1830 a Whig government was returned to power in London. Reform of Parliament was both its intention and its mandate from the British electorate. The Reform Bill was fought through in the Commons and rejected in 1831 by the House of Lords but eventually became law in 1832. The actual effect of the bill in Scotland was a modest increase in the number of people entitled to vote, but it was a small advance which anticipated further progress.

The intellectual climate of the times was progressive. More and more knowledge was being acquired and recorded in a host of subjects. Publishing houses were increasing in size and producing books in unprecedented numbers. Steam-powered presses rapidly produced larger print runs at lower unit production costs. The spread of Mechanics' Institutes and their libraries ensured that the new information was not restricted to scholarly circles. Each member paid a small subscription, which enabled the library to acquire a far wider range of books than any working man could hope to buy. Not all the workers spent their spare cash on drink and gambling at cockfights and boxing matches, popular as these activities were. People could learn as much as they wanted about a newly revealed, orderly world of scientific discovery, from anatomy to zoology, and they could see for themselves how machines were bringing enormous changes to industry, agriculture and daily life. In 1859, the ineffable Samuel Smiles published *Self Help*, promoting the notion of self-improvement and the benefits of education to ordinary people. Past certainties gave way to present excitements. The science of geology was largely established in Scotland. The hitherto sacred and unchallenged Biblical account of Creation began to be questioned. Outside the well-guarded stockade of religious faith, the tradition of Scottish thinking since the early eighteenth century had been pragmatic, questioning and sceptical. The recent past began to seem a time of naive rusticity. But in some areas of life, the past still reached out and stifled the spirit of progress. To the modern mind, it was a matter of scandal how hopelessly inadequate the Scottish system of local government had become.

The management of the Scottish burghs had become decrepit a long time before 1830. As the country changed from an agrarian state of peasants and small farmers to an industrial economy with more modern forms of agricultural practice, nothing changed in the way in which it was administered. The long years of Dundas patronage had intensified the reactionary behaviour of the burgh councils. Outgoing councils solemnly elected the incoming councils without any participation from the citizens. The same small groups of worthies exchanged positions. The position of provost was in many cases virtually hereditary and was often held by the largest of the local lairds rather than by a burgess. Throughout the later seventeenth and the eighteenth centuries burgh common lands were surreptitiously taken into private ownership. A typical example was in Cromarty as early as 1669, when Sir John Urquhart lent money to the council, which was in his control. It could not repay the loan, and he took the burgh's common land as payment. Semi-legal transactions such as this occurred all over the country. The Royal Commission on Scottish Burghs of 1835 remarked: 'If the large possessions which had been bestowed on Scottish burghs had been managed with common prudence and honesty, the taxes and burdens by which almost all of them are now weighed down would have been nearly unknown.'

A council position was an opportunity to gain wealth and exercise petty power at the expense of the rest of the community. Many councils kept defective or (like Edinburgh) fallacious accounts, or no accounts at all. In 1810 Aberdeen was given powers to raise £127,000 for construction of wet and graving docks. By 1819 the money had been raised and spent but there was no sign of any new docks. A committee of the House of Commons, set up in 1819, discovered Edinburgh, Aberdeen, Dundee and Dunfermline to be bankrupt. There were no sanctions available against such criminal conduct.

The office of Lord Chamberlain of Scotland, which had once exercised a degree of control over the burghs, had not existed since the seventeenth century. The Tory governments of the early nineteenth century and their Scottish managers could not correct the open abuses without toppling the whole worm-eaten structure of local government. To do so would destroy their own system of control and patronage along with it. Fifteen burgh members of parliament elected by the councils was a substantial number of obedient supporters in the voting lobbies of government. The councils stoutly defended their positions. Against the arguments of the reformers, the Convention of Royal Burghs claimed that change would 'unhinge a constitution which has stood the test of ages . . . and has been attended with as many advantages as could have been expected from any institution whatever.'

In 1833, the long efforts of the reformers resulted in the Municipal Reform Acts under which male householders with property worth ten pounds or more were allowed to have a vote in the election of burgh councillors. The Royal Commission of 1833 to 1835 recommended the immediate abolition of the burghs' economic privileges, and this was largely accomplished by 1846, although even in 1900 twenty-five burghs were still charging 'petty customs' on traffic through the town. Readers of John Galt's *The Provost*, published in 1821, can gain an accurate though somewhat rosy picture of municipal politics in a small Ayrshire town. Civic improvements did come about in Galt's fictional Gudetown, as in many real places, as long as the civic leaders could line their pockets in the process. They saw their behaviour as natural and traditional; as Justices themselves, they would have professed shock at its being considered criminal.

Development in the reform of larger places by-passed the self-electing councils by the use of Police Acts. These could be obtained by propertied men combining together in order to procure an act of parliament allowing specified developments in particular areas. 'Police' in this context meant civic management in matters such as paving, lighting and constraints on building; it was not necessarily policing in the later sense. Police Acts, when enforced, had to be locally funded and many local improvements, like the street lighting of Elgin, were achieved by the efforts of fund-raising committees.

SCOTLAND AND THE IRISH

In the 1840s and 1850s the population was swelled by a great influx of Irish from all the provinces of that country. This was the third great movement of people between the two countries, and it brought back to Scotland many of the descendants of the Plantation settlers of the early 1600s. It also brought into Scotland a substantial Catholic population, who were to have an impact on the political scene as well on the religious make-up of the country. Among the Irish were many who were simply taking refuge from desperate poverty and famine. They settled primarily in the Glasgow area since there was work available there and their predecessors had already established bridgeheads of settlement.

By 1841 the Irish made up sixteen per cent of the population in Glasgow. The Irish, whose own union with England in 1801 was more akin to a colonial relationship than the negotiated settlement between Scotland and England of 1707, were no respecters of the English and brought with them a tradition of demand for Home Rule and the willingness to use violence against what they regarded as a government sustained by military force and by an imported oligarchy of the wealthy. An inevitable part of their baggage was the entrenched antipathy nourished in Ulster between pro-Union Protestants and anti-Union Catholics. The two Irish factions did not intermingle, and the arrival of so many Catholics created some alarm within leading Presbyterian circles and something of a Protestant backlash.

Steps taken in the nineteenth century towards national and municipal order took place against a constant background of official and public fear of violence: the violence of militant Irish nationalism, of revolutionary anarchism and even the potential violence of Scottish working men who were now employed in army strength even in single factories, whose minds might be inflamed by agitators and who showed a disturbing tendency to organise themselves into united groups in order to put pressure on the employers.

WEALTH AND POVERTY

The rise and fall of industries, the introduction of labour-saving machines, the cyclic movements of the economy and the effects of wars abroad all ensured that there was no gentle or steady progress of the manufacturing economy, in which the population grew in proportion to the ability of industry to employ it. The economy was by no means unmanaged, but the disaster of the railway mania showed how little real impact parliament had on what was happening; the railways were an industry which the politicians had particularly set out to control from the start.

With a productive wealth far greater than in the eighteenth century, Scotland also found itself with a problem of poverty on a greater scale than ever before. Linked to poverty in a fatal union was disease. Sanitary concerns had never ranked high in Scotland. In the new and expanding towns and villages, builders had given no more consideration to private or public sanitation than previous generations. New homes very soon became slums. The single pump that supplied water to a street would also pour out cholera bacteria. Dirty water, raw sewage and the lack of washing facilities all promoted the spread of typhus. Lack of heating, damp, cold and overcrowded conditions for families in their 'single-ends' were the ideal means of passing on tuberculosis. The unemployed, the old, the chronically ill, the dying, the deserted wives, the very young all formed a mass of helpless people caught in the sump of social life.

The provisions of the Poor Laws in Scotland had never wholly coped with the country's poor, perhaps prompted by the inexorably reductive national sense of logic into assuming that too much available help would create a queue of non-necessitous cases. By the 1840s, with a depression in the textile industry, they were stretched beyond all reason. William Alison, professor of medicine at Edinburgh University, wrote in 1840: 'Let us look to the closes of Edinburgh, and the wynds of Glasgow, and thoroughly understand the character and habits, the diseases and mortality, of the unemployed poor, unprotected by the law, who gather there from all parts of the country . . . we must honestly and candidly confess, that our parsimony in this particular is equally injurious to the poor and discreditable to the rich in Scotland.'

The public health specialist Edwin Chadwick regarded Glasgow as the most insanitary city in Great Britain. Dr Alison's plea was eventually followed by some remedial action. In 1845, following a Royal Commission to investigate the Scottish Poor Law, the government of Robert Peel passed an act to transfer responsibility for poor relief from kirk sessions to approximately eight hundred parish boards. Parishes were authorised to raise a compulsory rate if funds were otherwise insufficient and to provide for medical relief as well as poor relief. The act still stipulated that relief could only be made available to those who were both destitute and disabled, although many doctors chose to interpret disability very widely. Certain districts of Glasgow and Edinburgh remained sinks of deprivation, and lesser pockets of equally appalling squalor existed in every other town. The failure of the potato harvests between 1847 and 1850 cruelly exposed the dependence of Highland inhabitants on this one crop, and the marginal nature of their existence. Highland parishes could scarcely fulfil even their most minimal statutory obligations to the starving. Rural poverty could provide scenes as desperate as any in the towns.

CHURCH AND STATE

The number of parishes in which immigrant Irish Catholics formed a high proportion of people in need was one reason why the responsibility for poor relief became a secular responsibility. Another reason was the convulsion in the Church of Scotland.

In 1843 the long-festering resentment of the Kirk against patronage had resulted in the Disruption, when two hundred ministers, led by the Moderator, walked out of the General Assembly and proceeded to form the Free Church of Scotland. The new church had no funds, no churches and no manses for its ministers. What the separatist ministers did have was the enormous mental energy generated by a momentous moral decision, and the almost complete loyalty of their congregations.

In an extraordinary effort of will and in a time of economic uncertainty, some five hundred churches were rapidly built. The Free Church, with highly intelligent men among its leaders, seized the opportunity to create for itself an administrative structure that suited the times, without prejudice to a spiritual outlook still firmly focused on the orthodoxy of the Westminster Confession. Inevitably, the situation in many parishes was confused, and sometimes there were hostile confrontations between supporters and opponents of the Free Church. The vision of a national and established Church was shattered.

But the high emotions of 1843 created the last occasion on which Church and People were two facets of a single entity. The established Kirk continued, retaining three out of every five ministers, but its claim to be the nation at prayer was no longer sustainable, nor could it exercise the old control on education. Inevitably, the civil power extended itself into charity and education. Even if the faces on the new parish boards were the same ones that decorated the old kirk session, they answered now to different masters. In the framing and administration of the poor law, however, the Kirk left a legacy that did not help the more unfortunate members of society.

Kirk sessions had always preferred to rely on voluntary generosity rather than compulsory contributions. The most influential minister of the time, Thomas Chalmers, one of the leaders of the Disruption of 1843, had already made a widely publicised attempt in the 1820s to apply a system of voluntary charitable work to the densely populated Glasgow parish of St Johns. It divided the parish into areas, each supervised by a sub-deacon who assessed the needs of his area. The linking of alms-giving to the Church had obvious inherent problems, both moral and social. Aid could be withheld from the troublesome or non-conformist. In a pluralist society, containing mutually intolerant religious beliefs, it was unworkable. Scotland was not the worst place to be poor in, since the poor always had company; it was one of the worst places to be poor and friendless in.

THOMAS GUTHRIE

B orn in Brechin in 1803, Guthrie was sent to university in Edinburgh at the age of twelve. Between 1826 and 1827 he lived in Paris, and on his return to Scotland became the minister of Arbirlot. He started a Savings Bank there, based on the pioneering example of the Reverend Henry Duncan at Ruthwell. In 1837 he moved to Old Greyfriars in Edinburgh, where he was shaken by the 'hideous scene of starvation and sin.' In the Disruption of 1843, he joined the Free Church and through his eloquence raised over £100,000 for buildings. Guthrie saw, more clearly than most, the links between poverty, ignorance, crime and disease. In 1847 he published *A Plea for Ragged Schools: or Prevention is Better than Cure*, and worked to set up schools for the children of the poor. He was also a strong supporter of the temperance movement, of half-holidays, and of better housing. He retired from the ministry in 1864 but went on to edit the popular *Sunday Magazine*.

CHARTISM

Nationalism was not a major political issue in the first fifty years of nineteenth-century Scotland. For the many people, both among the working class and the slowly growing middle class, who took up the cause of reform, there were more immediate problems to be addressed. Like the reforming Protestant party in the early 1650s, now the Scottish reformers of the later 1830s also drew strength and support from their English counterparts, although these were far from being in government. The Chartists of Scotland and England had the same ambitions, and few of the Scottish Chartists would have felt that political independence was the quickest way to fulfil their aspirations. Their organisation was formed in the wake of the Reform Bill of 1832, which had offered the prospect of better voting rights in Britain. By 1839 there were more than eighty local Chartist Associations in Scotland and the *Scottish Chartist Circular* had a weekly circulation of more than twenty thousand subscribers.

The Chartists had six main aims. They called for the extension of the franchise to all male voters. They wanted the abolition of the property qualification for voters. They believed that annual parliaments would be more effective and called for their institution. They wanted secret ballots at elections. They called for salaries to be paid to members of parliament. Finally, they wanted a fairer allocation of parliamentary seats. With hindsight, nothing could seem more respectable. Yet the Chartists spent many anxious

'TROCHTER'

'There was no Lunatic Asylum or Poor House in the North, and five or six half-witted creatures used to go about the streets, tormented often by idle boys. A poor creature was kept many years in the jail, who was said to have committed murder in a fit of insanity, and was condemned to confinement for life. He was placed in a cell with a small grated aperture for air and light, a pallet of straw for his bed, and bread and water his food. He lay there for many years, the community perfectly indifferent to his condition. . . .
We children were told that if we were not good we would be sent to "Trochter"; such was the name he was called, being the Gaelic for murderer. He used, in a stentorian voice, which was heard a long way off, up and down the street, to cry out in Gaelic, "Oh, yea, yea, Thighearn nan gras dean trochair orm," translated "O Lord of grace, have mercy on me." The people became so accustomed to the cry that they thought nothing of it; but in the middle of the night, when the shouts were frequent, the noise was very appalling.'
Joseph Mitchell (1803–83) on his boyhood in Inverness.

days arguing over whether it was right to use violence to achieve these goals, or not. The authorities in 1839 did not find the aims of the Chartists reasonable; they were seen to threaten the very fabric of society. Despite the industrial problems of 1840 to 1842, Chartism went into decline. It was essentially a political movement, like those of 1792, and it proved impossible to yoke its idealism to the new and basic aims of incipient trade unionism. But Chartism again exposed a strong radical strain in Scottish thought, which resurfaced in the formation of co-operative societies and socialist Sunday schools and also became linked to the temperance movement. This connection between political radicalism and prohibitionism shows up the Puritan, morally improving streak in the movement. Nevertheless, in the human degradation of slum areas, drinking created great social problems. Chartists knew that employers would cynically use cheap ale and whisky to placate a work-force which otherwise might rebel against the all-but-intolerable way of life imposed upon it.

Political nationalism was dormant, but the sense of a Scottish identity within the British and Imperial context was very strong. Preservation of the religious, legal and educational traditions played its part, but these were established institutions, part of daily life, and not to be marvelled at. Achievement was a new element in Scottish self-awareness.

By 1850, people in Lowland Scotland could look at a country that had been transformed within a lifetime and was still in change at a hectic rate. Horror might be mixed with admiration, but there was a vibrancy in the air, a sense of unstoppable progress. Such reactions were only Scottish in so far as they were felt in Scotland. Similar sentiments were common in other newly industrialised countries.

A CHANGE OF IDENTITY

What was essentially Scottish was the fictive, shadowy counterpart to political nationalism, the re-invention of the Scottish past. This process had begun with the 'Ossian' poems of James Macpherson in the seventeenth century but had been largely confined to a literary and antiquarian circle. The rapid growth in the popularity of the poems of Robert Burns after his death, in 1796, saw the early establishment of the Burns cult. The first Burns Club was formed in Greenock in 1801. On 27 January 1816, some of Edinburgh's leading literary men sat down to a Burns Supper, reported by the Edinburgh *Evening Courant* with the opening words: 'Scotland has long gloried in the fame of her divinest son.' Burns's Scotland was fading fast, along with Burns's language: the new huge printings of his works required glossaries of many Scots terms that were no longer current. Burns's works were appreciated by ordinary people for their true emotion, their humour, their frank satire and their democratic fire. But his visions of love in the cornfields, of gentle landscapes and tavern jollity, and his half-whimsical Jacobitism, catered to a growing nostalgia for a more placid, old-time, rural Scotland.

SOCIETY FOR VINDICATION OF SCOTTISH RIGHTS

This body was formed in 1852, to prevent Scottish interests being overlooked by the government. In its first report, the author James Grant (1822–87) wrote:

'The world is neither Scottish, English, nor Irish, neither French, Dutch nor Chinese, but *human*, and each nation is only the partial development of a universal humanity. . . . All true progress consists not in the eradication of the generic peculiarities of races, but in the wise direction of these peculiarities. England will not be better by becoming French, or German, or Scottish, but by becoming more truly and more nobly English; and Scotland will never be improved by being transformed into an inferior imitation of England, but by being made a better and truer Scotland.'

One of those who had dined on haggis and neeps in January 1816 was Walter Scott, not yet Sir Walter. As a one-man industry, he had already excited his countrymen, and soon the rest of Europe, with his narrative verse excursions into Scottish history, beginning with *The Lay of the Last Minstrel* in 1805. *The Lady of the Lake* in 1810 resulted in the beginning of a tourist industry in the Trossachs. In 1814 Scott changed horses from verse to prose, and embarked on his great series of the 'Waverley Novels'. *Old Mortality* had come out in 1816 and he was busy with *Rob Roy*. In 1820 he would be the stage-manager of the comic but triumphant visit of George IV to Edinburgh, the first

Etching of Sir Walter Scott, by H. W. Batley, after Sir Henry Raeburn, 1892

appearance of a reigning monarch in the city since Charles II. Scott's work ran like a fiery cross through the literary sensibility of Northern Europe, and marked the high tide of Romanticism. But his greatest impact was on the people of his native land, whose view of their own history was now firmly cast in the Scott mould. Pithy anecdotes, high-coloured dramatic scenes, romantic episodes and an artificially poetic language combined to create an alluring cloak of many colours which the sober work of modern historians is still unpicking to reveal the true forms beneath. But Scott had also made it a rather grand thing to be Scottish:

> 'Breathes there the man with soul so dead,
> Who never to himself hath said,
> "This is my own, my native land?"'

Even though for most it was a land of the roaring factory and the crowded insanitary street rather than the brown heath and shaggy wood, he had succeeded in establishing a national myth. Much later, another Scots poet, Edwin Muir, denounced this aspect of Scott as 'the sham bard of a sham nation'.

The visual arts contributed to the 'sham' and spurious image of Scotland.

The Royal Scottish Academy was founded in 1826 and provided exhibition space for artists to display and sell their works. Rural and historical themes were very much the preferred topics. There was no follower of Raeburn in portraiture. The demand was for uncontroversial art; religious scenes, for landscapes and sentimental pictures of cottage life. Artists like Robert Scott Lauder, David Scott and William Dyce, often with great technical skill, supplied it. The artist associated by most with Scotland was not a Scot at all. Sir Edwin Landseer was a Londoner who first visited Scotland in 1821. His image of the heroic deer on a wild hillside, *The Monarch of the Glen*, defined a mid-century view of Scotland.

THE HIGHLAND CLEARANCES

The Highlands, their past history romanticised by Scott's genius, were actually in a sad way. Kelp and cattle had been the main sources of employment. There had been attempts to develop and diversify an industrial base, such as the west coast fishery settlements of the 1780s and the spinning mill at Spinningdale in Sutherland in 1790. These remained isolated pockets of industry. From 1815 onwards, the kelp industry collapsed, brought down by cheaper Mediterranean imports and by industrial production of alkali. The price of black cattle fell sharply in the early 1820s. Domestic production of yarn and cloth in remoter areas was increasingly uneconomic as factory production increased. The end of the Napoleonic Wars meant that soldiers and sailors from the Highlands were no longer needed. The Highlands had very little to offer. The large population was fed mainly on a monotonous diet of potatoes and oatmeal, which kept families a little above subsistence level. The typical house was still the 'black house', a windowless cottage with a peat fire in the centre and an adjoining cattle byre. When improving minds, like that of the Sutherland factor, James Loch, looked at this vast area they could think only in terms of sheep rearing. The Cheviot breed of sheep could be farmed in large numbers with very little labour. But the sheep runs needed the richer grassland of the valley floors and lower slopes and could not coexist with all the little crofts and settlements in the glens. To the improving mind it was clear – the people had to go.

In the west, lairds had forbidden emigration because of the need to keep workers for kelp-gathering and burning. Now the same lairds were encouraging and compelling people to leave. Some landowners, like MacKenzie of Assynt, went bankrupt because of the collapse of the kelp industry. The people saw things in a different way. Even now, they still expected support from the chief or landowner, just as they gave it to him. They had an immemorial attachment to their land. Their patient and resigned attitude was the last sign of the old society of the Highlands. In future decades, they would learn to take action for themselves.

People began to leave the Highlands and Islands in great numbers. From the southern areas it was a relatively short journey to the industrial central belt, although it was an immense step in cultural and linguistic terms. For those farther north, Glasgow or Falkirk seemed almost as remote as Ontario or Otago; in some ways the colonies felt closer because the emigrant ships came direct to West Highland ports and anchorages.

As early as 1814, the clearances began in Sutherland when Strathnaver was turned over to sheep rearing. The inhabitants were forcibly transferred to coastal locations where they were expected to make a living by fishing. With next to no capital or other support and facing hostility from the established Moray coast fishermen, they were doomed to fail. The clearance policy continued in the Highlands without the half-hearted or cosmetic attempts made in Sutherland to alleviate the situation. The potato famine of the 1840s added to the miseries of the people. In the 1850s, emigration societies, including the quaintly named Scottish Patriotic Society, were formed, and emigration became an industry.

Even as communications improved in the Highlands, with long single lines of railway reaching beyond Crianlarich and Inverness, the countryside emptied. Estates that had once been populous clan territories were sold and resold. As the price of wool fell, more and more lands were made into deer forests owned by alien or absentee landlords with no personal or economic stake in the land and a vested interest in keeping people away.

> 'Ill fall the sheep, a grey-faced nation
> That swept our hills with desolation.'
> *Duncan Bàn MacIntyre*

CHAPTER TWELVE

The Nineteenth Century and Beyond: Part 2

VICTORIAN SCOTLAND

By the time Victoria became queen of Great Britain in 1837 the powers of the monarch were much more restricted than those of her eighteenth-century predecessors, and far less than the autocratic power, always greater in Scotland than in England, that kings had had before 1688. Parliament was sovereign, although the unelected House of Lords retained powers of veto over the Commons. The House of Commons itself was elected only by a minority of the adult population. By sheer longevity the Queen impressed herself on her subjects and gave her name to the high era of the British Empire. The royal family's purchase of Balmoral Castle in 1853, and the Queen's affection for things Highland, renewed a Scottish enthusiasm for the monarchy.

LIBERALS AND TORIES

In the later years of her reign, Victoria had two commanding figures as leaders of each of the political parties; William Ewart Gladstone in the Liberal Party which had emerged from the former Whigs; and Benjamin Disraeli, later Lord Beaconsfield, as leader of the Conservative Party, who also retained the name of Tories. The parliamentary confrontations and alternations in power between Gladstone and Disraeli codified the style of two-party politics that prevailed at Westminster, with the Labour Party largely replacing the Liberals after 1921. On the basis of Westminster electoral results, however, the Liberals would have remained consistently in power in a Scottish government from 1832 to 1900.

Throughout the century Scottish politics were dominated by the Liberals. Gladstone in particular made a strong impact on Scotland, and was for some years the member of parliament for Midlothian – once the parliamentary seat of Henry Dundas – whose electors he regaled with speeches of heroic duration. Gladstone received ecstatic welcomes on his travels throughout Scotland, on one occasion receiving the freedom of the burgh of Dingwall without actually getting off the train. Scottish Liberalism had roots in the radicalism of the decades that followed the French Revolution, and in the independent status of the Free Church. For those who believed in land-law reform and free trade, it was the only parliamentary party. Liberalism was also linked with a new impetus towards self-government.

Although the imperial parliament at Westminster was more highly organised than ever before, there were vast ranges of home, colonial and foreign affairs to be considered. The affairs of Scotland had to be fitted in with other demands on parliamentary time. The Scottish electorate, expanded by successive Reform Acts, and aware of the country's unresolved problems, pressed their parliamentary representatives for action. People began to question whether the tax and excise contributions from Scotland to the United Kingdom were adequately reflected by government expenditure in Scotland. In 1888 the government came up with the Goschen Formula, named after the Chancellor of the Exchequer. It set Scotland's share of government funds at eleven pounds for every eighty spent in England.

The separate nature of Scottish, Irish and English institutions made legislation for the whole of the United Kingdom a cumbersome business. As this became more apparent, a separate Scottish parliament seemed to many to be a practical solution as well as one that answered to a strengthening current of demand in Scotland itself.

The post of Secretary for Scotland, abolished in 1745, was reinstated in 1885. But the Scottish cause was of less pressing concern to the government than the demands of the Irish. The Scottish Liberal members were British before they were Scottish. They lacked the passionate intensity of their Irish counterparts, who focused their attention on Land Reform and Home Rule. Their urgings were muted by comparison.

But Ireland – unlike Scotland – had a Catholic majority who did not feel that Westminster could ever fulfil their aspirations. On the other hand Scotland – unlike Ireland – had an industrial economy that was intimately linked with that of England and had vested interests in the British Empire. If the nationalists of Ireland had the problem of Unionist Ulster to contend with, the people of Scotland had the problem of a more diffused but still vibrant unionism, particularly among the aristocracy and the leaders of commerce and industry. It was inevitable that Scottish devolution should stay well down in the order of government priorities. When Irish Home Rule was voted down in parliament in April 1886, the Liberal Party split between those who supported the idea of an Irish government and those who did not. There was no likelihood of a similar Scottish bill succeeding, but the movement for Home Rule remained alive.

THE SCOTTISH LABOUR PARTY

In 1883 the Scottish Labour Party was formed, two years before the Labour Representation Committee in London, and in the same year the first conference of the Home Rule Association took place. The Scottish founders of Labour had home rule very much on their agenda. James Keir Hardie stood for election as the very first of all Labour candidates in his home district of Mid-Lanark in 1888 but was defeated, and was later to represent English and Welsh constituencies. Parliamentary success came very gradually for Labour. In the early years of the twentieth century, it was an amorphous movement made up of a number of local parties and interest groups, which would not finally coalesce until the early 1930s. The era of the monolithic Labour 'machine' was still some way off.

In 1906, the year of an electoral landslide for the Liberals, they took almost fifty-seven per cent of the vote and won fifty-eight parliamentary seats. The comparable figures for Labour were 2.3 per cent of the vote and two parliamentary seats. It was 1922 before Labour won the largest share of the vote and the largest proportion of Scotland's 71 parliamentary seats.

Election poster for James Keir Hardie and the Labour Party, 1888

RELIGION — REVIVAL AND RECESSION

Scotland had by now a large Catholic community, drawn chiefly from the first and second generations of Irish immigrants in the central area. There were long-established Catholic congregations in some of the Hebrides and in the northeast, where Catholic landowners had sheltered the Old Church through centuries of difficulties. The Catholic Church in Scotland had its own hierarchy, appointed in 1878, twenty years after England and not without much ungracious Presbyterian growling.

From 1875 there was a campaign of religious revival, with mass meetings and hymn-singing, led by the evangelists Sankey and Moody. Thousands of people were 're-born'. Scotland largely remained a nation of church-goers in both town and country, but the defenders of strict Sabbatarianism were already fighting a rearguard action. On 3 June 1883 there was a riot at Strome Ferry to prevent the Sunday landing of fish and the running of a special train to take the catch to the east. Commercial interests were far less likely than erring individuals to be cowed by religious outrage. Even so, virtually every business closed on Sundays and farmers did not harvest their crops on Sundays, even if the sun was shining. Such universal observance, however, could not conceal the fact that the role of the Kirk in society was edging steadily back. Throughout the country the ascendancy of the kirk sessions was dwindling rapidly. It no longer seemed appropriate for moral backsliders to be admonished by the elders. There was a more secular spirit abroad in the country.

State-appointed bodies, like the Commissioners in Lunacy, and the elected town and parish councils, had taken over the management of society. Ministers and elders remained highly respected figures, but they had to be elected to councils in order to have influence outside the strictly religious sphere. Many ministers still sought to govern their congregations as completely as Andrew Melville would have liked to govern King James; and a shift in the ministers' emphasis towards social matters was much more apparent in the cities than in the small towns and country parishes, where traditional attitudes lingered on.

The small compromises of family life also meant that each generation of children, however irksome they found the Presbyterian Sunday, achieved a little less restriction than their parents had suffered. Religion still permeated daily life, and although most homes had abandoned family prayers, few would omit to say grace before meals.

EDUCATION FOR ALL

From 1872, under secular management, primary schools continued to teach Calvinist theology in the stately but incomprehensible language of the Shorter Catechism of 1643, and the parish ministers of both the Established and the Free Kirks called regularly to inspect the scholars' Bible knowledge. The Education (Scotland) Act of 1872, which made schooling compulsory for all children from the age of five to thirteen, brought the existing parish and burgh schools under the state control of a Scotch Education Department, based in London. The new drive for education created a rush of new school building projects and many new jobs for single women: the first professional opportunities for females.

Outside the burghs, education before had been largely in the hands of the churches, administered at a parish level, and run by the village dominie, who in theory, and often in practice, would teach bright children — boys only — from the absolute basics to university entrance level. The burgh schools were run by the councils, and in the cities there were other schools, some privately endowed, like Hutchesons' in Glasgow, some founded as philanthropic ventures, like the 'ragged schools' set up in Edinburgh by Thomas Guthrie and in Aberdeen by Sheriff Watson. Episcopalian and Catholic schools remained outside the system, funded by their own churches and parishioners, as did the private fee-paying schools. Secondary education was not compulsory and continued to be supplied by the grammar schools and academies, their fees often moderated by endowments and bursaries. The widening of the curriculum to include the sciences and the introduction of the Scottish Leaving Certificate in 1888 gave an impetus to secondary schooling, since the certificate inevitably set a standard that was used by employers and institutions. Until 1892, when all primary and most secondary education was provided free by the state, secondary schooling was essentially for the children of the better-off. For the poorer it was an economic and social struggle to send their children to the academy.

The Scottish burgh had always had a hierarchy and the Scottish countryside had always had its gentry. Simplicity of social structures had meant that there were elements of 'classlessness', as when the sons of the laird, the doctor and the cottar all sat on the same bench in the parish school, but their ways rapidly parted in early adolescence. The view of the employers and the professionals, that the employed should know their station, was one of the factors that enabled the working class to identify and organise itself. If the openness and quality of Scottish elementary education was something of a myth, there was always ample evidence of parents' enthusiasm for educating their children and readiness to make sacrifices to do so. The myth bore practical fruit in the nineteenth century when many bequests were made to the universities to assist poor students with the fees. These bequests were often restricted to promising scholars from specific parishes. Others were open to competition from all. Such bursaries were done away with by the universities in the later twentieth century, at a time when virtually all students had their tuition fees paid by their local authority. With ironic inevitability, personal fees were reimposed in 1998. Their abolition

---

'MOSQUITO' MANSON (1844–1922)

Sir Patrick Manson's life exemplifies, at a high level, the career of a Victorian Scot in the British Empire. His father was laird of Fingask and also manager of the local British Linen Company Bank. He began training as an engineer, switched to medicine and graduated at Aberdeen in 1865. His elder brother was already in China, and he went to Formosa as medical officer to the Chinese Imperial Maritime Customs. Through his search for a treatment for elephantiasis, he discovered the microscopic *filaria* worms in mosquito tissues. In Hong Kong he founded the medical school. He returned to Aberdeenshire in 1889, but lost his money and had to resume a medical practice, this time in London, where he became physician to the Seamen's Hospital. Here his interest in tropical disease was renewed, and he developed his theory of links between the mosquito and malaria. His association with Sir Ronald Ross began in 1894. Ross wrote, 'His brilliant induction so accurately indicated the true line of research that it has been my part merely to follow its direction.' Manson was one of the founders of the London School of Tropical Medicine.

---

would be the subject of stormy debate in the opening session of the new Parliament.

The universities were the pillars of the Scottish professional bodies in law, Church and medicine, and consequently were part of the establishment rather than engines of change. Their concerns were with classical education, evolved from the old curriculum, and the new 'pure' sciences. Honours degree courses were set up from 1858, reflecting a new seriousness in the pursuit of advanced scholarship and a significant extension of the universities' role from being places of general education to suppliers of more specialised learning. Undergraduates, who had in the eighteenth century arrived at an age as young as twelve, now normally came up to university at fifteen or sixteen. Secondary school was still not an essential preliminary stage though most students came from the burgh grammar schools.

The universities did not see themselves as handmaidens to industry, even if Glasgow, in particular, developed marine-related departments such as Naval Architecture. Industry required trained scientists and engineers. In Glasgow and Edinburgh, the two technical colleges, Anderson's and Watt's, taught draughtsmanship, engineering and practical science. More basic technical knowledge was acquired through the process of apprenticeship to a trade, and each trade within an industry, whether engineering or building, held itself separate from the others. This practical form of organisation worked effectively in the nineteenth century. It ensured a supply of skilled craftsmen for businesses and it formed a protective structure for the workers against a set of employers who were not motivated by a sense of fair dealing.

INDUSTRIAL RELATIONS

The mutual suspicion between workers and managers, with claims of incompetence on the one hand and of negative 'nineteenth-century' attitudes on the other, which inflamed industrial relations during the 1970s and 80s, when Scotland's industrial base collapsed, had always characterised industrial life.

By the 1850s that industrial base was still expanding and consolidating. To grow, it needed markets far beyond Scotland. Competition from Germany, France and Belgium as well as England meant that Scottish firms had to compete or die. With the exceptions of tweed cloth, whisky and the new linoleum, little that Scotland made was unique. Only more effective products or cheaper prices could hold the market, and even then protectionist

---

ELSIE INGLIS

S he exemplifies the determination of the generation of women who stormed the second most resistant redoubt of Academe, the medical faculties. Born in India in 1864, she was brought to Edinburgh as a young girl, and, supported strongly by her father, studied medicine and qualified as a doctor. She set up a medical school for women with the equally formidable Sophia Jex-Blake, Edinburgh's first woman medical graduate, but they fell out and Dr Inglis set up her own school in 1892. Having spent some time at the Elizabeth Garrett Anderson Hospital in London, she founded a maternity hospital in Edinburgh, staffed entirely by women, in 1901. The male-dominated legislation of the time, which allowed a husband to forbid any medical operation on his wife, appalled her. In 1906 she was a founder of the Scottish Women's Suffragette Federation. In the First World War she wanted to take a medical unit to the Front. When an English official said to her, 'My good lady, go home and sit still,' she promptly made the necessary arrangements with the French, and served in Serbia and Russia, setting up hospitals. Ill and exhausted, she was on her way home from Russia when she died in Newcastle in 1917.

tariffs could cut off trade. The linoleum producers of Kirkcaldy flourished but had to build factories abroad to get around local tariff barriers. The surest source of wealth was that of the primary producer, receiving royalties on coal or ore production. Next surest was perhaps the brewery trade, although it had grown to a point where foreign markets were essential.

THE RISE OF THE HERRING FISHING

Herring had always been caught off Scotland, notably in Loch Fyne, where the fishing was strictly controlled by the dukes of Argyll. In the second half of the nineteenth century, east coast fishermen began to exploit the huge shoals of herring that approached their coast each year between July and September. Instead of the traditional line with its baited hooks, they used drift nets, scooping up fish in industrial quantities. Bigger boats were wanted, and boat-building began to flourish. The catch would be gutted, salted and packed at high speed, and then shipped out, often to the Baltic ports. Harbours like Buckie, Macduff, Fraserburgh and Wick were extended. The newly built railways were able to move fish inland in large quantities. By the end of the nineteenth century, the herring fishers were turning from sailing vessels to steam drifters, and catches went up even more. To extend the season, they followed the shoals farther afield, to Shetland and Yarmouth, and the women who did the gutting and packing followed them in an annual pattern of migration and return. At the peak of the industry, around 1910–12, two million barrels of herring were sold. It was said that the wide harbour of Wick could be walked across from one side to the other, so closely packed were the herring boats.

Scottish women gutting herring in Yarmouth, 1924

Manufacturers could make fortunes but could also go bankrupt through over-trading or failure to keep pace with innovation. The Aberdeen textiles industry virtually disappeared between 1832 and 1848 in the textiles slump. Prices of commodities rose and fell. The American Civil War of 1861 to 1865 had a disastrous effect on imports from the American south but stimulated trade with the war economy of the north. The Franco-Prussian War of 1870 to 1871, although it left exporters to France with long delays in the payment of outstanding debts, generated another economic boom.

The successful captains of industry and commerce rewarded themselves well and built grand villas in salubrious areas, and prosperous suburbs and dormitory towns like Helensburgh spread with the railway. The blend of paternalism and exploitation with which the employers treated their work forces was not peculiar to Scotland but was certainly typical of Scotland. The natural extension of Adam Smith's ideas on political economy was to regard the workers as a resource to be used or set aside as demand required. The only way out of this for the working man was 'self-improvement', which meant adopting the same philosophy in order to join the class of managers and entrepreneurs. Trade unions were seen as a threat to the system and, by extension, to the whole fabric of society.

Every effort towards organisation for mutual support by groups of Scottish workers before the 1850s collapsed. Normally stimulated by a sense of excessive exploitation in the first case, they almost always led to strikes, that were broken by arrests, by threats and moral blackmail. The bitterness of the strikers was enhanced by the knowledge of the hostility that they faced from press, pulpit and law, as well as the employers. There was little opportunity for dialogue. It was only in the 1850s and 1860s that rudimentary industrial relations began and employers became prepared to negotiate with bodies like the United Coal and Iron Miners Association, which was founded in 1855.

Amongst employers the attitude remained vigorously against trade unionism, and the Clyde Shipbuilders' and Engineers' Association of 1886 had it as a prime aim to combine against the unionisation of their work forces. Political support for their point of view came strongly from successive Whig, later renamed Liberal, governments whose definition of Reform fell far short of workers' rights. But the extension of parliamentary voting to all adult males in 1867 opened up the way for a political party that could claim to represent the interests of workers. Industrial disputes continued to be bitter. They were sometimes large-scale and long-lasting, but the results were less one-sided than earlier in the century. In 1891 Motherwell railway station was wrecked by rioting strikers when the Caledonian Railway tried to evict employees from their tied houses. In 1894 sixty-five thousand miners were on strike from June to October, causing extensive lay-offs in coal-dependent industries. Perhaps only half the strikers were trade union members. Even in the largest industries, union members were in a minority. When the Scottish Trades Union Congress was founded in 1897, most of its constituent unions were small and local organisations, although by then trade union membership was rapidly growing and an era of merging and of amalgamating with English unions was beginning.

The High Victorian years of the early 1870s saw the peak rate of industrial expansion. The demand for labour was such that the market laws of supply and demand were on the side of the workers; pay went up and concessions in working hours were made. Holidays were introduced, leading to the establishment of the 'Fair', when whole towns virtually closed for a week, with the Glasgow Fair just the largest example. A sixty-hour or more working week was relatively common, and not until the 1880s was legislation introduced to limit working hours in engineering to fifty-one hours a week.

'CLYDE-BUILT' – DOMINANCE
IN SHIPBUILDING

The steel industry expanded fast in the 1870s, using the open-hearth production method, and by the mid-1880s was producing around 250,000 tons a year. It was now that the world dominance of Scotland in shipbuilding became plain. Ships were built all around the low-lying coasts of Scotland, even at the rural but timber-rich Spey Bay. Many ships were still wooden-hulled. Even as the marine steam engine chugged its way to dominance, the fastest sailing ships ever built were launched in the 1860s. But the racing clippers like the Clyde-built *Cutty Sark* and the Aberdeen-built *Thermopylae* were almost immediately made redundant by the opening of the Suez Canal in 1869. The future lay with the bigger metal-hulled ships. These were exactly what the Clyde shipyards were ready to supply.

By 1870 Scotland's shipyards were already launching nearly three-quarters of the iron-hulled tonnage in Great Britain and they now had a local source of suitable steel. The first steel-hulled steamship was launched, on the Clyde, in 1879. Expertise and experience in engine design and production were chiefly responsible for their leading position, and constant research and development kept them ahead of their competitors. Many fictional accounts of life at sea would feature the Scotch engineer, whose character would be rather idealistically summed up in Kipling's poem *MacAndrew's Hymn*. The steam turbine, developed by Sir Charles Parsons,

THE STRATHSPEY KING

This was the self-awarded title of the long-lived James Scott Skinner (1843–1927). He was born into a musical family, his father being a dancing master in Banchory, and the boy showed an early aptitude for the violin, the traditional source of country music. He spent six years in Manchester with a youthful orchestra, 'Dr Mark's Little Men', and received violin training from local musicians. Back in Scotland, he took the honours in a national fiddle competition at the age of nineteen, and from then on was a virtuoso concert performer. A prolific composer, adapter and improver, he brought more than 600 items into the Scots fiddle repertory. He performed throughout Scotland and to emigrant audiences in the United States. Recordings of his playing, made when he was already elderly, still exist.

was first installed in a ship at Dumbarton in 1884. From 1870 to 1914 the Clyde was the world's prime shipbuilding area, and, especially with the advent of the large passenger ship in the 1890s, a host of secondary industries arose, from cabinet-making to flag-making and from brassware to ropes and cables.

Through the 1880s, in Germany, the first splutterings of the internal-combustion engine resulted in a succession of self-propelled vehicles whose motive power was not steam. By 1895 motor cars were being assembled in Scotland, and the Albion Motor Company was founded at the very end of the century. Albion had a successful life as a truck-maker, but Scottish industry did not take up the petrol engine in a big way. Scottish manufacturers had an almost proprietorial interest in steam power, and a solidly established tradition. Having acquired its own mass and momentum, it could no longer be flexible. The spirit was managerial rather than entrepreneurial. Scots builders were to adapt slowly to the motor ship, and allow the technical leadership to pass elsewhere.

FUN AND GAMES

By 1881 the population of Scotland had reached 3.7 million. The majority now lived in towns and cities. Despite long working hours and the traditional disapproval of visible enjoyment of Sunday leisure, families still found ways of enjoying themselves. The nineteenth century bridges the divide between the games and pastimes of an earlier Scotland and those of the twentieth century. Calvinism had stamped out all but the faintest memories of the old holy days, but exuberance transferred itself to country fairs – including the 'holy fairs', where communion was taken by everyone – midwinter revels and harvest homes, some of these displaying a seasonal rite that went back before Christianity. The fires of Beltane and midsummer, scarcely Christianised as Johnsmas, burned on hilltops all over Scotland as a ceremony of renewal, whilst bold young men leapt across the still-flaming embers. By the end of the century such celebrations were rare and had to be deliberately and self-consciously recreated. The tradition of the night of Hallowe'en remained more vibrant, although it moved steadily down the age range. Instead of girls attempting to divine whom they would marry or how many children they would have, or young men dressed in masks and strange clothes representing the spirits of the dead, it became a 'tricks or treats' night for child guisers and as such lasted on into the next century.

Communal games involving men and older boys ranged up and down the streets of many towns and can still be observed each New Year in Kirkwall's Ba' Game, between the 'Uppies' and 'Doonies' on 1 January. The Border towns kept their Common Ridings, and many others celebrated an annual beating of the bounds, in all cases accompanied by fairgrounds, music, dancing and the public consumption of a great deal of alcohol. Quoits,

---

CHILDREN'S PASTIMES ON THE EASTER ROSS SEABOARD

'There were few toys so games had the minimum of equipment. They played Port (Hop Scotch) on the school's wide doorstep, or Spider's Web, drawn on a sandy part of an otherwise stony playground. They hopped neatly into sections of the web, and having completed the full round into the centre could write their initials in one 'box'. The next player had to hop over that space, made well-nigh impossible if the name was written near the centre where the boxes were much smaller and narrower. The player with the largest number of initialled boxes won. Boys played marbles, or raced each other on the roadway with girds or hoops.

'Every Friday night the Little Templars met in the school under the leadership of Mrs Watt, the headmaster's wife. They paid one penny to join, and had talks and readings on the benefits of temperance and the horrors of drink. Those of the children who were office-bearers had a splendid regalia – red velvet collars edged with gold braid and I.O.G.T. written on them.'

From *Down to the Sea* by Jessie Macdonald and Anne Gordon

---

cockfights and bare-fist boxing were all popular, and all provided opportunities for gambling as well as for social drinking. These events often took place in the open air, but premises were also built or adapted to put on such entertainments. Public disapproval turned such sports into furtive events, and as such they have not wholly disappeared.

SPORT IN SCOTLAND

Meanwhile other sports were encouraged. Golf, which had been popular with the Stewart kings as far back as James V, survived with equipment improved by the new technology, and the modern game took shape, with St Andrews as its capital. In 1860 the first Open Championship took place. The ancient winter sport of curling became popular and received a set of rules from the royally patronised Caledonian Curling Club (the use of the word 'Caledonian' in public titles frequently indicated a harking back to half-remembered or wholly imaginary Scots traditions).

In the Highlands, hill-running races and shot-putting became regular events in the communal Highland games that began in Braemar in 1817 and spread to many other places, often with spurious claims to origins in medieval times. While some form of football had been practised for centuries, it was essentially the two English forms of the game that were formally established in 1873 by the Scottish Football Association for soccer and the Scottish Football Union for rugby. The significance of these foundations goes beyond sport. There was no obvious reason not to form British associations. The related associations south of the Border did not always have the word 'English' in their titles, nor did they often proclaim themselves as 'British'. No one suggested that there should be differences between Scottish rules and English rules for games. Distance might have been a problem for Scots clubs affiliated to an English league; though reasonably rapid rail transport was possible, all-amateur clubs had but modest funds. That was not the crucial issue. With a habit of mind as automatic as a key turning in a well-oiled lock, the founders of these associations created them as Scottish institutions.

Nearly two hundred years of union with England had not diminished that primary sense of identity, nor had it removed a viable working context for that identity to display itself in. Something typically Scottish arose in the workings of the Scottish Football Association, albeit as an inheritance of the great Irish immigration. Religious rivalry became an element in the sporting contests between Glasgow Rangers, founded in 1873, and Glasgow Celtic, founded by Brother Wilfred in 1887 as a sporting club for Catholic youth. Very early in the history of the game, these two clubs became the dominant forces that they still remain.

PROFIT-INSPIRED ARCHITECTURE

On the streets and fields of Scotland, popular pastimes and sports flourished. Within towns and cities, civic energy and wealth and individual patronage by the rich created a mass of new buildings in a wild variety of styles. The sixteenth- and seventeenth-century tolbooths, the sober architecture of eighteenth-century public buildings, the studious Classicism of architects like Alexander Thomson of Glasgow were soon isolated specimens amid an architectural riot in which eclectic designers like J. J. Burnet borrowed and mingled elements from Byzantine, Egyptian, Gothic, Florentine Renaissance and Romanesque styles with a fine abandon. Most prominent among them is the very mixed style of 'Scotch baronial', associated with turrets, battlements, stepped gables and corbels. Churches, station hotels, museums, libraries, gateways to public parks, factories, town halls, fountains – all rose up between 1870 and 1914. There was a vigour and sometimes a cheerful vulgarity about this rush of building. David Bryce, arch-exponent of the Scotch baronial mode, was the architect of more than a hundred houses, castles and other buildings, including Fettes College in Edinburgh. But the archetypal structure of late-Victorian Scotland, symbolic in its massiveness, its materials and its function, was the Forth Railway Bridge, completed in 1890, a work of engineering not of architecture, designed chiefly by the Englishman Sir Benjamin Baker. It was not until Charles Rennie Mackintosh's new Glasgow School of Art building of 1896 that an architecture of originality and distinction appeared, able to link historic Scottish style with new European ideas in a manner that created something new rather than something borrowed.

In the sphere of town planning, Patrick Geddes, originally a botanist whose eyesight became damaged by harsh sunlight, turned to social and political issues. He felt that there could be effective strategic planning of the environment on the basis of combining 'Place, Work and Folk' in the correct relationship. Geddes, who coined the word 'megalopolis', was a world pioneer in town planning, and established the first 'Sociological Laboratory' in Edinburgh in 1892.

ART AND ARTISTS

For all its newly created wealth, the Victorian era was not a kindly one for the creative arts in Scotland. The unambitious style of narrative Scottish art can be found in pictures by artists such as William Quiller Orchardson. The tradition of landscape painting, which had been sustained by artists such as Samuel Bough and Horatio McCulloch, now began to develop into the grander landscape pictures of James Lawton Wingate and particularly of William MacTaggart who created a distinctively Scottish look. The Scottish Colourists formed a significant group of contemporary-minded artists at the end of the century.

The Glasgow School of Art formed a seed bed for designers and painters, such as the 'Glasgow Girls' and the 'Glasgow Boys' of the 1880s and 1890s, who applied their skills to books and furniture as well as paintings. Kirkcudbright became an art centre at the turn of the century, giving a home to such artists as Jessie King, who became a successful book illustrator and her husband, E. A. Walton. The best artists of the time, like George Henry, stayed in touch with what was going on in Paris, but Scottish art generally had subsided to a provincial level, rather than forming a national school.

THE DECLINE OF SCOTS

One of the victims of the century was the Scots language, which by the 1900s had become little more than a set of distinctive forms of pronunciation with a number of characteristic words and expressions of its own. Of the two large Scots dictionaries compiled at opposite ends of the century, Jamieson's *Etymological Dictionary of the Scottish Language* of 1808 refers to the Scots language; by 1911 Warrack's *Dictionary* refers only to the Scots dialect. No one was writing in Lowland Scots except for weakly humorous material in popular magazines and collections such as the *Scots Reciter*. The 'Doric' of the northeast survived better and maintained a school of local poets who could still use the language. The spread of commercial English helped to kill off written Scots, and the shared political, economic and literary culture was a hostile environment for Scots speech. Other factors helped. Although at a popular level the nostalgia for the so-recent innocent past spawned a multitude of well-loved songs of the 'Auld Hoose' and 'Rowan Tree' variety, at a slightly more exalted level there was a reaction against the perceived quaintness and rusticity of the eighteenth and early nineteenth centuries. Literary-minded people looked back to an antique Celtic era, their notion of its landscapes, faces and costumes largely inspired by Pre-Raphaelite painters. Its literature whether a modern imaginative effusion or a translation from Gaelic, was written in English. The nonsense of all this was summed up in the persona of William Sharp, a writer of real talent, who instead garbed himself in ladies' gowns to write spiritual Celtic romances under the pseudonym of Fiona MacLeod. This Celticism, dubbed the 'Celtic Twilight' by its critics, may have contributed something to the revived desire for devolved government, but its true nature was more apparent in the regular pan-Celtic congresses that solemnly discussed such matters as whether the Irish should have a national dress.

The best of the writers, Robert Louis Stevenson and George Macdonald, took refuge in historical romance or half-didactic fantasy. In the tumult of the nineteenth century, the great century of the novel, as the smokes thickened and the rivers ran black, no Scottish writers could face the conditions of their times directly and transmute the new, extraordinary human experience of their own country into creative life. Instead, those writers dubbed the 'Kailyard School' – the kailyard being the Scottish cabbage patch – wrote

Robert Louis Stevenson

third-rate sentimental tales of country life, populated by gossiping old wives, phthisic heroines, prosy ministers and earnest, gawky heroes, such as *The Stickit Minister* (1893) by Samuel Crockett or *Beside the Bonnie Briar Bush* (1894) by John Watson (Ian MacLaren).

THE CROFTERS' COMMISSION

The kailyard writers were perhaps a necessary product of a materialist age. Heine remarked that sentimentality and brutality are opposite sides of the same coin. No rhapsodies about ancient Celts deterred official action in 1882 when crofters on Skye formed a band to prevent the loss of their pasture rights. There were demonstrations, and when barricades went up against the police, the government sent two hundred marines and a gunboat to oppose them. The Skye protest mirrored anger and resentment elsewhere in the Highlands and Islands. Enforced evictions and clearances had largely ceased. Much of the land cleared for sheep farming was no longer farmed, as the price of wool had fallen steeply. The ground lay empty or was turned over to deer forest. Meanwhile, many crofts were too small to be vi-

SIR WILLIAM ROBERTSON NICOLL
(1851–1923)

Nicoll was one of the great opinion-formers of his time. He was born in Lumsden, where his father was a Free Church minister who had managed to accumulate a library of 17,000 books. At the age of fifteen, he went to Aberdeen University, graduated M.A. in 1870, then spent four years as a theological student in the Free Church's Divinity Hall. He became a minister, first at Dufftown, then Kelso, and also began to write as a journalist. Ill-health made him resign in 1885, and he was 'ordered south' by his doctor. He removed to Hampstead, and was appointed editor of *The Expositor*, an intellectual Christian journal which he ran until his death. But his real public influence came from the *British Weekly*, of which he became founder-editor in November 1886. High-volume printing and swift communication now made it possible to distribute newspapers and magazines in large numbers, and increased literacy and leisure time created a strong market. The new magazine was to be 'a penny religious journal of the best sort'. In Liberal homes throughout Great Britain it soon became required reading, shaping people's views towards an uncontroversial blandness on public affairs and literature. Nicoll wrote a column in it for thirty years, signing himself 'Claudius Clear'. He did not lose his Scottish contacts, and in some literary circles in London was regarded as the promoter, with his friend Sir J. M. Barrie, of Scottish writers to the detriment of English ones.

able. After some prison sentences had been handed out, the government took notice of the real underlying distress and set up a Royal Commission under Lord Napier. The resulting Crofters' Holdings Act of 1886 went well beyond the Napier recommendations and gave the crofters security of tenure and rent protection. A permanent Crofters' Commission was established to supervise their progress. It was not the end of trouble on the islands. Squatters on the Isle of Lewis, without benefit of croft protection, attempted a take-over of a deer forest, claiming that deer ruined their pasture lands.

Many areas of the Highlands and Islands were labelled as 'Congested Districts', holding a population that they could not support. Whilst the well-organised cottage tweed industry helped to stabilise life in the Outer Hebrides, the Highlands and the Inner Isles continued in a state of economic and social decline. Tourism, whisky distilling and forestry, none of which was labour-intensive, were the only sources of employment. Emigration continued, and many houses were left to fall in, or became empty for much of the year, the occupiers having moved south in search of work.

THE TURN OF THE CENTURY

Towards the end of the nineteenth century, the last large-scale British colonial war began in South Africa. Again there was a boom in shipping, cloth and munitions supplies, and a new recruiting call to the men of Scotland. The Boer War was not a wholly popular war, and there was a strain of pacifist and anti-colonial resistance. A strong element in the Liberal Party opposed the way in which the war was conducted; they paid for this with electoral defeat, even in Scotland, in 1900. The 'pro-Boer' Liberal member of parliament for Caithness was burned in effigy in Thurso. The war ended with the surrender of the Boers and the British annexation of the Transvaal in 1900.

Just after the Boer War, a bright young Scot of twenty-six went out to become private secretary to Lord Milner, High Commissioner for South Africa. His father was a Free Church Minister, and he had studied at Glasgow and Oxford. He exuded ambition and ability through every pore. On his return to Great Britain he would be a publisher, a best-selling author, a member of parliament for the Scottish universities and a journalist. He would become a baron and end his career as governor-general of Canada. John Buchan was the Empire Scotsman and Anglo-Scot *par excellence*. A rising man at the peak of Empire, his career seems to indicate a seamless union of the two countries at the heart of it.

The years between 1905 and 1914 nevertheless show a higher rate of emigration from Scotland than at any time in the nineteenth century. It was a time when prices were rising faster than wages, and the population, which was now over five million, was expanding faster than its opportunities. In the aftermath of the Boer War, and again between 1908 and 1910, there were sharp industrial recessions. By now factories built in a hurry in the previous century were seen as vile places to work in; their machinery, much of it no longer new, showed that the Scots had not lost their capacity to make do and mend. To more Scots than ever before, other lands seemed to offer more opportunities, and by now their emigration was a matter of choice rather than desperation or compulsion. Faster passenger ships went to more places, and very often there were contacts waiting to help; people could exercise control over their own future. During 1913, thirty-six thousand emigrants left by ship from the Clyde. There had always been suspicions that emigration deprived the country of its most energetic and enterprising young people, and somewhat discouraging inferences might be drawn by those who remained behind. In the early part of the twentieth century, under the gloss of Imperial confidence, there were deep cracks of uncertainty. Looking forward into the new century, most people with an interest in politics expected Scottish Home Rule within ten or twelve years; they would have been astounded to know it would take 99 years, and the collapse of the Empire, to bring it about. 'It's kittle shooting at corbies and clergy,' says an old Scots proverb; but shooting at the future is the most kittle business of all.

AD 79
- Julius Agricola begins the Roman conquest of North Britain.

84
- Battle of Mons Graupius.

c.85
- Agricola builds a line of forts between the Forth and the Clyde.

105
- Romans forced out of southern Scotland.

122
- Commencement of building of Hadrian's Wall.

c.126
- Disappearance of the Ninth Legion.

127
- Completion of Hadrian's Wall.

139
- Lollius Urbicus moves north with three legions: Antonine Wall begun.

c.143
- Completion of Antonine Wall.

c.155
- Uprisings force Roman retreat from southern Scotland.

158
- Romans return and re-garrison Antonine Wall.

180
- Romans forced back behind Hadrian's Wall.

196
- Maeatae overrun Hadrian's Wall.

208
- Emperor Septimius Severus rebuilds Hadrian's Wall and invades Caledonia.

296
- Further rebuilding of Hadrian's Wall.

c.350
- Birth of St Ninian.

360
- Picts and Scots invade across Hadrian's Wall, reaching as far as London.

369
- Theodosius reinstates the Roman frontier.

378
- St Ninian goes to Rome.

383
- Hadrian's Wall again broken through, no longer reconstructed.

397
- St Ninian's church at Whithorn dedicated to St Martin.

407
- Roman legions withdraw from the island of Britain.

410
- End of Roman rule in Britain.

431
- Death of St Ninian at Whithorn.

432
- St Patrick sails to Ireland.

498
- The Scots settlement begins. Formation of kingdom of Dalriada.

547
- The Angles control Lothian.

561
- St Moluag founds a monastery on Lismore.

563
- Columba comes to Iona and founds a monastery.

565
- Columba's mission to the Pictish king.

574
- Death of King Conall of the Scots. Accession of King Aidan.

575
- 'Synod' of Drumceatt: Scots of Dalriada ceases to pay tribute to Ireland.

584
- Death of King Brude of the Picts. Accession of Gartnait.

597
- Death of St Columba.

603
- Defeat of Aidan by the Angles.

608
- Death of St Baldred.

612
- Death of St Kentigern.

c.613
- Welsh-speaking Cumbria and Cambria cut off from each other.

623
- Death of Fergna, first recorded bishop, as distinct from abbot, of Iona.

634
- St Aidan sent from Iona to convert the Northumbrians.

657
- Oswy becomes overlord of the Scots.

664
- Synod of Whitby establishes the Roman practice in place of the Celtic Church's.

671
- Egcfrith defeats the Picts.

673
- Foundation of monastery at Applecross by Maelrubha.

681
- Trumwine is the first bishop of Whithorn of whom records exist.

684
- Battle of Nechtansmere: the Picts repel the Angles.
- Death of Tuathal, first recorded bishop of Fothrif (and abbot of Dunkeld).

c.700
- The Brecbennach or Monymusk Reliquary is made.
- First recorded bishop of Ross, Curitain.

710
- King Nechtan of the Picts makes his church conform to Roman practice and expels the clergy of Iona.

711
- Scots defeat North Britons at Loch Arklet.

728
- Civil war among the Picts.

730
- Dungal of Dalriada at war with the king, Eochaid, and provokes the Picts.

731
- King Aengus takes the Pictish throne and achieves overlordship of the Scots.
- The Venerable Bede's *History of the English Church* provides valuable information on Scotland.

736
- Aengus ravages Dalriada.

741
- Aengus defeats the Scots.

756
- Aengus with the Northumbrians subdues the Britons of Strathclyde.

c.760
- Founding of the cult of St Andrew at Kilrymont (St Andrews).

776
- Battles between Picts and Scots.

781
- Death of Fergus, king of the Scots. Scots under Pictish rule.

794
- Viking attacks begin.

c.800
- Compilation of the *Book of Kells* on Iona.

806
- Monastery of Iona sacked by Norsemen.

818
- Diarmit, Abbot of Iona, goes to Alba with the shrine of St Columba.

839
- Picts defeated by Norsemen. Kenneth MacAlpin becomes king of Scots.

c.843
- Kenneth MacAlpin becomes king of Picts and Scots.

846
- Founding of Dunkeld Cathedral.
- Kenneth defeats Drostan, a Pictish claimant to the kingship.

c.860
- Death of Kenneth MacAlpin. Accession of Donald I; new law of succession.

862
- Death of Donald I. Accession of Constantine I.

866
- Ketil Flatnose ravages Pictland with a Norse fleet and army.

c.875
- Orkney becomes a Norse earldom.

877
- Constantine I dies fighting Norsemen. Accession of Aed.

878
- Death of Aed. Accession of Giric.

889
- Accession of Donald II.

c.890
- Orkney, Shetland, Hebrides and Caithness become part of Harold Fairhair's kingdom of Norway.

900
- Donald II dies fighting Norsemen. Accession of Constantine II.

903
- Norsemen sack Dunkeld.
- Around this time St Andrews becomes the religious capital.

918
- Scots and Britons defeat Vikings at Corbridge.

926

- Athelstan takes possession of Northumbria.

934

- Athelstan invades from Northumbria.

937

- Battle of Brunanburh.
- Abdication of Constantine II. Accession of Malcolm I.

945

- Cumberland is ceded to Malcolm I.

954

- Death of Malcolm I. Accession of Indulf.

c.963

- Death of Indulf. Accession of Dubh.

967

- Death of Dubh. Accession of Culein.

971

- Death of Culein. Accession of Kenneth II.

c.971

- Edgar cedes Lothian to Kenneth II.

986

- Godred, king of Man and the Isles, fights off a Danish invasion from Ireland.

987

- Earl Sigurd of Orkney controls Sutherland, Ross and Moray.

995

- Death of Kennneth II. Accession of Constantine III 'the Bald'.

997

- Death of Constantine III. Short reigns of Kenneth III and Grig follow.
- Olaf Tryggvason forces the Norsemen of Orkney to adopt Christianity.

1000

- Around this time, a two-hundred-year spell of warmer weather begins over western and northern Europe.

1005

- Death of Grig. Accession of Malcolm II.

1006

- Malcolm II invades Bernicia but is defeated at Durham.

1014

- Battle of Clontarf in Ireland ends Norse overlordship.

1018

- Battle of Carham. Lothian permanently incorporated into Scots kingdom.

1028

- First recorded bishop of St Andrews, Maelduin.

1033

- Invasion of Cnut, king of Denmark and England. Malcolm II pays homage.

1034

- Death of Malcolm II. Accession of Duncan I.

1038

- Strathclyde is ravaged in a Northumbrian invasion.

1040

- Death of Duncan I. Accession of Macbeth.

1045

- Battle of Dunkeld between pro- and anti-Macbeth armies.

1054

- Earl Siward of Northumbria invades on Malcolm Canmore's behalf. Lothian and Strathclyde are taken over.

1057
- Death of Macbeth in battle at Lumphanan. Brief reign of Lulach.

1058
- Battle of Eassie. Death of Lulach. Accession of Malcolm III 'Canmore'.

1060
- Earl Thorfinn builds a cathedral on Birsay in Orkney.

1061
- Malcolm III invades Northumbria. Marries Ingibiorg of Orkney about this time.

1069
- Malcolm III invades Northumbria and Cumbria.
- Following Ingibiorg's death, Malcolm III marries Princess Margaret.

1070
- Malcolm III invades Northumbria and Cumbria.

1073
- William I of England invades. Malcolm III does homage at Abernethy.

1079
- Malcolm III invades Northumbria.

1091
- Further invasion of Northumbria by Malcolm III.

1092
- William Rufus takes possession of Cumberland and builds a castle at Carlisle.

1093
- Death of Malcolm III at Alnwick in Northumberland. Accession of Donald III 'Ban'.

1094
- Brief installation of Duncan II, his assassination and the resumption of rule by Donald III.
- Oldest extant charter of Scotland, a royal grant of land to the monks of St Cuthbert.
- St Serchan's 'Prophecies' compiled.

1097
- Deposition and blinding of Donald III. Accession of Edgar.

1098
- Magnus III 'Barelegs' of Norway devastates the Western Isles.

1099
- Death of Donald III: last king to be buried on Iona.

1105
- Edgar sends an elephant to the High King of Ireland, as a gift.

1107
- Death of Edgar. Accession of Alexander I.

1109
- First recorded bishop of Glasgow, Michael.

1113
- Selkirk Abbey founded.

1114
- The future David I becomes Earl of Huntingdon in England.
- Culdee monastery at Scone rebuilt by Alexander I.

c.1115
- Murder of Earl Magnus of Orkney by Earl Haakon.

1124
- Death of Alexander I. Accession of David I.
- First recorded bishop of Moray, Gregory.
- Aberdeen and Perth made royal burghs.

1128
- Holyrood Abbey founded. Kelso Abbey founded (removed from Selkirk).

1130
- Rebellion of Angus of Moray and Malcolm MacHeth.
- Founding of bishopric of the Isles (including Isle of Man): a Norwegian diocese.
- *Book of Deer* compiled around this time: oldest Scottish Gaelic text written on the margins.

1132
- First recorded bishop of Aberdeen, Nechtan.

1134
- The crown annexes the earldom of Moray.

1135
- David I begins to harry northern England.

1136
- Melrose Abbey founded, first Cistercian monastery in Scotland.

1138
- The Battle of the Standard (22 August).
- Founding of St Magnus Cathedral, Kirkwall, and Jedburgh Abbey.

1139
- Henry, Prince of Scotland, becomes Earl of Northumbria.

1140
- Wimund the Monk a claimant to the throne about this time.
- Somerled is by this time Lord of Argyll.
- Bishopric of Caithness established at Dornoch. Founding of Dryburgh Abbey.

1147
- Founding of Cambuskenneth Abbey.

1150
- First recorded bishop of Brechin, Samson.

1151
- Founding of Kinloss Abbey (from Melrose). First recorded bishop of Caithness, Andrew.

1153
- Death of David I. Accession of Malcolm IV 'the Maiden'.

1155
- First recorded Bishop of Dunblane, Laurence.

1156
- Division of the kingdom of the Isles between Dougal (son of Somerled) and Godred (king of Man)
- Grammar school founded in Aberdeen.

1157
- Release of Malcolm MacHeth from Roxburgh.

1158
- Walter FitzAlan is made High Steward.
- Somerled invades Man and takes control.

1159
- Malcolm IV joins Henry II's invasion of France.
- Treaty between Somerled and the King of Scots.

1160
- Revolt of six earls is put down, and Galloway revolt put down, with English assistance.
- Earliest likely date of the founding of Saddell Abbey, Argyll.

1163
- Founding of Paisley Abbey by Walter FitzAlan.

1164

- Revolt, defeat and death of Somerled, Lord of Argyll, whilst raiding Glasgow.

1165

- Death of Malcolm IV. Accession of William I 'the Lion'.

1171

- First record of Jews in Scotland. Abraham of Edinburgh lends £80 to Robert de Quincy.

1174

- Capture of William I at Alnwick by the English and subsequent imprisonment. Under the terms of the Treaty of Falaise William accepts English overlordship.

1178

- Arbroath Abbey founded by William I.

1179

- MacWilliam rising in the north.
- William I excommunicated in dispute over St Andrews bishopric; Scotland under interdict.

1181

- Roland of Galloway defeats Donald Ban MacWilliam; rising ends.

1187

- Rebellion in Moray put down with help of Galloway men.

1189

- The Quitclaim of Canterbury releases William I from his allegiance to England.
- Musselburgh Council agrees tax to pay Scotland's 'ransom'.

1190

- Berwick and Roxburgh established as royal burghs.

1191

- Dundee established as a royal burgh.

1192

- Scottish Church made a 'special daughter' of Rome.
- First recorded bishop of Lismore (Argyll), Harald.

1196

- William I takes control of the north from Harold, Earl of Orkney.

1200

- First reference in charters to coal mining: as a perquisite of the monks of Holyrood.

1203

- Ragnall of the Isles founds a Benedictine abbey on Iona.

1211

- Guthred and MacWilliams establish power in Ross.

1212

- Execution of Guthred.

1214

- Death of William I. Accession of Alexander II.
- Invasion of Moray by Donald MacWilliam and Kenneth MacHeth.

1215

- MacWilliam and MacHeth defeated by Fearchar MacTaggart.

1216

- Cistercian monastery founded at Culross.

1217

- Alexander II leads a Scots army as far as Dover.

1220

- Carles who fail to join the army when summoned are to be fined a cow and a sheep.

1221
- Alexander II marries Joanna of England.

1222
- Murder of the Bishop of Caithness; Alexander II leads a force there to assert authority. He also campaigns in Argyll.

1224
- Seat of the Bishop of Moray is moved from Spynie to Elgin.

1230
- Foundation of Beauly Priory (Valliscaulian).

1233
- 'Master of schools' recorded at Ayr.

1234
- Last Celtic Lord of Galloway dies. Revolt in Galloway defeated.

1236
- Bridge recorded at Ayr.
- See of Lismore established.

1237
- Treaty of York fixes Scottish border with England.

1238
- Death of Joanna. Alexander II marries a French bride.

1242
- Alexander II offers to buy the Hebrides from Norway.

1244
- Peace concord with England.

1247
- Record of shipbuilding at Inverness.

1249
- Death of Alexander II. Accession of Alexander III.

1250
- Canonisation of St Margaret.

1251
- Alexander III marries Princess Margaret of England (25 December).

1255
- Durward, supported by England, ousts Comyn as Alexander III's 'adviser'.

1257
- Comyn regency successful over Durward.

1258
- Death of Comyn. Alexander III establishes personal rule.

1263
- Haakon IV reasserts control over the Western Isles. Battle of Largs.

1266
- Treaty of Perth – Scotland gains the Hebrides and Isle of Man.

1274
- Devorguilla Balliol founds Sweetheart Abbey.
- Value of church lands put at £18,662; king's revenue £5,413.
- Birth of Robert Bruce, 11 July. Probable birth year of William Wallace.

1278
- Alexander III visits Edward I in London.

1281
- Princess Margaret of Scotland (dies 1283) marries King Eric of Norway.

1286
- Death of Alexander III. Accession of Margaret, 'Maid of Norway'.

1289
- Treaty of Salisbury.

1290
- Treaty of Birgham (March): Maid of Norway to marry crown prince of England. First documentary record of parliament.
- Death in Orkney of Margaret, Maid of Norway. The kingship in dispute.

1291
- Edward I of England in control of Scotland. Thirteen 'Competitors' claim the crown.

1292
- Edward I of England's traversal of Scotland reaches as far as Elgin.
- Kingship of Scots awarded to John Balliol; he is crowned in November.
- Sheriffdoms set up in Argyll and Skye.

1295
- First recorded French-Scottish alliance.
- Record of Court of Four Burghs meeting in Edinburgh.

1296
- Battle of Dunbar. Deposition of John Balliol by Edward I of England. Removal of Scotland's regalia and records, and of the Stone of Destiny. Compilation of 'Ragman Roll'. Sacking of Berwick.

1297
- Risings of William Wallace and Andrew Murray. Attack on the Justiciar at Scone. Defeat at Irvine. Battle of Stirling Bridge (11 September). Wallace named as Guardian.

1298
- Edward I invades again. Battle of Falkirk (22 July). Sir John Soulis becomes Guardian.

1299
- Scots take Stirling Castle.

1300
- Edward I agrees a truce to 1301. Pope Boniface VIII claims right of arbitration.

1301
- Sir John Soulis sends emissaries to Rome to plead Scotland's case before the Pope.

1302
- Robert Bruce submits to Edward I.

1303
- Battle of Roslin, 24 February. Edward I embarks on subjugation of Scotland.

1304
- Stirling Castle retaken by the English. Bruce and Bishop Lamberton make a band of alliance.

1305
- Edward I's Ordinance for the government of Scotland.
- Capture and execution (23 August) of Wallace.

1306
- Robert Bruce murders John 'the Red' Comyn, 10 February.
- Robert I (Bruce) crowned at Scone, 25 March.
- Battle of Methven, 19 June.

1307
- Battle of Loudon Hill (May). Edward I of England dies, 7 July.
- Robert I campaigns in the north.
- Battle of Inverurie, 24 December.

1308
- Battle of the Pass of Brander, 15 August.
- Death of Duns Scotus.

1309
- Robert I's first parliament, 16–17 March.

1310
- Edward II campaigns in Scotland, until 1311.
- Oldest written record of Scottish Gaelic.

1311
- Raids into England this year and next.

1312
- Treaty of Inverness, with Norway, 29 October.

1313
- Recapture of Perth (January).

1314
- Roxburgh and Edinburgh Castles retaken.
- Battle of Bannockburn (23–24 June).

1316
- Edward Bruce crowned king of Ireland.

1318
- Berwick recaptured (March).
- Death of Edward Bruce.
- Pope John XXII places Scotland under interdict.
- First mention of Lyon King of Arms, chief herald of Scotland.
- Consecration of St Andrews Cathedral.

1320
- Declaration of Arbroath, 6 April.
- Soulis Conspiracy and Black Parliament, August.

1322
- Raids into England, as far as Lancaster. Invasion attempt by Edward II fails.

1323
- Andrew Harcla tries to negotiate a peace for England.

1324
- Bruce's kingship recognised by the Pope.

1326
- Representation of burghs in parliament.
- Robert I establishes his home on the Clyde.
- Around this period Skye forms a separate bishopric within the archdiocese of Trondheim.

1327
- Invasion of England. Scots troops find cannon used against them for the first time.
- Dundee receives charter as royal burgh.

1328
- Scottish kingdom recognised by England, 17 March, in the Treaty of Edinburgh-Northampton.

1329
- Death of Robert I (7 June). Accession of David II, first king of Scots to be crowned with full papal sanction (24 November).
- Building of Brig o' Balgownie, Aberdeen.

1332
- Invasion and coronation of Edward Balliol. Renewal of war with England.
- Battle of Dupplin Moor (11 August).
- Flight of Balliol (December).

1333
- Battle of Halidon Hill (19 July). English retake Berwick. Return of Edward Balliol.

1334
- David II and Queen Joan are sent to take refuge in France (May).
- Earliest known Scots armorial bearings, on a seal of the Earl of Mar.

1335
- Invasion of Edward III reaches Perth. Sir Andrew Murray heads resistance.
- Imports of Scandinavian timber recorded.

1336
- Edward III causes destruction as far north as Elgin.
- First use of the title 'Dominus Insularum' (Lord of the Isles) by John of Islay.

1337
- John of the Isles negotiates with the English Earl of Salisbury.

1338
- Black Agnes defends Dunbar Castle against Earls of Salisbury and Arundel.
- Death of Sir Andrew Murray.

1341
- Edinburgh Castle retaken (April). Restoration of David II (June).

1346
- Battle of Neville's Cross (17 October). Capture of David II. The Steward assumes administration.

1349
- Ravages of the Black Death reach Scotland for the first time.

1350
- Revival of Lordship of the Isles.

1352
- David II's temporary return (February).

1354
- French alliance renewed. Negotiations for David II's return fail.
- First known document in which John of Islay refers to himself as Lord of the Isles.

1356
- Edward Balliol renounces his 'kingship'.
- Edward III's punitive expedition: the 'Burnt Candlemas'.

1357
- Treaty signed (October) for David II's ransom and release. Return of David II.
- First mention of a grammar school at Cupar.

1359
- David II makes diplomatic visit to London (February).

1360
- Murder of David II's mistress, Katherine Mortimer.

- Priory of Oronsay established by John of Islay, Lord of the Isles.
- New plague outbreaks.

1362
- First recorded feu charter: land granted in perpetuity.

1363
- David II faces down the Steward and his allies; marries Margaret Logie.

1364
- Parliament refuses a union with England and confirms the Steward (Robert II) as heir presumptive to the crown.
- Last recorded lawsuit for recovery of a runaway serf.
- Burgh merchants given monopoly of buying and selling within their burghs.

1365
- The French chronicler Jean Froissart visits Scotland and writes his impressions.

1369
- David II comes in force to Inverness. The Lord of the Isles brought to submission.
- Lanark and Linlithgow replace English-held Berwick and Roxburgh in the Court of Four Burghs (other two are Edinburgh and Stirling).

1370
- David II makes diplomatic visit to London.
- Composition of *The Pistill of Suete Susan*, about this time.

1371
- Death of David II (22 February). Accession of Robert II (The Steward).
- Treaty of Vincennes (28 October) renews Franco-Scottish alliance.

1375
- John Barbour's *The Brus* appears.

303

1378
- Donald MacDonald, future Lord of the Isles, is given a safe conduct through England to attend Oxford University.
- Export of hides at 44,559, compared to 8,861 in 1327.

1379
- Henry Sinclair of Roslin becomes Earl of Orkney.

1381
- John of Gaunt takes refuge in Edinburgh from the Peasants' Revolt.

1383
- Walter Wardlaw appointed first Scottish cardinal.

1384
- Parliament deplores lawlessness of the time. Passes an Act for the suppression of masterful plunderers, referred to as 'caterans'.
- Franco-Scottish raids into Northern England.
- John of Gaunt invades and holds Edinburgh to ransom.

1385
- French force arrives in Scotland. Richard II invades, sacks Edinburgh and retreats.
- Reconstruction of the church of St Giles, Edinburgh.

1387
- The chronicler John of Fordun, author of the *Scotichronicon*, dies, around this year.

1388
- Robert Stewart, Earl of Fife, appointed Guardian.
- Battle of Otterburn (5 August).

1390
- Death of Robert II. Accession of Robert III.
- Destruction of Elgin Cathedral by the king's brother.

1391
- Earl of Orkney's expedition to Greenland or North America, with the Venetian Antonio Zeno.

1396
- Staged clan battle on the North Inch at Perth between Clans Kay and Chattan (September).

1397
- Disorders of the times deplored in general council.

1398
- Stewart Earls of Carrick and Fife raised to dukes (Rothesay and Albany).

1399
- Duke of Rothesay becomes 'King's Lieutenant'.

1400
- Henry IV of England invades and retreats (August).

1401
- Albany Herald mentioned for the first time, among Scots heralds.

1402
- Duke of Rothesay dies in custody (March).
- Battle of Homildon Hill (14 September).

1404
- Duke of Albany becomes the King's Lieutenant.

1405
- Royal burghs south of the Spey are required to send a delegate to the Court of the Four Burghs.

1406
- Capture of Prince James (14 March).
- Death of Robert III (4 April). Accession of James I. Albany appointed Governor by parliament.

- James Resby, English Lollard priest, burnt to death at Perth (possibly 1407)

1408

- Only surviving record of a Gaelic charter from the Lord of the Isles.

1409

- Earl of Mar (later admiral of Scotland) captures a ship owned by London's Lord Mayor Whittington.

1410

- Disputes with Dutch over the North Sea fishing grounds.

1412

- Because of Scots piracy, the Hanseatic Diet seeks to suspend trade with Scotland.

1411

- Battle of Harlaw (24 July).
- Scotland's first university founded, at St Andrews, by Bishop Wardlaw.

1413

- Papal bull confirms St Andrews University.

1415

- Hanseatic trade forbidden to Scots because of piracy, until 1436.

1417

- Border raids and disorder until 1422.

1418

- End of the Great Schism: Scotland is last country to accept authority of Pope Martin V.
- Earl of Buchan leads a Scots army to France.

1420

- Death of Duke of Albany (September). Murdoch Stewart becomes Duke of Albany and Governor.
- Robert Henryson born (dies *c.* 1490).

1421

- Scots army in France defeats English at Baugé (22 March).

1422

- Scots first recorded as forming French king's bodyguard.
- At this time Andrew of Wyntoun (*c.*1350–*c.*1424) compiles his *Orygenale Cronykil of Scotland*.

c.1423

- Composition of The *Kingis Quair* by James I.

1424

- James I returns from captivity (April). His first parliament reveals far-reaching reform plans.
- Chamberlain's financial duties transferred to Treasurer and Comptroller. The crown claims rights to all mining of gold and silver.
- Completion of St Machar's Cathedral, Aberdeen.

1425

- Fall of the Albany Stewarts. Disputes with the Papacy begin.
- Sir Walter Ogilvy is first Treasurer; David Brown, chancellor of Glasgow Cathedral, is first Comptroller.
- James I founds Charterhouse at Perth, last Scottish monastery to be established. He warns the clergy against a decline in standards.

1426

- All laws other than the king's are abolished.

1428

- James I's coup against the Highland chiefs.

1429

- Power of the Lord of the Isles broken.

1430

- Bishopric of the Isles established.
- Sumptuary laws passed for restraint in dress. Football players to be fined fourpence.

1431

- Battle of Inverlochy: Donald Balloch defeats royal army.
- Plague in Edinburgh, again in 1432.

1433

- A Hussite heretic burned at the stake in St Andrews.

1434

- Prolonged severe winter weather this year and next causes hardship.

1435

- The future Pope Pius II visits Scotland as a papal ambassador.

1436

- James I fails to take Roxburgh Castle.

1437

- Assassination of James I (21 February). Accession of James II.

1438

- Warfare breaks out among the nobility.
- A plague year, continued in 1439.

1439

- Sir William Crichton appointed chancellor.
- Battle of Craignaucht Hill, between Boyds and Stewarts.

1440

- Earl William and his brother executed after Black Dinner of the Douglases (24 November).

1442

- Bishops dispute in the 'Little Schism'.

1444

- Deposition of Chancellor Crichton.

1445

- Garde Ecossaise formed as senior company of French Household Troops.

1446

- Warfare between Ogilvies and Lindsays.

1447

- Loch Fyne herring industry thriving: it produces 'in mair plenti than ony seas of Albion.'

1448

- English raid in Annandale and burn Dumfries; thrown back by Hugh Douglas, Earl of Ormond (23 October).
- Franco-Scottish alliance renewed at Tours (31 December).

1449

- Marriage of James II to Mary of Gueldres (3 July). Post of Admiral of Scotland is introduced.
- Death of Walter Bower, author of the continuation of the *Scotichronicon*.

1450

- Fall of the Livingstons. James II grants Glasgow Green to the town of Glasgow.
- Around now gypsies enter the south of Scotland.

1451

- University of Glasgow founded by Bishop Turnbull.

1452

- Murder of the Earl of Douglas by James II (22 February).

1453

- Richard Holland composes *The Buke of the Howlat* for Archibald Douglas, Earl of Moray.
- John Crukshanks is paid 30 shillings a year to maintain the common clocks of Aberdeen.

1454

- Parliament encourages landowners to plant trees and hedges.

1455

- Act of Annexation defines the crown's sources of finance.
- Final defeat of Black Douglases at Arkinholm (June).

1456

- Around this time Sir Gilbert Hay translates *The Buke of the Law of Armys*, from French, for William Sinclair, Earl of Orkney: the first literary prose in Scots.

1457

- Parliament again tries without success to ban football, also golf. Parliament encourages tenancy under feu-farm.

1460

- Death of James II in siege of Roxburgh Castle. Accession of James III.

1461

- Berwick retaken from England.
- Lord of the Isles attempts a coup in the north.
- *Book of Pluscarden* compiled, with much current information.

1462

- The Lord of the Isles makes Treaty of Ardtornish (13 February) with Edward IV of England for the partition of Scotland.
- The poet Robert Henryson recorded as graduating in Glasgow University.

1466

- Boyds and Kennedies rise to power as 'tutors' of the king.
- The coining of copper 'black money' tried and discontinued (1467).
- From now parliament keeps its own records, separate from the king's council.

1468

- The pledging of Orkney and Shetland.
- Marriage of James III to Margaret of Denmark.

1469

- Parliamentary commission set up to review and codify the law. Burgh elections regulated. The old council to select the new one.

1471

- Preparations made against English invasion.
- Collegiate Church of St Duthac established at Tain.
- Burghs and lords encouraged to build fishing boats to catch herring.

1472

- Formal Annexation of Orkney and Shetland. James III proposes to enforce his claim to be also duke of Brittany. Fall of the Boyds from power.
- St Andrews raised to archbishopric.

1473

- Parliament deplores the lack of gold and coin in the country.
- Edinburgh hat-makers form a craft guild.

1474

- Marriage treaty and truce with England.
- Laws passed to promote sea fishing. Town councils ordered to set up schools for musical education. These co-exist for a time with the grammar schools.
- Edinburgh skinners form a craft guild.

1476

- Submission of Lord of the Isles: earldom of Ross annexed to the crown
- James III grants a three-year safe-conduct to Florentine merchants.

1478

- Serious feuding and fighting in Angus, Sutherland and Caithness.

- Office of King's Advocate established (later Lord Advocate).
- 'Blind Harry's' *Wallace* appears.

1479
- Parliament (March) records trouble and fighting in many parts of the kingdom.
- Duke of Albany imprisoned in Edinburgh Castle, and escapes to France.

1480
- Battle between MacDonalds and MacKenzies in Wester Ross.

1481
- War with England
- Internecine strife in the Western Isles – Battle of the Bloody Bay.

1482
- James III's favourites murdered by the barons. Temporary imprisonment of James III. Richard of Gloucester enters Edinburgh. Final loss of Berwick to England. Return of Albany.
- Debasement of coinage raises prices and heightens scarcity of food and goods.

1483
- Flight of Duke of Albany (May).

1485
- Assay office known to be functioning in Edinburgh. Existence of a grammar school in Brechin is recorded.

1487
- Warfare in the north between MacKays and Rosses.

1488
- Rebellion against James III. Battle of Sauchieburn. Death of James III. Accession of James IV.

1489
- Fighting at sea between Sir Andrew Wood and English vessels.

- Provision made for building a grammar school in Elgin.

c.1490
- Rebellions against James IV put down.
- Drummonds burn 120 Murrays to death in church of Monzievaird.
- The composer Robert Carver writes church music for the Chapel Royal, Stirling.

1491
- Alliance with Denmark renewed.
- Bands and convocations within the burghs are forbidden.

1492
- Glasgow raised to archbishopric.

1493
- Lord of the Isles forfeited: his domains go to the crown.

1494
- James IV cruises up the west coast.
- First reference in the Exchequer rolls to the production of whisky.

1495
- The English Pretender, Perkin Warbeck, welcomed in Scotland.
- University of Aberdeen founded by Bishop Elphinstone.

1496
- Don Pedro de Ayala reports to Spain on conditions in Scotland.
- Education Act passed: barons and freeholders to send their eldest sons to grammar schools.

1497
- Venereal disease reaches Scotland; closure of brothels ordered in Aberdeen.

1498
- James IV holds court at Kilkerran (later Campbeltown).

- Plague attacks afflict the towns.
- Shore Porters' Society founded or re-founded in Aberdeen.
- First mention of coal mining at Machrihanish (Kintyre).

1500

- Population estimated at around 500,000.
- Earl of Argyll becomes King's Lieutenant in the west.
- King's College Chapel, Aberdeen, begun (till 1504). Iona Abbey rebuilding completed: raised to cathedral status. William Dunbar (c.1460–c.1520) is appointed court poet.
- Knitting is introduced to Shetland, from the mainland.

1501

- Earl of Huntly becomes King's Lieutenant in the north.
- James IV begins building of Palace of Holyrood in Edinburgh.

1502

- Death of the king's mistress, Margaret Drummond, and her sisters, after a suspect breakfast.

1503

- Marriage of James IV to Margaret Tudor (8 August).
- William Dunbar composes *The Thrissil and the Rois*.

1504

- Rising of Donald Dubh in the Western Isles (until 1507).

1505

- College of Surgeons and its Library established in Edinburgh.
- Guild of Barber-Surgeons given a monopoly on production of whisky.

1506

- Commissioners appointed to 'compose' feuds in the Western Isles.
- Building of the ship *Great Michael*.

1507

- Introduction of the printing press.

1508

- Annual royal audits held at Edinburgh from now on. Scottish ships sent to the Baltic to support the king of Denmark.
- Earl of Huntly appointed hereditary Sheriff of Inverness, with mandate to enforce peace in the Highlands.
- William Dunbar publishes *Lament for the Makaris*.

1509

- James IV ceases to hold parliaments.
- Bishop Elphinstone's Aberdeen Breviary, listing 70 Scottish saints. It provides a liturgy for Scotland, replacing Sarum liturgy.

1510

- James IV proposes a new Crusade.
- First curling club recorded, at Kilsyth.
- First record of gooseberries, grown as hedgerow bushes in the Dundee area.
- Around this time, Jean Damian tries flying from the walls of Stirling Castle (unsuccessfully).

1512

- *Book of the Dean of Lismore* compiled (until 1526).

1513

- Birth of John Knox (died 1572).
- French appeal for Scottish assistance against Henry VIII. Scottish ships bombard Carrickfergus.
- Battle of Flodden (9 September).
- Death of James IV. Accession of James V.
- Small quantities of gold mined at Crawford Muir.

1515

- Regency of the Duke of Albany begins.

1517

- Treaty of Rouen, renewing the French alliance.

1518

- Disturbances in Sutherland through Gunn-MacKay-Sutherland-Murray feuds (until 1522).

1520

- 'Cleanse the Causey' battle in Edinburgh.
- Murdoch Nisbet makes a version of Wycliffe's New Testament in Scots. This is not published (until the 19th century).
- Completion of St Machar's Cathedral, Aberdeen.

1521

- John Major (*c.*1470–1550) publishes his *Historia Majoris Britanniae*.

1524

- Scotland is effectively ruled by the 'Red Douglas', Earl of Angus.

1526

- Hector Boece's (*c.*1465–1536) *Historia Gentis Scotorum* published.
- Right of mining gold and silver leased to a group of Germans and Dutchmen.

1527

- Hector MacIntosh burns 24 Ogilvies in their own castle.
- Bridge of Dee built, Aberdeen.
- Barry Links recorded as a golfing site.

1528

- James V escapes from tutelage of the Earl of Angus: downfall of Douglas rule.
- The sheriffs of the north instructed to destroy Clan Chattan.
- Patrick Hamilton, Protestant martyr, burned at St Andrews (29 February).

1529

- Sir David Lyndsay's *Complaynt to the King* published.

1530

- Hanging of Johnnie Armstrong and other Border freebooters at the orders of James V.

1531

- Alexander of Islay takes an army into Ulster to support O'Donnel against the English.

1532

- Robert Henryson publishes *The Testament of Cresseid.*
- Inauguration of the College of Justice, or Court of Session. First president is Walter Mylne, abbot of Cambuskenneth. Origins of the Faculty of Advocates.
- North Sea fishery 'war' with the Dutch until 1541.

1533

- English officials in Ireland complain about increase of Scots in Ulster.
- Beginning of the Convention of Royal Burghs.

1534

- A new treaty of perpetual peace between Scotland and England is signed.

1535

- Parliament attempts to stop the land-owners imposing themselves on the burghs as provosts and bailies and profiteering from their positions.

1536

- James V visits France to marry the daughter of Francis I; she dies shortly after arriving in Scotland.
- John Bellenden publishes *Chroniklis of Scotland*, an English version of Boece's *History*.

1539

- A real tennis court is built at Falkland Palace.

1540

- James V sails round the north and west.

- James V recognises the gypsy kingdom of 'John Faw, lord and erle of Little Egypt', and allows his laws to appertain to his people.
- Sir David Lyndsay publishes *Ane Pleasant Satyre of The Thrie Estatis*.
- John Mosman of Edinburgh makes the (still extant) crown for James V.

1541

- James V fails to meet Henry VIII in York.
- Campveere recognised as sole Scottish staple port of the Netherlands.
- Salaries for judges introduced.

1542

- English fleet harries Scottish shipping. Battle of Solway Moss (November).
- Death of James V. Accession of Mary Queen of Scots. Regency of Earl of Arran.
- Around now the *Black Book of Paisley* is written, containing a text of the *Scotichronicon*, etc.
- The palace within Stirling Castle is completed.

1543

- Treaty of Greenwich (July) provides for Mary's marriage to Prince Edward of England.
- An Act is passed for publication of the Bible 'in Inglis or Scottis' – not carried out (15 March).
- The Setons begin Seton Palace, perhaps the first Scottish 'country mansion'.

1544

- English occupy and sack Edinburgh in Henry VIII's 'rough wooing' of Mary for his son.
- An English fleet under the Earl of Lennox devastates Arran.
- Battle of Blair-na-Leine between Frasers and MacDonalds of Clanranald.

1545

- Scots under Arran defeat the English at the Battle of Ancrum Moor (February).

1546

- Burning of George Wishart in St Andrews, 1 March.
- Murder of Cardinal Beaton in St Andrews Castle (May).

1547

- Battle of Pinkie (10 September). 'Black Saturday' (30 July): St Andrews Castle surrendered to French troops. John Knox exiled.

1548

- Queen Mary sent to France for her protection (August).
- John Knox publishes *Epistle on Justification by Faith*.

1549

- Many Hebridean mercenaries engaged in Irish wars against English occupancy of Ireland.
- Donald Monro publishes *A Description of the Western Islands* of Scotland.

1550

- *The Complaynt of Scotland* published in Paris.
- From about now until 1700 a comparatively colder weather period sets in, sometimes referred to as 'the little Ice Age'.

1551

- Frequent raids by the West Highlanders on the Irish coast.

1552

- Convention of royal burghs enacts that all burghs shall model their government on that of Edinburgh.
- First mention of golf being played at St Andrews.

1553

- Gavin Douglas publishes his translation of *The Aeneid* and the poem *The Palice of Honour*.

1554
- Mary of Guise becomes regent.

1555
- John Knox prompts Lord James Stewart to form the band of 'Lords of the Congregation'.
- The 'Bloody Vespers' of Elgin (1 January): battle in the cathedral between followers of William Innes and Alexander Dunbar.

1557
- Signing of the first Covenant, 3 December.

1558
- The English deputy in Ireland, the Earl of Sussex, carries out reprisal raids on the west coast.
- Marriage of Mary to the Dauphin Francis.
- Walter Mylne burned to death at St Andrews, the last pre-Reformation martyr (28 April).
- Knox publishes *First Blast of the Trumpet Against the Monstrous Regiment of Women*.

1559
- John Knox returns to Scotland. Stripping of churches begins, in Perth. Reformers take over Edinburgh; Mary of Guise retreats to Leith. Wars of religion begin.

1560
- Siege of Leith and departure of the French. Treaty of Edinburgh establishes Protestant dominance.
- The Reformation Parliament. Fall of the Catholic Church.
- Establishment of the General Assembly of the Kirk (20 December). Publication of the *Book of Discipline*. Publication of the Geneva Bible.
- Around this time Robert Lindsay of Pitscottie was writing his *Historie and Cronicles of Scotland*, not published until 1778.

1561
- Mary Queen of Scots returns to Scotland (19 August).
- Protestant Confession of Faith drawn up.
- Rioting in Edinburgh when magistrates enforce a ban on the Robin Hood pageant.

1562
- Mary rides to Inverness and Aberdeen; power of the Earl of Huntly broken.
- Ninian Winzet (1518–92) writes *Certane Tractatis for Reformatioun of Doctryne and Maneris*: a tract against Protestantism but in favour of reform.
- Lead mining is licensed to two Edinburgh burgesses.

1563
- Witchcraft made a civil crime.
- Bad harvest pushes up the cost of meal, with consequent hardship.

1564
- First Scottish Psalter printed.
- First mention of Fair Isle as a producer of coarse stockings.

1565
- Marriage of Mary to Lord Darnley. The Chaseabout Raid.
- Bad harvest causes food shortage, and again in 1567.

1566
- Murder of David Riccio in Holyrood Palace (March).
- Birth of the future James VI (June).
- Privy Council orders that 'nane molest the Hielandmen' coming to Lowland markets.

1567
- Murder of Darnley (9 February). Mary marries Earl of Bothwell. Deposition of

Mary. Accession of James VI. Regency of Earl of Moray.
- First book to be printed in Gaelic: a translation of John Knox's *Liturgy*.

1568
- Escape of Mary from Loch Leven. Battle of Langside (14 May). Escape and flight to England of Mary (19 May).
- George Bannatyne publishes *Ballat Buik*.

1570
- Assassination of Regent Moray.
- Meat eating banned during Lent for 'the commoun weill'.

1571
- Wars of religion. The 'King's Lords' besiege Edinburgh Castle, held by the 'Queen's Lords'. The archbishop of St Andrews is hanged, in Stirling.

1572
- Regency of Earl of Morton.
- Death of John Knox.
- Bad harvest makes a year of scarcity and high meal prices.

1573
- Edinburgh Castle surrendered, almost destroyed (29 May). Death of Maitland of Lethington and hanging of Kirkcaldy of Grange.
- Because of shortage, export of salt forbidden, except in ships that had brought in timber.

1575
- Unauthorised beggars to be scourged and branded, by act of parliament.

1576
- Fighting breaks out during a race meeting at Ayr.

1577
- 390 MacDonalds are suffocated in a cave on Eigg, by the MacLeods.

- Glasgow University is reformed in a 'Novo Erectio'.

1578
- James VI assumes government.
- Confirmation of privileges of Convention of Royal Burghs. Staple at Campveere confirmed again.

1579
- Arrival in Scotland of Esmé Stewart, soon to be made Duke of Lennox.
- Shortage of barley: whisky-making restricted to earls, lords, barons and gentlemen, for their own use. Merchants are forbidden to change nationality to benefit their business.
- First Bible printed in Scotland, purchase price £4 13/4d.
- Song schools made a burgh rather than a church responsibility.

1580
- Around this time, east coast fishermen begin to fish the Minch.

1581
- Fall and execution of Regent Morton.
- James VI publishes the Negative Confession, an attack on Catholicism, to mollify Protestants.
- Islesmen continue to raid Ulster. Orkney earldom and bishopric under Earl Robert Stewart.
- Inchcolm island noted as a den of pirates.

1582
- The Ruthven Raid.
- Constant feuding between MacKenzies and Glengarry MacDonalds as MacKenzie power rises; also between MacLeans and MacDonalds of Islay.
- Foundation of Edinburgh University.
- Publication of George Buchanan's *Rerum Scoticarum Historia*.

1584
- The 'Black Acts' enforce the king's superiority over the Kirk.

- Outbreaks of bubonic plague.

c.1585
- Death of 'The Admirable Crichton'.

1586
- Battle of Ardnary in Ireland: invading Highlanders defeated.
- Violent fighting between MacKays, Sutherlands, Gunns and Sinclairs in the north.

1587
- Execution in England of Mary (8 February). Act of Annexation: the crown takes over ecclesiastical holdings. Reforms to Court of Session.
- Parliament passes an Act 'for the quieting and keeping in obedience of the disorderit subjectis inhabitant of the Borders, Highlands and Isles'.
- Export of foodstuffs prohibited because of shortages.

1588
- Ships of the Spanish Armada driven north round Scotland by storms; some are wrecked, including one in Tobermory Bay.

1589
- James VI marries Anne of Denmark, leaving the country for six months.
- Six hundred Islesmen raid County Mayo.
- The High Kirk Session of Glasgow bans golf and shinty on Sundays and working days.

1590
- Witchcraft trial in North Berwick: witches suspected of making spells against the king.

1592
- Presbyterianism established by the 'Golden Act'. Murder of the 'bonnie' Earl of Moray.
- Parliament bans export of sheep and cattle because of food shortages.

1593
- Founding of Marischal College, Aberdeen.

1594
- Battle of Glenlivet: Earl of Huntly defeats Earl of Argyll (3 October).
- Parliament complains about the wild behaviour of university students and teachers.
- Chair of Law set up at Edinburgh University.
- Building of Provost Ross's House, Aberdeen.

1595
- Archibald Napier publishes *The New Order of Gooding and Manuring of All Sorts of Field Land with Common Salts*.
- Boys at Edinburgh High School mutiny, and shoot Bailie John McMorran.
- A famine year, with grain imports, high prices, and hardship among the poor.

1596
- Re-enactment of the 'Black Acts.' Appointment of eight Commissioners, 'the Octavians', to supervise the exchequer.
- Northern earls submit to James VI.
- Rescue of Kinmont Willie from Carlisle Castle by Walter Scott.
- Dysart and Culross fined £100 each for illegally exporting coal.

1597
- Import duty levied for the first time, at one shilling in the pound.
- Plantation of Lewis begins. Landholders in the Highlands and Islands ordered to produce charters or evidence of their territorial rights.
- James VI publishes *Demonologie*, a book on witchcraft.

1598
- General Assembly agrees bishops may sit in Parliament.
- James VI publishes *Basilikon Doron*, a book on monarchy.

- Feuds between MacDonalds and Mac-Leans cause bloodshed in the Western isles.
- Whisky listed among other exports to Ireland.
- Fynes Morison, an English traveller, notes that the Scots gentry use 'no Art of Cookery'.

1599

- Complaints about conduct of Earl of Orkney include piracy.
- Faculty of Physicians and Surgeons established in Glasgow.

1600

- First day of the New Year is moved this year to 1 January; previously on Lady Day, 25 March.
- The Gowrie Conspiracy. Bishops restored.
- Scots College established in Rome.
- Privy Council licenses one hundred foreign clothworkers to enter the country on advantageous terms, to pass on their skills.

1601

- Tax levied on wine 'to restrain drunkenness'.
- Feud on Skye between MacLeods and MacDonalds culminates in the Battle of Bencoullen.

1603

- James VI becomes also James I of England in the Union of the Crowns, and leaves Edinburgh for London.
- Massacre of MacKenzies, while at worship in the church of Kilchrist, by the MacDonalds.

1604

- First commission for a Treaty of Union.
- Earls of Argyll and Atholl combine to attack the proscribed MacGregors.
- Famine in the Highlands.

1605

- James VI sets up a Border Commission to reduce disorder.

1606

- Act of parliament allows for serfdom of coal and salt workers as 'necessary servants'.

1607

- English Parliament rejects Union.
- Earl Patrick's palace built in Kirkwall.

1608

- Plantation of Ulster begins.

1609

- The Statutes of Icolmkill. Plantation of Lewis abandoned.
- James VI acknowledges the status of the Beatons or MacBeths as physicians in the Isles.
- Justices of the Peace established around this time.
- Salt panning established on a large scale along the East Lothian coastline.

1610

- Proscription of the MacGregors.

1611

- Publication of the Authorized Version of the Bible.
- Glasgow receives charter as royal burgh.

1612

- Parliament grants a patent for the manufacture of sulphur and chemicals.

1614

- John Napier of Merchiston (1550–1617) publishes *Mirifici Logarithmorum Canonis Descriptio*, first work on logarithms.
- Coal exports run at around 14,000 tons, mostly to the Netherlands.

1615

- Earl of Caithness arrests Earl of Orkney

on Privy Council orders. Execution of Earl of Orkney.
- Hanging of John Ogilvie for refusing to deny supremacy of the Pope (later canonised – 1976).
- Great unrest in Kintyre and Islay with the rebellion of Sir James MacDonald. Crown forces brought from Ireland and Scotland.

1616
- An Act of Council proposes the establishment of parish schools. Local warfare endemic in the far north, between Earls of Caithness and Sutherland.
- Chiefs are instructed to send their sons to Lowland schools, and to keep only one galley.
- Status of Campveere as Scottish staple port reaffirmed.
- William Drummond of Hawthornden publishes his *Poems*.

1617
- James VI revisits Edinburgh (May).
- James VI presents Dumfries with 'Silver Gun of the Seven Trades' as shooting trophy.

1618
- The Five Articles of Perth.
- Coal mines at Culross extend beneath the sea.
- Matthew Taylor, 'the water poet', visits the Highlands.

1619
- First slate-roofed buildings in Sutherland.

1620
- Erection of Gladstone's Land, tall tenement in Edinburgh.
- George Jamesone (*c*.1588–1644), first recorded Scottish portraitist, active in Aberdeen.

1621
- Sir William Alexander receives charter

for the establishment of Nova Scotia (29 September).
- Nathaniel Udwort of Edinburgh purchases a monopoly on soap-making.

1623
- Failed harvest produces much hardship and many deaths through starvation.

1624
- The Privy Council threatens sanctions against those who visit 'Christ's Well' at Doune.
- Death of George Heriot (born 1563), goldsmith and money-lender: 'Jingling Geordie'.

1625
- Death of James VI. Accession of Charles I.
- Judges removed from Privy Council, to concentrate on Court of Session work.

1627
- Commission of inquiry reveals many parishes without school or schoolmaster.

1628
- Building of George Heriot's Hospital (now School) until 1659.

1630
- Numerous witchcraft trials during this time.

1631
- Earl of Stirling (Sir William Alexander) given monopoly on copper farthings.

1632
- Nova Scotia colonists forced out by the French.
- Construction of Parliament House in Edinburgh begins (until 1640)

1633
- Coronation in Edinburgh of Charles I. Act passed for the establishment of a school in every parish.

- Formation of a corps by Sir John Hepburn, to become the Royal Scots.

1635
- Scottish mercenary officers and soldiers begin returning from the Continent.
- First inland postal service, between Edinburgh and London. Proposal made to erect a lighthouse on the Isle of May (first in Scotland).
- A 'snorting and dowking' sea monster sighted off Aberdeen in July.

1637
- Promulgation of the new Scottish Prayer Book creates social disorder (23 July).

1638
- Signing of the National Covenant (28 February). General Assembly abolishes bishops (November-December).
- William Lithgow (*c.*1582–*c.*1650) publishes his *Totall Discourse of Rare Adventures and Painfull Peregrinations... from Scotland.*

1639
- The first Bishops' War, and Pacification of Berwick.
- The Trot of Turriff (14 May): Royalists scatter a Covenanting force.

1640
- The second Bishops' War. Scots occupy Newcastle. Harrying of Catholic clans by Argyll. Montrose makes the Cumbernauld Bond against Argyll.
- The Wedderburn brothers publish the *Gude and Godlie Ballatis* around this time.

1641
- Charles I visits Edinburgh in the hope of making allies.

1642
- Founding of the Scots Guards, 28 March.

1643
- The Solemn League and Covenant made with the English Parliament (13 October).
- The Westminster Assembly of Divines promulgates a Confession of Faith, Larger and Shorter Catechisms, etc.

1644
- Scots invade England.
- Siege of Newcastle and Battle of Marston Moor. Montrose named King's Lieutenant in Scotland. Campaigns of Montrose begin. Montrose's victory at Tippermuir (1 September).
- Parliament introduces excise duty of 2/8d per pint, on whisky.
- Outbreaks of bubonic plague frequent between now and 1649. Around a quarter of Edinburgh's population die in this outbreak.

1645
- Montrose's victories at Inverlochy, 2 February; Auldearn, 9 May; Alford, 2 July; Kilsyth, 15 August; defeated at Philiphaugh, 13 September.

1646
- Charles I surrenders himself to the Scots army (5 May).

1647
- Charles I handed over to English Parliament (30 January). The Engagement.

1648
- Battle of Preston (17 July).
- Cromwell in Scotland.
- The 'Whiggamore Raid' on Edinburgh: extreme Presbyterians take over government.

1649
- Execution of Charles I (30 January). Accession of Charles II; his proclamation in Edinburgh.
- Last visitations of bubonic plague.

1650

- Battle of Carbisdale (27 April). Capture and execution (21 May) of Montrose. Charles II lands in Scotland (June). Battle of Dunbar (2 September).
- Introduction of Metric Psalms.
- Famine in the Highlands.

1651

- Battle of Inverkeithing: Royalists defeated by Cromwellian army (2 July).
- Battle of Worcester (3 September).
- Dundee sacked by General Monk.
- Cromwell's rule extended over Scotland.
- *Mercurius Scoticus*, first Scottish newspaper, published in Leith; later banned.

1652

- The Scottish regalia hidden from Cromwell's troopers by James Granger, minister of Kinneff.
- English-Dutch war disrupts Scots-Dutch trade, until 1654.
- Thirty Scots members sent to join the Protectorate Parliament in London.

1653

- Scotland formally unified with England and Ireland under the Commonwealth.
- Sir Thomas Urquhart (*c.*1611–60) publishes the first two books of his translation of Rabelais.

1654

- General Monk defeats royalists under Middleton at Dalnaspidal.
- The Camerons are the last of the clans formally to submit to Cromwellian rule.
- Dundee offers free entry to merchants' guild, to combat the dearth of men and trade in the town.

1656

- Justices of the peace for Midlothian draw up pay scales for four separate grades of farm servant.

1658

- Oliver Cromwell claims to have freed

'the meaner sort' of Scots from the 'great lords'.

1660

- Restoration of Charles II.
- Oldest extant portrait of a figure in the belted plaid.
- From now on the importing of tea and coffee becomes significant. Coffee houses begin to open in Edinburgh.

1661

- The Drunken Parliament.
- Restoration of episcopacy.
- Execution of Marquis of Argyll.
- Ship *Elizabeth* is wrecked carrying state papers returned from England to Scotland, 18 December.

1662

- Acts are passed to discourage wine drinking in the Isles, thereby stimulating whisky-making, and against the use of Gaelic as a 'barbarous' language.
- Restoration of lay patronage.
- Forbes' *Songs and Fancies* published in Aberdeen – first secular music published in Scotland.

1663

- Expulsion of non-conforming ministers. Holding of Conventicles begins.

1664

- Lime trees first planted in Scotland, at Taymouth.

1665

- English-Dutch war again disrupts Scots-Dutch trade, until 1667.

1666

- The Pentland Rising (November). Battle of Rullion Green (28 November).

1667

- Commissioners of Supply are appointed in the shires.

- Glasgow creates a deep sea-going port at Port Glasgow.
- Twice a week post established between Edinburgh and Aberdeen.

1669

- Charles II's first Letter of Indulgence. Duke of Lauderdale fails to bring about a union of the Parliaments.

1670

- Founding of Royal Company for the Fishery of Scotland.
- Forth coalmines estimated to yield around 50,000 tons a year.

1671

- High Court of Justiciary established as central criminal court.

1672

- Parliament reduces the monopoly powers of royal burghs.
- Charles II's second Letter of Indulgence.
- Lyon Office established as central armorial registry.
- English-Dutch war again disrupts Scots-Dutch trade. Philip van der Straten, of Flanders, starts up the woollen industry of the Borders, at Kelso.
- Early mention of turnips, recorded as stolen from fields in records of baron court of Urie.

1674

- Heavy winter snow kills many cattle in the Borders.

1675

- First paper-works in Scotland, at Dalry.

1676

- Royal Company of Archers set up as sovereign's bodyguard.
- Foundation of the Physic Garden in Edinburgh.

1677

- Battle between two gypsy tribes, Faas and Shaws, at Romanno Bridge (1 October).

1678

- Duke of Lauderdale sends Highlanders to pacify Ayrshire.
- David Calderwood (1575–1651) publishes *History of the Church of Scotland*.
- Earl of Mar raises a regiment, later to become the Royal Scots Fusiliers (23 September).

1679

- Murder of Archbishop Sharp (May).
- Battles of Drumclog (May) and Bothwell Brig (June).
- Duke of York becomes Commissioner in Scotland.
- Rebuilding of Holyrood Palace completed.
- Earliest recorded pipe major in the army: Alexander Wallace of Dumbarton's Regiment.

1680

- Cameronians defeated by dragoons at Airds Moss, 22 July.

1681

- The 'Test' imposed, following passing of the Test Act. Acts passed to give tariff protection to certain industries.
- Edinburgh Assay Office begins to use letters to indicate dates.
- General Tam Dalyell raises a regiment, Royal Regiment of Scots Dragoons, later Royal Scots Greys (25 November).
- Viscount Stair (1619–95) publishes *Institutes of the Law in Scotland*.
- Foundation of the Royal College of Physicians.
- Annual wine import estimated at 1,600 tuns.

1682

- Foundation of the Advocates' Library, Edinburgh (now National Library).

1683
- Hearth tax introduced.
- First Scots gardening book, John Reid's *The Scots Gardiner*.

1684
- Start of the 'Killing Time'.
- The Dutch artist Jacob de Wit is hired to paint the kings of Scotland, from his imagination, for £250, to decorate Holyrood Palace.

1685
- Death of Charles II. Accession of James VII.
- Failed invasion by the Earl of Argyll against James VII's government; he is executed and the Campbell territories on the mainland ravaged.
- Two women Covenanters are drowned at Wigtown, 11 May.
- The Gaelic bard Iain Lom (*c.*1624–*c.*1710) visits the court of Charles II.

1686
- James VII's first Letter of Indulgence.

1687
- James VII's second Letter of Indulgence.

1688
- James VII's third Letter of Indulgence.
- Flight of James VII to France.
- Establishment of William II and Mary II.
- French wars with England have adverse affect on Scottish trade with France, until 1697.
- Central tower of St Machar's Cathedral, Aberdeen, falls in.
- Poor harvest and starvation on Skye.

1689
- Parliament deposes James VII (March) and claims the right to choose the monarch.
- William and Mary confirmed as joint sovereigns.
- Earl of Leven raises a Border regiment, later the King's Own Scottish Borderers (18 March).
- Earl of Angus forms the Cameronians into a regiment, 19 April.
- Battle of Killiecrankie (27 July), high point of the first Jacobite rebellion: death of John Graham of Claverhouse (born 1648), Viscount Dundee.
- Cameronians hold Dunkeld against the Highlanders.
- MacDonald of Keppoch defeats the MacIntoshes in one of the last clan battles.
- Ferintosh Distillery, near Dingwall, first bulk producer of whisky, burned down by supporters of James VII.

1690
- Jacobite forces defeated in Battle of Cromdale (1 May).
- Presbyterianism established as form of Church in Scotland.
- Royal supremacy over the Church abolished.
- Parliament passes first of numerous Acts for the Observation of the Sabbath.
- Rev. Robert Kirk has his translation of the Bible into Gaelic printed in London.
- First rope works in Scotland, in Glasgow.
- Maple and walnut trees first planted in Scotland.

1691
- Convention of Royal Burghs enquires as to the state of the burghs, revealing serious reduction in trade and activity generally.

1692
- Massacre of Glencoe, 13 February.
- Death of Robert Kirk, minister of Aberfoyle, author of *The Secret Commonwealth of Elves, Faunes and Fairies* and translator of the Bible into Gaelic.

1693
- MacGregor name proscribed again.
- First public music concerts in Edinburgh.

- John Slezer publishes his *Theatrum Scotiae*, views of Scottish towns.

1694
- Death of Mary II. Sole reign of William III.
- Bass Rock recaptured from Jacobite rebels.
- William Paterson (1658–1719) founds Bank of England.
- Act to support linen manufacture: all shrouds to be made of plain linen.

1695
- Company of Scotland Trading to Africa and the Indies founded. Bank of Scotland founded.
- Martin Martin publishes *Description of the Western Islands of Scotland*.
- First public concert given in Edinburgh.
- A General Post Office is set up in Edinburgh.
- Poor and late harvest causes hardship. The potato recorded as cultivated in Scotland and the Isles.

1696
- Education Act prescribes a school in every parish (*see* 1633).
- Another failed harvest causes much hardship. Duties lifted on virtually all food imports.

1697
- Paisley witch trials.
- Thomas Aikenhead hanged in Edinburgh for blasphemy and his corpse is burned.
- Records include mention of red and white varieties of potato.

1698
- The Darien venture is launched. Three ships leave on 1 July; two others follow later.
- Harvest fails again, causing starvations and deaths. Andrew Fletcher estimates the number of beggars at 200,000.

1699
- Grain export forbidden because of the shortage.

- A woollen manufactory is established in Glasgow.

1700
- Population estimated at *c*.1,000,000. Population of St Kilda counted at 200.
- News comes of the collapse and abandoning of the Darien colonial venture.
- James Macpherson, bandit and fiddle player, hanged at Banff.
- Salt panning consumes an estimated 150,000 tons of coal a year, and produces 25,000 tons of salt.
- Great fire in Edinburgh destroys many buildings around Parliament House.

1702
- Death of William III. Accession of Anne.
- Commissioners appointed to draft Treaty of Union.
- Further English-French war disrupts trade with France.

1703
- Scottish parliament passes Act of Security.
- John Adair publishes *Description of the Sea-Coast and Islands of Scotland*.
- Three women are scourged in the regality of Grant for bringing whisky to two men condemned to hang.

1704
- Dunkeld is last royal burgh to receive a charter.
- Alexander Selkirk is put ashore on Juan Fernandez: prototype of 'Robinson Crusoe'.

1705
- English parliament passes Aliens Act.
- The *Worcester* incident.
- Linen Act of 1694 repealed: shrouds must now be of wool, to protect the woollen industry.

1706
- Treaty of Union is drawn up in London and presented to Parliament in Edinburgh.

1707
- Act of Union, 16 January. Dissolution of the Scottish parliament and formation of the United Kingdom Parliament.
- Customs and Excise Service established in Scotland.

1708
- Abolition of the Scottish Privy Council.
- Edinburgh University first to abolish the 'regent' system of teaching.

1709
- The Kirk sets up Society for the Propagation of Christian Knowledge, for education in the Highlands and Islands. General Assembly recommends a library in each presbytery.
- Prolonged bad weather causes bad harvest and much hardship.

1710
- Dancing 'assemblies' begin in Edinburgh.
- Large-scale building of dry-stone dykes in Galloway to enclose land.

1711
- Export duty imposed on linen industry.
- Birth of David Hume (died 1776).
- Central tower of Elgin Cathedral collapses.

1712
- Patronage Act: lay patronage of Church ministers restored.
- Parliament attempts to increase malt tax: prevented by protests of Scottish members.

1714
- Death of Anne. Accession of George I.
- Catholic seminary set up by Loch Morar.

1715
- First Jacobite Rebellion, under the Earl of Mar. Jacobites take Perth. Battle of Sheriffmuir.
- Horse-post introduced between Edinburgh and Glasgow.

1716
- The Old Pretender lands at Peterhead, January, and leaves from Montrose, February. End of the Rebellion.
- Disarming Acts passed.

1717
- Horse-borne post introduced from Glasgow to Edinburgh and the north.

1718
- Glasgow and Greenock-owned vessels regularly cross the Atlantic, engaging in slave traffic as well as in goods.

1719
- Battle of Glenshiel; Jacobites and Spanish allies defeated.
- Allan Ramsay (1686–1758) sets up as a bookseller in Edinburgh, begins to publish his poetry.

1720
- First steam pumping engine in a Scottish coalmine, at Elphinstone, Stirlingshire.
- Around this time tea overtakes ale as morning beverage.

1721
- Robert Wodrow publishes *Sufferings of the Church of Scotland*.

1722
- Signet Library established in Edinburgh.
- The pheasant is introduced to Scotland.

1723
- Gilbert Burnet's (1643–1715) *History of My Own Times* published.
- Society for the Improvement in the Knowledge of Agriculture founded in Edinburgh.

1724
- 'Levellers' among the Galloway peasantry attack enclosed land.

1725
- Shawfield Riots caused by the Malt Tax.

- A new Disarming Act passed. General Wade commissions the Black Watch (42nd Regiment) to police the Highlands (12 May).
- Between now and 1736 General Wade constructs military roads in the Highlands. A six-horse chaise seen in Inverness for the first time.
- Allan Ramsay publishes *The Gentle Shepherd*.
- Dumfries town council puts an undermaster in charge of cock-fighting at the school. Scholars may bring a cock to fight on appointed days, for a fee of 12p Scots.

1727
- Death of George I. Accession of George II.
- Establishment of Commissioners and Trustees for Improving Manufactures and Fisheries.
- Founding of Royal Bank of Scotland, first bank to employ the overdraft method.
- Iron smelting begins at Invergarry.
- Inverness-Fort William road completed through the Great Glen.
- Last burning of a witch, at Dornoch.
- First larches planted in Scotland, at Dunkeld.

1728
- Allan Ramsay opens the first circulating library in Scotland.
- James Gibbs (1682–1754) publishes his *Book of Architecture*.
- Two million yards of linen are produced.

1729
- Foundation of Society of St Luke in Edinburgh, Scotland's first art institution.
- Edinburgh Royal Infirmary established.
- William Mackintosh of Borlum, imprisoned Jacobite commander, publishes *Essays in Ways and Means of Inclosing, Fallowing, Planting, Etc.*

1730
- Francis Hutcheson appointed Professor of Moral Philosophy at Glasgow: first to abandon lectures in Latin.
- Complete publication of *The Seasons* by James Thomson (1700–1748).
- Iron smelting at Abernethy, Speyside, using Tomintoul ore. Perth-Dunkeld-Inverness road completed.
- Edinburgh Royal Infirmary opened.
- The cedar of Lebanon tree is introduced to Scotland.

1731
- *The Poor Man's Physician* published in Edinburgh.

1732
- William Adam begins the new Haddo House.

1733
- The Original Secession from the Church of Scotland, led by Ebenezer Erskine.

1734
- John Cockburn establishes planned village of Ormiston.
- Sir Archibald Grant begins agricultural improvements at Monymusk.
- Death of Rob Roy MacGregor (born 1671).
- Robert Keith publishes *History of the Affairs of Church and State in Scotland*.
- First recorded reference to the sword dance, or *gille calum*.

1735
- Kelp manufacture begins, on North Uist.
- Mrs Henry Fletcher commences Holland linen manufacture. Glasgow has 47 ships engaged in the Atlantic trade.

1736
- The Porteous Riot in Edinburgh.
- Repeal of the Witchcraft Act of 1563.
- First purpose-built theatre in Edinburgh.
- Dr John Armstrong publishes *The*

Oeconomy of Love, a sex manual for newly-weds, in verse.

1737
- First Secession from the Church of Scotland.

1738
- Allan Ramsay the Younger (1713–84), portrait painter, removes to London.

1739
- Formation of the Black Watch as a regiment.
- Publication of Hume's *Treatise of Human Nature* and Anderson's *Diplomata*.
- *Scots Magazine* founded.
- Around this time, cultivation of the turnip is introduced and potatoes begin to become a staple rather than a luxury crop.

1740
- Tobias Smollett (1721–71), author, moves to London.
- Lord Lovat makes the first journey by coach from Inverness to Edinburgh.
- Aberdeen Royal Infirmary founded.
- Failure of crops throughout the country: subsequent hardship. Boys and youths kidnapped for sale to America.
- The Tay is frozen for six weeks from 1 January.

1741
- First Gaelic-English lexicon published.
- Granite starts to be used for buildings in Aberdeen.
- Press-gang activity of the Royal Navy snatches away many fishermen and seamen.

1742
- Edinburgh Ice Skating Club established.

1743
- Last wolf killed, either by Cameron of Lochiel in Inverness-shire or by Eoghan MacQueen in Perthshire.

1744
- Failure of French invasion plan.
- Original Seceders split into 'Burghers' and 'Anti-Burghers'.
- Honourable Company of Edinburgh Golfers established.

1745
- Prince Charles Edward Stewart lands and raises western clans.
- Capture of Edinburgh.
- Defeat of government army at Prestonpans.
- Invasion of England.
- Tennant's brewery set up in Glasgow.
- Edinburgh's first wallpaper merchant opens for business.
- Cattle plague breaks out in England, pushing up prices of Scottish cattle

1746
- Jacobite army retreats from Derby.
- Victory at Falkirk.
- Defeat at Battle of Culloden.
- Prince Charles Edward Stewart in hiding, then flees to France.
- British Linen Company receives its charter.
- Forest fire in Duach Valley, Moray, destroys 2.5 million trees.

1747
- *Aberdeen Journal* founded.

1748
- Act for the Abolition of Heritable Jurisdictions heralds final collapse of clan system.
- Petition for 'Augmenting the Salaries and Other Incomes of the Schoolmasters of Scotland'.
- Tobias Smollett publishes *The Adventures of Roderick Random*.

1749
- Aberdeen Banking Company founded: first outside Edinburgh. Younger's Brewery set up at Holyrood, Edinburgh.

- First stagecoach service from Glasgow to Edinburgh.
- First Scottish chemical works, a vitriol factory at Prestonpans.

1750

- Around this time the Norn language of Shetland finally becomes obsolete.
- Iron smelting using charcoal established in the Highlands at Bonawe.
- New shops in Glasgow include a silversmith's and a haberdasher's.
- It begins to be unusual for a farmer and his family to share all meals with the farm workers.
- Around this time the capercaillie becomes extinct.

1751

- Turnpike Road Act sets road improvement in motion.
- Towns with more than 10,000 people are Edinburgh-Leith (57,000), Glasgow (32,000), Aberdeen (15,500), Dundee (12,400). Only four other burghs exceed 5,000.

1752

- Calendar reformed; eleven days removed to bring Scotland and England into line with Europe. The 'Old New Year' continues to be celebrated in many places.
- The Appin Murder: Colin Campbell of Glenure ('The Red Fox') killed, 14 May. James Stewart ('James of the Glens') tried and hanged.

1753

- Slight shocks from the great Lisbon earthquake are felt throughout the country (1 November).

1754

- James Justice publishes *The Scots Gardener's Director*.
- Society of Golfers formed at St Andrews.
- Allan Ramsay, the painter, returns to Edinburgh.

1755

- Society for Encouraging Art, Science and Industry formed in Edinburgh.
- Journeymen Woolcombers' Society begun in Aberdeen.
- Alexander Webster publishes *An Account of the Number of People in Scotland*, estimating the population at 1,265,380, of whom 51 per cent live north of the Tay. Perthshire is the most populous county, at 120,116, followed by Aberdeen with 116,168, then Midlothian, 90,412.

1756

- Death of William McGibbon, Scotland's leading eighteenth-century composer.
- Around now, inoculation against smallpox is becoming increasingly common.
- Duke of Argyll has 29,657 trees planted at Inveraray, including many foreign species.

1757

- Greenock becomes a burgh (of barony).
- James Watt (1736–1819) appointed mathematical instrument-maker to Glasgow University.

1759

- Birth of Robert Burns (25 January).
- William Robertson publishes his *History of Scotland* (from 1542 to 1603).
- Foundation of the Carron Iron Company.

1760

- Death of George II. Accession of George III.
- James Macpherson (1736–96) begins publication of his Ossian poems.
- Thomas Braidwood (1750–98) opens Britain's first school for the deaf and dumb.
- Edinburgh School of Design established.
- Banks begin to be established in country towns.
- Carpet weaving begins in Hawick and Kilmarnock.
- Coke smelting of iron begins.

- Around now the fashionable dinner hour is advanced to three, or even four, o'clock.

1761

- Completion of the Royal Exchange, Edinburgh.

1762

- St Cecilia's Hall built in Edinburgh: first purpose-built concert hall.

1763

- A windmill is erected at Stromness, Orkney, for milling grain.

1764

- Joseph Black demonstrates that a balloon filled with hydrogen will rise.

1765

- Alison Cockburn (1713–94) publishes her version of *The Flowers of the Forest*.
- Society for the Importation of Forest Seeds established in Edinburgh by Dr John Hops, professor of botany.
- By this time wooden-tracked waggonways are in common use in the Fife collieries, using horse-power.

1767

- Work begins on the New Town of Edinburgh.
- James Small patents the chain plough – use of it spreads rapidly.

1768

- William Smellie launches the *Encyclopaedia Britannica* in Edinburgh.
- Gaelic poems of Duncan Bàn MacIntyre (1724–1812) published.
- Famine in the Western Isles and West Highlands, and again in 1769.

1769

- Fenwick weavers form the first Co-operative Society (9 November).
- James Watt patents a separate steam condenser.

1770

- William Hunter (1718–83), anatomist, establishes his 'Hunterian Museum' in London; to be bequeathed to Glasgow University.
- Death of the Gaelic poet Alasdair Mac-Maighstir Alasdair (born *c*.1695).
- Town of Ballater founded, around mineral wells.
- The Crieff Cattle Tryst in disuse.
- Act passed to establish Clyde Trust.
- Thirteen million yards of linen are produced.
- John Broadwood (1732–1812) founds his piano manufactory in London.
- James Bruce discovers the source of the Blue Nile.
- By now potatoes are the main item of diet in the Highlands and Islands.

1771

- Tobias Smollett publishes *The Expedition of Humphrey Clinker*. Henry Mackenzie publishes *The Man of Feeling*.
- Value of tobacco imports peaks at around £490,000, three times the value in 1755. Re-exported tobacco accounts for 51 per cent of Scottish export value.

1772

- Gavin Hamilton (1723–98) paints an Ossian cycle in Penicuik House.
- Collapse of the Ayr bank of Douglas Heron.
- Calico manufacture begins in Lanarkshire.
- Smeaton builds a new bridge over the Tay at Perth.
- North Bridge of Edinburgh completed.
- James Riggs sets up his Spade-making Works at Sanquhar.

1773

- Robert Fergusson (1750–74) composes his poem *Auld Reekie*.
- Building of Culzean Castle by James Adam (finished 1790).
- John Erskine of Carnock (1695–1768)

publishes his *Institutes of the Law of Scotland*.
- *Edinburgh Medical Journal* established.
- Dr Samuel Johnson and James Boswell tour the Highlands and Islands.
- James Watt removes to England to pursue development of his improved steam engines.
- Death of James Gibbs (born 1682), architect of nave of St Nicholas, Aberdeen, and numerous London churches and buildings.

1774
- Register House, Edinburgh, built by Robert Adam.

1775
- Partial emancipation of coalminers and salt-pan workers from serfdom.
- Iron smelting established at Furnace, Kintyre (to 1813).

1776
- American War of Independence has a disastrous impact on Glasgow's tobacco trade.
- Gaelic poems of Mary MacLeod (*c.*1615–*c.*1707) first published.
- Adam Smith (1723–90) publishes *The Wealth of Nations*. Lord Kames publishes *The Gentleman Farmer*.

1777
- Thirlage to local mills is ended, although money payments have to be made to compensate for multures.
- The Highland Light Infantry formed.
- Weatherby's Racing Calendar records a five-day race meeting at Ayr.

1778
- Atholl Highlanders raised by Duke of Atholl, still in existence as a 'private army'. Seaforth Highlanders raised by Earl of Seaforth.
- Death of the Gaelic poet Rob Donn MacKay (born 1714).

- Edinburgh is estimated to have 400 illicit stills.

1779
- First large water-powered spinning mill is opened at Rothesay.
- A large iron-works is established at Wilsontown.

1780
- Value of linen manufacturing has increased almost six-fold since 1730.

1781
- Private distilling (not for resale) is made illegal. Existence of around 1,000 small distilleries is estimated.
- The Mound in Edinburgh begins to be built up, continuing to 1820.
- First Highland Games are held, at the Falkirk Cattle Tryst.

1782
- Highland dress again allowed.
- First umbrella seen in use in Edinburgh.
- Bad harvest causes famine and deaths in the Highlands. Grain shortage results in efforts to ban whisky distilling.

1783
- Beginning of the rule of Henry 'The Ninth' Dundas as political supremo of Scotland.
- Royal Society of Edinburgh founded.
- *Glasgow Advertiser* (later *Glasgow Herald* then *The Herald*) founded. Glasgow Chamber of Commerce established.

1784
- Forfeited estates of Jacobites restored.
- Death of Allan Ramsay, portrait painter (born 1713).
- Elspeth Buchan (1738–91) proclaims herself the Woman of Revelation.
- Founding of the Royal Highland and Agricultural Society.
- J. Tytler makes the first hot air balloon ascent in Scotland, from Comely Bank to Restalrig, Edinburgh.

1785

- By now soft fruit bushes are commonly found in cottage and house gardens.
- The Ayrshire breed of cow and the Dunlop cheese are both in active development at this time.
- James Hutton (1726–97), pioneer geologist, expounds his *Theory of the Earth* to Royal Society of Edinburgh.
- Signor Lunardi, Italian balloonist, makes flights from Glasgow and Edinburgh, including one over the Firth of Forth.

1786

- Robert Burns publishes the Kilmarnock edition of his poems.
- John Anderson (1726–96) publishes *Institutes of Physics*.
- Northern Lighthouse Board is set up.
- Stagecoaches introduced between Edinburgh and London.
- David Dale (1739–1806) institutes cotton mills at New Lanark.

1787

- Andrew Meikle's (1719–1811) threshing mill completed. The world's first fully successful thresher.
- Kinnaird Head lighthouse built.

1788

- Prince Charles Edward dies in Rome.
- Alexander Nasmyth (1758–1840) paints Robert Burns's portrait.
- William Symington (1763–1831) launches a paddle steamer on Dalswinton Loch.
- British Fisheries Society establishes port at Ullapool.
- Direct Glasgow-London stagecoach service begins.
- The Northern Meeting is established at Inverness (June 11).

1789

- William Cullen publishes *Treatise on Materia Medica*.
- The Old Quad, Edinburgh University, built by Robert Adam.

1790

- Bernera Barracks, Glenelg, abandoned.
- First publication of pibroch music.
- James Bruce of Kinnaird (1730–94) publishes *Travels to Discover the Source of the Nile*.
- Opening of the Forth and Clyde Canal.
- By now the Clydesdale horse breed is established. Duke of Atholl establishes the first deer forest.

1791

- Publication of the *Statistical Account of Scotland* begins (until 1799)

1792

- Association of Friends of the People for Parliamentary Reform started by Thomas Muir and William Skirving. They hold three conventions this year and next.
- Opening of the Monkland Canal.
- Sir Alexander Mackenzie (1764–1820) is first European to cross the Rocky Mountains.
- James Adam (1730–94) designs the Glasgow Infirmary.
- Robert Adam (born 1728) architect of Register House, Edinburgh, and many other buildings, dies. William Murdoch develops gas lighting.

1793

- War with France begins. Political trials of suspect 'radicals' this year and next. Thomas Muir sentenced to 14 years' transportation for sedition.
- Cameron Highlanders regiment raised by Cameron of Lochiel.
- Work begins on the Crinan Canal.

1794

- Duke of Argyll raises the Argyll Highlanders; Duke of Gordon raises the Gordon Highlanders.
- Board of Agriculture publishes *The General View of Agriculture* to encourage progressive techniques.

1795

- Aberdeen obtains a Police Act for civic order, street paving, etc.
- Opening of Glasgow Royal Infirmary.
- Regular race meetings are established around now in Ayr, Edinburgh, Dumfries, Kelso, Hamilton, and other places.

1796

- Opening of the Andersonian Institution, Glasgow, later Royal Technical College, ultimately University of Strathclyde.
- Work begins on the Aberdeenshire Canal, later converted to railway track.
- Death of Robert Burns (21 July).

1797

- Militia Act. Riots in Tranent against conscription.
- George Mealmaker, radical weaver of Dundee, transported for sedition.
- Edinburgh opens its first Magdalene Asylum, for the reformation of 'fallen women'.

1798

- Ayrshire Yeomanry raised by Earl of Cassilis.
- Opening of Dundee Infirmary.
- St Rollox Chemical Works established in Glasgow.

1799

- Napoleonic Wars begin.
- Liberation of the coal miners.
- Mungo Park (1771–1806) publishes *Travels in the Interior of Africa*. Robert Burns's *Love and Liberty* poems published as *The Jolly Beggars*.
- Sir Henry Raeburn (1756–1823) paints a famous portrait of the violinist Niel Gow, among many other cultural and social figures.

1800

- Ayrshire is first county to establish a rural police force.
- Aberdeen New Streets Act passed: building of Union Street commenced.

1801

- First official census shows population as 1,608,000.
- The world's first paddle steamer, *Charlotte Dundas*, used as a tug.
- Robert Brown (1773–1858), botanist, sails with Flinders to survey Australia.

1802

- Sir Walter Scott publishes *Minstrelsy of the Scottish Border*.
- Foundation of the *Edinburgh Review*.

1803

- Highland Roads and Bridges Commission established.
- Thomas Telford begins road construction.
- First all-iron swing plough developed by Gray of Uddingston.

1804

- Construction of Caledonian Canal begins.

1805

- Building of the Hunterian Museum, Glasgow.
- Sir David Wilkie (1785–1841), artist, leaves Edinburgh for London.
- Sir Walter Scott publishes *The Lay of the Last Minstrel*.
- Around this time weaving of Paisley pattern shawls begins in Paisley.
- Royal Highland and Agricultural Society offers a prize for a practicable mechanical reaper.

1806

- Glasgow, Paisley and Johnstone Canal begun.

1807

- Construction of the Bell Rock lighthouse, completed 1811, by Robert Stevenson.
- Death of Niel Gow, celebrated fiddler and composer of strathspeys (born 1727).
- Measles epidemic causes many deaths.

1808

- The Court of Session is reorganised into

two divisions under the Lord President and the Lord Justice Clerk.

- Jamieson's *Etymological Dictionary of the Scottish Language* published.
- Hugh Watson, pioneer of Aberdeen-Angus cattle breeding, starts his farm.

1809

- Completion of the first complete topographical survey of Scotland.
- Death of Sir John Moore at Corunna (born Glasgow 1761).
- Caledonian Horticultural Society established.
- The bothy system is coming into use in larger farms in Angus and the northeast.
- Lachlan MacQuarie appointed governor of New South Wales.

1810

- Surveys confirm Ben Nevis as highest mountain; previously thought to be Ben Macdhui.
- Sir Walter Scott publishes *The Lady of the Lake*.
- World's first savings bank established, the Parish Bank Friendly Society of Ruthwell, by the Rev. Henry Duncan (20 June).
- Lead mining still carried on; yield is 1,400 tons.
- John Loudon McAdam (1756–1836) begins road construction.
- Commercial Bank of Scotland founded (24 March).
- Hunters for cairngorm stones haunt the Cairngorm Mountains.

1811

- Census shows population as 1,806,000.
- Crofting system begins to oust runrig in the Highlands and Islands.
- Death of David Ritchie, 'the Black Dwarf', 3 feet 6 inches tall, born 1735 near Peebles.

1812

- American War does severe damage to cotton trade (to 1814).

- Henry Bell (1767–1830) builds steamship *Comet*.
- Lanarkshire weavers jailed for 'combining' in a trade union.
- Strawberries grown commercially at Roslin.

1813

- Dissatisfaction and unrest among workers in the post-war slump, especially handloom weavers. Court of Session fixes their pay but employers ignore this.

1814

- Strathnaver Clearances in Sutherland.
- Anonymous publication of Scott's *Waverley*.
- Last sea-witch in Orkney sells winds to sailors.
- Earl of Buchan sets up a colossal Wallace statue, near Dryburgh.
- Heavy storms, with numerous shipwrecks, 16–17 December.

1815

- The Corn Laws push up food prices, creating hunger among the unemployed and further unrest.
- Establishment of trial by jury in civil cases.

1816

- Sir Walter Scott begins building of Abbotsford.
- David Brewster (1781–1868) invents the kaleidoscope.
- Small Stills Act helps reduce illegal distilling.

1817

- Treason trials of radical agitators.
- Tax of 4d put on newspapers and magazines.
- Edinburgh's first Police Act.
- Founding of *The Scotsman* newspaper and *Blackwood's Magazine*.
- First Scottish steam railway (goods only) between Kilmarnock and Troon.

- Union Canal, from Edinburgh to Glasgow, begun.
- First Braemar Highland Gathering.

1818
- Sir Walter Scott publishes *Rob Roy* and *Heart of Midlothian*.
- Measles, typhus and whooping cough epidemics.
- First iron passenger ship launched on the Clyde.
- Colonel 145, first animal in the Aberdeen-Angus herd book, is born.

1820
- Government arrests twenty members of Glasgow Radical Committee.
- Skirmish of Bonnymuir between Radical marchers and Kilsyth Yeomanry (5 April). Fifty men tried for treason, three hanged, nineteen transported.
- Around now 'tweed' becomes a popular fabric in Glasgow and London.
- The Edinburgh Botanic Garden resited at Inverleith.

1821
- Census shows population as 2,092,000.
- Edinburgh School of Arts established, later the Watt Institution, ultimately Heriot-Watt University.
- John Galt (1779–1839) publishes *Annals of the Parish*. Lady Nairne (1766–1845) publishes her songs pseudonymously in *The Scottish Minstrel*.

1822
- King George IV visits Edinburgh.
- Licence fee on distilling reduced to £10; duty reduced: smuggling dies away, development of the whisky industry begins.
- Jute first imported to Dundee.
- The kelp industry of the west collapses.
- Opening of the Caledonian Canal (November).
- First Highland Agricultural Show.

1823
- Foundation of the Bannatyne Club. Sir

Henry Raeburn (1756–1823) appointed King's Limner and Painter in Scotland.
- Dick Veterinary College founded, Edinburgh.
- White Star Line founded in Aberdeen.
- Lifting of import duties on salt (January) has a severe effect on Scottish salt industry.
- Charles Macintosh (1776–1843) patents his 'proof cloth': his invention of rubberised waterproofing leads to the 'Macintosh' coat.
- Hugh Clapperton (1788–1827) crosses the Sahara.

1824
- James Hogg publishes *The Private Memoirs and Confessions of a Justified Sinner*.
- Sir Walter Scott publishes *Redgauntlet*.
- Edinburgh sets up the first municipal fire brigade.
- William Burn (1789–1870) designs Edinburgh Academy.
- Ayrshire Colliers' Union established.

1825
- The cotton industry is estimated to employ 151,000 people.
- Abolition of salt duty ruins the Scots salt-pan industry.
- Edinburgh Royal High School built by Thomas Hamilton (1784–1858).
- James Chalmers (1782–1853) invents adhesive postage stamps.
- David Douglas (1798–1834) discovers the giant fir in North America.

1826
- Royal Scottish Academy founded.
- First Scottish public railway, between Monkland and Kirkintilloch (steam and horse).
- Incorporation of Edinburgh-Dalkeith Railway (horse traction) and Dundee and Newtyle Railway (horse and cable).
- First Scottish tile-works, at Cessnock.
- Dr Robert Knox (1791–1862) opens his anatomy school in Edinburgh.
- Glasgow City Mission founded.

1827

- The High Court sentences its youngest criminal, a nine-year-old boy, to eighteen months for theft.
- Captain James Stirling founds Perth, Australia.
- Patrick Bell (1799–1869) invents the first effective reaping machine.
- Robert Wilson invents the screw propellor.

1828

- Population of the island of Rum is cleared out to America.
- Home Drummond Act begins licensing of public houses. Pubs must close for the hour of divine service.
- Publication of Rob Donn MacKay's (1714–78) Gaelic poems.
- J. B. Neilson (1792–1865) invents hot-blast iron-refining.
- Building of the lighthouse at Cape Wrath.
- Patrick Bell, minister of Carmyllie, develops the first practicable machine reaper in the world.

1829

- Trial of Burke and Hare for body-snatching in Edinburgh; Burke hanged; Hare turns King's Evidence.
- Building of the Royal Exchange, Glasgow.
- Catholic Emancipation Act passed.
- Restoration of High Kirk of St Giles in Edinburgh.
- Damaging floods in Moray

1830

- Death of George IV, accession of William (III of Scotland, IV of England). Whigs come to power in Westminster Parliament.
- Sir Charles Lyell (1797–1875) publishes *Principles of Geology* (completed 1833).
- Aeneas Coffey's patent still gives boost to whisky-making.
- First iron steamship, *Lord Dundas*, built on the Clyde.

- David Hutcheson organises steamboat services from the Clyde to Argyll.
- From around now, Shetland ponies are extensively used in coalmining.

1831

- Census shows population as 2,364,000.
- Norse chessmen dating from *c.*1200 found on Lewis.
- Sir James Ross (1800–1862) locates the Magnetic North Pole.
- Scotland's first effective steam railway, Glasgow to Garnkirk.
- James Smith publishes *Remarks on Thorough Drainage and Deep Ploughing*.
- Cholera strikes for the first time, with deaths estimated at 10,000.

1832

- Reform Act passed: 40,000 people march in celebration in Edinburgh.
- Scottish MPs increased from 45 to 53.
- Franchise extended to 60,000 men (householders of £10 in the burghs and proprietors of £10 or tenants of £50 rental in the country districts).
- Dundee and Newtyle Railway completed.
- Death of Sir Walter Scott.
- Continuing outbreaks of cholera cause at least 10,000 deaths.

1833

- Slavery abolished in British dominions.
- Burgh Reform Act extends electoral rights in burgh elections to all rate-payers.
- Abbotsford Club founded to publish historical source material. Thomas Carlyle publishes *Sartor Resartus*.

1834

- General Assembly passes Veto Act, empowering congregations to reject the choice of a patron. House of Lords rejects this.
- Countess of Dunmore organises first sales of Harris Tweed in London.

332

- Thomas Carlyle moves to London from Scotland.
- Thomas Henderson (1798–1844) becomes first Astronomer Royal for Scotland.
- Society of Golfers becomes the Royal and Ancient Golf Club. First Scottish cricket championship, between Perth and Glasgow Cricket Clubs.

1835
- Dalkeith Scientific Association is formed.
- A cockpit is erected in Hope Street, Glasgow, with much gambling activity.

1836
- First iron ship is built on the Tay, at Perth.
- Three-month strike of cotton workers.
- North of Scotland Bank founded, Aberdeen.
- Serious typhus epidemic in Glasgow and other urban areas, with many deaths.
- First Champion Clydesdale Horse competition.
- First ascent of Sgurr nan Gillean on Skye, by Principal James Forbes of St Andrews University.

1837
- Death of William IV, accession of Victoria.
- J. G. Lockhart publishes *Memoirs of the Life of Sir Walter Scott* (completed 1838).
- Thomas Carlyle publishes *The French Revolution*.
- James Forbes (1809–68) discovers the polarisation of heat.
- The capercaillie is re-introduced, from Sweden.

1838
- Chartism becomes a force for political reform.
- Five leaders of the 1836 cotton strike sentenced to transportation (given a free pardon in 1840).

- Clydesdale Bank founded in Glasgow. Caledonian Bank founded in Inverness.
- Royal Caledonian Curling Club founded.

1839
- By now over 80 local Chartist Associations have been formed.
- James Nasmyth (1808–90) develops the steam hammer.
- First Aberdeen clipper, *Scottish Maid*, launched.
- Sir James Ross begins Antarctic exploration.

1840
- Kirkpatrick Macmillan makes the first true bicycle.
- Glasgow School of Art founded.
- Architectural Institute of Scotland founded.
- Great auk ceases to breed in the Hebrides.

1841
- Census shows population as 2,620,000. Sixteen per cent of Glasgow's population is Irish-born (44,000 out of 270,000).
- Sheriff Watson establishes 'ragged schools' in Aberdeen.
- Thomas Carlyle (1795–1881) publishes *On Heroes and Hero-Worship*.
- Hugh Miller (1802–56) publishes *The Old Red Sandstone*.
- Sir Thomas Dick Lauder (1784–1848) publishes *Legends and Tales of the Highlands*.
- Robert Napier starts first yard for all-iron ships, at Govan, and builds first iron warship for the Royal Navy, HMS *Jackal*.
- 'Tennant's Stalk', 455-foot smoke-stack, built at St Rollox Chemical Works, Glasgow.

1842
- Chadwick Report condemns Glasgow as most insanitary town in Britain.

333

- Scottish Patriotic Society founded to encourage emigration.
- James Forbes invents the seismometer.
- Edinburgh and Glasgow are joined by railway.
- Donaldson's Hospital, Edinburgh, built by W. H. Playfair (1789–1857).

1843

- Employment of women in the mines ceases.
- Disruption of Church of Scotland – establishment of Free Church. Around 500 churches are built in the year following.
- First performance of *The Messiah* in Glasgow.
- Robert Adamson (1821–48), pioneer of photography, develops calotype process.
- James Braid writes first medical paper on hypnosis.

1844

- Incorporation of the North British Railway Company; its first line from Edinburgh to Berwick.
- Skerryvore lighthouse constructed.

1845

- Board of Commissioners for Poor Relief established.
- Poor Law Act extends residence requirement for someone to be eligible for parish relief from three to five years.
- Efforts to stop the 'bondager' system of unpaid female labour in Lothian fail.
- Electric telegraph begins operation.
- Incorporation of the Caledonian Railway Company, between Glasgow and Carlisle (opened September 1847).
- Robert William Thompson (1822–73) patents a pneumatic tyre.
- Completion of the Scott Monument in Princes Street, Edinburgh.

1846

- Burgh Reform Act removes old trading monopolies of burghs and gilds.
- Corn Laws repealed.

- Serious typhus epidemic sweeps through Glasgow, with many deaths.
- The Famine Relief Committee finds that potatoes represent up to 88 per cent of the diet in the Highlands, and 25 per cent in the Lowlands.
- Public Money Drainage Act makes £2,000,000 available for land drainage loans.

1847

- Failure of the potato crop causes famine in the Highlands between now and 1850.
- Thomas Guthrie (1803–73) publishes *Plea for Ragged Schools*.
- United Presbyterian Church founded.
- Educational Institute of Scotland founded.
- Sir James Young Simpson (1811–70) originates use of ether at childbirth.
- James 'Paraffin' Young (1811–83) establishes the paraffin oil industry from shale deposits.

1848

- Ten thousand Chartists demonstrate on Calton Hill, Edinburgh; Chartist riots in Glasgow (March).
- Pure jute cloth first produced in Dundee.
- Leather golf balls replaced by gutta-percha.
- Representatives of 200 bowling clubs meet in Glasgow to agree a standard set of rules.
- Outbreaks of cholera throughout the country this year and next.

1849

- Seventy people crushed to death in false fire alarm in a Glasgow theatre.
- David Livingstone (1813–73) begins missionary activity in Central Africa.
- Private Money Drainage Act stimulates founding of companies to finance drainage and land improvement.
- World's first train ferry built by Napier at Govan, the *Leviathan*.

1850

- Lothian shale-oil industry begins.
- Completion of the Glasgow and South-Western Railway, Glasgow to Dumfries (October).
- World's first train ferry established across the Firth of Forth, from Granton to Burntisland, North British Railway.
- Scotland has 21 poorhouses.
- By now, runrig cultivation has almost vanished in the Highlands.

1851

- Emigration Society founded on Skye.
- Completion of Donaldson's Hospital, Edinburgh. Glasgow Natural History Society founded.
- David Hutcheson & Company establish steamer routes in Western Isles.
- Alexander Bain develops an electric clock.

1852

- Highland Emigration Society formed.
- An amateur dramatic society is formed in Falkirk.
- Triangulation Survey of Great Britain is completed; surveyors celebrate in the open air with a giant pudding.

1853

- Formation of the National Association for the Vindication of Scottish Rights.
- Public drinking of alcohol is restricted to licensed premises. Sunday closing of pubs is introduced.
- Opening of the Deeside Railway.
- Purchase and rebuilding of Balmoral Castle by Albert, Prince Consort.
- John Ruskin's *Edinburgh Lectures* help to popularise the Gothic style.
- The Royal National Lifeboat Institution has seven stations in Scotland.
- A 28-gram nugget of gold is found at Kildonan, Sutherland.

1854

- Crimean War begins – Scottish regi-

ments sent out. The 93rd Highlanders hold the 'thin red line' at Balaclava.
- Opening of the Great North of Scotland Railway between Aberdeen and Huntly (September 19).
- Hugh Miller publishes *My Schools and Schoolmasters*.
- Outbreaks of cholera throughout the country.

1855

- United Coal and Iron Miners' Association of Scotland founded.
- 89 per cent of men can sign their names on marriage certificates; 77 per cent of women.
- Glasgow begins to build the pipeline for the supply of pure water from Loch Katrine.
- Inverness to Nairn railway, first in the Highlands.
- David Livingstone discovers the Victoria Falls.

1856

- Henry Cockburn's (1779–1854) *Memorials of His Time* published.
- Eliza Edmonston's *Sketches and Tales of the Shetland Islands* first popularises Fair Isle knitting.

1857

- Indian Mutiny breaks out. Scottish regiments in action, including the relief of Lucknow.
- Board of Commissioners in Lunacy established.
- First steel steamship constructed on the Clyde.
- Crash of the Western Bank.
- Madeleine Smith tried in Glasgow for murder of her lover, verdict not proven (September).
- David Livingstone publishes *Missionary Travels in South Africa*.
- Donald MacLeod publishes *Gloomy Memories of the Highlands of Scotland*, first in Canada.

1858
- Honours degree courses instituted at the universities.
- Free Church builds the Assemby Hall on the Mound, Edinburgh.
- George Macdonald (1824–1905) publishes *Phantastes*.
- R. M. Ballantine publishes *The Coral Island*.
- Edinburgh Academicals Football Club formed (to play rugby).

1859
- Large numbers of men (five per cent of eligible population) join the Volunteer Movement, sparked by French invasion fears.
- Loch Katrine water is piped to Glasgow. Queen Victoria opens the scheme, 15 October.
- Scottish National Gallery opens (21 March).
- Samuel Smiles (1813–94) publishes *Self-Help*.

1860
- Union of King's and Marischal Colleges as Aberdeen University.
- *The Book of Deer* (eleventh/twelfth-century gospels with Gaelic marginal notes) is found in Cambridge University Library.
- J. F. Campbell (1822–85) begins to publish *Popular Tales of the West Highlands*.
- Glasgow Choral Union holds its first music festival.
- *The Scotsman* reports that in Europe only Austria has a higher illegitimacy rate than Scotland.
- Portable steam sawmills now in use in lumber industry.
- Golf Open Championship introduced.

1861
- Census establishes Scotland as having 787 islands, of which 602 are uninhabited.
- American Civil War creates huge growth in Dundee jute industry and hits the cotton industry.
- Founding of the Royal Scottish Museum in Edinburgh.
- Tom Morris (1821–1908) becomes golf professional at St Andrews; wins British Championship Belt four times.
- Queen's Park Football Club formed, 9 June.
- John McDouall Stuart is first man to walk across Australia, north-south.

1862
- Burgh Police Act, enabling local authorities to enforce building regulations.
- Salmon Fisheries Act.
- Osgood Mackenzie begins to establish the gardens at Inverewe.

1863
- James Clerk Maxwell (1831–79) develops theory of magnetic waves.

1864
- Last public execution in Edinburgh: George Bryce for the razor murder of a young woman.
- Completion of railway from Perth to Inverness; incorporation of the Highland Railway Company.
- James Augustus Grant (1827–92), explorer, publishes *A Walk Across Africa*.

1865
- Last public execution in Glasgow: Dr E. Pritchard for murder of his wife and mother-in-law.
- Sir Archibald Geikie (1835–1924), geologist, publishes *The Scenery of Scotland*.
- Cattle rearing is heavily hit by rinderpest coming in from the Continent.

1866
- Glasgow 'tickets' small houses to stipulate maximum number of dwellers.
- Police Act to suppress brothels and street prostitution.

336

- The fort at Fort William abandoned and largely demolished.
- Church of Scotland permits use of organs.
- Cholera outbreaks throughout the country.

1867
- Franchise extended to all adult males. Scottish Women's Suffrage Society formed, in Edinburgh.
- Public Health Act for Scotland passed.
- Singer Sewing Machine factory established near Dumbarton.
- Building of the Albert Institute, Dundee.

1868
- Scottish Reform Act passed (13 July). Franchise extended to all male householders.
- Scotland's first Ladies' Educational Association formed, in Edinburgh, to promote higher education for women.
- Scottish Co-operative Wholesale Society founded.
- Queen Victoria publishes *Leaves from a Journal of Our Life in the Highlands*.

1869
- Female householders are given right to vote in municipal elections.
- Peak of pig-iron production, at 1,206,000 tons.
- Sailing ship *Cutty Sark* launched at Dumbarton, 22 November.
- Ramblers About Glasgow Club formed.

1870
- New Glasgow University buildings on Gilmorehill completed (November) except for the spire (1887).
- Medical students riot in Edinburgh against women attending anatomy lectures.
- Thomas Lipton (1850–1931) opens his first grocery shop in Glasgow.
- The Kildonan gold-field in Sutherland is closed down by the land-owners.

- Powderhall racing track set up, in Edinburgh.

1871
- Gaelic Society of Inverness founded.
- Paisley Museum established.
- Tramcars begin to run in Edinburgh.
- North British Railway introduces the first 4–4–0 express locomotive.
- Scotland win the first Rugby International against England.

1872
- Voting in elections by secret ballot introduced.
- Dundee Museum and Art Gallery established.
- Steel Company of Scotland founded.
- Education Act ensures universal education from age five to thirteen.
- Scottish Education Department set up.
- First international soccer match, Scotland-England, results in an 0–0 draw. Second Rugby International is won by England.

1873
- James Clerk Maxwell publishes *Treatise on Electricity and Magnetism*.
- Alfred Nobel establishes a dynamite factory at Ardeer.
- Dundee has ten steam-powered whaling ships.
- Death of David Livingstone at Ujiji, Africa.
- Sankey and Moody begin a ten-year religious revival campaign throughout the country.
- Severe summer storms with several deaths (22–23 July).
- Formation of the Scottish Football Association, with seven member clubs.
- Scottish Football Union formed (3 March) for Rugby Football. Scottish Football Association Cup Competition set up, won by Queen's Park. Rugby International a draw with England. Founding of Glasgow Rangers FC.

1874
- Repeal of the Patronage Act.
- Wick and Thurso linked to Inverness by rail (July).
- Caledon Shipyard founded in Dundee.
- Building of the harbour at Buckie (until 1880).
- SFA Cup won by Queen's Park. Rugby International won by England.

1875
- Artisans' and Labourers' Dwellings Act passed.
- Factories Act raises minimum age of child workers to ten years; ten–hour working day established.
- Cockburn Association founded in Edinburgh (first civic society).
- Episcopal Church founds an Orphanage at Aberlour.
- Eighteen gypsy families found still living around Kirk Yetholm.
- The 1745 Monument erected at Glenfinnan.
- Institute of Scottish Bankers founded in Edinburgh: first professional banking body.
- SFA Cup won by Queen's Park. Rugby International drawn with England.

1876
- Residence requirement for someone to be eligible for poor relief is restored to three years.
- Tramcars begin to run in Dundee.
- W. F. Skene (1809–92) publishes *Celtic Scotland* between now and 1880.
- The staff-head, or *coigreach*, of St Fillan is acquired by the Museum of Antiquities from its hereditary keeper, Alexander Dewar.
- Alexander Bain (1818–1903) founds the journal *Mind*.
- Alexander Graham Bell (1847–1922), inventor of the telephone, emigrates to the USA.
- SFA Cup won by Queen's Park. Rugby International won by England.

1877
- Several companies amalgamate to form The Distillers' Company Ltd.
- Galloway Cattle Society founded.
- Clydesdale Horse Stud Book set up.
- SFA Cup won by Vale of Leven. Scotland beat England in Rugby International.

1878
- Crash of the City of Glasgow Bank.
- Roman Catholic episcopal hierarchy re-established.
- Fine Art Institute Building, Glasgow, designed by John James Burnet.
- First Tay Bridge opened (1 June).
- Dollar Academy founded.
- William MacGonagall (1830–1902) publishes his first collection of verse.
- African Lakes Company founded in Glasgow 'to advance the Kingdom of God by honest trade'.
- SFA Cup won by Vale of Leven. Rugby International drawn with England.

1879
- Collapse of the first Tay Bridge (28 December).
- Sir James Murray (1837–1915) commences work on *The Oxford English Dictionary*.
- Establishment of Edinburgh Dental Hospital.
- Building of Central and St Enoch Stations, Glasgow.
- David Hutcheson & Company becomes David MacBrayne & Company.
- Formation of Aberdeen-Angus Cattle Society.
- SFA Cup won by Vale of Leven. Rugby International drawn with England.

1880
- Around now, week-long summer holidays for workers become usual (normally unpaid).
- First Ordnance Survey maps of Scotland published.

- Society of Antiquaries founded (18 December).
- Callander-Oban Railway completed (July).
- SFA Cup won by Queen's Park. England win Rugby International.

1881

- Census shows population at 3.7 million.
- The 91st and 93rd Regiments are combined as the Argyll & Sutherland Highlanders.
- Foundation of Queen's College, Dundee.
- Foundation of the Highland Reel and Strathspey Society.
- First torchlight procession of Up Helly Aa in Lerwick, Shetland.
- SFA Cup won by Queen's Park. Rugby International drawn with England.

1882

- Formation of the Highland Land League.
- 'Battle of the Braes' in Skye between crofters and police, 11 April.
- R. L. Stevenson (1850–94) publishes *Treasure Island*.
- The 'Glasgow Boys' group of artists flourishes between now and *c.*1895.
- Academy of Music for Scotland established in Edinburgh (September).
- Chair of Celtic Studies founded at Edinburgh University; Gaelic taught at university for the first time.
- Scottish Texts Society founded.
- Slight earthquake shock felt over the whole country (2 February).
- SFA Cup won by Queen's Park. Scotland beat England in Rugby International.

1883

- The 'Crofters' War' continues: appointment of Royal Commission.
- Steamer *Daphne* capsizes at launch on the Clyde; 124 die.
- Explosions at Glasgow Gasworks (January) and the Forth and Clyde Canal aqueduct at Keppoch Hill (February) are ascribed to Irish terrorist activity. 'Glasgow Dynamiters' sentenced to penal servitude.
- Deer forests take up 1,709,892 acres.
- Sir William Smith (1854–1914) establishes the Boys' Brigade.
- First Carnegie Free Library opens in Dunfermline.
- Alexander Mackenzie publishes *The Highland Clearances*.
- SFA Cup won by Dumbarton. England win Rugby International.

1884

- Third Reform Act extends voting rights to farm labourers, among all male occupiers.
- Twelve additional Scottish MPs (total now 70) and constituencies are re-aligned.
- Uig crofters band to resist eviction, on Skye. Government sends a gunboat and 250 marines.
- W. Y. MacGregor paints *Vegetable Stall*, a fine painting in the new French style.
- Miss Cranston's Tearooms open in Glasgow.
- Royal Scottish Geographical Society founded. Observatory established on summit of Ben Nevis (until 1903).
- Heavy thunderstorms cause death and destruction in Edinburgh (August).
- A five–foot salmon, weighing 80 pounds, is netted in the Tay (December), believed to be the biggest ever.
- SFA Cup won by Queen's Park. England win Rugby International.

1885

- Creation of the Scottish Secretaryship.
- Five crofters from Valtos (Lewis) sentenced to short terms for defiance of writs from Court of Session.
- Coatbridge is made a burgh.
- Monday holidays become common, as a substitute for the no longer observed fast days.
- Steel output reaches 241,000 tons.
- Founding of the Federation of Burns Clubs.

- Founding of Aberdeen Art Gallery.
- J. M. Robertson publishes *The Perversion of Scotland*, critique of contemporary culture.
- National Museum of Antiquities begun in Edinburgh (opened 1890).
- Heavy snow in May causes many deaths of cattle and sheep in the northeast.
- A brilliant display of over 600 meteors occurs on 27 November.
- Two remarkable results in the SFA Cup: Arbroath 36, Bon Accord 0; and Dundee Harp 35, Aberdeen Rovers 0. Cup won by Renton. No Rugby International.

1886
- Crofters' (Holdings) Act passed. Crofters' Commission set up.
- Scottish Home Rule Association formed.
- Six Skye crofters sentenced to six months each for mobbing and rioting.
- Glasgow's first underground (steam) railway opened.
- Six people die in a 'novel accident' at Crarae granite quarry, choked to death by fumes.
- Over 30,000 people celebrate centenary of Kilmarnock Edition of Burns, at Kilmarnock (August).
- Stevenson publishes *Dr Jekyll and Mr Hyde* and *Kidnapped*.
- Mrs E. Mouat of Shetland is rescued off the Norwegian coast, only survivor from a small boat that drifted away accidentally (November).
- Earthquakes shake Uist and Shetland (October).
- SFA Cup won by Queen's Park. Rugby International drawn with England.

1887
- Queen's Golden Jubilee celebrations include a dinner for 6,000 poor people in Glasgow.
- Riots by Blantyre miners destroy shops and property; the military are called (February).
- Seventy die in pit explosion, Blantyre (28 May).

- Squatters on Lewis invade deer forests, claiming the deer are ruining pasture land (November).
- Completion of the new Tay Bridge.
- Unveiling of the Wallace statue at the national Wallace Monument, Stirling (25 June).
- Sir David Bruce (1855–1931) identifies the *Brucella* bacterium.
- Gaelic Society of Glasgow founded.
- Glasgow Rangers FC moves from Kinning to Ibrox Park. Glasgow Celtic FC founded by Brother Wilfred.
- SFA Cup won by Hibernian. Rugby International drawn with England. The Cairngorm Club founded.

1888
- The 'Goschen Formula' assesses Scottish/English share of government expenditure as 11/80.
- Dundee is made a city.
- Formation of Scottish Labour Party.
- First conference of the Home Rule Association.
- Seventy miners die in a fire at Mauricewood Colliery, Midlothian.
- Reformatory ship *Cumberland*, in the Clyde, set on fire by inmates: 400 escape.
- John Boyd Dunlop (1840–1921) develops the pneumatic tyre.
- Higher and Lower Grade school leaving certificate introduced.
- A plague of rats afflicts many parts of the Lowlands.
- SFA Cup won by Renton. Renton defeat English Cup-holders West Bromwich Albion on 19 May to become 'world champions'. No Rugby International.

1889
- Institution of elected County Councils.
- J. M. Barrie (1860–1937) publishes *A Window in Thrums*.
- Opening of National Portrait Gallery, Edinburgh (15 July), and completion of Glasgow Municipal Building, George Square (7 October).

- George Henry paints *Galloway Landscape*, fine Impressionist-style work.
- Eight hundred Catholics make a pilgrimage to Iona in honour of St Columba.
- First burning of a longship in the Up Helly Aa celebration, Lerwick, Shetland.
- First milking machine patented by William Murchland of Kilmarnoock.
- Dairy School for Scotland established near Kilmarnock.
- Earthquake damages houses in Inverness and Forres. A violent gale wrecks numerous vessels (16 November).
- SFA Cup won by Third Lanark. No Rugby International. Scottish Mountaineering Club founded.

1890

- Mr Gladstone addresses Midlothian electors at the Corn Exchange, Edinburgh, for two hours 'without apparent fatigue'.
- Sir James Frazer (1854–1941) begins publication of *The Golden Bough*.
- An arm bone, allegedly a relic of St Giles, is found in restoration of his High Kirk in Edinburgh.
- Completion of the Forth Bridge. Railway strike paralyses transport, December-January.
- Scottish Football League established, eleven members in the first season. Glasgow Rangers and Dumbarton are joint champions. SFA Cup won by Queen's Park. England win Rugby International.
- White-tailed sea eagle extinct in Scotland by this year.

1891

- Elementary school fees abolished.
- James Keir Hardie elected as first Independent Labour member (for a London seat).
- Founding of An Comunn Gaidhealach, First National Mod, at Oban.
- Motherwell station wrecked in riot during railwaymen's strike.

- Sir Hugh Munro publishes his tables of mountains over 3,000 feet in the *Scottish Mountaineering Journal* (September), listing 283 summits.
- Professor Norman Collie, FRS, sees the Grey Man of Ben Macdhui.
- Twentieth football International with England, at Blackburn. England win 2–1 (4 April). SFA Cup won by Heart of Midlothian. Scotland beat England in Rugby International.

1892

- Secretary of State becomes a member of the Cabinet.
- Commission on Deer Forests appointed.
- Miners go on strike (March).
- Scottish universities allow women to become undergraduates.
- Sir Patrick Geddes (1854–1932) establishes world's first 'sociological laboratory' in Edinburgh.
- Glasgow's first women doctors employed at the Samaritan Hospital.
- H. E. Moss of Greenock builds the first of the 'Moss Empire' halls, in Edinburgh.
- Last gypsy king, Charles Faa-Blythe, crowned at Kirk Yetholm. By now only a handful of gypsy families remain.
- Widespread flu epidemic (January).
- Plague of fieldmice reported in several country districts (April-June).
- SFA Cup won by Celtic. England win Rugby International. Scottish Bowling Association founded in Glasgow (12 September).

1893

- Lord Mayors of London and Dublin make a state visit to Edinburgh.
- Last whaling trip is made from Peterhead, by the *Windward* (18 April).
- Glasgow Art Gallery begun.
- Professionalism finally accepted in football. Football League sets up a Second Division. SFA Cup won by Queen's Park, for the last time. Scotland beat England in Rugby International.

- Camanachd Association formed in Kingussie to regulate shinty.

1894
- Local Government Board for Scotland takes over responsibility from Board of Commissioners for Poor Relief.
- William Sharp (1855–1905) publishes – as Fiona Macleod – *The Sin-Eater*.
- The West Highland Railway links Fort William to Glasgow (August). The Highland Railway builds Britain's first 4–6–0 locomotives.
- Strike by 65,000 coalminers from June to October. 20,000 steel workers laid off.
- Sewage treatment system installed in Glasgow; it no longer flows raw into the Clyde.
- Exhibition of Highland Industries in Inverness (September).
- Edinburgh University awards medical degrees to women.
- Severe hurricane causes damage across south.
- SFA Cup won by Rangers. Scotland beat England in Rugby International.

1895
- Deer Commission schedules 1,782,785 acres of deer forest as suitable for crofting purposes.
- Railway 'races to the north' cut London-Aberdeen journey to 8.5 hours.
- Strike by 30,000 jute workers in Dundee.
- Thirteen die in colliery explosion at Denny.
- Completion of Sule Skerry lighthouse, most remote in Britain.
- Theatre Royal, Glasgow, largest in the country, burns down, without casualties (March).
- Exceptional snowfall in February.
- SFA Cup won by Renton. Scotland beat England in Rugby International.

1896
- James Connolly (1868–1916) leaves for Ireland.

- Charles Rennie Mackintosh designs the new Glasgow School of Art.
- Mr A. Usher announces his gift of £100,000 to build a hall in Edinburgh.
- First commercial cinematographic show, at the Empire in Edinburgh (April).
- Alfred Austin, poet laureate, unveils the Burns statue in Irvine (18 July).
- New Royal Observatory opens on Blackford Hill, Edinburgh.
- Glasgow District Subway (electric) opens (14 December).
- First large hydroelectric generating station, at Foyers.
- Socialist Sunday Schools begin in Glasgow, 3 February.
- SFA Cup won by Hearts. Scotland beat England in Rugby International.

1897
- Formation of the Scottish Trades Union Congress (25 March). Establishment of the Congested Districts Board.
- Sir Ronald Ross (1857–1932) identifies cause of malaria.
- Dingwall-Skye Railway extended from Strome Ferry to Kyle of Lochalsh (November).
- John Stirling makes first car to be assembled in Scotland: the Stirling.
- Beacon fires from Caithness to the border mark Queen Victoria's Diamond Jubilee, and loyal demonstrations are held throughout the country (June).
- SFA Cup won by Glasgow Rangers. England win Rugby International.

1898
- Opening of the People's Palace, Glasgow (22 January).
- Deer forests take up 2,510,625 acres.
- Scottish Records Society founded.
- Wireless telegraph in use.
- Black houses are still being built on Lewis.
- SFA Cup won by Glasgow Rangers. Rugby International drawn with England.

1899

- Boer War begins: Scottish regiments sent out to South Africa. Yeomanry units are mobilised, and troops' comforts' funds are started.
- Assembly of Arrol-Johnson motor cars begins in Paisley.
- Albion Motor Company established to build lorries, 30 December.
- SFA Cup won by Celtic. Scotland beat England in Rugby International.

1900

- Dr Clark, the 'pro-Boer' MP for Caithness, is burned in effigy in Thurso.
- J. P. Coats of Paisley gives a library of books to each Board School, on condition they contain 'no religious works'.
- Clyde shipbuilding totals 491,832 tons.
- Scotland is now one of the world's main locomotive builders; more are built here than in England.
- A Conciliation Board is established to fix miners' wages.
- Free Church resolves on union with the United Presbyterian Church. Dissenters stay on and claim the Free Church's assets.
- Unaccountable disappearance of the three Flannan Isles lighthouse keepers.
- Smallpox in Glasgow results in 200 deaths.
- Scotland has 65 poorhouses, capable of holding 15,500 people.
- Argyll Car Works open (January).
- Hen houses come into use.
- Gales cause damage to the Shetland fishing fleet (December).
- SFA Cup won by Celtic. Rugby International drawn with England.

1901

- Death of Queen Victoria, accession of Edward I (VII of England).
- Number of Gaelic speakers is 230,806; Gaelic-only speakers number 28,107.
- Education Act makes fourteen the school-leaving age; attendance at school compulsory for under-twelves; exemptions are still possible for children aged twelve–fourteen.
- Scottish Prohibition Party founded.
- George Douglas Brown (1869–1902) publishes *The House with the Green Shutters*.
- Around this time motor cars become increasingly frequent.
- West Highland Railway extended to Mallaig (April).
- On the Clyde 519,000 tons of shipping are launched.
- Andrew Carnegie offers £2,000,000 as a Trust Fund to the Scottish universities. First Chair of Scottish History established, Edinburgh University.
- Heavy gales in November disrupt the telegraphic link with England, and the coastguard vessel *Active* is wrecked on Granton breakwater with nineteen deaths.
- SFA Cup won by Hibernian. Scotland beat England in Rugby International.

1902

- Liberal League formed by Lord Rosebery for a 'sane imperialism', making a split with his leader, Campbell-Bannerman. Young Scots group formed to maintain the Gladstone tradition.
- In Glasgow a Citizens' Union is formed to protest at plans to build council houses.
- Centenary number of the *Edinburgh Review* is published (October).
- Hugh Miller's centenary is celebrated in Cromarty (August).
- Sir Ronald Ross (1857–1932) wins the Nobel Prize for Medicine.
- The United Free Church proceeds against Dr George Adam Smith, of its Theological College, for heresy: he is let off with a caution.
- Glasgow's Hampden Park opened, world's largest stadium at the time.
- In a whale hunt at Hillswick in Shetland, 166 whales are driven ashore and killed.

- SFA Cup won by Rangers. England win Rugby International.

1903
- Most industries are depressed, especially steel and textiles. Shipbuilding on the Clyde is 484,853 tons. Wages are reduced in the engineering, coal and steel industries. A strike of engineers is repudiated by the Amalgamated Society of Engineers.
- North British Locomotive Company formed in Glasgow by amalgamation: largest privately owned locomotive works in Europe.
- A train hits the buffers at St Enoch Station, Glasgow, causing 15 deaths (27 July).
- Fire at Dailuaine (September 27) leads to 700,000 gallons of whisky being lost.
- Serious flooding in the Clyde Valley causes extensive damage (February).
- SFA Cup won by Celtic. Scotland beat England in Rugby International.

1904
- *Scottish Historical Review* founded.
- Scottish Motor Traction Company (SMT) founded (June), with first route from The Mound to Corstorphine.
- Clyde shipbuilding is 417,876 tons. Sir William Ramsay (1851–1939), joint discoverer of argon, receives Nobel Prize for Chemistry.
- The vessel *Scotia*, with the Scottish Antarctic Expedition, arrives in the Clyde (21 July).
- Charles Rennie Mackintosh builds The Hill House, Helensburgh.
- St Kildan wren protected by act of parliament.
- SFA Cup won by Third Lanark. Scotland beat England in Rugby International.

1905
- Royal Commission on the Scottish Ecclesiastical Question sits.
- Edward VII reviews 38,000 volunteers in Holyrood Park and a column of ten motors.
- Tonnage of ships launched on the Clyde amounts to 540,080. Beardmore's take over Arrol-Johnson.
- Gaelic admitted as an examination subject in schools.
- Total eclipse of the sun visible in the south (30 September).
- SFA Cup won by Third Lanark. Scotland beat England in Rugby International, but in their first International with New Zealand, Scotland lose 12–7, in Glasgow.

1906
- Scottish Women's Suffragette Federation founded.
- Shipbuilding tonnage is 601,658 tons. *Lusitania*, liner of 35,200 tons, is launched on the Clyde (7 June).
- Boilermakers' and riveters' strike for a five per cent pay rise (October-November) is defeated.
- British Linen Company changes name to British Linen Bank.
- Vatersay is 'invaded' by crofters from Barra, seeking more land.
- New buildings of Marischal College, Aberdeen, opened (September) in time for University's 400th anniversary celebration.
- Founding of the Glasgow Orpheus Choir by Hugh Roberton.
- Socialist weekly *Forward* founded, October.
- Serious railway accident with many deaths at Elliot Junction, Arbroath (28 December).
- Earthquake shock felt in Perthshire.
- Aberdeen is cut off for four days by snow (December).
- SFA Cup won by Hearts. Scotland beat England in Rugby International. In first Rugby International with South Africa, Scotland win by two tries to nil.

1907
- Scottish Grand Committee formed in Parliament.

- Third Pan-Celtic Congress is held in Edinburgh.
- Volunteer units are re-formed into the Territorial Army.
- Clyde shipbuilding totals 619,919 tons.
- Explosion at Ardeer nitroglycerine works kills three.
- Caledonian Bank is merged into Bank of Scotland.
- Failure of the Argyll Motor Company.
- Universities of Edinburgh and Glasgow adopt the three-term system (previously two).
- Campaign to preserve the Auld Brig of Ayr succeeds.
- Movements are started for the cultivation and increased use of Scots and Gaelic.
- Fifty small boats with holiday fishers are blown out to sea from Dunoon; most are recovered; two people drowned (15 August).
- Dr Bruce's Scottish Arctic Expedition, reported missing, turns up in north Norway.
- SFA Cup won by Celtic. Scotland beat England in Rugby International.

1908

- Scottish Liberal Federation supports disestablishment of the Church, votes for women and home rule (October).
- School boards are required to ensure medical inspection of children and to provide meals in 'necessitous' cases.
- Clyde shipbuilding falls to under 400,000 tons: lowest since 1894. Increasing unemployment creates disorder; workers try to force an entry into Glasgow City Hall. Trade and industry generally are depressed.
- Interim report of Royal Commission on Whisky Industry declares that the name of whisky should not be denied to spirit made with malt, or with malt and grain.
- The ten Vatersay 'invaders' sentenced to two months jail each.
- Royal Commission for the Inventory of Scottish Historical Monuments is established.
- Dunkeld Cathedral is restored.
- Fiftieth anniversary of the death of Robert Owen is commemorated in Lanark (6 June).
- SFA Cup is won by Celtic. Scotland beat England in Rugby International.

1909

- Unemployment in the Glasgow area is estimated at 19 per cent of the work force.
- Shipbuilding on the Clyde is 427,325 tons.
- Campbeltown whisky output is down by 25 per cent.
- Scottish Textiles College established at Galashiels.
- Aberdeen imports 27,000 tons of Scandinavian granite for its granite-cutting and polishing industry.
- Construction of naval dockyard at Rosyth begins.
- Legislation is made to preserve the Moray Firth fish stocks.
- Glasgow Waterworks extended to Loch Arklet.
- Marjorie Kennedy Fraser (1857–1930) publishes *Songs of the Hebrides*.
- John Buchan (1875–1940) publishes *Prester John*.
- Glasgow Repertory Theatre founded.
- SFA Cup is withheld. Scotland beat England in Rugby International.

1910

- Death of Edward VII, accession of George V.
- Twenty Liberal members set up a Scottish National Committee to promote self-government.
- General Assembly of the Church of Scotland deplores the fall in the number of children attending Sunday schools.
- First World Missionary Conference is held, in Edinburgh (14–23 June).
- Iron ore deposits found on Raasay.

- Death of William MacTaggart (born 1835), leading Scottish painter of his generation.
- Production of knitted jerseys begins on Fair Isle.
- James Braid (1870–1950) wins the Open Golf Championship for the fifth time.
- SFA Cup won by Dundee. England win Rugby International.

1911

- Census shows the population as 4,760,904. Population of Glasgow now exceeds 1,000,000 (101,000 in 1811).
- Scottish Unionist Party formed.
- Coal Mines Act: boys under thirteen no longer allowed to work underground.
- Scottish Land Court set up.
- Shipbuilding tonnage on the Clyde is 630,583.
- Carters and dockers strike in Dundee; riots take place and the military are called in.
- Quincentenary of St Andrews University celebrated, 13–15 September.
- New Mitchell Library opened in Glasgow, 16 October.
- Chapel of the Thistle dedicated in St Giles during a visit by the king (19 July).
- Heavy storms in December. Liner *Busiris* lost off the Galloway coast, 23 December.
- SFA Cup won by Celtic. England win Rugby International.

1912

- Royal Commission on Housing set up (reported in 1917).
- Scottish Board of Agriculture set up.
- Crofters' Commission and Congested Districts' Board merged in Scottish Land Court.
- Liberal Unionists merge with Conservative Unionists.
- Young Scots group join with Liberal Home Rulers to promote self-government.
- Coal strike in March involves 130,000 miners: additional 6d a day awarded.

- Shipbuilding tonnage on the Clyde is 641,908.
- Textile industry benefits from economic recovery.
- Deer forests take up 3,584,966 acres.
- Severe weather makes access to St Kilda impossible; HMS *Achilles* makes a relief visit
- SFA Cup won by Celtic. England win Rugby International.

1913

- During the year 36,000 people leave from the Clyde, mostly for Canada.
- The number of Gaelic speakers is assessed at 202,398; Gaelic-only speakers number 18,400.
- Government of Scotland bill (for home rule) dropped at the committee stage.
- Temperance (Scotland) Act passed.
- Scottish suffragettes begin sabotage operations, and burn church at Whitekirk.
- Glasgow has 44,354 single-end houses; 111,451 room-and-kitchen houses, the vast majority sharing water closets.
- Dockers of Leith strike from June to August; riots in July are met by naval and military force.
- Shipbuilding tonnage is 756,976 tons. *Aquitania* launched on the Clyde.
- A record year for the jute industry.
- SFA Cup won by Falkirk. England win Rugby International.

1914

- War declared on Germany (August).
- SFA Cup won by Celtic. England win Rugby International. Cup and International matches suspended until 1920.

1915

- First wartime strikes on the Clyde. '2d an hour' strike of engineers, February; rent strike, October-November.
- Major railway disaster at Quintinshill, Gretna, with 200 deaths.
- HMS *Natal* blows up in the Cromarty Firth, with the loss of all hands (30 December).

- Mary Slessor (born 1848), missionary, dies in Calabar, West Africa.

1916
- HMS *Hampshire* sunk off Orkney; Lord Kitchener drowned.
- Grand Fleet leaves Scapa Flow for Battle of Jutland (31 May).

1917
- HMS *Vanguard* explodes in Scapa Flow; 804 killed.

1918
- First World War armistice, 11 November.
- Voting in parliamentary elections extended to all men over 21 and all women over 30.
- Number of Scottish seats now 74.
- Women can now stand for parliament.
- John Maclean, first Soviet consul, tried for sedition (May).
- The *Iolaire*, with 200 returning soldiers and sailors, founders outside Stornoway harbour (31 January); all are drowned.
- School leaving age raised to fifteen. Catholic schools brought into the state education system.
- Islands of Lewis and Harris acquired by Lord Leverhulme.

1919
- The German High Seas Fleet is scuttled in Scapa Flow (21 June).
- Riots in George Square, Glasgow, put down by tanks (31 January). The 48-hour week is established for industry.
- Shipbuilding tonnage is 2.6 million tons.
- Housing and Town Planning (Scotland) Act.
- Forestry Commission set up.
- William Craigie proposes what will eventually become *The Scottish National Dictionary*.

1920
- Massive slump in prices for agricultural produce.

- Prohibition in the USA has a dire effect on whisky production and revenue.
- Around this year the last cattle drove is made, from Knapdale to Stirling.
- David Lindsay publishes *A Voyage to Arcturus*.
- SFA Cup won by Kilmarnock. England win Rugby International.

1921
- James Ramsay Macdonald forms first British Labour government.
- Railways Act passed, 19 August; Scottish railway companies merged into LMS and LNER.
- SFA Cup won by Partick Thistle. England win Rugby International.

1922
- Return to Lanark from Canada of the silver badge from the box that held the Silver Bell, the world's oldest racing trophy.
- First King's Cup Air Race, from Croydon to Glasgow and back (8–9 September).
- SFA Cup won by Morton. England win Rugby International.

1923
- First Scottish radio broadcasting station, in Glasgow.
- Erection of Scottish National War Memorial, until 1928, by Sir Robert Lorimer (1864–1929).
- Disaster at Redding Colliery, Stirling: 40 miners killed.
- Unemployment is at 14.3 per cent.
- Highland, Caledonian and Glasgow and South-Western Railways are merged into the London, Midland and Scottish Railway (LMS); Great North of Scotland and North British are merged into the London and North-Eastern Railway (LNER), 1 January.
- Lord Leverhulme abandons efforts to modernise Lewis and Harris.
- John MacLeod wins Nobel Prize for Medicine.

- Royal Scottish Country Dance Society founded.
- SFA Cup won by Third Lanark. England win Rugby International.

1924
- Buchanan's Home Rule Bill fails.
- SFA Cup won by Airdrie. England win Rugby International.

1925
- Beet sugar subsidy creates the beet sugar industry, until the 1970s.
- SFA Cup won by Celtic. Scotland beat England in Rugby International.

1926
- Seven-month miners' strike leads to the General Strike, 4–12 May.
- Hugh MacDiarmid (1892–1978) publishes *A Drunk Man Looks at the Thistle*.
- John Logie Baird (1888–1946) first demonstrates television (27 January).
- SFA Cup won by St Mirren. Scotland beat England in Rugby International.

1927
- Unemployment is at 10.6 per cent.
- Death of James Scott Skinner, fiddler and composer, 'The Strathspey king' (born 1843).
- Last Arrol-Johnson cars are built, in Dumfries.
- SFA Cup won by Celtic. Scotland beat England in Rugby International.

1928
- Women receive the vote on same terms as men.
- Sir Alexander Fleming (1881–1955) discovers penicillin.
- First plane to visit Lewis is seaplane S1058.
- The 'Wembley Wizards' beat England 5–1 at football. SFA Cup won by Rangers. England win Rugby International.

1929
- Local Government Act defines three classes of burgh: four cities, nineteen large burghs, 178 small burghs. Parish councils abolished. Responsibility for poor relief, education and public health transferred to county councils and large burghs.
- Unemployment is at 12.1 per cent.
- Hunger march of unemployed from Glasgow to London.
- Fire at Glen Cinema, Paisley: 70 die (31 December).
- Church of Scotland and United Free Church amalgamate.
- Usable reserves of iron ore virtually exhausted; only 25,000 tons mined against 3,000,000 tons a year in the 1870s.
- Last trams run in Perth (19 January).
- SFA Cup won by Kilmarnock. Scotland beat England in Rugby International.

1930
- Rationalisation of the shipbuilding industry. Work on RMS *Queen Mary* suspended until 1933.
- Inhabitants of St Kilda evacuated: island group now unpopulated.
- Scottish Pipe Band Association formed.
- SFA Cup won by Rangers. Rugby International drawn with England.

1931
- Cuts in the pay of Naval personnel, up to 25 per cent, provoke a mutiny in the Atlantic Fleet on a visit to the Cromarty Firth. Ships are sent back to their home ports.
- National Trust for Scotland founded.
- The Scottish Youth Hostels Association and the Clarsach Society are formed.
- Excavations begin at Jarlshof site in Shetland.
- Neil Gunn (1891–1974) publishes *Morning Tide*.
- Hannah Institute for Dairy Research founded.
- SFA Cup won by Celtic. Scotland beat England in Rugby International.

1932

- Unemployment is at 27.7 per cent.
- Interest in Home Rule increases, as a possible answer to econmic problems: Secretary of State says it is an academic question.
- Edinburgh University celebrates its 350th anniversary (October).
- Lewis Grassic Gibbon publishes *Sunset Song*, first in *Scots Quair* trilogy.
- The *Flying Scotsman* train runs non-stop from London to Edinburgh in 7 hours 27 minutes, a record timing.
- First combine harvester at work in Scotland.
- SFA Cup won by Rangers. England win Rugby International.

1933

- Labour gain control of Glasgow City Council.
- Repeal of Prohibition in the USA leads to re-expansion of the whisky industry.
- Scottish Milk Marketing Board created.
- The Byre Theatre opens in St Andrews.
- SFA Cup won by Celtic. Scotland beat England in Rugby International.

1934

- Unemployment is at 23.1 per cent.
- Kurt Hahn founds Gordonstoun School.
- First internal airmail service in Britain, Inverness-Kirkwall.
- RMS *Queen Mary* launched at Govan, 81,235 tons (28 September).
- SFA Cup won by Rangers. England win Rugby International.

1935

- William Soutar publishes *Poems in Scots*.
- Edwin Muir publishes *Scottish Journey*.
- Export demand for cured herrings is down by two-thirds from pre-war years, home demand by one-third. Fishermen's earnings for the season average less than £10.
- SFA Cup won by Rangers. Scotland beat England in Rugby International.

1936

- Death of George V, accession and abdication of Edward II (VIII of England), accession of George VI.
- Saltire Society established.
- Unemployment is at 18.7 per cent.
- An estimated one million people watch the new *Queen Mary* leave the Clyde, on 24 March.
- The LMS Railway's new Pacific locomotive runs from London to Glasgow in 5 hours 35 minutes.
- SFA Cup won by Rangers. England win Rugby International.

1937

- Building of St Andrew's House on Calton Hill, Edinburgh.
- Scottish Gaelic Text Society established.
- Scottish Special Housing Association established.
- Trains collide at Castlecary: 35 dead, 179 injured, 10 December.
- World's largest football crowd recorded at Hampden Park for Scotland v England: 149,547.
- SFA Cup won by Celtic. England win Rugby International.

1938

- Unemployment is at 16.3 per cent.
- Classification of 22.8 per cent of Scottish working-class housing as overcrowded.
- SFA Cup won by East Fife. Scotland beat England in Rugby International.

1939

- Second World War begins. Conscription introduced.
- Tom Johnston appointed Commissioner for Civil Defence.
- Unemployment is at 13.5 per cent.
- HMS *Royal Oak* sunk in Scapa Flow by a U-boat (October). First air raid of the war is aimed at Rosyth (October), and first German pilot of the war shot down over the Forth Bridge (16 October).
- Disaster at Valleyfield Colliery, Fife: 35 miners killed.

- SFA Cup won by Clyde. England win Rugby International. Cup and International matches suspended until 1947.

1940
- Evacuation of Dunkirk (1–4 June). Many Scots captured as Highland Division holds rearguard.
- Formation of Local Defence Volunteers (later Home Guard).
- Food rationing introduced. Free milk provided to schools and to expectant mothers.
- Marriage by declaration abolished.
- RMS *Queen Elizabeth*, world's largest passenger steamer, launched on the Clyde (83,673 tons) and used first as a troopship.

1941
- Tom Johnston appointed Secretary of State, February.
- Blitz attacks on Clydeside in spring, killing 1,200 people (March). Greenock raid in May leaves 280 dead.
- Rudolf Hess, Hitler's deputy, lands in Scotland (10 May).
- SS *Politician* wrecked, 5 February: provides the story for Compton Mackenzie's *Whisky Galore*.

1942
- Committee of Enquiry into Hydroelectricity recommends use of hydroelectric power to regenerate the Highlands (December).
- Personal petrol allowance abolished.
- Maximum penalty for black marketeering is raised to fourteen years' penal servitude.
- Three-day gale in the north during January, with 100 mph winds; part of Peterhead harbour is washed away.

1943
- Hydroelectric bill gets its second reading, 24 February.

- Bombing raid on Aberdeen leaves 43 dead.
- Coal strikes intermittent between July and November.
- Farm workers' pay is raised, to protests from farmers.
- Glasgow Western Infirmary employs its first women doctors.
- Glasgow Citizens' Theatre founded.

1944
- HMS *Vanguard* launched on the Clyde, 30 November: Britain's largest battleship at 44,500 tons.
- 4,400 members of the Women's Land Army are employed in Scotland. There is also a Women's Forestry Corps.

1945
- Victory in Europe, 8 May.
- General election, 5 July, with sweeping victory for Labour.
- Sir Alexander Fleming is joint winner of the Nobel Prize for Medicine.
- Choral Society formed at Haddo House.

1946
- Bread and flour rationing introduced, 21 July.
- Scottish National Party publishes its constitutional plan.
- Scottish Games Association formed.
- Strong winter gales, with 99mph recorded at Stornoway.

1947
- Coalmines brought into public ownership, 1 January.
- Scottish National Assembly takes place in Glasgow.
- Unemployment is at 6 per cent.
- Glasgow dockers' strike, March-May.
- Coal exports resume, to Sweden and Ireland.
- *Caronia*, 34,000 tons, is launched on the Clyde (30 October).
- Prestwick becomes a civil airport.

- A KLM plane crashes at Auchenweet Farm, Ayrshire: 39 are killed.
- Severest winter of the century.
- SFA Cup won by Aberdeen. England win Rugby International.

1948

- National Health and National Insurance Acts passed, 5 July. Much former social legislation, including the Poor Law Act, is repealed. Separate parliamentary seat for Scottish universities is abolished.
- East Kilbride and Glenrothes become Scotland's first 'New Towns'.
- Miners moved from Lanark to Fife.
- First Edinburgh International Festival.
- First post-war hydroelectric schemes at Loch Sloy, Loch Tummel and Fannich.
- SFA Cup won by Rangers. Scotland beat England in Rugby International.

1949

- John MacCormick (1904–61) organises the Scottish Covenant (for a Scottish Parliament within the UK): over a million sign.
- Nobel Peace Prize is awarded to John Boyd Orr (1880–1971).
- First 'forestry village' at Ae, Dumfriesshire.
- 30,000 buyers come to Scottish Industries Exhibition in Glasgow.
- Scottish Craft Centre established.
- SFA Cup won by Rangers. England win Rugby International.

1950

- General election: 37 Labour, 31 Tory, 2 Liberal, 1 Independent members returned.
- Unemployment is at 2.7 per cent, twice the average for Great Britain. Tonnage of ships built on the Clyde is 444,000. Clydesdale and North of Scotland Banks merge.
- Unauthorised removal of Stone of Scone (Stone of Destiny) from Westminster.
- Scottish National Orchestra founded.

- St Salvator's College, St Andrews, celebrates its quincentenary (27 August).
- Sir Harry Lauder, archetypal Scots comedian, dies on 26 February (born 1870).
- Scottish Mountain Rescue Committee formed.
- SFA Cup won by Rangers. Scotland beat England in Rugby International.

1951

- General election: 35 Labour, 35 Conservative, 1 Liberal members returned.
- Census shows population at 5,095,969. Glasgow has 1,089,555 people, Edinburgh has 446,761.
- Unemployment level is 2 per cent of working population.
- Coal production is at 23,526,000 tons.
- Tonnage of ships built on the Clyde is 427,000.
- Total number of cattle is 1,600,000; of sheep 6,859,000; of poultry 9,921,000. Working horses number 67,500. White Fish Authority established.
- Glasgow begins construction of 'high-rise' municipal flats.
- The first National Nature Reserve is established, around Beinn Eighe in Torridon.
- SFA Cup won by Celtic. England win Rugby International.

1952

- Death of George VI, accession of Elizabeth I (II of England).
- Government sets up Royal Commission on Scottish Affairs.
- Stone of Destiny turns up in Arbroath Abbey.
- Whisky revenue to the Exchequer exceeds £60,000,000. Bank of Scotland and the Union Bank amalgamate.
- Television broadcasting begins from Kirk o' Shotts (4 March).
- 27,000 acres of new trees planted.
- Highly successful herring season, 60 per cent up on 1951.
- Foot and mouth disease, imported from

the Continent, breaks out in Aberdeenshire (April-August): 19,000 animals are slaughtered.
- Ospreys return to breed in the Cairngorms.
- Outbreaks of myxomatosis kill off much of the rabbit population.
- SFA Cup won by Mctherwell. England win Rugby International.

1953
- Food rationing abolished.
- The *Prestwick Pioneer* is first plane to be designed and built in Scotland.
- An experimental peat-burning power station is set up at Altnabreac, Caithness.
- Royal yacht *Britannia* is launched on the Clyde.
- Historic Buildings Council for Scotland established. Scottish Official Board of Highland Dancing established.
- Whisky is recorded as Britain's biggest single export, by value. More record herring catches create a glut.
- Great storm in January sinks passenger ferry *Princess Victoria* in North Channel (133 die); 47 million cubic feet of timber laid low by the gale.
- SFA Cup won by Rangers. England win Rugby International.

1954
- Crofters' Commission re-established.
- Report of Royal Commission of 1951 makes no positive recommendations on devolution.
- Tonnage of ships built on the Clyde is 477,805.
- New brickworks established at Brora to use local clay.
- Cairngorm National Nature Reserve established, 9 July.
- Fair Isle acquired by National Trust, 4 September.
- Uruguay beat Scotland 7–0 in football World Cup. SFA Cup won by Celtic. England win Rugby International.

1955
- General election: 36 Conservative, 34 Labour, 1 Liberal returned. Scottish Standing Committee formed by parliament.
- Tonnage of ships built on the Clyde is 485,438, highest since 1930.
- Forth Road Tunnel mooted.
- Beef cattle number 927,000, dairy cattle 797,000; sheep 7,336,000.
- Heavy snow early in year isolates many communities.
- Billy Graham, evangelist, claims 2.5 million people have heard his message (March-April).
- SFA Cup won by Clyde. England win Rugby International.

1956
- Cumbernauld New Town started.
- Five new coal pits sunk.
- Chapelcross and Dounreay nuclear reactors begun.
- Tonnage of coal mined in Scotland is 21,480,325. Tonnage of steel produced is 2,518,900. Tonnage of pig iron produced is 931,400. Scotland's 21st Industrial Estate is opened at Inverness (May).
- Tramcars cease to run in Dundee (20 October) and Edinburgh (16 November). Electrification of Glasgow's suburban railways announced.
- Unemployment is at 2.5 per cent.
- National Library building opened, 4 July.
- Scottish Georgian Society established.
- SFA Cup won by Hearts. England win Rugby International.

1957
- Commercial television established.
- Creation of the Ravenscraig steelworks. Hunterston nuclear power station begun. Whiteinch Tunnel begun under the Clyde.
- Abolition of horse-breeding grant spells the final end of the farm horse.
- Sir Alexander Todd wins Nobel Prize for Chemistry.
- Skiffle music is highly popular. Lonnie

Donegan reaches No 1 in the hit parade with *Cumberland Gap*.
- Rum, St Kilda and Caerlaverock are named as National Nature Reserves.
- SFA Cup won by Falkirk. England win Rugby International.

1958

- Unemployment at 4.4 per cent remains at double the average for Great Britain. Coal production falls below 20,000,000 tons, and the closure of 20 pits is forecast. Dixon's Blazes, the Govan ironworks, close after 119 years.
- Last tram runs in Aberdeen.
- Amalgamation of Scottish regiments is proposed, with controversy over whether combined Royal Scots Fusiliers and Highland Light Infantry (Royal Highland Fusiliers) should wear trews or kilt.
- Hoard of seventh- or eighth-century silver found on St Ninian's Isle.
- SFA Cup won by Clyde. Rugby International drawn with England.

1959

- General election: Labour majority in Scotland (38 Labour, 32 Conservative, 1 Liberal) but Conservatives win overall in Great Britain.
- Oil and gas reserves discovered in the North Sea.
- Auchengeich Colliery fire: 47 miners die.
- The Broughty Ferry lifeboat capsizes, with the loss of her crew (8 December).
- Unemployment is 4.3 per cent.
- Deep-water terminal at Finnart constructed.
- Industrial projects include steel-strip mill for Ravenscraig and wood-pulp mill for Corpach in Lochaber.
- Tonnage of ships built on the Clyde is 388,539.
- Prestonpans Salt Works closes down.
- National and Commercial Banks combine in National Commercial Bank.

- Bovine tuberculosis finally eradicated. Cattle numbers total 1,892,411. Sheep population is highest ever at 8,883,659. The Deer Act is passed to conserve red deer stocks and prevent large-scale poaching.
- The Church of Scotland rejects the 'Bishops' report', 6 May. Iona Abbey, rebuilt, is reconsecrated, 28 June.
- SFA Cup won by St Mirren. Rugby International drawn with England.

1960

- Announcement (November) of American nuclear submarine base in Holy Loch.
- Employment Act encourages job creation.
- National service is abolished.
- Lothian shale mining comes to an end. Shipbuilding order books fall.
- Cattle numbers exceed 2,000,000 for first time. Working horses are now down to 18,294.
- North Ford Causeway joins Benbecula to South Uist. Queen Elizabeth makes the first visit to Shetland by its reigning monarch since Haakon IV in 1263.
- Six towns begin to bid for a new university.
- Oxford and Cambridge expedition to Loch Ness reports inconclusive findings.
- SFA Cup won by Glasgow Rangers. England win Rugby International.

1961

- Census records population at 5,178,490.
- Number of Gaelic-speakers 76,580; number of Gaelic-only speakers 1,097.
- Plebiscite Fund opened to seek £100,000 to ascertain people's view on self-government (31 November).
- Demonstrations take place against Holy Loch Polaris base, as USS *Proteus* arrives to set up depot on 3 March.
- Seaforth and Cameron Highlanders combined in a single regiment as Queen's Own Highlanders.

- Muriel Spark (1918–) publishes *The Prime of Miss Jean Brodie.*
- Toothill Report on Scottish economy (22 November) asks for more industrial/commercial planning by government.
- Rocket-firing range set up on South Uist.
- Lorries being assembled at Bathgate by BMC, and Rootes Group announce car factory for Linwood.
- Ben Cruachan pumped storage hydroelectric scheme and Greenock Dry Dock begun.
- Scottish fishing industry numbers 3,000 vessels. Aberdeen trawler *Red Crusader* is shelled by a Danish warship off the Faeroes.
- SFA Cup won by Dunfermline. England win Rugby International.

1962
- King Olaf of Norway makes state visit to Edinburgh.
- Moderator of the Church of Scotland makes historic visit to the Pope.
- Establishment of Livingston New Town.
- Unemployment is at 4.7 per cent. Sixteen further collieries are closed down, and 27 listed for closure.
- Glasgow tramways close down, 4 September, with last tram to Auchenshuggle.
- Wood-pulp mill established at Corpach.
- Foundation of Scottish Opera (28 January).
- Fixed Sunday opening hours for pubs spell the end of the 'bona-fide traveller' era. Glasgow opens the first municipal anti-smoking clinic.
- SFA Cup won by Rangers. Rugby International drawn with England.

1963
- The Reid Committee proposes sweeping changes in land law, first since 1617.
- Scottish peers are all made eligible to sit in House of Lords: previously they elected sixteen of their number.
- Last capital punishment in Scotland: Henry Burnett is hanged for murder at Craiginches Jail, Aberdeen.

- The Beeching Report heralds sweeping cuts in railway services.
- Rootes car factory opens at Linwood (2 May), making Hillman Imp car. Denny shipyard on the Clyde goes into liquidation; Harland & Wolff at Govan is put on a care-and-maintenance basis. Work begins on Tay Road Bridge (29 March).
- The Royal College of Science and Technology, Glasgow, becomes University of Strathclyde.
- Aberdeen trawler *Millwood* is arrested by Icelandic gunboat *Odinn* (28 April).
- SFA Cup won by Rangers. England win Rugby International.

1964
- General election (October). Labour government at Westminster. Scottish result: Labour 42, Conservative 26, Liberal 4.
- Harris Tweed established by law as a product spun and finished in the Outer Hebrides.
- Scotland's railway network substantially reduced, including many branch lines and Stranraer-Dumfries main line.
- Forth Road Bridge opened (4 September), also first stretch of M8 motorway (20 November).
- Contract signed for construction of *Queen Elizabeth II* at Clydebank.
- *Solway Barrage Scheme* published (August).
- Epidemic in Aberdeen leads to 400 cases of typhoid, from corned beef (May-June).
- Stirling selected as site for a new university (17 July). Queen's College, Dundee, gains university status (16 September).
- The Kirk refuses to have women ministers.
- SFA Cup won by Rangers. Scotland beat England in Rugby International.

1965
- Establishment of the Scottish Law Commission and the Highlands and Islands Development Board. Capital punishment abolished.

- Post Office Savings Bank HQ to be moved to Glasgow. Cruachan hydroelectric scheme (15 October).
- First Sunday ferry to Skye meets a hostile demonstration.
- Ingliston racing circuit opened (11 April).
- Princes Street Station, Edinburgh, closes (September).
- Heriot-Watt College, Edinburgh, becomes a university.
- SFA Cup won by Celtic. Rugby International drawn with England.

1966
- General election: Labour government returned at Westminster. Scottish result: Labour members 46, Conservative 24, Liberal 3.
- Royal Commission on Scottish Local Government is set up.
- Unemployment is at 3.6 per cent.
- Geddes Report calls for reorganisation of shipbuilding into larger units.
- Redundancies begin at Bathgate and Linwood motor plants; workers reject work-sharing.
- Major gas discoveries in the North Sea.
- Tay Road Bridge opened (18 August).
- Two Glasgow railway termini, St Enoch and Buchanan Street, close down.
- General Assembly of the Kirk allows women elders.
- General Teaching Council for Scotland set up.
- *Historical Dictionary of Scottish Gaelic* begun.
- Smallest public theatre in the world is opened at Dervaig, Mull.
- SFA Cup won by Rangers. Scotland beat England in Rugby International. Walter McGowan wins the World Flyweight title (14 June).

1967
- Scottish National Party wins Hamilton by-election.
- Establishment of the Scottish Arts Council and Scottish Civic Trust.

- Unemployment is at 3.8 per cent.
- Clyde shipbuilding rationalised into two consortia. *Queen Elizabeth II* launched at Clydebank (20 September).
- Last steam puffer in general trade, *Invercloy*, is broken up.
- Fire at Michael Colliery, East Wemyss: 9 men are killed, and the pit is closed down.
- Biggest ever pearl found in the Tay, at 44.5 grams; christened 'Wee Willie'.
- SFA Cup won by Celtic who also are first British club to win the European Cup, in Lisbon. England win Rugby International.

1968
- Countryside Commission for Scotland established.
- Scottish Transport Group set up to co-ordinate steamer and bus schedules.
- The Cameronians regiment is disbanded. Argyll and Sutherland Highlanders also to be disbanded.
- Irvine New Town founded.
- Decimal coinage is introduced (23 April).
- Hurricane force gales cause 20 deaths (15 January).
- Glasgow warehouse fire leads to the death of 22 people (18 November).
- The Church of Scotland allows women to become licensed as ministers.
- SFA Cup won by Dunfermline. England win Rugby International. Jim Clark, three times world motor racing champion, killed in a crash at Hockenheim circuit, Germany (7 April). Andrew Cowan and Brian Coyle win London-Sydney car rally, 18 December.

1969
- Age of majority and voting lowered to eighteen. Scottish Select Committee set up in parliament.
- Wheatley Report on Local Government. Three Glasgow Labour councillors jailed for corruption: London HQ takes over the Glasgow Labour Party.

- British Linen Bank merges with Bank of Scotland.
- The Waverley rail route from Edinburgh via Hawick to Carlisle closes (5 January), the Edinburgh-Perth route on 15 October.
- Burntisland Shipbuilding Company goes bankrupt.
- Aberdeen trawlermen strike, June-August.
- Scottish Fisheries Museum set up at Anstruther.
- Monsignor Gordon Gray becomes Scotland's first resident cardinal since before the Reformation (April).
- The Longhope lifeboat founders in the Pentland Firth, with the loss of her crew of eight (18 March).
- A gunman is shot dead in Glasgow after wounding twelve people.
- SFA Cup won by Celtic. England win Rugby International.

1970

- General election: 44 Labour, 23 Conservative, 3 Liberal, 1 Nationalist members. Scottish Labour majority outweighed by Tory win in England. Conservative government formed.
- Argyll and Sutherland Highlanders are 'reprieved', though only at Company strength.
- Unemployment at 103,000 is highest for eight years.
- Hydroelectric power schemes now number 54. Home (UK) sales of whisky exceed 10,000,000 gallons for the first time. Export sales are 62,000,000 gallons. Albion Motors becomes part of British Leyland.
- Open University founded, with Scottish network.
- M8 motorway completed from Edinburgh to Glasgow.
- Fraserburgh lifeboat founders; only one of her crew survives (21 January).
- SFA Cup won by Aberdeen. Scotland beat England in Rugby International.

1971

- Census records population as 5,230,000.
- British Summer Time is ended: mornings are lighter.
- Argyll and Sutherland Highlanders are restored to battalion strength. Royal Scots Greys and 3rd Carabiniers are combined in Royal Scots Dragoon Guards, 2 July.
- Crisis, work-in and demonstrations at Upper Clyde Shipbuilders.
- Scottish fishing industry numbers 2,600 vessels.
- Invergordon Aluminium Works begin production (25 May).
- Collapse of safety barriers in Ibrox Stadium causes 66 deaths. Gas explosion at Clarkston kills 21 (21 October).
- Government ceases distribution of free milk to schools.
- A bomb explodes at Edinburgh Castle during the Military Tattoo (28 August).
- SFA Cup won by Celtic. Centennial Rugby International, Scotland beat England. Chay Blyth sails single-handed 'wrong way' around the world. Ken Buchanan wins World Lightweight Boxing Championship, 12 February.

1972

- Great Britain joins the European Common Market (22 January).
- 'Cod war' with Iceland begins.
- Rockall formally annexed by the United Kingdom as part of Scotland, 11 February.
- Edinburgh has a Labour Lord Provost for the first time.
- Local authorities clash with the government over imposing increases in council house rents. Court of Session instructs Glasgow to comply.
- Students at Stirling University demonstrate against cost of the queen's visit.
- George Mackay Brown publishes *Greenvoe*.
- Royal Scots Dragoon Guards reach No. 1 in the hit parade with their recording of *Amazing Grace*.

- Unemployment is at 5.8 per cent in December. Workers at British Leyland, Bathgate, strike for nine weeks, February-March.
- Major North Sea oil activity includes digging of the world's largest graving dock, at Nigg.
- Seven men are lost with the *Nautilus*, of Fraserburgh (January). Seven fire-fighters die in a fire in Glasgow (August).
- SFA Cup won by Celtic. Scotland beat England in Rugby International. Rangers win European Cup-Winners' Cup in Barcelona, but fans' behaviour brings them a two-year suspension from European competition.

1973

- Kilbrandon Report recommends some form of Scottish Assembly.
- Clydebank is fined twice for not implementing council rent rises.
- Clayson Committee recommends changes in licensing hours.
- Oil shortage results in the 'three–day week'.
- Unemployment is at 3.7 per cent.
- Piper and Thistle oil fields discovered. St Fergus Gas Terminal approved, September.
- First strike of fire-fighters in Glasgow, 26 October–4 November 4.
- Work begins on Strathclyde Regional Park, at Hamilton.
- The 7:84 Theatre Company produces John McGrath's *The Cheviot, The Stag, and the Black, Black Oil*.
- Death on 5 December of Sir Robert Watson-Watt, inventor of radar (born 1892).
- SFA Cup won by Celtic. England win Rugby International. Jackie Stewart, three times world champion racing driver, retires (October). Scotland through to finals of the 1974 World Cup.

1974

- Two general elections, with Scottish results helping to secure minority Labour government and then a small majority for the same party; 11 Nationalist MPs elected (October). Scottish Council of Labour rejects its own executive's opposition to a Scottish Assembly. Scotland experiences net immigration for the first time since 1945: arrivals exceed departures by 7,800.
- Ninian oil field discovery announced (2 April). Sullom Voe and Flotta oil terminal plans agreed. Highland One, world's largest oil platform, launched at Nigg, 16 August. Petrol supplies restricted by tanker drivers' strike, May-June.
- Glasgow *Evening Citizen* ceases publication.
- Professional football played on Sunday for the first time (27 January).
- SFA Cup won by Celtic. Scotland beat England in Rugby International. Scotland exit from World Cup.

1975

- Referendum on membership of European Community: 1,332,286 in favour, 948,039 against; only Shetland and the Western Isles record a majority against it (6 June).
- Reform of local government: new local authorities established: 9 regions, 53 districts and 3 island councils replace 430 previous councils.
- Scottish Development Agency established.
- Convention of Royal Burghs becomes Convention of Scottish Local Authorities. Scottish Ombudsman (Commissioner for Local Administration) appointed in August.
- King Carl Gustav of Sweden makes a state visit, 8–10 July.
- Announcement of nuclear power station for Torness (February).
- Govan shipbuilders receive £17.2 million of state aid.
- Headquarters of British National Oil Corporation to be in Glasgow.
- 'Tartan Army' claims responsibility for

bomb damage to pipelines. Six members of 'Army of Provisional Government' jailed, April and May.

- Troops move 70,000 tons of Glasgow's rubbish during dustmen's strike.
- The Bay City Rollers reach No 1 in the hit parade with *Bye Bye Baby*.
- Mount Everest climbed by the southwest face for the first time by Dougal Haston and Doug Scott (September).
- Scottish Football League restructured: Premier Division has 10 clubs, First Division has 14, Second Division has 14. SFA Cup won by Celtic. England win Rugby International.

1976

- Crofting Reform Act enables crofters to buy their land. Licensing (Scotland) Act passed. Divorce Act abolishes 'matrimonial offence' as cause and substitutes 'irretrievable breakdown of marriage'.
- William Ross, longest-serving Secretary of State, resigns.
- Two Scottish MPs form a breakaway Scottish Labour Party.
- 'Scotland is British' pro-union campaign launched on 23 November.
- Unemployment 7.5 per cent.
- Base of the world's largest concrete structure, for the Ninian field, is floated out of Loch Kishorn.
- Canonisation of St John Ogilvie, 17 October.
- Exceptionally hot and dry summer this year.
- SFA Cup won by Rangers. Scotland beat England in Rugby International.

1977

- Scottish National Party make large gains in local elections.
- Unemployment 8.4 per cent.
- Boilermakers agree to end demarcation at Govan Shipbuilders.
- Flotta oil terminal inaugurated.
- First licences are granted for Sunday opening of pubs (October).

- Football fans dig holes in the Wembley pitch, London, after 2–1 win over England in soccer international.
- SFA Cup won by Celtic. England win Rugby International. Scotland through to the finals of the 1978 World Cup.

1978

- Unemployment falls during the year from 9.2 per cent to 7.8 per cent.
- British Leyland factory in Bathgate is on strike for seven weeks in August-September; the company announces reduced investment in the plant. Chrysler plant at Linwood on strike for five weeks, July-August. Singer factory at Dumbarton is largely shut down (December). Last open-hearth steel works shuts down, at Glengarnock (December).
- Herring fishing banned on west coast, except for the Firth of Clyde, to conserve stocks.
- Protests lead to reduction of a planned large-scale seal cull in Orkney.
- SFA Cup won by Rangers. England wins Rugby International. Scotland exits from the World Cup, winning one out of three games.

1979

- Devolution referendum fails to gain the necessary support of 40 per cent of the electorate (1,230,937 in favour: 32.85 per cent; 1,153,503 against: 30.78 per cent. 36.37 per cent abstain (1 March).
- General election returns Tories to Westminster under Mrs Thatcher (4 May). In Scotland, Labour have 44 seats, Tories 22, Liberals 3, SNP 2. First European elections arouse little interest (8 August).
- Lorry drivers' strike paralyses much of industry and commerce in January. Scottish branch of Confederation of British Industry asks churches to pray for industrial peace. Collapse of Penmanshiel Tunnel disrupts east coast railway line from Edinburgh to Newcastle.

- Iona is acquired by the Sir Hugh Fraser Trust.
- Extremely cold weather enables first Grand Bonspiel for sixteen years to be played on Lake of Menteith (February).
- SFA Cup won by Rangers. Rugby International drawn with England. Jim Watt wins World Lightweight Boxing title.

1980

- Scottish Radio Orchestra is disbanded by the BBC, but Scottish Symphony Orchestra is retained.
- Alan Wells wins the Olympic Gold Medal in the 100 Metres.
- Earthquake, centred on Longtown, Cumbria, affects southwest Scotland.
- SFA Cup won by Celtic. England wins Rugby International.

1981

- Unemployment at 325,000.
- The Linwood car plant is closed down with loss of 4,500 jobs; the Bathgate tractor plant and the Corpach wood-pulp mill also close.
- More than 40,000 people now work in the electronics industry, and around 100,000 in oil-related industries.
- Alasdair Gray publishes *Lanark*.
- Glasgow University opens a Science Park.
- Death of Sir William MacTaggart (born 1903), central artist of the Edinburgh school and grandson of William MacTaggart.
- SFA Cup won by Rangers. England win Rugby International.

1982

- Unemployment at 333,000.
- The Carron Iron Company goes into liquidation, and the aluminium works at Invergordon is closed down.
- Work begins on Coulport nuclear submarine base.
- The Pope visits Scotland (May).
- Most local authorities ban corporal pun-

ishment in schools after an adverse European Court decision.
- SFA Cup won by Aberdeen. Rugby International drawn with England. Jocky Wilson is World Professional Darts Champion (again in 1989).

1983

- General election: Labour have 41 seats, Tories 21, Liberal/SDP 8; Nationalists 2.
- Unemployment at 311,500.
- A new coalmine opens, at Castlebridge, near Kincardine.
- Scott-Lithgow yard has an £85,000,000 oil rig cancelled, with 4,000 jobs lost.
- Opening of the Burrell Collection galleries in Glasgow (October).
- Following purification schemes, salmon are once again found in the River Clyde after more than 100 years.
- SFA Cup won by Aberdeen, who also win Cup-Winners' Cup. Scotland beat England in Rugby International.

1984

- Election for European Parliament: Tories lose 3 of their 4 seats; Labour now have 4, the SNP one.
- Coalminers' strike.
- The Burrell Collection is Scotland's biggest visitor attraction.
- Unemployment is at 326,000 (December). Scotland has three of Great Britain's ten unemployment 'black spots'; one of them is Irvine New Town.
- North Sea oil production is 127 million tonnes – fifth most productive in the world.
- SFA Cup won by Aberdeen. Scotland beat England in Rugby International and win the Grand Slam.

1985

- Unemployment at a post-war record, with 340,000 out of work.
- Property revaluation causes large rises in rates.
- Teachers on strike throughout the year

for an independent pay review body, and many schools provide only part-time education.

- Oil production is at record level.
- The wettest summer on record. Hay production is down 85 per cent in some areas.
- The High Court rejects the claim of two brothers to the right of trial by combat.
- Ex-SAS man Tom McClean lives on Rockall for 40 days.
- SFA Cup won by Celtic. England wins Rugby International. Scotland through to finals of the Football World Cup. Sandy Lyle wins the Golf Open.

1986

- Edinburgh hosts the Commonwealth Games, but 31 countries boycott the event as a protest against sporting links with South Africa. Games have a £4,000,000 deficit.
- Edinburgh has a growing AIDS problem. Twenty-two new-born babies already infected.
- Riots and disturbances in several prisons, including Perth, Saughton, Peterhead and Barlinnie.
- Falling oil prices cause recession in the oil industry and more widely.
- Gartcosh steel-rolling mill closes.
- First drive-on car ferries to Lewis.
- A Chinook helicopter crashes near Sumburgh Head, with the loss of 45 lives.
- Fall-out effects from the Chernobyl nuclear disaster are found throughout the country, especially on uplands.
- SFA Cup won by Aberdeen. Scotland beats England in Rugby International. Scotland exits from the World Cup tournament.

1987

- General election. Conservatives returned to power at Westminster but win only 10 out of 72 Scottish seats: their 'right to govern' is questioned. Mrs

Thatcher, Prime Minister, dismisses prospect of devolution.

- After two and a half years of strikes, teachers win a pay increase but with stringent service conditions (January).
- Disruption in prisons continues. Governors complain about conditions (3 March).
- SFA Cup won by St Mirren. England wins Rugby International. Dundee United fails to win the UEFA Cup, but their fans win a good behaviour award.

1988

- Privatisation of the two electricity boards announced.
- Fire on the Piper Alpha oil rig, in the North Sea, kills 166 men (6 July).
- A terrorist bomb brings down a Pan-Am jumbo jet on Lockerbie, causing the deaths of 259 passengers and 11 inhabitants of the town.
- Seafield Colliery in Fife is closed.
- James Whyte Black wins Nobel Prize for Medicine.
- Glasgow hosts the Third International Garden Festival.
- SFA Cup won by Celtic. England wins Rugby International.

1989

- Poll tax is introduced in Scotland as a trial for UK. Protests increase throughout the year.
- Government launches a Rural Enterprise programme to help rural industry.
- Two of the three remaining collieries are closed.
- A nuclear re-processing plant is announced for Dounreay; environmentalists launch protest movement.
- Torrential rain causes flood in Inverness and washes away the Ness railway viaduct.
- SFA Cup is won by Celtic. England wins Rugby International. Richard Corsie is World Indoor Bowling Champion (again in 1991).

1990

- Glasgow is European City of Culture this year.
- Sale of council homes to tenants reaches 200,000.
- Scotland is estimated to produce a third of Europe's personal computers.
- Clydesdale Tube Works, Bellshill, closes down (November).
- Fishing vessel *Antares* sunk by a submarine in the Firth of Clyde; Royal Navy promises better information on submarine movements.
- Scotland exits from Football World Cup in first round. SFA Cup won by Celtic. Scotland wins Rugby's Grand Slam and Calcutta Cup in final match of the season at Murrayfield. Stephen Hendry is World Snooker Champion (again in 1992).

1991

- £1,000 million of poll tax estimated as unpaid, since its introduction. Poll tax replaced by new Council Tax.
- Farm incomes estimated as 27 per cent down on year before.
- Western Isles Council loses investment of £24,000,000 with the collapsed BCCI bank.
- Unemployment level 9.2 per cent in June.
- Shipbuilding now employs 14,000 people, compared to 77,000 in 1951.
- SFA Cup won by Motherwell. England win Rugby International. Liz McColgan is World Champion in Women's 10,000 Metres.

1992

- General election returns 11 Tories (up 2) and only 3 SNP members.
- Unemployment is almost 250,000.
- Scotland estimated as fourth largest financial centre in Europe.
- 4,000 fishermen and their families demonstrate against EU fishing quotas.
- United States' Polaris base at Holy Loch is closed down.

- Centennial National Mod takes place in Oban.
- Ravenscraig Steelworks closed down (June).
- SFA Cup won by Rangers. England win Rugby International.

1993

- Strong opposition is expressed to government plans to privatise Scottish water supplies.
- Unemployment at 9.2 per cent in December.
- £1,300 million plan to prolong activity in the Brent oilfield until 2008.
- Timex factory in Dundee closes after a long dispute between management and work force.
- Oil tanker *Braer* runs aground off Shetland (5 January): 85,000 tonnes of oil are spilled but stormy weather prevents pollution disaster.
- Irvine Welsh publishes *Trainspotting*.
- SFA Cup won by Rangers. England win Rugby International.

1994

- Scotland's 65 regional and district councils are replaced by 28 single-tier authorities.
- Elections for European Parliament return 5 Labour and 1 Nationalist MEPs.
- John Smith MP, Leader of the Labour Party and MP for Monklands, dies.
- Unemployment is at 8.7 per cent.
- Go-ahead is given for developing the first oilfields to the west of Shetland. Edinburgh HQ of British Gas is closed down.
- A Chinook helicopter crashes on the Mull of Kintyre, killing all 29 service staff on board (June). Official report blames pilot error.
- James Kelman publishes *How Late It Was, How Late*, and wins the Booker Prize.
- Football League establishes a Third Division, making four in all. SFA Cup won

by Dundee United. England win Rugby International.

1995

- Scottish National Party wins Perth and Kinross by-election, pushing Tories into third place after Labour.
- Unemployment at its lowest level in 15 years.
- Scottish nuclear plants to be privatised together with English ones, despite protests, but HQ of new company to be in Edinburgh.
- Assynt Crofters in dispute with landowner.
- The number of drug-related deaths in Strathclyde causes concern.
- Opening of the Skye bridge over Kyle Akin, with controversial toll charges (16 October).
- SFA Cup won by Celtic. England win Rugby International.

1996

- The Stone of Destiny is ceremonially returned to Scotland and placed in Edinburgh Castle.
- Fifteen Labour councillors in Monklands District are suspended from office.
- Unemployment is at 7.9 per cent.
- Sixteen children and their teacher are killed by a gunman entering their primary school in Dunblane (16 March).
- In Lanarkshire, and surrounding areas of Central Scotland, 15 people die, and around 50 are hospitalised because of *E. coli* 0157 poisoning from infected food.
- The Rosyth Naval Dockyard sold to a private company (November).
- A girl first bears the standard at Duns Common Riding.
- SFA Cup won by Glasgow Rangers. England win Rugby International.

1997

- General election (1 May): no Conservative MPs are returned in Scotland. Labour government formed.

- Devolution referendum results in vote for a Scottish parliament with tax-varying powers: 1,775,045 vote in favour of a parliament and 614,400 against in a 60.1 per cent turnout.
- Following public pressure over the Dunblane shootings, MPs vote to make the ownership of all handguns illegal from autumn 1997 (June).
- Professor Hugh Pennington reports on the *E. coli* 0157 outbreak, with 32 recommendations for improving hygiene in shops, abattoirs and farms.
- The island of Eigg is bought by its inhabitants for £1.5 million.
- Scientists at Roslin Institute breed a sheep by cloning. She is named 'Dolly' (February).
- Four fishermen drown when their boat capsizes 100 miles off the Scottish coast.
- SFA cup won by Kilmarnock. England win Rugby International with their highest score in a home international.

1998

- Government announces that the Dounreay nuclear plant is to close.
- *Silvery Sea*, Scottish trawler, struck by a German coaster: five fishermen drown.
- Farmers' incomes recorded as falling by 42 per cent from 1997 level.
- Four climbers die after being hit by an avalanche on Ben Nevis; three others survive.
- Museum of Scotland in Edinburgh opened by Queen Elizabeth.
- John Barr – the butcher whose shop sold the contaminated meat that caused the *E. coli* epidemic in Lanarkshire – fined £2,250.
- Stephen Hendry defeated in snooker world championships: first time since 1990. SFA cup won by Celtic. Scotland knocked out of the World Cup in the first round. Rugby International won by England.

1999

- First Scottish Parliamentary elections in May return 62 Labour, 38 SNP, 22 Conservative, 18 Liberal-Democrat, 1 Green, 1 Scottish Socialist and 1 Independent as the first MSPs.
- Queen Elizabeth opens Scottish Parliament (1 July). Donald Dewar is First Minister, David Steel is President.
- Glasgow is UK City of Architecture and Design this year.
- A Cessna plane crashes near Glasgow Airport: 8 die and 3 survive (September).
- Last solar eclipse of the millennium is seen in partial form across Scotland.
- The Sutherland Royal Commission on care for the old recommends universal free care for old age pensioners (March).
- The Kingston Bridge in Glasgow is moved 2 inches by hydraulic jacks.
- A Larkhall family are killed in a gas explosion that totally destroys their home.
- British Open Golf Championship at Carnoustie is won by Paul Lawrie from Stonehaven. SFA Cup won by Glasgow Rangers. Euro 2000 play-offs: Scotland beat England 1–0 at Wembley; England beat Scotland 2–0 at Hampden Park. Craig Brown, Scotland manager, receives the CBE. Scotland are Five Nations Rugby Champions.

2000

- Flu outbreak is the worst in 10 years. Hospitals under pressure.
- The *Solway Harvester* fishing boat sinks off the coast of the Isle of Man killing all of its 7-man crew.
- The Scottish Executive proposes the repeal of Section 28 (Clause 2A) which bans the discussion of homosexuality in schools. In the 'Keep the Clause' campaign's private referendum, funded by Brian Soutar, 86 per cent voted in favour of retaining the clause. The Executive still plans to repeal.
- Parliament agrees that Scottish students who study at Scottish universities will have their tuition fees paid by the state.
- Two Libyans are accused of the bombing of the Pan Am Flight 103 which crashed over Lockerbie in 1988. Scots Law trial begins in Holland in May.
- Sean Connery receives a knighthood.
- August: 5,000 Scottish pupils receive the wrong Higher and Standard Grade exam results or do not receive any at all. Scottish Qualifications Authority chief Ron Tuck resigns. 150,000 students must have their results double-checked.
- Three days of blockades of fuel depots by truckers, haulage firms and farmers in protest against the level of fuel tax. Petrol shortage lasts for over a week.
- Donald Dewar, first First Minister of Scottish Parliament, has operation in May to replace faulty heart valve. He returns to work 3 months later but dies on October 11, following a brain haemorrhage.
- Henry MacLeish is elected First Minister. John Swinney is elected leader of the Scottish National Party, following Alex Salmond's resignation. Michael Martin MP is elected Speaker of the House of Commons, first Catholic to hold this post since the Reformation.
- British Open Golf Championship at St Andrews is won by Tiger Woods of the USA. Celtic knocked out of SFA Cup by Inverness Caledonian Thistle. Rangers win the League Championship and the SFA Cup. England win the Six Nations Rugby championship; Scotland win the Calcutta Cup. David Coulthard wins Monaco Grand Prix.

2001

- Westminster Parliamentary Election (June): Labour win 56 seats, Liberal Democrats 9, SNP 5, Conservatives 1.
- Scottish Parliament agrees to advance proposals for universal free care of old age pensioners (January 25).

- House of Lords votes to set up a select committee to reinvestigate the Mull of Kintyre Chinook crash of 1994.
- The extra-territorial court at Camp Zeist, Netherlands, finds Abdel Baset Al-Megrahi guilty of the murder of 270 people at Lockerbie, and sentences him to life imprisonment. The second accused Libyan, Al-Amin Khalifa Fhimah, is acquitted. The trial is estimated to have cost £62,000,000.
- Severe outbreak of foot-and-mouth disease from England affects many farms in Dumfries & Galloway, with many thousands of animals slaughtered and burned.
- Cardinal Thomas Winning dies (June).
- Plans to spread asylum seekers throughout the UK include 3,700 additional places in Glasgow.
- New plans for the derelict Ravenscraig Steelworks site in Motherwell centre as a recreation and retail complex.

- Scottish Parliament votes for a ban on foxhunting and other hunting with dogs (September).
- Henry MacLeish resigns as First Minister (October) and Jack McConnell is elected as Scotland's third First Minister (November)
- Scottish tourism industry hit hard by the after-effects of the foot-and-mouth outbreak and the terrorist attack, on the Pentagon and twin towers of New York's World Trade Centre, on 11 September.
- British Open golf championship at Royal Lythum and St Anne's won by David Duval of the USA. John Higgins completes a hat-trick in snooker: the Champions Cup, Regal Masters and Stan James British Open. Stephen Hendry wins the European Open. Celtic win 'The Treble' Scottish Championship, SFA Cup and CIS Insurance Cup. Martin O'Neill is appointed as the team's new manager.

SELECT BIBLIOGRAPHY

Anderson, A. O. *Sources of Early Scottish History* Edinburgh 1922
Barron, E. M. *The Scottish War of Independence* Inverness 1934
Barrow, G. W. S. *The Anglo-Norman Era in Scottish History* Oxford 1980
Barrow, G. W. S. *Robert Bruce* London 1965
Brown, A., McCrone, D. and Paterson, L. *Politics and Society in Scotland* Basingstoke 1996
Checkland, S. G. and O. *Industry and Ethos: Scotland 1832–1914* London 1984
Dickinson, W. C. and Donaldson, G. (Eds.) *A Source Book of Scottish History* London 1950–54
Dodgshon, R. A. *Land and Society in Early Scotland* Oxford 1981
Dodgshon, R. A. *From Chiefs to Landlords* Edinburgh 1998
Ferguson, T. *The Dawn of Scottish Social Welfare* London 1948
Graham, H. G. *The Social Life of Scotland in the 18th Century* London 1899
Grant, I. F. *Economic History of Scotland* London 1934
Gregory, D. *The History of the Western Highlands and Isles of Scotland* London 1881
Hanham, H. *Scottish Nationalism* London 1969
Harvie, C. *Scotland and Nationalism* London 1977
Houston, R. A., and Whyte, D. (Eds.) *Scottish Society 1500–1800* Cambridge 1989

Hunter, J. *The Making of the Crofting Community* Edinburgh 1976
Hutchison, I. G. C. *A Political History of Scotland* Edinburgh 1986
Lenman, B. *Economic History of Modern Scotland* London 1977
Mackinnon, J. *A Constitutional History of Scotland from Early Times to the Reformation* London 1924
Mackintosh, J. *A History of Civilisation in Scotland* Paisley 1895
Mathew, D. *Scotland Under Charles II* London 1955
Mitchell, D. *History of the Highlands and Gaelic Scotland* Paisley 1900
Nicholson, R. *Scotland in the Later Middle Ages* Edinburgh 1974
Piggott, S. *Scotland Before History* London 1958
Piggott, S. *The Prehistoric Peoples of Scotland* London 1962
Plant, M. *Domestic Life in Scotland in the 18th Century* Edinburgh 1952
Ritchie, R. L. G. *The Normans in Scotland* Edinburgh 1954
Sanderson, M. H. B. *Scottish Rural Society in the 16th Century* Edinburgh 1982
Skene, W. F. *Celtic Scotland* Edinburgh 1876
Smout, T. C. *A Century of the Scottish People* London 1986
Wainwright, F. T. (Ed.) *The Problem of the Picts* London 1955
Withers, C. W. J. *Gaelic Scotland* London 1988
Wormald, J. (Ed.) *Scotland Revisited* Edinburgh 1991